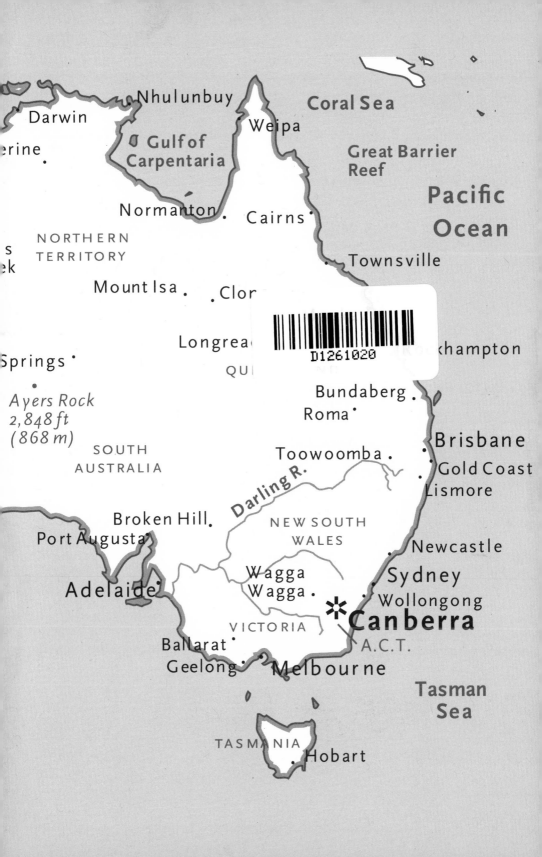

Darwin

Nhulunbuy

Weipa

Coral Sea

Gulf of
Carpentaria

Great Barrier
Reef

erine

NORTHERN
TERRITORY

Normanton

Cairns

Pacific
Ocean

Townsville

Mount Isa

Clor

Longrea

QU

khampton

Springs

Ayers Rock
2,848 ft
(868 m)

Bundaberg

Roma

SOUTH
AUSTRALIA

Toowoomba

Brisbane

Gold Coast

Lismore

Darling R.

Broken Hill

NEW SOUTH
WALES

Port Augusta

Newcastle

Wagga
Wagga

Sydney

Adelaide

Wollongong

VICTORIA

*Canberra

A.C.T.

Ballarat

Geelong

Melbourne

Tasman
Sea

TASMANIA

Hobart

D1261020

AUSTRALIA
& THE SOUTH PACIFIC

Canadian Foreign Service Memoirs
PENUMBRA PRESS · Manotick, ON · 2009

AUSTRALIA
& THE SOUTH PACIFIC

LETTERS HOME, 1965–1972

SHEILA MENZIES & ARTHUR MENZIES
Canadian High Commissioner

To Deanne Bass and Michelle Trottier
with best wishes and thanks for your
arranging visits to the National Arts
Centre, etc.

Arthur Menzies
27/4/09

Copyright © 2009 ARTHUR MENZIES
Published by Penumbra Press

No part of this publication may be
reproduced, stored in a retrieval
system or transmitted, in any form or
by any means, without the prior
written consent of the publisher or a
licence from The Canadian Copyright
Licensing Agency (Access Copyright).

PENUMBRA PRESS, *publishers*
Box 940 · Manotick, ON · Canada
K4M IA8 · penumbrapress.ca

Photographs are from the collection of
the author. Where uncertainty over
copyright arose, every effort was made
to source and obtain permission; in
many cases, this proved fruitless. In
the event of errors or omissions with
respect to copyright, the publisher will
gladly correct them in subsequent
editions of this book.

Library and Archives Canada
Cataloguing-in-Publication Data

Menzies, Arthur, 1916–
Menzies, Sheila, 1918–1998
    Australia and the South Pacific:
    Letters Home, 1965–1972 /
    Arthur Menzies & Sheila Menzies.
    Includes index.
    ISBN 978-1-897323-92-2
    1. Diplomacy—Canada
    2. Australia—Politics and
        government—1965–
    3. High commissioners—Canada
        Biography
    I. Title
CT120.R63   2009 920.071
    C2009-906548-1

CONTENTS

MY APPOINTMENT as Canada's High Commissioner in Australia in 1965 was in several ways a logical extension of a lifelong narrative that began with my birth in China as the son of a Canadian missionary and continued with my elementary schooling in China and five years of secondary education in Japan. These early experiences left me with a deep affection for the people of East Asia. However, my mixed Scottish and English ancestry and my more immediate family background in Ontario placed me firmly in the centre of British-Canadian culture, with a paternal great-grandfather who left Scotland in 1832 to settle on stony land near Milton, Ontario, and whose son David eventually bought a farm and general store at Staples, near Windsor.

My father, after earning a degree in civil engineering at the University of Toronto, was inspired by some of the great missionary speakers of the time to turn to the study of divinity. He graduated in that discipline in 1910 and became a missionary in North Henan Province of China for the Presbyterian Church. During his studies in divinity he had met Annie Belle Sedgwick, of Windsor, who was training to become a deaconess of the Anglican Church. She became a missionary as well, and preceded him to China. After travelling to China by way of Scotland, Ireland, and the Trans-Siberian railway, he sought her out and, in 1911, married her. I was born in 1916 in Zhangde, North Henan, my parents' fourth and youngest child; my only brother died in early childhood.

Both my parents learned Chinese, but Father went much further than mere proficiency in the language. He became fascinated with the great thinkers of China and, more particularly, with the early history of that ancient civilization. His alert observations during his travels through the region in which he carried on his missionary work (which happened to be very near the last capital of the Shang, or Yin dynasty [1100-1039 B.C.]), his curiosity, and his scholarly turn of mind led eventually to serious archaeological study. He became fascinated with the pictographs that appear on what are called "oracle bones." This is the beginning of the Chinese character system. Eventually he produced a book entitled *Oracle Records from the Waste of Yin* (Shanghai: Kelly & Walsh, Ltd., 1917), which includes 2,369 line drawings of inscriptions from these bones.

The First World War interrupted Father's archaeological studies and disrupted the orderly sequence of my education as a "mish-kid," as we offspring of missionaries were called. Because he had been trained as a civil engineer and spoke Chinese, he was called up in 1917 to serve as an officer with the Chinese Labour Corps—some 96,000 Chinese civilian labourers who were recruited to serve in France to replace British and French soldiers killed in trench warfare. Meanwhile my mother, my two sisters, a Chinese nursemaid, and I moved back to stay with my Menzies grandparents in their farm home near Staples until Father was released from service, which did not happen until 1920.

In 1921 we returned to China. My sisters and I attended a Canadian Mission school at Weihui, 100 kilometres south of our home in Zhangde, where my parents resumed their missionary work. We continued our schooling there until 1927, when we were evacuated to the British Concession in Tianjin because of civil war in Henan. Our mission school was moved to British Army barracks. In the autumn of 1927 Father was invited to lecture on Chinese history, culture, and religion at the North China Union Language School in Beijing (known at that time in the West as "Peking"), and also to continue his archaeological research. We three children attended the Peking American School.

In 1929 my father was due for a year's home leave, so I was

8

able to refresh my Canadian identity once more, this time in Edmonton, where my grandparents had relocated. The eight-month journey home to Canada left me with a powerful and abiding sense of many of the countries of Asia, because we travelled the long way home, via India, the Persian Gulf, Mesopotamia, Syria, Lebanon, and Palestine. Father stayed three extra months in Palestine to work on two archaeological excavations while Mother took us three children back to Canada by way of Egypt, Cyprus, Constantinople, Athens, Italy, Paris, and London.

When we returned to Asia in August 1930, we children were dropped off at the Canadian Academy in Kobe, Japan, which followed the Ontario Department of Education curriculum. This was close enough to our Chinese home that we could be with our parents for summer holidays. My two sisters graduated from high school in 1932 and 1934 respectively and returned to Canada. I finished Grade Thirteen in 1935. Father, meanwhile, had been appointed Professor of Archaeology at Cheeloo University in Jinan, Shandong Province, a large Christian university supported by a half-dozen Protestant missions, where the teaching language was Chinese. Because he was the first to lecture on archaeology in Chinese, his teaching notes were printed by the Cheeloo University Press. After I graduated from high school my father and I toured several archaeologically and historically important Chinese sites. This trip, and Father's explanations, enabled me to begin to understand, appreciate, and share more fully his great interest in Chinese archaeology, history, and culture.

Father returned on leave to Canada in 1936 and enrolled at the University of Toronto in courses leading to a PhD in archaeology, thinking that he would return to China the following year and complete his thesis there. However, by 1937 the conflict between Japan and China had begun, and the United Church of Canada Board of Overseas Missions refused to approve his return. He remained in Toronto, having been offered a five-year position funded by the Rockefeller Foundation as research assistant in the East Asiatic section of the Royal Ontario Museum of Archaeology. He also was able to complete his PhD thesis. In 1942, after the United States had joined the war against Japan and Germany, he took a position as a Chinese cultural adviser to the United States Office of War Information in San Francisco, and later in Washington. In June 1946 Father suffered two heart attacks. He returned to Toronto in 1949, and continued his researches until his death in 1957.

In 1935 I returned to Canada to attend the University of Toronto, where I took a four-year honours degree in Philosophy and History, graduating in 1939. I then proceeded to Harvard University to take post-graduate studies in Far-Eastern History under John King Fairbank and Edward Reischauer. In December of that year I wrote the qualifying examinations for Third Secretary in the Department of External Affairs, and was put on the eligible list. After a brief posting in the Toronto Passport Office I took a nine-month educational leave to complete my MA and then take my general and oral examinations for a PhD, after which I was posted to the Passport Office in Windsor.

During my first year at Harvard I had met Sheila Skelton, a graduate of Queen's University and a graduate student in American History at Radcliffe College. She was the daughter of Dr. O.D. Skelton, Canadian Under-Secretary of State for External Affairs from 1925 until his death in 1941. I was quite captivated by this highly intelligent young lady with long blond hair, and by the end of the academic year in June 1940 our friendship had developed into something more. After receiving her Harvard MA, Sheila proceeded to earn a specialist teaching certificate in English and History at the Ontario College of Education, and then taught in schools in Sudbury and Montreal. We were married in June 1943.

During the twenty-five years between my joining the Department of External Affairs and my appointment as High Commissioner to Australia in 1965 I held many positions, nearly all of which made use of my familiarity with the Asia-Pacific region, and a good many of them turned out to be specifically helpful in preparing me for the work I would be doing in the South Pacific from 1965 to 1972. At the outbreak of war in 1939, Canada and the other old Dominions—Australia, New Zealand, Ireland, and South Africa—had agreed to establish diplomatic missions in each other's capitals, so by 1944, when I was first assigned to the

China desk, I had had many opportunities to meet representatives from Australia. Furthermore, one of my principal responsibilities was to oversee the establishment of the Canadian embassy in Chungking, West China. As Australia was opening its embassy there at the same time, there were many reasons to consult and exchange information.

Of course, the Canadian perspective on the Pacific Ocean, which focused on its northeast region, was different from that of the Australians. When, after the attack on Pearl Harbor, the Japanese moved to bring the whole of Southeast Asia under its control, Australia felt itself directly threatened. We too felt some concern about the possibility of an attack, initially via the Aleutian Islands in the northeast Pacific, but it soon became clear to us that Japan had little interest in pursuing that possibility, and in any case we had no forces available to deploy in the Pacific theatre for the war with Japan until after victory in Europe. Having committed almost everything we had to the European campaigns, Canada had limited naval forces available for the protection of our British Columbia coast. It was only after VE Day that we began to recruit the Sixth Division under Major General Hofmeister as the Canadian contribution to the Allied assault on Japan. Canadian participation in the assault on Japan ended with the dropping of the atomic bomb.

The direct threat that Australia had experienced during the war with Japan led to a post-war relationship with the United States that was different from ours. It led, for instance, to Australian participation in the Vietnam War, whereas Canada refrained, because it had been a member of the International Commission for Supervision and Control to oversee the ceasefire agreements in Vietnam, Cambodia, and Laos, which was signed in Geneva in 1954.

I was appointed Head of the Far Eastern Section of the American and Far Eastern Division of the Department of External Affairs in 1946, and Head of the Division in 1948. One of our most important concerns during this period was the Far Eastern Commission, which met in Washington to examine policies and plans for the occupation of Japan. Australians were even more deeply concerned in that process than we were, as they had been directly threatened by Japan, and had troops among the occupation forces.

In early 1950 I accompanied Lester B. Pearson, Secretary of State for External Affairs, on a trip to the first meeting of Commonwealth Foreign Ministers in Colombo, Ceylon. This turned out to be a round-the-world trip for Mr. Pearson, with stops in the Middle East, Pakistan, India, Burma, Singapore, Hong Kong, and Japan (where he lunched and conferred with General MacArthur), and in my opinion it helped give him the confidence to take a more direct role in these areas.

In November 1950 I was appointed Head of the Canadian Liaison Mission in Japan, accredited to General Douglas MacArthur, Supreme Commander for the Allied Powers in the occupation of Japan. Sheila and I and our two little children moved into the large Marler House in Tokyo in December. During Herbert Norman's time in Japan the Canadian priority had been the reform of Japanese government, and I continued to attend to that responsibility, as well as to the negotiation of the Japanese Peace Treaty, which was signed in April 1952, and the North Pacific Fisheries agreement. But much of my time was taken up with keeping an eye on Canadian participation in the Korean War, where we had 3,000 troops in the Commonwealth Division, three destroyers, and an air transport squadron.

In January 1953 the Honourable R.W. Mayhew arrived as Ambassador and asked me to stay for six months to help him adjust. During my two and a half years in Japan I maintained very close relations with my old Commonwealth colleagues; we had a common interest in the role of the Commonwealth Division in Korea. Canadian troops used Australian facilities at Kure for preparatory training, and wounded Canadians were sent to the Australian hospital at Ebisu, in Tokyo. Australian General Bridgford represented participating Commonwealth countries on the Allied Council for Japan.

We returned to Ottawa in the summer of 1953, and I returned to my old job as Head of the Far Eastern Division. My principal preoccupations were the Geneva Conference, which, although it failed to agree on a peace treaty to nail down the armistice in

Korea, did come up with a ceasefire in Indochina, and Canadian acceptance of membership in the three-country International Commissions for Supervision and Control in Vietnam, Cambodia, and Laos, on which Canadian diplomats and military officers served until 1972. Australia had diplomatic offices in South Vietnam, Cambodia, and Laos, and followed the work of the International Commissions closely.

In 1956 I accompanied the Honourable Paul Martin, Minister of Health and Welfare, on a round-the-world flight in the old C-5 to San Francisco; Honolulu; Manila; Hanoi and Saigon in Vietnam; Phnom Penh, Cambodia; Vientiane, Laos (all to visit the Canadians on the tripartite International Supervisory Commission); Djakarta; Melbourne (for the Olympics); Canberra; Wellington, New Zealand (for a Colombo Plan conference); Singapore; Rangoon; Colombo; Delhi; Karachi; and then home, via Europe. I got a good education as a tour co-ordinator, press officer, speech writer, note taker, and report writer. In all the capitals we got good background briefings from our Australian friends. Then in 1957 I made a trip to Saigon for a Colombo Plan conference as adviser to the Honourable W.J. Browne, Minister Without Portfolio in the Diefenbaker government.

In 1958 I was posted as the first Canadian High Commissioner to the Federation of Malaya (now Malaysia), and concurrently as the first Ambassador to Burma. In both these newly independent countries we worked closely with the Australians.

Returning to Canada in 1961, I was appointed Head of Defence Liaison (I) Division responsible for politico-military affairs. We exchanged views with our Australian colleagues on United Nations peacekeeping activities and on the training of armed forces officers for newly independent Commonwealth countries.

By the time of my appointment as High Commissioner to Australia in 1965, then, I had had considerable experience working with Australian diplomats, armed forces officers, and trade officials, because of our common interest in the Asia-Pacific area.

ACKNOWLEDGEMENTS

THE AUTHOR and publisher would like to thank the following people for their valuable contributions in preparing this work for publication: Serge Arpin, J. Larry Black, Douglas Campbell, Dennis Choquette, Christopher Cook, Mary Culham, Melissa Cutler, Paul Dole, Patricia Marsden-Dole, Kenneth Menzies, Norah Menzies, Andrea Segal, Amie Silverwood, and Mary Jane Starr.

PREFATORY NOTE

THESE LETTERS were written as an informal record of the activities of a Canadian high commissioner and his partner wife during the period in which they represented Canada in Australia and the South Pacific. We tried to share with our immediate family members in Canada what we learned about Australia (and later the South Pacific islands we visited) and the people we encountered. These family-oriented letters were distinct from the confidential or unclassified telegrams and letters from the office that I sent to the Department of External Affairs and other departments in Ottawa.

Some of our earliest letters from Australia are quoted in an introductory chapter; letters written in December 1965 and later are marked "A" if they were written by me, and "S" if they were written by my wife, Sheila. As we went on, Sheila wrote more letters than I did, as she had more time. But she knew my mind, because we had a strong mutual understanding and bond.

There are gaps in the story, because we did not take our typewriters on trips out of Canberra. I had hoped to fill these gaps by including official reports dictated at the office when I returned from trips, but these reports have not been found by Library and Archives Canada. I have, however, supplemented the letters with newspaper stories, a report on a trip to the Northern Territory, an article on Fiji's independence I wrote for the External Affairs monthly bulletin, and a speech I delivered to a subcommittee of the Australian House of Representatives and Senate.

I hope that the story we have recorded will serve to tell a fairly comprehensive and happy account of our sojourn.

ARTHUR MENZIES

INTRODUCTION

In the late summer of 1965 I was asked by Marcel Cadieux, Undersecretary of State for External Affairs, if I would be interested in an appointment as Canadian high commissioner to Australia. Having worked for four years at External Affairs headquarters, for the most part as Head of the Defence Liaison (1) Division charged with conferring with the Department of National Defence on such matters as North American defence co-operation with the United States, Canada's role in NATO, UN peacekeeping, and military assistance to newly independent Commonwealth countries, I recognized that it was time to move on.

Cadieux said, "Consult your wife Sheila, and let me have your answer soon." Marcel and I had shared an office on the ground floor of the East Block with Gordon Robertson (who later became Clerk of the Privy Council) and Gordon Hilborn (who later worked in Historical Division) when I first came to Ottawa in May 1942. We were good friends, and I realized that his proposal was an acknowledgement of my years of interest in the Asia-Pacific area.

Sheila's reaction was positively enthusiastic! Australia shared with Canada a common British heritage and, in particular, a common loyalty to the British Crown and to British legal and parliamentary traditions. We enjoyed a generally similar way of life. That Australia was an English-speaking country was a distinct plus for Sheila because she would not have to learn a new language, as we both had in Cuba, Japan, and Malaya.

We had a score of good Australian friends who had served with us in Ottawa, Tokyo, Kuala Lumpur, and Rangoon. One special friend was David Hay, who is the same age to the day as I am. He was educated at Geelong Grammar School, Oxford, and Melbourne University, served in the Australian Army from 1939 to 1945, and re-joined the Australian Department of External Affairs in 1946. He served as First Secretary in the Australian High Commission in Ottawa from 1950 to 1952, and returned to serve as High Commissioner to Canada from 1961 to 1964, when I was at Defence Liaison (1). He was Ambassador to the UN from 1963 to 1965. David went on to become the last Australian Administrator of Papua New Guinea, from 1967 to 1970, and finished his public service as Secretary of the Department of External Territories from 1970 to 1973. Along the way he was awarded the CBE, and consequently he was addressed as Sir David Hay. We have maintained a close friendship.

Sir David Hay was succeeded as Australian High Commissioner to Canada in 1964 by Sir Kenneth Bailey, a respected legal scholar and a former secretary to the Attorney-General's Department. Sir Kenneth took a great interest in comparing Canadian federal and provincial legislation with Australian federal and state legislation, and he wrote up his findings for the legal officers at home. I found his observations thought-provoking and, although not trained in the law, I was stimulated to pursue some of his comparisons. Sir Kenneth was kind enough to write letters of introduction for me.

Evan Gill, who served as Canadian High Commissioner to Australia from 1962 to February 1965, spoke to me enthusiastically about the appointment. He also sent letters of introduction to friends he had found helpful, including some property-holders around Canberra with good fly-fishing streams stocked with rainbow trout.

So, with Sheila's whole-hearted endorsement, I told the Undersecretary that I would feel honoured to be appointed High Commissioner to Australia.

Here it was then, another assignment to the Asia-Pacific area. This time, though, it was to the South Pacific, and a continent unknown to Europeans until Captain Cook claimed it for the British in 1770. This was a land that, a century earlier, Portuguese explorers secretly referred to as Terra Australia Incognito; others called it the Great Southland. My assignment would be as High Commissioner of Canada to Australia, but I extended it to include a concurrent interest in Canadian relations with South Pacific islands such as Papua New Guinea, Nauru, and Fiji. Happily, our children, Kenneth and Norah, could visit us in Australia once a year at public expense until they reached the age of twenty-one; this would give them an opportunity to experience our new Australian and South Pacific environment before they went their separate adult ways. Sheila, whom I had met at Harvard, where she was doing her master's degree, looked forward to this posting as an opportunity to learn about Australian history at the Australian National University, and to give talks about Canada to women's groups and schools. She relished the idea of being an active but independent partner in the relationship—formal as well as informal—between the Menzies and the Australians. This relationship with Australians had a nice homey (but not genuinely familial) ring about it, because the Australian Prime Minister at that time was also a Menzies, Sir Robert Gordon Menzies. Our shared surname was a windfall for me, as Sir Robert was a very popular leader at the time both at home and within the Commonwealth, although one with whom our own Prime Minister, Lester B. Pearson, did have occasional differences.

During our seven years in Canberra we recorded our adventures faithfully in weekly letters to the family at home. We began these letters as of October 28, 1965, just as we left Ottawa:

> So these notes, if maintained, will record some of the events and impressions of our trip to Australia. Of course we leave Canada with mixed feelings—leaving behind our children, our relatives, our home, our pets, our way of life among friends in Ottawa, and my work in the Defence Liaison (1) Division, which I have enjoyed. But we know that this is part of a Foreign Service officer's career, and we look forward to the new assignment and a new life in an Australia we cannot but already know we will like.

During the flight from Ottawa to Vancouver I then summed up for our family what I looked upon as the messy business of leaving:

Well, what a business, getting away from Ottawa. First it was getting Norah, age seventeen, off to grade twelve in Albert College boarding school in Belleville, a prospect she disliked, as it meant leaving all her close friends at Lisgar Collegiate in Ottawa. Kenneth was returning to a familiar environment at Queen's University in Kingston, taking his third-year honours course in Politics and Economics. Then there was the clear-up in the yard and in the cellar. I'm afraid I spent too much time tinkering and painting. Farewell parties took much time. All our friends were so good to us. Several had dinners. There were two or three big receptions. The Australian High Commissioner had a black-tie dinner for us and included us in many other functions, including one last night for the Australian Minister of Health, Reginald Swartz.

Packing and sorting before that was quite an undertaking, with our four years' accumulation. There were several lots: (a) things to be left in our house attic; (b) things to be stored in Ottawa by Moloughney's; (c) a sea shipment of pictures, books, winter clothes, etc., for Australia (leaving Montreal October 30 and arriving Sydney December 4); (d) an air cargo shipment of clothes to Australia; and, finally, (e) the sixty-six pounds we were each allowed on our air tickets, including warm clothing for Canada and Japan and light clothing for the tropics and the Australian summer, into which we are going.

Thankfully, that organizational challenge was over and done with as we left behind us the first frosty flakes of yet another cold Ottawa winter. On the flight from Toronto to Vancouver I wrote,

Prime Minister and Mrs. Pearson, Jim Cootes, his appointments secretary, Annette Perron, his private secretary, and some other members of his party are aboard. The P.M. asked me when I passed his seat why I hadn't turned up for a 6:00 p.m. appointment the other day at 24 Sussex Drive. The word had not got through to me. He said he had been thinking of me as a possible representative in Peking if we ever recognized the government there. He spoke warmly of Sir Robert Menzies, although they didn't see eye to eye on all matters. He said to tell him that a CBC team that went to New York recently to get popular reactions to the Canadian elections found little interest. One chap who was asked who the prime minister of Canada was replied, "Sir Robert Menzies"—which shows that Australians are very popular in the U.S.A. today, especially since they sent troops to Vietnam.

On the way down, we were able to spend a fortnight visiting old friends in Tokyo, Hong Kong, Saigon, Kuala Lumpur, Singapore, and Djakarta to get an update on these East Asian countries before flying on to Australia. In a letter from Saigon dated November 9 I described briefly the tense atmosphere there:

We have had two very interesting days here. I have had a number of useful talks, including one with the Foreign Minister and one with General Westmoreland, who commands the 165,000 U.S. troops here. It is hot and humid, although nearing the end of the monsoon season. This city is rather dirty, and seething with people, many of them refugees from the disturbed countryside. At night one can hear the crump-crump of 500-pound bombs being dropped outside Saigon on some Vietminh positions. Our host here has been Blair Seaborn, the Canadian Commissioner on the International Commission for Vietnam. He is a member of our service and a good friend of ours.

This brief visit to war-torn Vietnam brought into sharp focus the decade-old struggle for control of the country, with which I was intimately involved from July 1954 to January 1958 as Head of the Far Eastern Division. In this capacity I directed the establishment and the first years of operation of the Canadian delegations to the International Commissions for Supervision and Control in Vietnam, Cambodia, and Laos, in accordance with the Geneva Conference agreements. The war in Vietnam, to which Australia had by then committed troops in support of the South Vietnamese and American forces, while Canada stayed out because of our semi-judicial role on the International Commission and our prior commitment of Canadian forces to NATO, was to be the most contentious issue during my nearly seven years in Australia.

After visiting Djakarta, the capital of Indonesia, Australia's closest Asian neighbour, we flew out early in the morning of November 15 on a big Qantas aircraft heading to Australia. After crossing the island of Java, we flew about 1,400 miles over the ocean and entered Australian airspace at Broome, on the northwest coast of Western Australia. Leaving the coast, we peered out the plane windows at 35,000 feet and saw the Great Sandy Desert, a reddish-brown wasteland. Later the plane flew over the Macdonnell Ranges and over Ayers Rock and Alice Springs in the south of the Northern Territory. Flying on, we crossed the northeastern corner of South Australia, the southwestern corner of Queensland, and then northern New South Wales. When we reached the Pacific coast we were about 3,600 miles from Djakarta.

We were making a half-circle out over the ocean when the captain suddenly told us to put our seatbelts on for landing. I craned my neck to look down upon the approaching golden coastline of the Sydney beaches. There it was: our home for the next seven years. The sun shone brilliantly from a cloudless sky as we flew over the headlands that provide a setting for the magnificent jewel that is Sydney Harbour, at the centre of which we could see the spectacular white sail-like roofs of the nearly finished Sydney Opera House. The harbour was full of multicoloured sails of all sizes; the summer sailing season had already begun.

We were met at the airport by John Stiles, the Canadian Trade Commissioner and Commercial Counsellor, and by his wife Margaret, who had attended Queen's University with Sheila. How wonderful it was to be able to start this new adventure with old friends! John, with whom I would be working closely over the next two years, was the head of our historic Sydney Trade Office, the first Canadian government office on foreign soil. Also at the airport to greet us were a Sydney-based protocol officer from the Department of External Affairs, four journalists wishing to interview me, and two female journalists to interview Sheila. We were ushered into the VIP lounge for a short time while awaiting our flight to Canberra.

From the VIP lounge we had a view of the aircraft parking area and the luggage trains and service vehicles. I was struck by the shimmering bright light and the dryness of the air, very different from the warm humidity of the Southeast Asian capitals we had just visited. There were beds of flowers in their full summer bloom outside the terminal building.

I soon realized that we would need to attune our ears to Aussie pronunciations. The loudspeakers were announcing the arrivals and departures of the two domestic airlines. They announced that the "TII" flight for Brisbane was arriving. Only after I checked the board did I learn that it was a TAA (Trans Australia Airline) flight. Similarly, the "INI" aircraft whose departure was announced was really an ANA (Australian National Airways) flight. We learned later that although the graduates of the public (private) schools, strongly influenced by many English schoolmasters, spoke the King's English, the working class spoke Aussie talk, referred to by native Australians and outsiders alike as "Strine." Much later, when Sheila and I were playing doubles tennis with Australian friends, the husband exclaimed, "Look, she's got lace on her panties under her tennis frock just like Gorgeous Gussy" (the American lady tennis pro). But to our ears what he seemed to be saying was not "lace," but "lice."

We were greeted in Canberra by a senior officer from External Affairs, six Commonwealth high commissioners, and members of the Canadian High Commission. Sheila and I felt that we had been warmly welcomed. Tom Read, First Secretary, and his wife Penny drove with us and Andrew Jansen, our new chauffeur, to install us in our home, at 32 Mugga Way. On November 28, 1965, I wrote a letter to introduce our family to our new home:

This is my first letter from Canberra, although we have been here for nearly a fortnight. So I will try to give you a few first impressions. I had visited Canberra in December 1956, during my around-the-world trip with the Honourable Paul Martin. In the nine intervening years the city has been transformed, in appearance at least, by the flooding of the sandy flats of the Molonglo River to make six-mile-long Lake Burley Griffin, several sections of which are over half a mile wide. The lake divides the city into northern and southern sections, linked by two scenic six-lane bridges. Canberra is set in rolling sheep country at an altitude of about 2,000 feet, about ninety miles from the coast and roughly halfway between Sydney, 250 miles to the north, and Melbourne, 350 miles to the south. Between Canberra and the sea is the Great Dividing Range, while in the west and southwest the Snowy Mountains rise, at heights of 5,000 to 7,000 feet. We can drive to the coast or the Snowy Mountains in two to three hours.

Red Hill, which rises 500 feet or more directly behind our house, gives a fine view of the city and its sprawling suburbs. A little over a mile north is a lower hill called Capital Hill, and State Circle runs round it. A number of broad avenues run into State Circle. We reach Melbourne Avenue from Mugga Way, which skirts the foot of Red Hill. Our office is on Commonwealth Avenue, which runs north from State Circle and continues across the lake over one of the main bridges. The Parliament Buildings and the main government offices are not far from us. North of the lake is City Centre, the main shopping area, with some high-rise office buildings and one large department store, David Jones, as well as many smaller stores. Still on the North Side, to the west is the Australian National University, and to the east the great War Memorial, the Defence Headquarters, and Duntroon Military College.

Yesterday afternoon the weather was in the mid-seventies and delightfully sunny, like a day in early June in Canada, so Sheila and I took a drive around the lake in our official 1962

Pontiac. To the northwest there is quite a high hill, called
Black Mountain, with a good road up to the TV transmitters
and some nice picnic spots and lookouts. There was a
wonderful view from up there, with the city spread out below
us. There were over fifty two-passenger and three-passenger
sailing boats on the lake, making a most colourful scene.
Later we went down to one of the shorefronts, where the
boats were being launched. Almost all have buoyancy tanks
to keep them afloat. We saw three boats go over in ten
minutes, but the crews seemed not to have too much
difficulty righting them. There are a couple of cruise boats
on the lake and two or three police launches. Otherwise
motorboats are not allowed.

Most of Australia is pretty dry. The annual rainfall here is
twenty-five to thirty-five inches. The country looks dry and
feels dry, like Mexico or the southwestern U.S.A. Indeed,
Canberra might be mistaken for a university town in the
southwestern U.S.A. The soil is a red laterite. Grass, except
where it is watered, is everywhere a yellow-green. Gum trees
of the eucalyptus family, with scraggly bark and leathery
leaves, are the natural trees of the area. Many pines and
other trees have been planted, but the gums are the most
typical.

I wish you could see our house and garden. Vancouver
Street runs up to Mugga Way in front of our house. There is
a fifteen-foot stretch of grass next to the road, then a
sidewalk, and on our property a single-width road makes a
complete oval in front of our house. Then there's the most
gorgeous bank of pink roses, stretching eighty feet across the
front. Along the sides are great poplars and feathery
Southern Pines. We have a flagpole with a nylon Canadian
Maple Leaf flag that is renewed every month. The house
itself is fronted by another bed of flowers. It's a Spanish-style
house in white stucco with an orange tile roof. It is old, and
quite cut up inside, but it has been very nicely decorated and
furnished by the government. It was first rented in 1940 and
then bought about 1947. It is too small for large-scale

entertaining, but it is homey, and pleasant for getting to know small groups of Australians, and we will try to make the best of it that way. At the side of the house, reached by a screened porch from the dining room, is a secluded side garden with a great willow tree, a fish pond, a rough patio, and a nice sheltered lawn. At the back of the house we have quite a large vegetable garden and some fruit trees. Just now a fine crop of raspberries is ripening.

We get all manner of strange birds here. There is a magpie the size of a large crow. These are very cheeky birds. Last Sunday I was watching a cricket game, and a magpie kept swooping close to a small boy who was trying to post the scores on the board at the end of the field. The crows make the strangest noises, like babies crying. There are some lovely whistlers. And yesterday Sheila and I saw a magnificent red, green, and yellow parrot in our backyard, fully fifteen inches long. We have some nice big brown house spiders about two inches in diameter. Across the road there is a fine old honey-coloured Labrador dog. A good deal of riding is done here and there are horses grazing on the hill behind us.

Our office was completed two years ago. It is a fine-looking building with a good deal of glass. I have a nice office, decorated in green and white. My secretary is Joan Cameron. Tom Read is First Secretary, Philip Slyfield is on his first assignment abroad as Third Secretary, and our Administrative Officer is Charles Campbell, a man of fifty-five. On the commercial side we have Bernie O'Neill as Counsellor and Doug Campbell as Second Secretary. There are some Canadian clerks and stenos. With wives, our Canadian group totals about twenty, and there are about as many Australian staff.

The entertainment side of a high commissioner's job is normally the responsibility of his or her spouse. Sheila had had over twenty years of experience in entertaining, especially in our postings in Japan and Malaysia. One of our first undertakings in this regard when we arrived in Canberra was to advertise for an experienced cook and caterer. We were very fortunate to find Edith Dorn, a German-Australian in her mid-fifties who had worked for a wealthy Australian businessman in Sydney. Edith was an excellent cook, planner, and organizer of mid-sized lunches and dinners at our residence and larger receptions at our office building. Sheila and Edith would plan ahead, and Edith would cook and put in our freezer any dishes that could be prepared in advance, or order special dishes from caterers. Edith would calculate the number of waiters required, and gradually collected a group of experienced waiters whom she could count on. She had a small bedroom at the back of our residence, which we enlarged into a comfortable small apartment for her.

Edith claimed to have been the first woman to swim the English Channel. She was also a trophy-winning lawn bowler. Her previous employer had owned a stable of racehorses, so Edith had learned about horseracing, and enjoyed betting on the weekend in Sydney and Melbourne. I tried a few flutters myself, but had no luck.

Edith stayed with us during our nearly seven years in Australia. She had a few moody periods and some ill health, but we remained good friends. Sheila continued to correspond with her, and sent birthday and Christmas cards until Edith's death at the age of ninety.

§ My primary tasks in Australia were, first, to call on the Governor General, the Prime Minister, the Minister for External Affairs, the Minister of Trade, and other key federal cabinet ministers, and later the state premiers and the key senior public-service officers, so that I could count on their friendship and understanding if I needed to take up a Canadian issue with them. Second, I was expected to promote Canadian trade with Australia—and sometimes in competition with Australia. In doing so it was important to work closely with my commercial counsellor in Canberra and our trade commissioners or commercial counsellors in Sydney and Melbourne. I also wanted to meet Canadian businessmen to offer any help we could give. Third, I wanted to meet Canadians living in Australia, such as university professors, exchange teachers, and the thirty or so graduate students who were studying at the Australian National University in Canberra. Fourth, I called on heads of diplomatic missions. My fifth concern was public relations in general. This involved accepting as many invitations to speak to Australian audiences as possible. I encouraged all the Canadian staff to accept talk requests. When we visited state capitals and other centres, I indicated in advance that I and my wife would be glad to speak to academic, social, and other interested groups.

The letter of November 28 continued:

We have had a lot of official calls to make and receptions to attend in these first few weeks. I have called on the Prime Minister, Sir Robert Menzies, who was genial, and called me "kinsman." I have also called on the Minister for External Affairs, Mr. Paul Hasluck, officials of the departments, speakers of the Senate and the House of Representatives, and various diplomats. On Friday Sheila and I went to call on Lord and Lady Casey at Government House. We each had half an hour's chat, and then had lunch with Their Excellencies and their staff. As a former minister for External Affairs, Lord Casey does an excellent job as governor general. He gave me two of his most recent books, *Personal Experience: 1939 to '46* and *The Future of the Commonwealth*.

A variety of incidents from these first months in Australia illustrate some of the ways we were made aware that the new world we were going to be living in was a mixture of the different and the familiar. Early in our Australian tour we visited Broken Hill, in the Far West region of New South Wales. This is the site of the richest silver-lead mines in the world, and BHP (Broken Hill Proprietary Company) is the biggest Australian mining company. The union, the Barrier Industrial Council, really runs the town of 25,000, as well as the mines. We were told that the high-paying underground mining jobs were completely union-controlled, and that jobs were passed on from father to son.

I gave a talk in the union hall, drawing comparisons with nickel mining in Sudbury and coal mining in Cape Breton. When refreshments were served, one of the men said, "You're from Hawaii." I thought he regarded Canada as being so far from their tight-knit closed society that it seemed to him as exotic as pictures he had seen of Hawaii. Later, when I drew this expression to the attention of Sir Harold White, the National Librarian and our neighbour in Canberra, he smiled and told me that what he was probably saying, with a strong Strine accent, was "You're from away."

The Australian Capital Territory, or ACT, is a small, specialized preserve similar to Brasilia, the inland capital of Brazil, and it is about the size of our National Capital Region—Ottawa, Gatineau, and Gatineau Park. Quite a number of my Australian colleagues had cottages (which they called shacks) in the bush, perhaps by a pool in the Murrumbidgee River, where, in early winter, they would stock trout that by springtime would be large enough for fly-fishing. Australians, like Canadians, enjoy that type of bushy outdoor living, which, when the occasion arose, I found a refreshing change from sitting behind my desk reading papers and dictating dispatches to Ottawa.

I recall that just before leaving for Australia we went to Christ Church Cathedral in Ottawa to hear the Anglican Bishop of Western Australia speak. In order to show that he was a man of the people he remarked that "it was nothing for his parishioners to see their bishop going to the outback in his shorts." This was meant to conjure up the vision of the intrepid bishop striding off into the bush in very informal wear, but for some in the Canadian audience it produced the image of a reverend gentleman heading to an outhouse in his underpants.

Besides directing us to his fly-fishing friends, Evan Gill had given us a letter of introduction to John and Pam Hyles, who owned Booroomba sheep station, to the south of Canberra in the Australian Capital Territory. On our first visit John took us out in his truck to show us how he moved grazing sheep from paddock to paddock. After seating us beside him on the broad front seat he pursed his lips and sounded out a piercing whistle, which brought two border collies running. "Good dogs!" he said; then, "Git in," and they jumped into the back of the truck. We drove to a paddock where sheep had cropped off most of the grass. John opened the gate to drive in, and the gate to the neighbouring paddock, where the grass was long. He called out, "Go git!" and the two dogs jumped out and crouched at two strategic positions on the far side of the paddock. John whistled a further command and the collies started to round up the sheep and herd them to the open gate leading to the next paddock. Sheila and I were very impressed by the way the dogs chased the sheep into a compact mob, quickly cut off any wandering sheep, and then hounded them through the gate and into the next paddock. John praised the dogs and fed them each a biscuit before he commanded them again to "Git in" for the return trip. During our years in Australia we never tired of going to watch sheepdog trials.

The Hyleses would invite a few privileged diplomats to a barbecue at Booroomba station. I recall one evening being invited out with the American Ambassador, Ed Clark, and his wife. Ed Clark was a proud Texan with a booming voice who loved to boast about how almost everything in Texas was bigger and more modern than anything in Australia. As we sat out on the porch having a drink before the barbecue, three kangaroos hopped in from the bush to nibble the well-watered green grass around the house. Ed observed this scene for a moment and then declared, "Well, my friend, I do have to admit that your grasshoppers are bigger than ours in Texas!"

I was thrown into my new job and didn't have much of an opportunity to adjust before I found myself in front of the media arguing on Canada's behalf. The day after we arrived, the newspaper headlines read, "Canadian Bluetongue Invades Australia." It happened that a grazer from upstate New South Wales had picked up a couple of Thermos bottles of Charolais semen in Vancouver to upgrade his cattle. Many Australians have the habit of going to a pub at the end of the afternoon to have a beer with the boys. This grazer did just that, and he blabbed about what he had done.

30

So he got caught. The Australian sanitary authorities decided to make an example of him, so they sent up the Army with blow-torches, and they burned about a square mile of bush on his property, killing all the cattle, which they then buried and covered with lime. Right away I had sessions with the press, trying to convince them that we had never, ever had bluetongue in Canada. This didn't matter to the Australians, because there had been two or three cases down in Texas and they might have come across the open border. It was just a little reminder that we were in a different country, and that it had its own rules, which we had to learn to live with.

ONE

1965

December 12, 1965 · *Canberra*

s » We have had our first visit from a Canadian cabinet minister and his wife. Senator John Connolly is Government Leader in the Senate and Minister Without Portfolio. They couldn't have been nicer, so it was very lucky for us. We tried things out on them that we now know will work or won't work when we have other important visitors from Canada. They had been at the Commonwealth Parliamentary Conference in New Zealand. He has just been elected chairman of this group, and thus Canada will be the host country for the conference next year. Within the year he is supposed to travel all over the Commonwealth and visit the parliaments. Thus it was chiefly to see parliamentarians that he came here. The only catch was that Parliament was due to adjourn Friday for the long holiday recess, so we were very busy trying to round up members the evening before, when they were trying to finish up House business. We had a buffet supper here from 6:00 to 8:00—come at 6:00, have one drink, sit down and eat at 6:30, and finish up quickly so that they can be back in the House before the evening session at 8:00. Most members don't have their wives in Canberra, so we were able to have nine members, including the Speaker of the Senate and the Leader of the Opposition. The latter, Mr. Calwell, stayed on later and gave a wonderful talk, reminiscing along historical lines about people such as

General MacArthur. Later on, Arthur and Senator Connolly went down to the House and Senate. Friday morning we all toured the ACT headquarters, viewing plans for future buildings, etc. So far they have a great feeling of space everywhere, and lots of trees in parks, rather like the greenbelt around Ottawa. It certainly is attractive.

It is hard to realize that we have only been here three weeks. The people are very friendly and very like Canadians. I have to keep reminding myself that I'm not at home and just talking to a group of Canadians. The climate has been wonderful since we arrived. It's actually been very changeable, at times cool so that you want the furnace on, at other times 80 degrees outside and you're glad to return to a cool house. On the whole it's getting warmer each day, and most people will spend Christmas at the beach or in some sort of outdoor holiday activity. The only catch is the flies. They're not a biting variety, but like small houseflies, and they just stick to you. People are always waving their hands around their faces, because the flies just come in and land on you. It is especially funny at the airport, because visitors think people are waving to welcome them. It is called the Canberra wave! Evidently there is no cure—you can put on a cream to try to keep them off, and use a sort of DDT, but they are still a general nuisance. In the breeze of the evening they disappear, and it is very pleasant.

A » I'll start by adding my piece about the Connolly visit. They came to our lovely new chancery building Friday morning and, after a tour, had coffee with all the staff, to whom Senator Connolly spoke informally. Friday noon he and I attended a luncheon given by the Department of External Affairs for him and other visiting parliamentarians. Then after lunch we visited the Australian National University here in Canberra. In the beginning ANU consisted of two parts: undergraduate facilities for civil servants, including night school, and a graduate research centre. These have now been joined together, with an enrolment of about 2,500. We got a briefing first from the Vice-Chancellor, Sir Julian Huxley. (The title "Sir" is accorded to all sorts of big shots here, as in Britain, some for merit, and some for their contributions to party funds. Huxley would be in the first class.) Then we went to University House, the graduate residence, where we had tea with about twenty Canadian graduate students and research fellows, who are studying on Commonwealth and ANU scholarships in such diverse fields as nuclear physics, geology, geography, philosophy, public finance, and English. This gave Connolly a good idea of the connections between Australian and Canadian universities, and also enabled us to meet most of these fellow countrymen for the first time.

Another visitor in the past week was John Fisher, chairman of the Canadian Centennial Commission. I was glad to have the opportunity to talk over with him the plans—or the lack of plans—to assist posts abroad in marking the Centennial. I gave a men's lunch for him so that he could meet newspapermen and officials of the Australian Commission and discuss their part in Expo 67 in Montreal.

December 19, 1965

s » I have just been reading a book that emphasizes the importance of the cities of Australia. It says that although to most people Australia means gum trees and kangaroos, sunburnt plains and lonely stockmen, bush fires and Aborigines, the more important Australia is actually that of Sydney and Melbourne, the great cities of the coast. Well, this past week we had three nights and two full days in the bright lights of the great city of Sydney. Compared with the 80,000 of Canberra, it has two and a half million, so it is rather like going to New York from little Ottawa. However, I did not find the traffic as terrific as in Tokyo, Hong Kong, and some other Asian cities. For one thing, there are few scooters or bicycles. Roads are much, much poorer than American ones, though. There are too many bends, and they are very narrow, so you can't make good time travelling. There are more small European and Australian cars than large American ones. We stayed with Margaret and John Stiles. John is the Canadian Trade Commissioner there. I went to Queen's University with Marg, and John is a very capable Trade and Commerce officer, quiet and slow-spoken but very helpful and efficient, so we find them very congenial. They have three children, a live-wire aged three, a boy of twelve who had just started his holidays, and a boy of sixteen whom we didn't see, as he was off at cadet camp, instructing. They have a German maid they brought from their last post, in Germany. In the past two years they have been faced with the big job of finding and then furnishing the house that the Canadian government owns. It is located in Vaucluse, on the south shore of Sydney Harbour, and there is an old fifteen-foot lighthouse on the property, still used for navigation purposes. It is a good district, overlooking one of the lovely bays of Sydney Harbour, and the house is spacious for entertaining. They had dinner for twenty-four—six small tables of four—in their large dining room, which gave us a good opportunity to meet the Canadian community of Sydney. We made calls on several Australians, which I'll leave for Arthur to describe.

A » Sydney is the air and shipping port of entry to Australia for Canadians. The harbour entrance was noted by Captain Cook in 1770 and named Port Jackson, before he anchored in Botany Bay, a little way south. In 1788 the "First Fleet" of convicts went first to Botany Bay, but in a few days they moved north to Port Jackson and established themselves at Sydney Cove.

For over a hundred years, until the completion of the Canadian Pacific Railway through the Rocky Mountains in 1876, British ships commanded by men like Captain Cook, Captain Vancouver, Captain Bligh, and many others, after sailing out from England around the Cape of Good Hope, were re-provisioned in Port Jackson before they proceeded across the Pacific, where they explored, settled, and supplied the west coast of British North America.

Unlike other major cities in Australia, which were laid out with broad avenues by British surveyors, Sydney grew in a higgledy-piggledy way around the harbour and the many little bays and inlets running off it. The harbour divides Sydney into two areas, north and south, which are joined by the great Harbour Bridge, often congested by traffic. The south side, served by

George and Pitt streets, is the centre of the city, with tall office buildings and shopping centres. To the east of the Harbour Bridge is a promontory on which the striking Sydney Opera House, with its soaring sail roofs, is located. Jorn Utzon, a Dane, won an international contest for his design, but after over ten years of construction overruns and design difficulties there are severe tensions between him and the city management.

Sheila and I paid a joint call on the Governor of New South Wales, Sir Kenneth Street, in the impressive Government House in downtown Sydney. He's an old man of about seventy, I should judge, and he is filling in until the arrival of Mr. Roden Cutler, the first member of the Australian diplomatic corps to be taken on as governor. His daughter, a Mrs. McKay, is a friend of friends of ours in Ottawa, the Ross Tolmies.

With John Stiles I called on the Chief Justice of the Supreme Court of Australia, Sir Garfield Barwick. He had been Minister for External Affairs from 1961 to 1964, and spoke very critically of Duncan Sandys and his handling of the independence of Malaysia, saying that the confrontation with Indonesia need not have occurred if there had been more flexibility. Another interesting meeting I had was lunch with Sir Philip Baxter, Vice-Chancellor of Sydney University (8,000 students) and chairman of the Australian Atomic Energy Commission. He is pressing the government for the establishment of a nuclear power plant near Adelaide, in South Australia, by 1972, and is interested in co-operating with either Canada or Britain on this project. The Premier of New South Wales, Mr. Askin, received me and gave a men's reception to enable me to meet members of his cabinet, and others with a connection with Canada. This was an agreeable affair, and it provided a number of useful contacts. Of course we expect to return to Sydney quite often, so these early contacts should prove useful, especially since Sydney is more business-oriented than other state capitals.

December 29, 1965

s » Wednesday we held an office party. On some occasions it has been held at the residence, but the thought of forty-one adults and twenty-seven children in this confined space made us decide to use the office building. It is very large, and the basement floor is equipped with a kitchen, a cafeteria, and a large room for showing films. We had all the Canadian staff and their families and all the local staff and their families, including people like the janitor, the gardener, and the driver, so it was a really complete party, and they all mixed together very well. At 5:30 we had fifty minutes of films —geared for children mostly, but because even the children are of mixed ages and many are at the stage when they can be considered young adults, only two of the films were of the cartoon variety, and then, to appeal to the older ones, there was one about beavers and one on choosing a dog. Then came the food part—hot dogs and hot mince pie with ice cream, mostly beer for the adults and Coca-Cola for the kids. Hot dogs are almost unknown here, and a real novelty. The shop where I had ordered the buns made a mistake, and we had to scrounge around to about ten different other shops to get buns enough of all sorts and descriptions. Our cook, Edith Dorn, had made the mince pies. We heated them here, and they were very good. Then everyone went upstairs to the lobby, where we had put up a live pine Christmas tree—a little straggly by Canadian standards, but quite acceptable—and sang Christmas carols in a circle around it. Last of all I gave a gift to each of the children. I had quite a time shopping for them, not knowing the children well yet, having only their ages and names, but all seemed pleased.

A » For our Christmas present this year we bought an Australian car called a Holden. Holden was a coach-builder in Australia like Fisher in the U.S.A., and when General Motors came out here they linked up to build a GM/Holden car, which is about the size of a Ford Falcon or a British Ford Consul. Our car is a Holden Special 179 Sedan, with automatic drive. It is Corinth blue and has blue upholstery. We have British-type over-the-shoulder seat belts, which we will use for out-of-the-city driving. It is a pleasure driving without a gearshift.

Christmas Day we went to a morning reception at the home of a neighbour, Harold Cox of *The Melbourne Herald*, then had a chicken dinner here. In the evening we went to the grounds of the Parliament Buildings, where the YMCA had arranged a "carols by candlelight" observance. There was a band and microphones and loudspeakers, and about three thousand sat on the grass with song sheets and candles, singing carols.

Next day we drove down to the seacoast, which is ninety-five miles away. Leaving the Canberra Valley one climbs up over a range of hills and then enters wide-open sheep country with a few sleepy towns and small dried creeks, until one reaches the Coast Range at Clyde Mountain, where the pass is 2,470 feet. From there we had quite a run down to the sea, where there is a resort at Bateman's Bay, crowded with holiday-makers. We visited a new surf beach about five miles away over very dusty roads, then turned back to the main coastal highway and went south toward Melbourne for about fifteen miles through a New South Wales state forest reserve of gum trees. Just beyond Bimbimbie (don't you love the names?) we turned back to the sea at Broulee. Here my third secretary commercial's wife has a family cottage on a lovely headland. To the south there is a perfect eight-mile sand beach with wonderful surf. We stayed for a short while, then headed home. We did 245 miles in the round trip. So now we have some sense of the lie of the land: there are the Snowy Mountains to the west of us, with winter skiing, to be reached in two and a half hours, and on the other side of the Great Dividing Range, also about two and a half hours away, there is the sea, which is supposed to provide a good holiday for about six months out of the year.

TWO

1966

January 9, 1966

A » Today we decided to explore the country to the northwest of Canberra. We drove thirty miles north through sheep country with low rolling hills, to Yass. At the bottom of each valley there is a creek or a dried creek bed, along which, if there is a trace of water, you'll see some green grass and willows. The hills are covered with sparse grass that has turned yellow now. Occasional gum trees provide shade for dirty, dust-coloured sheep or cattle. The home-steads look like our summer cottages, with big six-foot-diameter galvanized tanks outside to store rainwater from the eaves. Some windmills raise water for stock reservoirs. There are a few galva-nized sheep-shearing sheds and baled-hay sheds, but no barns as we know them. Everywhere the sun shines—indeed it beats down all day, and the land is parched and dry. The towns have mainly Victorian-style hotels, and the stores are only beginning to get modern storefronts. Inside they have the same goods as in North America. We visited a couple of park entrances to the Burrinjuck Reservoir, which is perhaps twenty miles long. These were dusty down-at-the-heel spots, but the people were well dressed and drove new cars, and they had trailers and fine speedboats for waterski-ing, etc. We drove west of Yass to a village with the delightful name of Wee Jasper, on the Goodradigbee River. Near there we lunched under an old gum tree with a nice little breeze but about two hundred flies, despite spray on exposed places. Then we made our way back over a reasonably marked road called Captain's Flat Road. This became a very rough hill track that took us for twenty-five miles over hill and dale, mainly through gum tree forests. Sheila had to get out and open and shut stock gates a dozen times, and we had some pretty precipitous hills to climb and descend. Fortunately the road was dry and firm, if rocky, and apart from getting very hot and dusty, we made it, and furthered our education.

January 23, 1966

A » The retirement of Sir Robert Menzies has been the highlight of the week's news here. It seemed to me to take considerable strength of will to decide to retire while still fit and in full political control, with no one audibly urging him to go. He had been prime minister from 1939 to 1941, a period when he showed his intellectual arrogance and lost control of his party, which disintegrated. He patiently built the Liberal Party thereafter, and in 1949 he won the prime ministership again, and has held it since in a coalition with the smaller Country Party. He has been a dominating figure through the brilliance of his mind and his oratorical eloquence. His government rode the surf-wave of economic development and prosperity here in Australia with a pragmatic program reasonably responsive to what the people asked of it. Internationally Sir Robert was rather Churchillian in his ideas of the Empire and Commonwealth. Although through the pressure of events he learned something about his Asian neighbours — and even these he rarely visited, preferring to go to England — he seemed to have insufficient understanding of and sympathy for the new nationalism of Africa. So Australia stayed away from the Lagos Conference. Well, he decided he did not want to fight another election, due at the end of this year, so he wisely and courageously decided, as many others have not, to retire while on top. Mr. Harold Holt, 57, the former minister of finance, takes over. He does not have the colour of Sir Robert, but is cautious and has long experience in government. I hope he goes further in reflecting the views of younger Australians in foreign affairs.

This week the Department of Immigration held its sixteenth annual Citizenship Convention, with representatives of voluntary groups—three of them—discussing the problems of migrants, whom Australia takes in at the rate of 140,000 a year. Canada is a competitor for good immigrants, and so is interested in what is done here.

January 30, 1966

s » Last night Arthur gave his first big speech in Australia, to the Australian Highland Club and Burns Club. The Scots here are really organized and, with over five hundred members and a permanent building, they have one of the five real clubs in the world. They had a big turnout for the dinner—between 120 and 150 people, a cross-section of society that we would not usually come into contact with, and one that is not often exposed to Canadian speakers—so it was a good opportunity for Arthur. He did very well, having done a lot of homework on Burns, his poetry, and the Scots influence in Canada and in Australia. It was a colourful evening, with the haggis being piped in to the dining room, the Scotch whisky poured on it, and then an address to the haggis delivered in the broadest Scotch by an old man of eightynine who had come up from Sydney especially for the occasion. The local butcher who prepared the haggis gave the recipe in the paper: 6 lbs. liver, 6 lbs. oatmeal, 4½ lbs. onions, 1 lb. suet, 3 oz. each black pepper and pimento—all in a plastic bag instead of the traditional sheep's paunch. A great tragedy occurred: it exploded in the boiler while they were cooking it! However, they salvaged enough for the head table, so we were not spared. Arthur said that it tasted better than the haggis he and Kenneth had one day in London this summer. I just took two bites and like many others was able to pass it down to someone at the other tables to give them a rare treat. By the time they toasted the Queen, Scotland, kindred clubs, the Lassies, the Land of Their Adoption, the press, the artists, as well as Arthur's main one, "the immortal memory of Robert Burns," and sang Scottish songs, it was midnight when we returned.

Officially Australia Day is January 26, the same as the Indians' national day, but here it is celebrated by a public holiday on Monday January 31. So this is a holiday weekend, and as school resumes on Tuesday, February 1, it is rather like the Labour Day weekend, the last fling at the beach for many before starting a new school year.

February 6, 1966

A » The most interesting event of the week was the visit of the British Minister of Defence, Mr. Denis Healey, who put to Australians and New Zealanders the proposition that if Britain had to give up its bases in Malaysia and Singapore it would have to take its forces home, unless alternative facilities were built in advance in Australia. I went to a National Press Club luncheon, where he gave a good talk and answered questions in such a way that the questioners thought they were getting something pretty frank. I had to busy myself behind the scenes to get a full account of what had been discussed.

Another event was the press conference Friday afternoon in which the new Prime Minister, Mr. Holt, announced the scope and the nature of the Australian participation in Expo 67. The Australians expect to spend $3.6 million on their 30,000-square-foot pavilion. They exhibited a model of it. There will be a kangaroo and wallaby enclosure outside and a tank for barrier reef fish. Inside there will be displays showing such things as the Snowy Mountains hydroelectric scheme, bauxite and iron mining, art, Aboriginal art, sport, and scientific achievement. This week we have two Canadians from Expo coming to discuss Australian artistic participation. More anon.

February 12, 1966

S » Monday, February 14, is the changeover date to decimal currency. As you likely know, both currencies will be in use for about two years here, to give them a chance to get all their cash registers and such equipment changed over. They have been conducting quite an educational campaign on TV, radio, the press, etc., but there is going to be a period of confusion in making change for a few weeks, because although £1 converts exactly to $2, the pence and cents don't work out so neatly. 1d equals one cent, but both 2d and 3d equal two cents, etc. It means that a lot of prices for things like milk or bread or newspapers will go up or down a fraction, and all retailers naturally see it as an opportunity to put prices up, so there is a great outcry. As the Canadian dollar is worth $2.40, not $2.00, we will still have some converting to do, but from our point of view it will be a great improvement over the £.s.d. After three months I'm still slow calculating in them.

March 6, 1966

A » We returned last evening from our first official visit to the state of Victoria, concentrated almost entirely in Melbourne, its capital city. As we saw little of the state, I am not going to try to lecture you on it. Suffice it to give just a few orientating facts. Victoria is in the extreme southeast corner of Australia, opposite the island of Tasmania. With an area of 87,884 square miles, it is three times the size of New Brunswick but only one-thirtieth the size of Australia; it has a population of over three million, one-quarter of Australia's people. Victoria was cut out of New South Wales on July 19, 1851, and for much of its length the border between the two follows the Murray River. Much of the northeastern corner of the state is occupied by the Australian Alps, where the skiing takes place in the Australian winter. The Great Dividing Range crosses the state from east to west. Victoria is quite well watered, by Australian standards, and the state has done a great deal to store water in reservoirs. It has fine wheat fields, dairy and sheep farms, and orchards. However, Victoria is probably most noted for the industries about Melbourne, which has a population of 2.1 million, as well as the financial activity, the schools and universities, and the cultural life and horse racing of a metropolis.

Canada has had a trade commissioner's office in Melbourne since 1892. We buy about $18 million worth a year through Melbourne—sultanas, canned pears and peaches, mutton and wool, and quite a variety of manufactured goods. We sell much more—newsprint, autos and parts, lumber, plastics and synthetic rubber, stainless steel, sulphur, and a long list of manufactured goods. We have a fair-sized Canadian community there, and connections in Melbourne University, etc. Prince Charles is at Timbertop, the mountain branch of Geelong Grammar School, whose main campus is in the industrial and port city of Geelong, about thirty-five miles southwest of Melbourne. Both the former Prime Minister, Sir Robert Menzies, and the current P.M., Mr. Holt, are Melbournians.

We flew down to Melbourne on Monday, February 28, taking an hour and a half to fly the three hundred fifty miles in a Super Viscount. We were met by representatives of the Premier's department, and our Commercial Counsellor Adrian Gilbert and his wife. We were interviewed by press and radio and television at the airport, and tried to give them something reportable about trade, the need for more frequent air service between Canada and Australia, and the desirability of more inter-university exchanges of staff and students. It was a lovely warm summer day, and Melbourne looked its best for our arrival. It takes about forty-five minutes to drive into the centre of the city, through miles of suburbs with neat brick bungalows, each with its small rose garden. Toward the centre the buildings become bigger. There are many fine old ornate Victorian stone buildings of four to six storeys, but beside them there are springing up twenty-storey modern apartment and office buildings. O-Y-O (own-your-own) apartment house schemes are popular. Melbourne streets are broad and laid out on a square pattern. There are large parks, and the narrow Yarra River runs through the centre, emptying into Port Phillip Bay. There are excellent sand beaches right in the city. We stayed at the Windsor Hotel, opposite the imposing Parliament Buildings with their Grecian facade.

I recall that when I visited Melbourne in November 1956 with the Honourable Paul Martin to see part of the Olympic Games, en route to a Colombo Plan meeting in New Zealand, I was detained on business at the airport, and so arrived at the Windsor Hotel after the main party. When I went up to the desk and asked if they had a room for Menzies, the elderly clerk replied rather peremptorily, "Yes, and what's that to you, young man?" It developed that the Prime Minister, Sir Robert Menzies, was staying at the same hotel at that time. The hotel is genteel and Victorian, in the manner of the Windsor in Montreal, but quite comfortable. As all hotel accommodation in Australia is on a bed-and-breakfast basis, I enjoyed some fine steaks for breakfast, just to lay a foundation for the other two big meals we were entertained with each day.

Our first function was a call at the enormous Government House, far bigger than Rideau Hall in Ottawa. Here we were received by the Governor, sixty-year-old Major General Sir Rohan Delacombe, and Lady Delacombe. He is a retired British Army officer, a descendant of the commander of the British Army detachment on San Juan Island in the Strait of Georgia back in 1858, when an American settler shot a prize pig belonging to the Hudson's Bay Company—an incident that almost brought on a war. Sir Rohan ended his military career as commander of the British sector of Berlin from 1959 to 1962, where he knew our Canadian representatives, George Grande and Bert Hart. Other guests at the luncheon were the British High Commissioner in Canberra, Sir Charles Johnston, and Lady Johnston, who were down for the opening of a British goods week at George's, a swank Melbourne store. After lunch we went out to inspect the pool and the garden, which was at its peak for a Red Cross garden party. It seemed a bit incongruous to us to see a British governor and British Army aides in 1966.

After lunch, Adrian Gilbert joined me for a call on Sir John Williams, Chairman and Managing Director of the Herald and Weekly Times Ltd. He is a rather crusty old chap who publishes one of the great mass circulation (250,000) papers of Australia. His firm owns the Boyer Newsprint Mills in Tasmania, which mixes two-thirds Canadian long-staple pulp with eucalyptus pulp. He also buys a lot of Canadian newsprint. Then we went on to call on Mr. E.K. Sinclair, the editor-in-chief of *The Age*, one of the more sophisticated Australian papers, which maintains correspondents in Singapore, London, and Washington. He is the current president of the Australian Associated Press, which combines with the British news agency Reuters to cover the Far East. He had some interesting comments on the growing interest of Australians in background news about Asia.

Our next call was on the Honourable Sir Henry Winneke, Chief Justice of the Supreme Court of Victoria, and solicitor general of the state from 1951 to 1964. He was very interesting in his comments on the co-ordination of legislation between the states on such matters as company law, and also on the relations between the Commonwealth (federal) government and the states.

From there Gilbert and I went to call on Dr. David Myers, Vice-Chancellor (principal) of La Trobe University, the third of the city's universities (the other two are the University of Melbourne and Monash University), which is supposed to open to receive its first students in March 1967. Buildings are being erected on a 500-acre site in the northern Melbourne suburbs of Preston and Heidelberg. Dr. Myers, an Australian, was Dean of Engineering at the University of British Columbia for fifteen years before returning last year to take on this job. He has two or three grown-up children in Canada. At a little reception given by Dr. Myers was Dr. Galbraith, Chancellor of the University of Alberta and publisher of *The Red Deer Advocate*, who is on a world cruise.

Monday evening Gwen and Adrian Gilbert gave a small dinner party for us at their home. Other guests were Mr. and Mrs. Gene Marshall—he is architect of the Melbourne Tramways, and the son of a British missionary in China whom we had befriended as a young Canadian Army N.C.O. in Ottawa twenty-two years ago, before he went to Australia with a radar team and became engaged and decided to stay on—and Bill and Barbara Wilcock; Bill is manager of the Commonwealth Bank Mint in Melbourne, and we had known him in Malaya when he was helping to set up the Central Bank of Malaya. Bill gave us an example of Strine from his visit to Ireland: he asked for scotch and soda and got scotch and cider! Figure out that pronunciation if you can.

Tuesday morning began with a wreath-laying ceremony at the Shrine of Remembrance. This is a massive granite structure set in a fifty-acre park on the highest hill in Melbourne. Australian and British flags flanked the Canadian flag, flown in honour of my visit, while the Canadian maple, planted three years ago, still struggles to adjust to the reversal of seasons. The shrine is like a great Greek temple; within the sanctuary the Stone of Remembrance is lowered in a square in the floor, so that you have to bow your head to read it. A unique feature is a small hole in the roof so placed that a beam of sunlight moves across the inscription on the stone—"Greater love hath no man"—precisely at eleven o'-clock on November 11, and has only failed to do so because of cloud on two occasions since the shrine was completed in 1933.

Next we went to call on the Lord Mayor of Melbourne in the Town Hall. This is an imposing building. The Mayor, Mr. Beaurepaire, is a youngish man whose family owns a motor-car tire concern. He told us that the city of Melbourne, which (like the city of London) comprises only one square mile of downtown Melbourne, has a resident population of 80,000; the rest live in suburbs.

From the Town Hall I went to inspect Gilbert's office. He has two Canadian assistants, John Tennant and Ray Lucas, a local office manager, and half a dozen clerks. They have two thousand square feet of modern office space in a good building and present a good impression of Canada. Most of their work is commercial, but in addition they handle quite a volume of consular and information work, which has presented some problems that I wanted to discuss.

Then on to the Parliament Buildings to attend a Cabinet luncheon tendered by the Premier, Sir Henry Bolte. This fifty-seven-year-old Liberal politician has been premier for nearly eleven years, and is obviously in full command of the state. We had a spirited conversation about the division of powers between the federal and state governments here and in Canada. As Sir Henry puts it, "It's all wrong. Our constitution leaves the residual powers with the states, but we gave up taxing during the war to the federal government to help the war effort, and can't get them back, while your constitution leaves residual powers with the federal government, which is now busily turning many of these back to the provinces." After lunch we exchanged speeches. Sir Henry

47

dealt with the subject mentioned above, as well as the assistance they have been getting from a Dr. Hetherington of Calgary in regard to the development and distribution of the natural gas that has been found in Bass Strait off the Victoria coast. After lunch the leader of the opposition Labor Party, Mr. Stoneham, took me on a tour of the Parliament Buildings, which had been lent to the federal government until the Parliament Buildings were built in Canberra in 1927. We also visited the Library of Parliament, which has quite a call for Canadian legislation, etc.

You'd think I would be tired then—and I was—but I picked up Sheila and Gwen Gilbert at 2:45 for a visit to the University of Melbourne, where we called on the Vice-Chancellor, Sir George Paton. The University of Melbourne has 14,000 students, and together with the University of Sydney has fifty-two percent of all university students in Australia. They are now introducing quotas in all faculties, because they can't accommodate the applicants. We talked about problems of university exchange between Canada and Australia—to good purpose, as he asked me to write him so that he could raise the subject at the vice-chancellors' conference. We inspected some of the buildings, then went over to St. Hilda's College, a women's residential and tutorial college in the University of Melbourne, whose principal, Mrs. Kenneth Smart, is the widow of a distinguished Australian general. Before her marriage she worked as an information officer in our department in Ottawa and New York, as Marjorie Gordon, daughter of Dr. Charles Gordon, alias Ralph Connor, author of *Glengarry School Days* and other Canadian books. I had known Marjorie reasonably well some eighteen years ago, so was pleased to see her. She has gained a great reputation here as a speaker and teacher. She had a number of members of her board of governors in to tea to meet us and then showed us through the College. It is new and well planned. Each student has a separate room, with one bathroom between each two rooms.

Tuesday night we were guests of Sir Douglas and Lady Copland at the Alexander Club. He is a distinguished seventy-five-year-old economist who served as Australian high commissioner to Canada from 1953 to 1956 and whom I knew well then. He was a very popular after-dinner speaker with a wonderful collection of droll stories. Sir Douglas is now chairman of the Australian Committee for Economic Development, which prepares and publishes studies on problems of economic development in Australia.

Wednesday morning Gilbert and I went to visit the Melbourne Stock Exchange, where we were received by the president, Mr. E.A. Mellor, who answered questions and took us onto the floor to see the trading taking place. Most Australian stocks are valued at one to two dollars, so there appears to be a greater turnover than the real value would indicate. The market has been rather depressed recently, but in the long run the value of investments in Australian stocks should rise, with the development of the mining and other resources of this country, which has such great potential.

We called on Mr. D.G. Anderson, Director General of Civil Aviation, one of the federal departments still located in Melbourne. Our discussion revolved around negotiations that have been proposed to consider the Canadian request for an increase in the frequency of Canadian Pacific flights to Australia and Qantas flights to Canada. Anderson is a tough bargainer, but fortunately his assistant secretary for international affairs, Trevor Pyman, was Australian counsellor in Ottawa about ten years ago and is a good personal friend.

Next I went with Sheila and Gwen Gilbert out to Monash University, the second university in Melbourne, which has been in operation for three years. It is out in the suburbs and has very modern buildings, including a twelve-storey arts building with elevators and escalators. Here we were entertained at lunch in the faculty dining room of the student union by the Acting Vice-Chancellor, Dr. Donald Cochran, an economist, and his wife, and the principal of the medical college. We then toured some of the buildings. The enrolment is now under 5,000, but is to rise 12,000 as more buildings are completed. Here too they have far more qualified applicants then they can accommodate—hence the expansion and the building of La Trobe University.

That evening I was entertained at dinner by officers of the Melbourne branch of the Australian Institute of International

Affairs, and later spoke to about fifty on "Canada and Southeast Asia," and answered questions for an hour.

I'm going to skip Thursday and let Sheila tell you about our visits to the Botanic Gardens and the animal and bird sanctuary at Healesville, the reception for Canadians by the Gilberts, and dinner with Dr. Callaghan of the Australian Wheat Board.

I'll jump to Friday, when Gilbert and I went out to visit the plant of the Ford Motor Co. of Australia, Ltd., at Broadmeadows. This is a wholly owned subsidiary of Ford of Canada and imports about $10 million worth of parts from Canada each year. The plant manager, Mr. W.A. Marr, is a Canadian and there are two or three other Canadians there. The total staff is about 3,000, with others at sub-assembly plants in Geelong and Sydney. They assemble mainly the Ford Falcon, with 95 percent Australian content, and the Ford Cortina. They have a terrific labour turnover, because in order to compete they pay minimum wages, and get migrants who will work there until they can find something that pays better or where the wife can work, etc. It was quite interesting getting a full account of the operations, especially since we toured the plant on golf carts.

I was lunched by the executive of the Melbourne Club, whose president, Sir Clive Fitts, is a distinguished surgeon. This is the classic Victorian men's club, with a membership of seven hundred. I was given an honorary membership for the duration of my stay in Australia. In the afternoon I went to call on Sir Charles Spry, Director General of the Australian security services, and discussed their operations. You may recall that after we had our Gouzenko case in Canada in 1946 the Australians had the defection of Petrov in 1954. Then the Russians closed their embassy here from 1954 to 1959. Soon after it reopened an Australian girl counteragent trapped the First Secretary, Spirov, into trying to pass some codes and transmitting equipment to an agent in Adelaide, and he was declared *persona non grata*. The Australians took a telephoto sequence of the meetings where possible, and also recorded the conversations, which were picked up by a mic in the girl's handbag. I have seen a film they made of this story.

Later I went to call on Sir William Dunk, Commissioner of the

British Phosphate Commission, which exploits the phosphate rocks at Nauru and Christmas Island. Eighty-five percent of the rock is used in Australia and New Zealand to make fertilizer. Last year they imported $4 million worth of Canadian sulphur to make superphosphate.

Well, we were free Friday evening and Saturday morning to shop and stroll about. I'll leave it to Sheila to tell you about this and our return to Canberra Saturday afternoon. From my point of view this was a useful visit, as it gave us about as much of an introduction to Melbourne as we could have expected to work in, given the time we had. We met state and civic officials and some of the federal officials based in Melbourne, made contact at the three universities, met Canadians, saw something of industry, and saw our friends. In addition I think my talk to the AIIA was worthwhile.

s » As Arthur said, I will tell you something of our visit to the Botanic Gardens. The Melbourne ones are among the few in the world allowed to be called "royal"—and this is typical of much of Melbourne. There is still great respect for things British and a following for British royalty and tradition here that is not so apparent in other parts of the country. Anyway, we drove, mostly, and partly walked through a sampling of the forty acres of lawn, and looked at trees and plants in the other forty acres of cultivated area. I find it difficult to get used to the seasons here. Even talking to people you get different ideas. The conclusion seems to be that "every season is different," so no one can tell for sure if roses will bloom twelve months of the year or just nine, or if azaleas will flower once or twice, etc. Anyway, this present time is fall, and winter is due to start gradually. This means it's the time when officials can apologize for the poor show and the lack of flowers. When, however, we see as many flowers as at midsummer at home, we are quite impressed. Naturally, though, there were not many flowering shrubs or trees in the park at this season. We saw the "Separation Tree," the gum tree under which was celebrated the authorization of the separation of the colony of Victoria from that of New South Wales on July 1, 1851. Both Adrian Gilbert and

Arthur were quick to note the significance of July 1, and it will be included in the future speech on Canada Day I'm sure.

The Sir Colin MacKenzie Sanctuary at Healesville is one of the chief tourist attractions of Australia. Because Australia was separated from the other land masses of the world at a very early stage, many animals were left to live and evolve here independently. Thus there are animals that still survive in Australia of which we find only fossils in Europe. Animals like the platypus are said to be the missing links that show the evolutionary connection between mammals and egg-laying, cold-blooded reptiles. Thus the platypus bears fur and secretes milk for its young, but lays soft-shelled rounded eggs and has a very variable body temperature. We also saw the only other living egg-laying mammal in the world, the anteater, more generally known here by the name of echidna. Because they have to travel continuously in search of ants, they have no permanent homes and therefore no nest, so the eggs are carried and kept warm in the pouch in which the milk glands are situated.

The sanctuary is a vast and beautiful parkland. Although there are cages and enclosures for some of the animals, many are allowed to roam in a very large area. The kangaroos, wombats, and emus, for instance, are not penned up, although they have a half-enclosed area they can retreat to when thousands of children stream through on weekends. There's one cage they have developed that's especially good. It's a wire enclosure as big as a small barn with many, many kinds of parrots, or wild birds, or whatever they are exhibiting. You are allowed to walk right through the centre of it among the birds, because they have built a sort of double-door system: you go inside one way or door into a porch-like part and then open the second door into the main enclosure. So far they have lost none from the inside. An even fancier arrangement is made to house a pair of lyrebirds. People donated through automobile clubs to build this large aviary, two hundred feet long, one hundred feet wide, and about thirty-five feet high. The aim was to recreate as nearly as possible the conditions they're accustomed to. This involved making a dam and a small creek, then having an overhead water spray system that lets down the equivalent of one inch of rainfall every three hours. This builds up the rich growth of vegetation underneath—ferns, shrubs, and trees —so that it's as tropical as possible. Again, you're allowed into this enclosure through a double set of doors, and the birds, although very timid, are used to people a bit now and can often be seen. Visiting hours are just two to four in the afternoons. The keeper took us just ahead of the crowd, and we got a good view of the male—like a small peacock. It is famous for putting on a real dancing display to distract others from the eggs, but of course this was not the season for that. Oh yes—you stay on a set path in the enclosure.

Just a bit about two other exhibits. This is the first time in Australia that I have seen koalas. As you likely know, they do not belong to the bear family at all, and have very different habits. They are marsupials, like the kangaroo. Their diet consists almost wholly of the leaves of certain kinds of eucalyptus or gum trees, and they have a digestive system to cope with them. They do not normally drink water—they get their moisture from the leaves. This diet is the reason they cannot be exported to zoos in other parts of the world. They used to be very common in Australia, but now, because of disease and bush fires, only a small number remains. They are much smaller than I had imagined, and they have really big claws on their front paws, which can dig in if they're excited, so although they look cute and cuddly they may not be so sweet.

Have you ever heard of brush turkeys? If so, you are ahead of me. Anyway, they use their claws to scrape together brush, leaves, sticks, and all into a huge pile that looks like a small haystack. The male digs a hole in this pile and the female deposits an egg, then he digs another hole and she deposits another egg, and so on, so that in all about twenty eggs are deposited separately in the mound and left to hatch, as in an incubator. The male can gauge the temperature of the stock very accurately, and never lets it vary more than a couple of degrees, by covering or uncovering the eggs with more or less straw. Once the eggs hatch, the male shoos the female away from the mound to get her own meals farther afield, while he scurries around close by to feed the twenty or so hungry babies. We saw the mounds, but not the birds, I'm afraid.

So we, like the 300,000 visitors they get each year, found the visit to the 432 acres well worthwhile. We were fortunate to have an excellent day for the drive; it is thirty-eight miles from Melbourne.

Our night on the town was at The Top of the Town, a restaurant at the top of a twenty-storey building. We were guests of Dr. Callaghan, chairman of the Australian Wheat Board, and Mrs. Callaghan. The only other guests were Mr. Dorman of the Wheat Board and his wife, and Mr. and Mrs. Gilbert. There is a spectacular view of the lights of Melbourne on all sides. The area around is pretty flat, more so than in either Sydney or Canberra, so you see just an ocean of lights in all directions. We had an elaborate meal and there was dancing between courses, so it took three hours. We were all pretty tired by the end.

Victoria has the most active Canadian Club group in Australia. We were pleased to meet about half of the 140 members at the reception the Gilberts gave at the office. Some are Canadians, some are married to Australians, and they all like to keep up their Canadian interests. To be a member, one must have lived three years in Canada. They represent quite a cross-section, so were an interesting group to meet. Another time we will concentrate on a smaller number of the most useful connections. I also had an opportunity to meet separately with the executive of the Women's Canadian Club at a supper at the home of the president the evening Arthur was making his speech. They had twelve there, and we had a good natter about differences between life in Australia and Canada. I found them a friendly group.

Besides separate calls on the wife of the Premier and a tour of the Parliament Buildings, I also found the visit to one of Melbourne's large hospitals they had arranged for me very interesting. I went not to the biggest or the new one for children, but to an old one, the Queen Victoria Memorial Hospital. For a very long time it was run by women and for women. They now have a few men on the board, and since they became affiliated with the new University of Monash two years ago as a teaching hospital they have taken on a few male doctors as consultants. However, the going concern behind all this enterprise is Dame Mabel Brooks, who is president of the board and the one who showed us around. She has held this job for forty years! She has written books about Napoleon's exile on St. Helena, and evidently is as great a historian as she is an administrator. We went on a typical tour—premature babies, maternity ward, then a general ward, and charity work. I was most impressed with all the bright sunshine in the rooms, and the use made of bright sun porches that they get the patients out into every day. Although an old building, it was all cheerful and bright.

March 13, 1966

S » Wednesday night Arthur gave a talk to the Australian Institute of International Affairs. The meeting was at the University. It was a "closed" meeting—that is, for members only. About fifty were there. Arthur spoke very well on "Canada's Far East Policy" for about fifty minutes, then answered questions for another half-hour. He was quite at home with the subject, naturally, and spoke forcefully and easily. Beforehand we had dinner with one of the executives, a professor, now assistant registrar at the University. Although he has been here thirteen years, his English origin was still very apparent, and we had quite an amusing time at the table with him, his wife, and their two teenage sons, both of whom had just bought second-hand cars.

A » This week we had a six-man Canadian Fisheries delegation in Canberra for an evening and a day. We had them in to the residence on the evening of their arrival to meet the Canadian staff and wives. They are interested in expanding existing sales of Canadian tinned salmon and sardines, and frozen salmon and fish sticks. Next day we had a meeting in my office and a luncheon attended by Australian officials and the Minister of Primary Industry, Mr. Adermann. Another visitor this week was a Mr. Lee, a representative of the National Film Board, whom I took to see the Postmaster General, Mr. Hulme, in hope that the ABC will buy more NFB documentaries.

Parliament reopened on Tuesday of this week without Sir Robert Menzies. Mr. Holt made an introductory speech in which he announced that Australia would replace its 1,500-man battalion in Vietnam with a task force of 4,500, including about one-third National Servicemen. This was a courageous decision in view of the national elections due in November or December, and will be attacked by the Labor opposition, which does not want a larger role in Vietnam and opposes sending conscripts there.

March 27, 1966

s » Another busy week! Some of the women's groups I have become involved in were especially active this week, and some of their activities even involved Arthur and other males. The Pan Pacific and South East Asia Women's Association — known as "Pan Pa Se Wa" said quickly, and written PPSEAWA — held its national conference for Australia here this week. In a way I find it a rather nebulous organization, which just talks friendship in the area, and mixes Asians and others. However, in some centres it is much more active than in others and does more good. Canberra has a really active branch that makes a real effort to mix Australians and Asians, whether students, diplomats, or visitors. Australians have sent a pretty good calibre of delegate to the international conferences as well. Anyways, the International President, a very charming retired social worker from Honolulu, was here, as well as the National President, from Victoria, and delegates from most states. I went to a luncheon they held at the University, but missed a coffee party, because this year's Pakistan National Day was celebrated by a film showing in a local cinema at 10:00 a.m. Many people busy like Arthur don't find that hour the most convenient one to take off nearly two hours to watch films, no matter how artistic. However, Arthur also came to the official opening of the PPSEAWA conference one evening. The keynote speech, given by the economics editor of *The Canberra Times,* was on ways to encourage cooperation in the Pacific — lots of ideas but rather rambling. This paragraph should prepare you — I've agreed to go on the Executive, and promised to help them with a film show at our chancery to raise money to send a teacher from a Pacific island for training.

A » Diosdado Macapagal, president of the Philippines until December 1965, was here this past week and we went to a dinner for him and his wife at the Philippine embassy. He had been on a three-month tour of all the countries of South America and spoke most interestingly of his impressions. As Spain governed the Philippines for 350 years, and most of the people were converted to Catholicism and educated in the faith, there is a strong bond with the South American countries similarly influenced by Spain. He seemed to think that the South American countries were beginning to pick up some economic development momentum, having been subsidized by the U.S. Alliance for Progress and having established the Latin American Free Trade Area. For the Philippines, he hoped for continuation of land reform, so that the peasantry would not become too dissatisfied.

April 3, 1966

S » I guess we are having the equivalent of Canadian Indian summer. It was very chilly, and then a heat wave struck and the temperature shot up to 84. I had just spent a while putting away summer clothes and getting out winter wools, and now I have to reconsider what to take to Sydney for three days beginning tomorrow. The difference between an Australian hot day and a Canadian one is that here it will be very warm at noon but it turns cooler much more quickly in the afternoon and by evening it is always cool or chilly. Last weekend we were pleased to have an invitation to lunch in the country at a "property." People here speak of owning a "property" the way they would own a "farm" in Canada or an "estate" in England. This Dr. and Mrs. Davy are cousins of people we knew in Kuala Lumpur. He was a surgeon in Sydney, but when he retired two years ago they bought this place, very close to the property where his wife was born and where a son still lives. Arthur asked a lot of questions about sheep and cattle and generally acquired a basic background for the Royal Easter Agricultural Fair, which we are going to this week.

While walking over the paddocks ("fields," to me) we picked a huge basket of mushrooms. This is the peak season for them, and as we ate them there for lunch with no ill effects I was pleased to bring home a supply. We had mushrooms on toast, and as an entrée for dinner with guests had mushroom-filled pancakes, a specialty of Edith's, and we tried freezing some. We will have a packet of them for lunch today, so it was a profitable trip.

A » Parliament has risen here for the Easter recess, but not without a continuation of the acrimonious debate on conscription for military service in Vietnam that has stirred the House. When Prime Minister Holt addressed a by-election meeting in Kooyong, a Melbourne suburban riding formerly held by Prime Minister Sir Robert Menzies, he had a very rough time from hecklers. The Liberals retained the seat yesterday, but with a reduced majority. The Australian Labor Party is itself split by a leadership dispute between the leader, Mr. Calwell, an aging (69), witty, rough-and-tumble Irish politician, and Gough Whitlam, a young and brilliant, if at times erratic, moderate socialist. Politics here are working up to November general elections.

April 11, 1966

s » On April 4, the seven Commonwealth high commissioners and their wives gave a luncheon in honour of the Queen Mother, who had come out to Australia to open the Adelaide Festival. We were all lined up to meet her, and she had an interested word for each, her blue, blue eyes sparkling and a radiant smile on her face. We had group photos taken, then went into a good but not too heavy lunch; then another word with each, and she was off.

A » Later that afternoon Sheila and I flew to Sydney. After checking in at the Hotel Australia we went out to see Jill Perryman in *Funny Girl*, a brassy, sassy, fast-moving musical play about a Ziegfeld Follies girl in the First World War period. The production, the staging, the scenery, and the dance numbers were very good. Jill Perryman is Australia's own version of Barbra Streisand, and sang out—indeed belted out—the songs with great gusto. I found it great fun; Sheila found it a bit brassy and noisy.

Tuesday we went to Sydney University in the afternoon to see one of our commercial secretaries get an MA in economics. The University is big—16,000 students—with a fine mixture of old and new buildings. The second New Guinean to get a university degree got his in architecture at the same ceremony, to loud applause. Wednesday morning I visited the University of New South Wales, which, even though it was only started in 1950, has 12,000 students.

One of the reasons for our visit was to give a reception for Senator Harry Hays, ex-Minister of Agriculture, a judge at the Royal Easter Show. There were eighty guests—cattle-breeders and the like. In the afternoon we had gone out to the opening of the Show with John Stiles, the Trade Commissioner, and his wife Margaret. The Governor, Sir Roden Cutler, a former member of the Australian diplomatic service and a Second World War Victoria Cross holder, gave a good short speech about what he had seen of the effects of the drought in the northwest of New South Wales. Then there was a parade of certainly over a thousand horses and cattle, with each breed well labelled. They were marched around the arena in concentric circles. After this the New South Wales mounted police did their musical ride, with horses backing up, sashaying sideways, and doing a great many intricate manoeuvres to the music of a band. We left after seeing a couple of young German stunt people shot about 150 feet out of a cannon onto a net.

Another event of our visit to Sydney was dinner with the Governor and Lady Cutler. There were about thirty people there—a rather formal event in the great Government House, which occupies a commanding position in a park on the edge of Sydney Harbour.

On Saturday, April 9, I attended a ceremony at the National War Memorial to mark the twenty-fifth anniversary of the siege of Tobruk, in North Africa, in which Australians were the principal defenders. Some nine hundred out of the two to three thousand veterans of Tobruk were on hand for the parade and ceremony. There were representatives of veterans from Britain, New Zealand, India, Israel (Palestine Transport Company), and the Polish Legion, but none of the four Canadian naval officers who were involved could come. The organizers were the Rats of Tobruk Association.

April 24, 1966

s » It seems that each week some special feature is added to the usual round of events and work, and it takes over and fills every minute. Each of these extras is interesting, and provides opportunities for wider contacts with Australians, but it means there's a terrific steady pressure on Arthur to get the never-ending office work done as well. Last week the meetings of the Interparliamentary Union were held here. The Canadian delegation had Senator Desserault and Herman Batten, Liberals; ex-Minister of Agriculture Alvin Hamilton, still a real ball of fire who never stops talking, P.C.; Barry Mather of the N.D.P.; and a secretary, Mr. Small. We had a cocktail party with about forty-five guests and then took some hangers-on out to dinner.

Thursday night we had our most high-powered dinner here yet. It was in honour of Sir Valston and Lady Hancock. He is the Australian Commissioner General in charge of their Expo 67 participation. There is a board of top industrialists and the like to advise him, and we had its chairman, Sir Frederick White, who is head of their equivalent of our Research Council, and Lady White. We also had Sir William Hudson, another member of that board and head of their large Snowy Mountains hydroelectric scheme, and Lady Hudson—they motored in from seventy miles away and had to return that night after dinner.

A » Yesterday I went on my first trout fishing expedition, with Eric Conybeare, a Canadian professor (called "senior lecturer" here if not the head of a department) of petroleum geology at the Australian National University. We started at 6:00 a.m. and in an hour and a half we drove about forty miles to the west over the first big range of mountains to a lovely valley with the smallish Goodradigbee River running through it over boulders and pebbles. We covered about five miles of the river, fishing the pools with spinners, and later with worms on hooks. I caught none; he caught four. But it was a delightful warm day and the air and the scenery were superb.

May 8, 1966

s » We had a busy week away in Mildura and Geelong, and a busy week on our return. We flew back instead of motoring with Andrew, mainly because I had committed myself to have a benefit film show at our office for the Pan Pacific and South East Asia Women's Association to raise money to send a Pacific Island trainee to teachers college. They sold fifty tickets at one dollar each. We showed five Canadian films, mostly from the National Film Board, but two Crawley documentaries as well, about an hour and a half in all. Then we had coffee and cakes, etc., that members had brought.

Thursday night we had a dinner in honour of Lady Bailey, the wife of the Australian High Commissioner in Canada, who is home on a bit of leave, visiting her son here. The son works in the prime minister's department, and is very interesting too. Other guests, mostly academic, included the National Librarian and his wife, who live across the road, a law professor from the University here, and Professor McDougall, from Carleton University, who is here for six months as a visiting Commonwealth Professor at Australian National University. He is the director of the Institute of Canadian Studies, which is responsible for publishing the Carleton Library Series of reprints of Canadian books in paperback form, which has brought out Dad's *Laurier* and, more recently, Dad's *Galt*, so we had connections with him before he came here. He's a very pleasant chap.

An interesting Canadian girl named Ruth Parker looked me up here this week. She was with me at Guide camp, and we had only slightly heard of each other in the twenty years since, but it is amazing how Canadians abroad will be Canadian-conscious enough to follow up such a connection, whereas they wouldn't at home. She trained as a nurse at the Montreal General, then specialized in radiotherapy in England, and since has taken working holidays, mostly as a nurse—a year in England, a year in France, and now four years in New Zealand and Australia. She has nursed on an Aborigine reserve eighty miles from Alice Springs in the central desert and on a government Aborigine station in Darwin. She has also picked tobacco, been a domestic on a large sheep station, and generally seen the life here. At present she is taking a refresher course in general nursing and working in a big hospital in Melbourne, and has just had a weekend holiday in Canberra. She hopes to make enough money to return to Canada this summer, stay with her mother in Niagara-on-the-Lake for a year, then likely take off again—perhaps for Peru! Needless to say, she has not married, and with nursing experience always in demand she is able to lead this wandering life. A very attractive blond, she's nearly forty now.

May 15, 1966

A » Even though I'm a fortnight late, I'm going to tell you something in this letter about our trip to Mildura and Geelong from April 26 to May 2. By good fortune our new official car, a 1966 Pontiac Parisienne, arrived ten days before our trip, and with considerable pushing we managed to get it cleared and on its way to Canberra so that we could use it on our trip. We left at seven o'clock for the 545-mile trip. Out of Canberra we drove thirty-five miles north through rolling merino sheep country to Yass in order to get through lower passes in the Great Dividing Range. Then on about sixty-five miles to Gundagai through moderately hilly sheep country. On the way there is a monument to the famous "Dog on the Tucker Box," a faithful dog that stood guard over his master's tucker (food) box for a long time after his master had died. At Gundagai we crossed the Murrumbidgee River, which, with the Murray, is one of the main irrigation rivers on the western side of the Great Dividing Range. We followed the river more or less closely much of the rest of the way, turning off the Melbourne highway eighty miles short of the Victoria border. After we had gone about two hundred miles west from Canberra we got out onto flat plains. At first they were like our prairies, with fine wheat fields, but these soon changed to grazing land. Then we went on to an almost treeless plain, with salt bushes. For the last hundred miles or so we passed through a number of irrigation settlements, then finally crossed the Murray after dark, and reached Mildura at about 7:00 p.m.

One of the purposes of this trip was to take up an invitation from the Australian Dried Fruits Board to visit the centre from which about $4 million worth of sultana raisins and currants are exported to Canada annually. Mildura has a particularly interesting history for Canadians, because two Chaffey brothers from Brockville, who had developed the engineering science of irrigation in California, were persuaded in 1886 by Premier Alfred Deakin of Victoria to apply their technique in Australia. Mildura was selected as the site, and an elaborate program was developed for pumping water up out of the Murray into irrigation channels, which were to distribute it to an initial fifty thousand acres. Various financial difficulties were encountered, but in the end a successful settlement was developed at Mildura, and another at Renmark in South Australia. Today the settlements flourish, and many more have been established. But the credit is given to the Chaffey brothers, whose house is a local landmark and whose first giant pump was taken out of service only in 1955.

Our hosts in Mildura were Mr. and Mrs. John Gordon. Mr. Gordon is deputy chairman of the ADFB, and a modestly wealthy owner of eighty acres of grape vines. They were very congenial and helpful throughout. Indeed, our experience has been that most Australians are just as nice and helpful and understandable as English-speaking Canadians and that it is very easy to get on a very friendly basis with them, despite the title of "His Excellency the High Commissioner for Canada" with which we are draped. The Gordons came to the hotel—the Mildura Grand Hotel—after supper on the evening of our arrival to give us a rundown on our program.

Next day, April 27, we were picked up at 9:30 and taken on a visit to the Chaffeys' house, and then on to a park at one of the locks in the Murray River. Water is so precious in Australia that the levels in the rivers are maintained by a series of dams and barrages, or weirs. In the lower reaches the river is navigable, so there are locks, as in the Rideau River. Very little fresh water is permitted to run into the sea.

On an island in the river they have a number of koalas, and we were able to find one sleeping propped in the fork of a tree. We had seen them in Tasmania, but it was fun to see one again in Mildura.

At 10:30 we were guests of honour at a reception given by the Mayor of Mildura, Councillor Roy Burr, and the President of the Shire of Mildura, Councillor Alex Smart. Sheila and I were led around in different directions to meet the husbands and wives and chat with them. Then we had an exchange of speeches, in which the Mayor referred to the Chaffey brothers, and the Shire President referred to the value of the Canadian market for Australian dried vine fruits. After the reception we toured the city, seeing high schools, technical schools, schools for students with special learning needs, libraries, an Olympic swimming pool, a harness racing oval, cricket pitches, etc.

In the afternoon we went out to inspect the irrigation works, including the big pumps and the main and lesser channels. Each landholder is entitled to four irrigations a year for a fixed sum of one dollar per acre each time. If additional water is available he can get extra irrigations during the season. The water is delivered to the highest corner of a block of land, then after that the farmer deals with it.

We went on to Mr. Gordon's farm, where we saw the acres of grape vines and learned of the problems of growing good strains, disease control, weed control, irrigation, etc. The sultana he grows is a white grape, called the Thompson seedless in California. After they're picked, the grapes are spread on wire racks about eight inches apart in layers under a tin roof. The sun dries the grapes to raisins in one to two weeks.

That evening the ADFB gave a dinner for us at the hotel, with about sixty of the principal personalities and their wives present. I had not been told in advance that a speech was required, but gave it some thought over the shaving and dressing period. Next day I was reported in *The Sunraysia Daily* under the heading, "Raisin Pie Lifts Sultana Sales!" The item began, "Canada's insatiable appetite for raisin pies presented a wonderful market for Australia's dried fruits, High Commissioner for Canada Menzies attests." Canada takes nearly twenty thousand tons of Australian dried vine fruits, or twenty-three percent of the production, so that one of the other speakers said that twenty-five cents in every dollar he earns comes from Canada. That made us popular. And Sheila has had to send back recipes for raisin pie, Canadian-style.

Thursday morning we visited a packing house, where the dried fruits are received, weighed, conveyed on belts through shakers that take off their stems, cleaned, and packaged. In another plant they have machines that push the seeds out of dried grapes by an ingenious system of rollers and needles. The packing houses work for a fee, and ship the packed fruit in accordance with arrangements made by the ADFB.

In the afternoon we went to the local branch of the Commonwealth Scientific and Industrial Research Organization to see research work done on the growing and processing of grapes. Then we went on to the Mildura Winery, where we were shown through the sherry, wine, and brandy processes. Here we met Herbert Chaffey, a son of W.B. and a retired secretary of the winery. His wife, well over seventy, was born in Ottawa and recalls the old days in her home there on McLeod Street. In the evening we went out to the Gordons' for an after-dinner coffee and chat.

On Friday we were taken over by the Apex Club of Wentworth, twenty miles down the Murray River on the New South Wales side. First we went to the orange farm of John MacDonald and inspected the orchard, from the planting of saplings, the grafting, the irrigation, and the spraying to the picking of the oranges and mandarins. We took away quite a gift of fruit with us. Then we went out to visit a sheep-shearing shed on a big station of 100,000 acres that carries about 7,000 sheep. The owner gets around in either a jeep or a motorcycle. One side of his property is thirty miles long and another fourteen miles long. One paddock is 7,000 acres. He runs one sheep to twelve to fourteen acres, because the soil is so poor.

In the evening we were given a welcome and a reception by the president and councillors of the Shire of Wentworth. Another speech was called for. Then we went into the local hall for a combined Apex and Rotary dinner, with wives present, at which I was the guest speaker. The hall was quite cool and drafty but no one got up and walked out.

Saturday morning we left at eight o'clock for Geelong, some 350 miles to the south, on the coast forty miles west of Melbourne. At first we drove through vineyards, then mallee scrub, but eventually entered fine wheat-growing country. Around Mildura they get about ten inches of rain a year, in some places farther south about thirty-five inches. We got into Geelong at about 4:00 p.m. This is an old city of 100,000 with many industries, a good port, and a lot of famous boarding schools. Prince Charles is attending Timbertop, a hillside outpost of Geelong Grammar School.

Sunday noon we had lunch with Mayor Roy Fidge, his wife, and another couple. Then in my striped trousers and short black coat and hat I went to review a march past of eight bands and 3,500 high school students in honour of Commonwealth Youth Sunday. Almost all were in school or organization uniforms; some marched well, others didn't. Later the young people were assembled in a park for a brief service at which I spoke over a microphone for ten minutes about the Commonwealth and what they could do about it. There was a big tea afterwards at which Sheila and I went around and spoke to groups of head boys and head girls, who seem very much the same as those in Canada at that age: poised and pleasant and quite able to carry their end of the conversation. In the evening we went to a small evening gathering of the Geelong Australian, Canadian, and American Association.

Monday morning Mayor Fidge, who is also the chairman of the Geelong Harbour Trust, took us out by launch for a tour of the harbour. It was a fine calm day and we had a splendid trip to the Aluminum Company of America plant at Point Henry, then to the Shell Refinery, to two fertilizer plants, and to Jackson's Frozen Meat export warehouses, now over fifty-percent owned by Canada Packers.

Later in the morning we went to the Huyck Factory, which had just been opened as a subsidiary of Kenwood Mills, Arnprior, a division of Huyck Canada Ltd., in turn a subsidiary of Huyck of Albany, N.Y. This plant produces paper-makers' felts. The pulp solution is spread onto one of these felts and then run through a series of rollers to compress it and dry it until, presto, out the other end comes paper. There are a number of Canadians on the staff of the factory. We had lunch with the manager and his assistant.

Monday afternoon we went off to Belmont, a suburb of Geelong. Our first visit was to the C.S.I.R.O. Wool Textile Research Centre. Here they have a lot of spinning and weaving machinery that they experiment with, as well as labs of various kinds. They have developed a shrink-proofing system for wools that they expect will come into wide usage in a year or two. Next we had another Shire reception. Then on to Oldham College, the oldest independent agricultural college in Australia. The principal, I.A. Dean, explained the program, then took me on to a Rotary supper, where I was guest speaker. Next day we drove to Melbourne and then flew back to Canberra, while Andrew drove the car back.

s » When Kenneth arrived in Australia on May 6, we did not know whether he could stay until May 11 or May 18—it depended on when the flights to Noumea were leaving. His boss there is away travelling, so doesn't need him until a later date, but as the number of flights alternates between one and two flights a week, there is quite a bit of pressure to get prior booking on the planes. We did not hear till the morning of May 10 that he definitely had a flight on the later date. Naturally we were very pleased to have his company a little longer. Fortunately, Arthur was able to arrange something of interest to Kenneth and to us, a three-day tour (Thursday to Saturday) of the Snowy Mountains scheme. As the Australians are very proud of this large civil engineering construction, it is one thing they plan for VIPs to see. The Scheme has a public relations department to make itineraries, and one of their twenty-two public affairs officers is assigned to look after such parties as ours. The same people at other times conduct coach tours around the Scheme. (The three-day bus tour, complete with bed and three meals a day, costs just $35). The basic idea of the Scheme is to divert the water of the Murray and Murrumbidgee rivers and all the little streams and tributaries in their valleys inland across the mountains before it rushes to the sea as before, and to use it, first, for hydroelectric purposes, to produce power, and, secondly and more importantly in this dry land, for irrigation. This imaginative and costly scheme was begun in 1949 and will not be all completed until 1975. Unlike complicated engineering schemes in most parts of the world, this one is actually ahead of schedule and within estimated costs.

We were very fortunate in the weather. As much of the construction in the mountains is at the four- or five-thousand-foot level, and as May is equivalent to about November in Canada, it could have been very cold and blowy. However, the only snow we saw was on the mountaintops; where we were, frost was on the ground only in the mornings. Therefore, although I got out my fur coat and Arthur his winter coat we had no need for them. I just wore a raincoat over a suit, and Kenneth just his corduroy jacket. I was very glad to have my heavy fleece-lined boots, however. They made all the difference between comfort and discomfort for me. Also I have become quite Australianized and now wear a "spencer" on most occasions. When I came here and heard people talking of spencers I was a little vague, but as the winter season approaches one sees the full range of such a garment in every department store. It is a fine wool shirt, but differs from any I have seen in Canada because it is cut with a scoop neck that does not show under clothes, and may have either short or long sleeves. It does the job of old-fashioned underwear, but is so fine and soft it is easy to conceal. Therefore one tends to see people outdoors dressed quite normally on the outside, and often in a dressy silk material or, say, just a suit, but one knows full well that the reason they are not cold and shivery is that they have had the good sense to put on the soft woolly layer next to their skin. So now, to the two cotton shirts I bought in Ottawa on Dr. Law's recommendation as good preventatives for arthritis, I have added one long-sleeved spencer and one short-sleeved one, and so can sally forth in most any weather. As many Australian houses do not have central heating, or have inadequate heating by Canadian standards, it is just as often indoors as outdoors that one feels the need and comfort of such a garment.

May 29, 1966

A » Tuesday noon we had a ceremony at the chancery at which Mr. Bury, the Minister for Labour and National Service, presented on behalf of the Australian timber industry three Aboriginal *pukamuni* ritual poles carved in bloodwood, about seven feet high and brightly painted, used to appease the souls of dead tribesmen. I accepted the poles for transmission to Vancouver, where they will be displayed in return for a B.C. totem pole now erected in Sydney. We had a reception afterwards, which helped to get out the newspaper and TV men.

Wednesday we went down to Melbourne, where I had some talks with government people. That evening we gave a dinner for some of our Canadian colleagues, followed by *Busybody*, a hilarious comedy starring Irene Handl about a daft but canny cleaning woman and the uncovering of an office murder.

Thursday I had meetings all day to review trade with Australia and hear of John Stiles's visit to Canada. In the late afternoon we gave a reception for about fourteen members of the Canadian Sub-Branch (Victoria) of the Returned Servicemen's League and their wives. These were chaps who had served in the Canadian Forces in the First or Second World War, some of them over 80.

Thursday night we were patrons at the Beavers Canadian Ball, organized by a fundraising committee in support of one of the Opportunity Youth Clubs of Melbourne. The committee had decided to use the Canadian beaver theme as an indicator of their eagerness and persistence. They had borrowed Canadian flags and posters from our office and menu cards from the C.N.R., dressed up two security men as R.C.M.P., and generally did a lot of work to create an atmosphere for the ball. Oh yes—and the day before, I was taken out to the zoo to be photographed with Aileen and Hector, the two beavers from Granby Zoo in Quebec, who since their arrival in 1962 have acclimatized well and have had two litters of pups. I could not have got near them without taking off half my clothes and getting in their pool, but we got some shots of each that got good coverage in the local paper. Well, they had a capacity crowd of four hundred young people, two hot bands (one, The Groop, after midnight, was in the style of the Beatles), and a terrific loudspeaker system so that you had to shout into your neighbour's ear to be heard. But the young people had a great time with all the latest dance contortions. We were sedate most of the time with the other patrons, a local MP and a local businessman and their wives, and the president and secretary of the club. We were introduced to Miss Queensland, a real beauty, off on a four-month trip as a reward, and Miss Victoria. There were some lovely-looking girls there. At about 1:30, when we left, the party was still going strong; we weren't. Friday we returned to Canberra to clean up the week's work.

June 12, 1966

A » I gave a major speech to three hundred members of the Sydney Rotary Club on "Canada's Policies in Asia." In the afternoon John Stiles and I drove out to visit the Australian Aluminum Company Ltd. plant in Granville, a Sydney suburb. It is owned by Alcan Aluminum Ltd. of Montreal and produces some thirty thousand tons per year of sheet, foil, extrusions, etc. In the evening John and Margaret took me to see an Australian intimate review called *A Cup of Tea, a Bex and a Good Lie Down*. Bex is a local headache powder. The professional cast did thirty skits and songs spoofing Australians in England and Americans in Australia, some hilarious.

Wednesday we lunched with a couple of Canadian travel people at the "Skol" Club, a monthly meeting of executives in the travel and hotel trade. We were exploring ways of promoting Australian travel to Canada for Expo 67. Later we called on the general manager of the Overseas Telecommunications Commission, which runs the Pacific cable here and is putting out tenders for a ground station for the International Communications Satellite Consortium, in which Canada also has an interest.

Thursday I was given a lunch by officers of the Common-wealth Bank, and we had a lofty discussion on financial and economic matters. Later I called on Dr. H.C. Coombs, Chairman of the Reserve Bank of Australia, which is like the Bank of Canada.

Sheila came down Thursday noon. She got in after a fog delay in the nick of time to meet her luncheon guests, and then joined John and Margaret Stiles and me for a four-o'clock tour of the Sydney Opera House. I am sure that you have all seen articles in magazines about this famous architectural experiment, with roofs that look like glowing white sails on the Sydney waterfront. A Danish architect, Joern Utzon, won an international competition for the design about five years ago. As a result of political hasti-ness and his prima donna qualities as an architect, Utzon was left to solve his architectural problems as he went along, spending profits from the state lottery for the building. Well, early this year, with a change of state governments, the new minister of Public Works began to ask questions, and Utzon resigned in a huff. The outside will be quite spectacular, but the inside appears not to have been so well thought out, as the stages will take many people to operate, and the main theatre as designed will hold less than half the required number. The whole subject is much in the press here, so we were glad to be shown around.

Thursday night we went to a ball given by the Royal Common-wealth Society of New South Wales in honour of the Queen's birthday. The Governor, Sir Roden Cutler, and many decorated cit-izenry were among the three hundred guests. Today we saw part of the ball on TV as a prelude to a debate on the monarchy. There is some republicanism here among young intellectuals and non-British immigrants, but most Aussies are more automatically roy-alist than Canadians, because we do not have such exclusively British traditions.

June 26, 1966

s » The Australians have retained many customs of the aristocratic English. Although these are dying out with the younger genera-tion, one such that is kept, even if not on as large a scale as a few years ago, is the Presentation of Debutantes at a Deb Ball, usually sponsored by one of the district churches. There were twenty such young ladies presented to Arthur at a ball at the big Albert Hall this week. Each one, beautifully gowned in full white evening dress, had to walk up a long red carpet singly and hold Arthur's hand and curtsy. Then they went off to the side, where they were joined by their escorts. After this the twenty couples performed a little dance, mostly fancy curtsies, for which they had practised twice a week for three weeks, the last two rehearsals being in the big hall. The girls seem to like the fancy setup, but I marvel that they get boys to go through the formality with them. Of course there were a lot of other people at the ball, mothers, fathers, people from the church and from all sorts of other districts—even some who pay to watch from the balcony. Evidently people here like the tradition. We now feel that having seen it once, unless it's out of town where we would have some additional interests, we have done that particular duty for our tour. Oh yes—Arthur had to make a five-minute speech, which he handled very aptly, with lots of jokes and stories. He didn't know until that morning.

A » Thursday evening I gave a talk on the integration of the Canadian Armed Forces to the Canberra branch of the Young Liberals Association. It involved some preparatory note-taking, but was well received, and there were lots of follow-up questions.

Wednesday evening we went on short notice "to have a drink" with the Prime Minister and Mrs. Holt. There were only about ten of us there, quite an informal and intimate gathering. He goes off Monday afternoon for a trip to the U.S.A. and Britain. I had hoped that he might visit Canada, but it couldn't be fitted in this time. He will certainly be there next year.

The SEATO Foreign Ministers Conference begins tomorrow. I went to a Press Club luncheon today to hear the British Foreign Secretary, Michael Stewart, speak on "East of Suez."

July 3, 1966

s » Thank goodness the celebration of Canada's 99th birthday is now over. We decided to have everyone at one evening celebration this year. Having made the decision we were committed, but we are not sure now that it is over whether we will do the same next year or not. Anyway, in the beginning about five hundred were invited—we knew that all the MPs were likely to be out of Canberra, because the House is not in session. We got about a hundred regrets, and then there were a hundred we didn't get answers from—or just on the last day, when all the plans had been made. I did my calculating on the basis of three hundred for food, with Edith doing a hundred and a caterer doing two hundred, and enough drinks for four hundred. In the end we had no more than about three hundred, so all worked out well. We used not only the large front hall at the office, but had the partition pushed back in the library, and the desks and furniture there for extra stenographers, etc., were taken out to make a second large room. We were honoured by the attendance of the New Zealand Prime Minister and his wife, here for the SEATO meetings. They dropped in for five minutes and stayed for more than an hour. As usual, many of the young Canadian students and such stayed quite long. We watched Arthur on a portable TV set giving a Canada Day interview. We sure were tired by the time I paid off the twenty-one waiters, waitresses, etc. We tidied up the next day, and office staff will reconstruct the furniture, etc., on Monday. Amen 1966.

A » The big news in Canberra this week has been the SEATO and ANZUS Council meetings. Monday morning Sheila and I, along with a thousand others, attended the formal opening of the SEATO conference, with two hours of opening speeches from the Prime Minister and all the foreign ministers present. This was the occasion to say anything for which public support was wanted. Rusk, Holyoke of New Zealand, and Holt and Hasluck of Australia all spoke about the firmness of their backing for South Vietnam. The Thai Foreign Minister, Thanat Khoman, said that there would have been no invasion of South Vietnam if SEATO had intervened collectively in Laos in 1961. The British Foreign Minister dealt Britain out of the Vietnam War as a co-chairman of the Geneva conference. The French sent only an observer and the Pakistani was very reserved. Secret meetings followed, with their contents pretty fully divulged to the press. Then there was the Australia/New Zealand/U.S.A. ANZUS meeting, with more expressions of mutual solidarity. In between I gather there were some useful private talks. In connection with these meetings we attended a public lecture by Stewart, the British Foreign Minister, which he read, followed by a much more lively question period. Friday Rusk performed brilliantly for the National Press Club without a text.

July 31, 1966

s » We are having perfectly wonderful weather for the last day of July—midwinter in theory, but beautiful sunshine outside, in the sixties by day and the thirties by night. We had a phenomenon this past week: pink rain. There is so much red dust in the air over so much of Australia from the drought that if the wind blows from a certain direction while rain is falling the combination comes down as pink rain. In the mountains they get pink snow! It sounds very pretty and romantic, but actually it is filthy; it has to be scrubbed off porches and cars, and ruins clothes if they're caught on the line. Anyway, it made a harmless topic for Judy LaMarsh to comment on—because she had also brought a snowstorm to Wellington, New Zealand.

The whole week has been dominated by the visit of Miss LaMarsh. The one thing I was at that Arthur wasn't was the talk she gave Tuesday morning to the Women's International Club, the biggest women's club audience, I think, of any in Canberra (half are Australian women, half foreign). Miss LaMarsh spoke very candidly about the job of getting elected to Parliament and the special effort required of a woman, giving all sorts of examples from her campaigning in Niagara Falls as well as other Canadian examples. She was very informal and spoke easily and well without notes for about thirty-five minutes. As with her other speeches, I think she did her job well.

Norah and I went by plane to Sydney Friday morning so that

we could have a whole day to shop in the big city of two and a half million people (their shops really impressed Norah) before connecting at John Stiles's office to drive out with him to the house and connect with Arthur, who had come on a late-afternoon flight. I'm glad we were able to stay with the Stileses. They have three children, and Mark, the oldest, is the same age as Norah, so things like a football game he was in and a trip to the zoo (in Judy's honour, to see the koala bears and get publicity with them) meant that Norah and the younger Stiles children could also see things. It worked out well.

A » I suppose I should add a few lines about our Judy. She rested last weekend and so was fitter for the week before her. She came to us Sunday evening to meet staff and Canadian professors and grad students at the Australian National University. Monday, after getting her hair done in the morning (something one doesn't plan for in men's programs), she spoke to the National Press Club luncheon on "Canada 1966," giving an exposé of French-English relations and federal-provincial relations. As a cabinet minister she carried conviction and a sense of participation. Monday evening she came to our home again for our reception for cabinet ministers and senior officials. Then on the Tuesday, after her Women's International Club speech, she called with me on the Prime Minister and then attended a luncheon hosted by the P.M. In the afternoon there was a call on the Minister of Health, and then she left for Melbourne. I gather that her program worked out well there, and also in Sydney, where she was particularly happy with the attention paid her by the koalas. Indeed, because of some administrative uncertainties, about all we can say is that Miss LaMarsh's visit was a "koala-fied success."

Our family visit to Sydney was more successful. In addition to the shopping and the visit to the zoo and Bondi Beach, "one of the great surf beaches of the world," we went last night, after seeing Miss LaMarsh off, to see Jill Perryman in *Funny Girl*. Sheila and I had seen it a couple of months before, but I enjoyed introducing it to Norah (who knew North American recordings of

Barbra Streisand) and to the Stileses, with whom we feel most compatible.

September 4, 1966

A » We got back from our twenty-day trip to the Pacific Islands a bit tired and worn out from the steady pace and the steady heat, but very, very glad we had seen so much of the world—an unbelievable part that will soon disappear with civilization.

I haven't written any letters along the way this time and don't feel that I can now undertake a full essay on the subject. The full three weeks was certainly a wonderful experience for me, and gave me a much better perspective on the problems of development in the Southwest Pacific. During the Second World War Australia, New Zealand, and the United States were involved in heavy fighting in the neglected islands and decided to do something about their development after the war. This was the reason for the establishment of the South Pacific Commission. But then the peace treaty with Japan, the Korean War, the Indochina situation, the emergency in Malaya, etc., deflected attention to farther north in Asia, and Britain and France were preoccupied with the problems of decolonization in Africa and elsewhere. The Southwest Pacific territories did not shout for attention, and until after 1956 were not accorded development priority. France's policy in the Pacific is to retain its possessions there as integral parts of France in order to project French grandeur and culture in the area, retain control of the valuable nickel ores in New Caledonia and the nuclear test site south of Tahiti, serve as a link in its round-the-world air service, and serve tourism. New Caledonia has about 3,500 Frenchmen, and seems very much a part of the French world. The French seem intent on preserving the unique Anglo-French condominium of the New Hebrides as a sort of buffer to New Caledonia. This is a remarkable arrangement, acceptable for a period of extreme underdevelopment but in my view quite unworkable with the emergence of an indigenous elite.

We only had a short time in the British Solomon Islands, but my immediate impression was that it would be wise for the British to develop the islands in close association with Papua and New Guinea. One of the Solomon Islands, Bougainville, is already a part of Papua New Guinea, and the rest are really so backward and undeveloped that it seems to me it would make more sense to develop them in conjunction with the much larger Australia-administered territory with which their Melanesian people are affiliated.

I was surprised and delighted with the foundations for growth that the Australians have laid in Papua and New Guinea, mostly in the last ten years. Before the war they spent $40,000 a year there; now they spend $70 million. They have built and staffed primary, secondary, and technical schools, as well as specialized administrative, agricultural, forestry, medical, nursing, and teacher training colleges. This year they have 10,000 in high school and expect 300 graduates; by 1970 they will have 30,000 high school students and 1,000 graduates. The new University of New Guinea is being built, and a preliminary year is in training. Goodness knows it is needed, because there have only been two university graduates so far. All of this is most helpful and hopeful for the future, because the country needs unification of its seven hundred different language groups, pocketed as they are in various small coastal plains and valleys, and in hilly sections and high plateaus. There is an amazing diversity in conditions. In northern New Britain, around Rabaul, and in Papua, around Port Moresby, there has been settlement and mission education for eighty years, but the million people living in the Highlands were only discovered in 1937, shortly before the Second World War, and are still very primitive.

September 11, 1966

A » This has been a glorious spring weekend, with a warm sun and temperatures in the sixties. The golden wattle is in rich bloom everywhere. Something like an acacia, with masses of powdery golden blossoms, it is native to Australia. Then Canberra has been planted liberally with flowering plums, cherries, and quinces. The apples, pears, peaches, and apricots are to come

New Guinea is her talking point

from The Canberra Times, September 8, 1966

If merits were given to enthusiastic tourists the administration of Papua-New Guinea should award a high mark to Mrs. A. R. Menzies, wife of the High Commissioner for Canada, who has just returned from a trip around the Pacific.

She describes it as a family expedition timed to take advantage of the summer vacation in Canada.

"We had our son Kenneth and daughter Norah with us. They were on vacation from school and university in Canada," she said.

The family entered New Guinea from the north after travelling through New Caledonia, New Hebrides and the Solomon Islands. "Most visitors arrive at Port Moresby but we touched down at Rabaul in New Britain and went on to Wewak and Maprik in New Guinea."

They gathered a treasure trove of souvenirs at the administration craft centre at Maprik—a black mask from the Sepik district, a giant wooden hook (on which natives hang meat and other food from the rafters to keep it safe from pigs and dogs), clubs, ceremonial figures and intricately woven strings of lantro seeds.

NO TOURIST TRAPPINGS

"Things are not exactly geared for tourists at present. You don't get paper, string or boxes with the things you buy and they are bulky and heavy. The colours rub off a bit too but we'll give these a coat of lacquer before we hang them," she said.

Mrs. Menzies spoke enthusiastically about developments she saw in Papua and New Guinea. "Tea and coffee were being grown together on plantations in the highlands which is unusual. In Asia they would be in quite different areas."

The tea is a fine variety and of good flavour. "In Canada we already use coffee and cocoa from New Guinea which we get through the London exchange and I'm sure the tea will be popular too."

Visits to schools and colleges were made as a family group. "When we gave talks about Canada and our education system to students who are to become teachers, my husband always got a laugh by telling them to ask Kenneth and Norah the hard questions and leave the easy ones for him. The children got on well with the young people in New Guinea."

Hospitals they visited varied from small, primitive places with slat beds often run by Canadian missionaries to well-equipped modern buildings in the larger centres.

"And of course the administration arranged for us to meet any Canadians in the district. The king of the crocodile hunters is a Canadian and we came across anthropologists, teachers and agriculturists."

She says there are splendid opportunities for young workers in Papua-New Guinea...."Not just in offices or shops but out in the field. For instance, we met a woman who was an agricultural officer. The authorities reason that as women do most of the cultivation they are more likely to take advice from a woman agriculturist."

---

later. Our garden has many daffodils. They last well here, as they don't get spattered with rain. Before lunch we went over to our neighbours' place across the road to look at their garden. The Harold Whites have three acres, with many fine shrubs and flowering trees. They had one exquisite pink camellia. Then this afternoon we went to a wildflower show at Albert Hall. Canberraites are keen gardeners, so there is much interest in the shows. They have some lovely specimens of red warratah (which is three inches across and looks like a giant chrysanthemum just opening), a native tree flower, and pink banksia (a cone-like flower with soft down outside, which also grows on a bush). They also had magnificent displays of Western Australian wild flowers, daffodils, and carnations.

The first black African representative, a high commissioner from Ghana, has arrived here. He seemed affable and well educated. He has quite a job trying to inform the Aussies about Africa, about which they are both ignorant and, for the most part, unconcerned.

September 25, 1966

A » On Friday, September 30, we fly to Sydney and Brisbane, and then up across the continent to Darwin, an all-day expedition of 2,426 miles. We stay in Darwin, the hot and humid capital of the Northern Territory, over Saturday. Then we fly to Kununurra, just inside the Western Australian border, to visit the Ord River Scheme, a cotton-growing project opened up four years ago by the building of a barrage across the Ord. From there we fly over the Kimberley cattle-grazing ranges to Derby, which is the headquarters of the Northwest. We make a side trip from there to Yampi Sound and Cockatoo Island to see iron ore extraction. Then on to Port Hedland, an iron ore loading port, and Wittenoom Gorge to see asbestos mining; motor to Mount Tom Price to see more iron; then Carnarvon and Geraldton, cattle and wheat ports; and thence to the capital, Perth, where we are to stay for three days at Government House, from October 9 to 13. From Perth we motor down through the prosperous southwest corner of Australia, farmland, forests, and dairy country, to Albany; then on to Esperance, where great tracts of land are being opened up with the addition of a simple trace element. We drive north then to Kalgoorlie, the centre of gold mining, and take the train back across the great Nullarbor Plain to Adelaide, from which we fly back to Canberra on the night of October 21, by which time we will have covered about seven thousand miles.

Monday of this past week I went to a National Press Club luncheon to hear Mr. Douglas Jay, the president of the British Board of Trade, talk on Anglo-Australian trade. Britain has invested over $2.5 billion dollars in Australia since the war and is still this country's greatest supplier and market. Of course Australia is largely a raw material and food supplier, while Britain would like to see Australian tariffs lowered to admit more of her manufactured goods.

September 30, 1966 · *en route from Canberra to Darwin*

A » It is not quite a month since our return, on September 1, from New Guinea. Getting caught up with hold-over business, writing trip reports, and doing current work left no time to read in preparation for this trip. Sheila has done some and I've brought a briefcase of papers. But basically we are approaching the great West with open minds.

We were supposed to leave at 9:40 this morning but didn't get off until nearly 10:30 because of rain. We flew through cloud to Sydney, where John Stiles and Fred Palmer, the new representative of the Canadian Government Travel Bureau, met us and drove us in to the office, where we had sandwiches and a chat about matters of mutual concern.

September 30, 1966 · *en route from Mount Isa to Darwin {9:15 p.m.}*

A » We are now en route from Mount Isa to Darwin. At first the rolling, eroded hills were pretty thickly covered with eucalyptus. This opened into red soil with sparse vegetation. Mount Isa is a famous copper-mining area. Nearby is the "mothballed" Mary Kathleen uranium mine. We had turbulence during the latter part of our trip to Mount Isa; after a twenty-minute stop we are heading northwest again to Darwin. When we get there we will have covered 2,472 miles from Canberra, by turbo-prop Viscount and Elektra.

I have been reading some articles on Northern Development covering North Queensland, the Northern Territory, and the northern portion of Western Australia. This area is tropical, with thirty to sixty inches of rainfall coming in summer monsoons, and hot and dry conditions for the rest of the year. Rich bauxite and iron ore deposits have been found. There are more rivers to be dammed in the north than elsewhere. Some agricultural projects are being started in river valleys. The raising of beef cattle is the main industry. The area is still very lightly populated, and for strategic reasons the Australians would like to settle the area more in the next decade.

October 1, 1966 · Darwin

A » After turning our watches back half an hour we got into Darwin at 10:10 p.m. We were met by a Northern Territory official and by Mrs. R.L. Dean, wife of the Administrator of the Northern Territory. Mr. Dean is representing Australia at the Independence celebrations of Botswana (Bechuanaland) on September 30 and Lesotho (Basutoland) on October 4. We were driven to the old Government House, where we were to be guests. It is a lovely old bungalow-type residence by the bay, surrounded by a broad verandah. I had stayed here in November and December 1956 when accompanying Hon. Paul Martin around the world.

This morning we were taken on a tour of the city by an Administration driver. Darwin has a population of 22,000 and is said to be growing at a rate of eleven percent a year. One can quite believe it from the new areas, new houses, and new schools being built. There are some fine new administration buildings and a handsome courthouse. There is an RAAF base, and Army and Navy establishments. There is quite a good shopping area, the biggest north of Alice Springs. One hundred miles south a one-million-ton-a-year iron mine is being opened, the Francis River Iron Mining Company (FRIMCO), owned by a man called Duval. Another, half that size, is closer to Darwin. Then at Rum Jungle, fifty miles out, a fabulous lead, silver, and zinc strike has been found that should produce a very rich mine. All these things give Darwin business.

Darwin is just about to emerge from its long dry season. The soil is rocky and leached, the rank grass yellow, the scrub trees covered with dust. Decrepit galvanized iron shacks and junk mess up the country. But where the Administration has taken over it has put in sealed roads and ensured proper standards of housing. Most houses are on ten-foot reinforced concrete stilts, as a protection against termites, for coolness, for car parking, and for laundry hanging. Some gardens are attractive, with frangipani and bougainvillea, palms, etc.

The Northern Territory has a population of 55,000. Of these, 22,000 are full-blood Aborigines. These have been exploited by stockmen and others, but are now getting a better deal. By 1968 they are to be paid equal wages. This is good, but it creates problems, because many of the older ones do not have the necessary education or the home background. Aboriginal children go to the public schools in Darwin and other towns, but as most of the Aborigines live on cattle stations or on reserves they usually attend mission schools, which only offer the primary grades. Because they get little encouragement at home from illiterate parents, very, very few go on to high school. It is thought that it will likely take a couple of generations before they adjust more.

The Northern Territory used to belong to South Australia, but was handed over to the federal government about sixty years ago, because South Australia could not afford to run it. The budget is $100 million, of which only $50 million is raised locally. In addition there is considerable defence spending on airfields, etc.

The Northern Territory, like Papua and New Guinea, comes directly under the Minister for Territories. He is represented by an administrator, an assistant administrator, etc. There is a council, with six official members, three nominated members representing the mining, pastoral, and commercial interests, and eight elected members. It passes all local legislation. There are four administrative districts: Darwin, Katherine, Tennant Creek, and Alice Springs (from north to south). A railway runs three hundred miles south, but then there is a gap of seven hundred miles of road to Alice Springs.

On Saturday evening, October 1, we had dinner with the Assistant Administrator, Mr. Adkins, and his wife, and a Mr. and Mrs. Nicholas Paspaley. Of Greek origin, Mr. Paspaley was brought up in Broome, which was the old West Australian centre for a fleet of luggers that harvested mother-of-pearl for buttons. His principal current interest is in cultured pearls. As he explained it, Australia has the original mother-of-pearl oyster; what the Japanese have is just a make-do. He has three luggers, each of which carries two or three divers in diving suits who search the bottom of the bays for mother-of-pearl oysters at thirty to fifty fathoms for an hour at a time. If they find thirty oysters during the hour they are down that's good. The best oysters are four to five years old. When raised to the surface the oysters are put in tanks, and every week a mother ship takes them up to Port Essington Bay, about two hundred miles northeast of Darwin and east of Melville Island, where the first attempt at settlement in the north was made in 1824 by Captain Gordon Brenner. It's in Port Essington Bay that Paspaley has his oyster project. The oysters are placed in wire baskets, ten to a basket, and suspended from oil-drum rafts in four to five fathoms of water. After resting for four to five months they are opened and a small piece of mother-of-pearl is inserted in the flesh of each one. In about twenty-five percent of these oysters a pearl of superior quality is formed in twenty months, compared to the four to five years required in Japan. They also put in small pieces on the shell face itself, and the oyster covers these over to make half pearls for earrings, etc. He uses Japanese divers and technicians.

November 27, 1966

A » The Australian general elections were held yesterday. The issues were pretty well narrowed down to two. The Liberal-Country Party governing coalition supported participation in the war in Vietnam as a means of keeping potential enemies a long way from Australia, supported the American alliance so that the U.S.A. will come to the rescue of Australia in time of trouble, and stood on its administrative record and economic growth. The

Australian Labor Party, led by seventy-year-old Arthur Calwell, said it would bring home conscripts from Vietnam and end the Australian involvement there as soon as reasonably possible, and made extravagant promises of improved social benefits. Some weeks ago I predicted the return of the government "plus or minus four seats." Last evening we were fortunate enough to go to the national central tally room in Albert Hall in Canberra as guests of the Chief Electoral Officer, who has had an extensive connection with Canada. They had all the candidates in each constituency listed on the boards around the room. The room was more than half filled with radio, TV, and press men, who prepared their commentaries as the returns were posted by Australian National University students putting up figures like hymn numbers in the various slots. We had various guides to indicate the constituencies that might swing one way or another on a slight change in the popular vote. The polls closed at 8:00 p.m. By 9:00 p.m. several were predicting that the Government would stay in, and by 10:00 p.m., even before returns came from Western Australia, which is two hours behind the East, as B.C. is behind our East, it was apparent that the Government would pick up some additional seats. Here they have a fancy system of proportional representation, or preference vote. If one candidate does not get an overall majority, then they eliminate the one with the smallest vote and allot his ballot to the person the voter has given his second preference to, and so on. This means that persons voting for one of the splinter parties can often decide the winner by getting their supporters to mark their second preferences for one of the two leading parties. Well, it isn't all settled yet, but it looks as if the government coalition will have added three to nine seats. Probably Mr. Calwell will resign.

Sir Valston Hancock, Australian Commissioner General for Expo 67, and Lady Hancock left for Canada this weekend to take up residence there and supervise their pavilion, etc. We attended a reception they gave, and on Wednesday night gave one of our own for them that was attended by about fifty people. We are fortunate to have such a pleasant and efficient man in charge of the Australian show at Expo.

December 4, 1966

s » Remember, remember the 29th of November! We had a triple celebration this year—three men, all born on the same day in the same year, so all celebrating their fiftieth birthday this Tuesday, Arthur being of course Number One; then David Hay, Administrator Designate for New Guinea and Papua, who was Australian high commissioner in Canada before Sir Kenneth Bailey, the present one, and therefore a good friend of ours from those days; and thirdly, Lindsay Brand, an assistant secretary to the Treasury Department and a good friend of David's. With wives, that made six, then we added three other couples, also good friends of the Hays and ourselves: Sir John Bunting, Secretary of the Cabinet, and Lady Bunting, the Shanns—he was most recently Australian ambassador to Indonesia—and the Jamiesons, also External but now retired, at one time posted in Ottawa, and ended up as Australian ambassador to Russia. It made quite a congenial group, with lots of easy good conversation. I had three nice carnation corsages, or rather buttonholes, for the three birthday-men. At the table we had three separate birthday cakes, which they cut and shared so that each of us received one candle, which we all blew out simultaneously. David and Lindsay brought a wrapped-up present that looked like a bottle of something. And so it was—a drink that is half lemon squash and half water, so it is called "50-50." Clever, eh? Oh yes—we had champagne at dinner too. Another strange coincidence is that David Hay has a niece who has a birthday on November 29, just as Arthur has Alexandra, and they're both eighteen!

December 11, 1966

a » The principal event of the past week was our annual staff meeting on Thursday and Friday. We had sixteen officers at the meeting reviewing the events of 1966 and looking ahead at what we might expect in 1967. I led off with a review of foreign-policy relations between Canada and Australia, stressing the differences occasioned by our different geographic positions, ours in North

America and the North Atlantic and Australia's on the edge of Southeast Asia. Then Bernie O'Neill talked about trade policy and how Australian policy affects the prospects for Canadian trade. Next we had a review of trade, item by item, and the prospects for 1967, which we hope will see an increase from $120 million to $235 million. This year for the first time we had a new Canadian Government Travel Bureau representative here. He expects 12,000 Australians to visit Canada in 1966 and hopes to see that figure rise to 15,000 next year. Immigration from Australia to Canada is running at about 4,000 a year and raises administrative problems. Quite a range of other subjects was discussed. We ended with a talk about how we plan to celebrate Canada's Centennial next year. An annual session like this helps to give the specialists some idea of what we're all doing.

Thursday night we had twenty-six in for refreshments and then went up to the Carousel Restaurant on Red Hill for dinner. There was other entertainment during the two days. We had Marg and John Stiles stay with us.

Tuesday night I got caught to give an address at the annual speech night of Ainsley Primary School, the oldest in Canberra. We went at 7:50 and were met by the principal, senior teachers, and other guests. There were about six hundred in the hall, about two hundred of whom were in the two choirs, which sang very well for us. I tried in my fifteen-minute speech to pitch my remarks mostly at a level that would hold the attention of the children and yet get something to parents as well. After my talk a lot of prizes were given out; one boy from Nauru got two of them.

December 19, 1966

s » Arthur and I left Saturday morning; it was about a two-and-a-half-hour drive up toward the Snowy Mountains region to a large lake that is part of the hydroelectric scheme. We were at a motel in the village of Adaminaby, which is actually about four miles from the lake, but is the little shopping centre. They had to move because of the flooding of the old townsite by the new dam. We had lunch at the motel, then rented a boat with a motor and went fishing for the afternoon. It was a good way to get away from it all. If we stay in Canberra it is very difficult not to get involved even on weekends, and we just decided we would like peace and our own company for two days. Arthur caught two rainbow trout. Sunday we went out again in the boat and were out from nine to four, and in that time he got three more fish, one a really big size—but not as big as the beauty that escaped just as we were trying to land him in the boat. I'm afraid I wasn't too efficient as an assistant with a small new landing net we had. It was windy on the water, and the boat tended to blow around, though the 9½-horsepower motor was efficient. I spent most of the time working it and had no time to fish too. We now know the setup of such a place and its facilities. We intend to try a couple of other places in the next month or two.

A » Wednesday I went down to Melbourne on the "steak and eggs" flight (breakfast time to you). In the morning I visited the banknote printing division of the Reserve Bank. The elaborate and detailed precautions taken in engraving the plates and printing the lines and colours on banknotes discourages me from becoming a forger. Australia has had a lot of printing experience recently, with the changeover to decimal currency. I also saw postage stamps being printed, some with magnetic colours so that the sorting machines can handle them. I went to a Rotary Club lunch. In the afternoon I went to George's Department Store to discuss an exhibition of portraits by Yousuf Karsh next March, which I am to open. Then in the evening I went out to the suburb of Beaumaris, where I was guest speaker to 350 members of the Returned Services League at their Christmas Special Meeting. Returned to Canberra early Thursday morning.

Recollections of Australia
By Norah Menzies

I spent the summer of 1968 (the Australian winter) working as a volunteer at the Royal Guide Dogs in Melbourne. I will never forget my first day there as an impressionable seventeen-year-old meeting their PR person Helen Leckie. How exotic she looked in her rust-coloured suede jacket and short, short miniskirt, smoking cigarillos. Her generosity and warmth encircled me. She swooped me up to accompany her on a weekend trip upcountry, where she was to give a speech at the local Lions Club, thanking them for a donation for a guide dog. She said of course I could share her hotel room, and of course they won't mind another body, especially a Canadian—and off we went. And my memory is of our Aussie hosts being totally delighted at the unexpected guest and making me feel honoured rather than an interloper.

This Australian trait of going with the flow and the unexpected, appreciating it, and grabbing it for all it's worth really spoke to me and enthralled me. I was very fortunate to come across Australians who embraced me with their wide-open friendship, and this is what I will always keep in my heart.

My impressions of Australia as a teenager in the late 1960s really revolved around the amazing people I met. Before I travel now, I read up about the country's social justice record, its political parties, culture, etc. As a teenager I just plunged in totally unprepared and unaware, and joyfully, luckily, had an incredible time!

In the summer of 1969 my Canadian roommate Sonja Kekkonen ventured to Australia with me. My parents generously lent us a Datsun car and we jaunted off across the outback—totally unprepared. Our "survival kits" were bottles of Coke and little else. Big four-wheel-drive vehicles with their "roo" bars out front (for hitting kangaroos, as I gathered to my horror) and winch cables in the back, incredulously passed us with a cheery wave and a toot. We, on the other hand, in our little Datsun, crept at dusk—and I do mean C-R-E-P-T—through the zillions of rabbits crisscrossing the endless dirt road, so as not to hit any!

Out in the middle of literally nowhere we picked up Rod, a handsome Aussie hitchhiker, who nobly earned his keep every time we came to a large puddle (read "pond"!) that engulfed the road (read "track"!). Rod would climb out and with a long stick wade through the puddle/pond and show us the shallowest place to drive! Likewise, we would come to a "bridge" (read "sign indicating that beneath this rushing water there is supposed to be a road/bridge that, with an enormous leap of faith, you may drive over sight unseen providing the tall ruler by the riverside indicates that your truck/jeep [and in our case our tiny Datsun] will not be submerged"). Sonja and I were incredulous, but Rod happily trotted across, proving there really was something we could drive on, and we inched across behind him.

A welcome gas station in the interior had me politely asking for the bathroom, in answer to which the owner, without batting an eye, proudly took me to a small room in his house that contained only a bathtub. I quickly learned to specifically ask for the toilet!

We made it to the coast, where Rod was squatting in some stone ruins and living on a fifty-pound sack of potatoes and salt that he shared with us. The Hilton was not for us! (2008)

Kenneth and the South Pacific Commission,
New Caledonia, May to August, 1966

The Secretary General of the South Pacific Commission, Mr. W.D. (Bill) Forsyth, headquartered in Noumea, New Caledonia, was a personal friend of mine in the Australian Department of External Affairs. To educate his children in English he kept a home and his wife in Canberra. I lunched with him one day to get a description of the economic and educational development work done by the S.P.C. During our lunch I got the idea that Kenneth, who was in his third year of Honours Political Science and Economics at Queen's University in Kingston, might benefit from taking a Canadian summer job with the S.P.C. It would provide him with practical first-hand knowledge of the work in the international headquarters of an economic development organization and some knowledge of a very widespread area of the South Pacific. Living in French-speaking Noumea but doing his work in English seemed to me about the best arrangement he could hope for to develop his bilingual capacity. Ken agreed.

Bill said he would be glad to take Kenneth on as a Volunteer Assistant to himself, and as his Administrative Assistant. He couldn't pay him much, but could offer free accommodation at the Commission's Transient Quarters.

As the Canadian Department of External Affairs would pay his way out to Canberra and back, I arranged for him to spend a night with friends in Vancouver, a night in Honolulu, two days with a friend, Paul Gabites, New Zealand High Commissioner in newly independent Apia, Western Samoa, two days in Fiji, and then on to visit us for a few days in Canberra before flying to Noumea.

Kenneth benefited from and greatly enjoyed his three-month service, from May to August, with the South Pacific Commission, whose Secretary-General was very kind to him. Furthermore, he was able to make good use of his experience when he wrote a thesis, which he submitted in April 1967, in partial fulfilment of the requirements for his Bachelor of Arts degree from the Department of Political Studies at Queen's University, in Kingston, Ontario. This 88-page, seven-chapter study is supported by seven pages of bibliography, which indicates that while in Noumea and while preparing his thesis he did a considerable amount of reading. The chapters are entitled, I: "The South Pacific"; II: "The Function of the South Pacific Commission and Its Formation"; III: "Institutional Structure"; IV: "The Development of the South Pacific Commission"; V: "The South Pacific Conferences"; VI: "The Effectiveness of the South Pacific Commission"; and VII: "Conclusions."

I shall not try to summarize the history of these seventeen island units that cover an area greater than North and South America combined. Only one, Western Samoa, was independent in 1966. The Japanese invasion and occupation of the area from 1941 to 1945 had changed the sleepy colonial life of the islands forever. Australia and New Zealand in particular recognized the need for international co-operation in the development of these territories.

Kenneth's study deals with the need for inter-island co-operation through the establishment of the University of the South Pacific in Fiji, an institution that anticipated "distance education" by electronic means such was we now have in Northern Canada. He makes a good background argument for the co-operative advantages of the South Pacific Commission.

When Kenneth's service was completed Sheila, Norah, and I flew to Noumea, where we picked him up, and the four of us made our three-week exploratory tour of the Southwest Pacific islands. (A.M. 2008)

THREE

1967

January 2, 1967

s » Australians usually take their chief holiday between the middle of December and the end of January, during the children's summer holidays from school. Many offices, even government ones, are therefore very generous with holidays over Christmas and New Year's. As a result many people are out of town and not too much business gets done. Well, to add to the numbers of the holidayers and take advantage of this slack period we went away for four days. We just returned, at 6:30 this evening, Monday, well sunburned and a bit tired, but very pleased at what a successful and pleasant change we have had.

Arthur had been in touch with the minister in the New South Wales government who looks after parks—he is at present on a trip to Canada and the U.S. Through him he heard that there was a lodge in Kosciuszko State Park. We were told by letter that it had eleven beds, so it sounded quite a size, and we felt it was a bit presumptuous to occupy it all by ourselves. Therefore we invited Philip Slyfield, the young second secretary in the office, his wife Jinny, his mother, who is visiting here from Canada for a couple of months, and his young son Christopher, aged two, to be our guests. We were not sure just what sort of place we were getting into, but took food and provisions, fishing gear and sports clothes, and started off Thursday morning. The Slyfields came Friday afternoon. They returned this morning and we this afternoon. Art will continue—I'm going for my turn in the bath now.

A » Kosciuszko State Park embraces 2,100 square miles of the "roof of Australia," and includes 7,314-foot Mount Kosciuszko and four other peaks over 7,000 feet. Kenneth came with us in May when we made a tour of the Snowy Mountains hydroelectric and irrigation scheme. The park covers part of this area and is being developed, like North American parks, for recreation and the preservation of the unique fauna of the wilderness area. There are two fair-size skiing centres in the park, one at Thredbo and one at Perisher Valley. They run in our summer months, but even this morning we walked down from Mount Kosciuszko onto a big drift of snow that had not yet melted. On two of the days we were there we drove for about a hundred miles to explore areas of the park. On one of these drives we went over the Slink Pass down to Geehi, where we got wonderful views of the western ramparts, sometimes called "the China Wall" because it rises so steeply (for Australia). Another time we dropped down about 3,000 feet to the canyon of the Lower Snowy River, a wild and lovely valley filled with cypress trees that looked like our Canadian evergreens. Two other occasions were given over to fishing, once in the Thredbo River and another time on Lake Eucumbene, where we got more sun than fish. Altogether we packed in quite a bit during our four days there and a day travelling about 120 miles to and fro.

January 22, 1967

S » This has been a short week in Canberra because of our five-day holiday—Saturday, Sunday, Monday, Tuesday, and Wednesday, a real English weekend. One day last year we motored to the South Coast, south of Canberra, just for the day, but this was a chance to really get acquainted with the chief holiday area near here. Now, with school holidays, accommodation is difficult to find. Fortunately we had made reservations long ago at this hotel in Ulladulla. It was recommended by friends, but people have such different tastes that we were rather suspicious until we were actually there. It turned out to be very satisfactory. It is well off the main road—about three blocks—and it has a large garden all around it and a lovely view of the sea. We had a nice clean room with twin beds and a small kitchen equipped with stove and fridge, so we were lucky. As in most Australian hotels or motels, the cost included breakfast, which was the only meal served by the management, and in true Australian style it was substantial: choice of fish, or chops, or bacon and eggs, etc. They insisted you eat at eight o'clock. It might not suit a holidayer like Norah, but all their customers—about twenty-five of them—were on hand and tucked in. For swimming we went by car to a beautiful beach with good surf.

A » During our time at the seashore I tried my hand at various forms of fishing—from the rocks, surf-casting, and long-lining. We were interested to see the locals catching sandworms at low tide. An old chicken's foot on a string or a nylon stocking filled with rotting meat would be dragged slowly along the water's edge. The worms, smelling the delicacy, would poke their heads out of the sand and get nipped by a pair of pliers carried by the fisherman. Only luck I had was when I was taken out deep-sea fishing by a local fisherman. I caught a good snapper, a morwong (like a snapper but not red), two maoris (a red fish), two rock cod, and two sweepers. I bought a plastic bucket and some party ice and brought the better fish home. A bluebottle wrapped itself around my knee while I was surfing. These bluebottles are akin to jellyfish. They have a bladder the size of an egg, which is inflated with air and floats on the surface, trailing a three- to ten-foot tail that looks like thin blue yarn and stings painfully when it comes in contact with flesh. My knee hurt for three hours and I was left with a line of welts. Ricketts Blue is supposed to be good for it, but I think its effect is mainly psychological.

On our way back to Canberra we drove north on the coast as far as Nowra and then climbed up over the Coast Range, which at that point catches quite a bit of rain and has lovely tree ferns, something quite unusual in this dry continent. We ate our picnic lunch at the lookout on the top of the range, then descended into Kangaroo Valley, a lush farming area famous for its cattle stud properties. We climbed another ridge to get out, and at the top were in Morton State Park, with an outlook over the Fitzroy Falls. This country is like the Blue Mountains area that so effectively enclosed the early settlers around Sydney. There is a plateau about two thousand feet high laced with deep valleys with precipitous sides. The Fitzroy Falls drop about a thousand feet down into one of these valleys—not much water in Canadian terms, but still quite a sight. We drove back to Canberra via Goulbourn and Lake George, arriving at 7:00 p.m.

From the Australian national point of view, this week has been enlivened by the visit of Prime Minister Ky of South Vietnam. Arthur Calwell, the elderly leader of the Australian Labor Party, had announced in advance that he would lead protest marches against this fascist dictator, so security precautions were very strict. Ky gave a very good account of himself in English (his third language, after Vietnamese and French) in a televised talk to the National Press Club and a question period afterward, which I attended. He showed a grasp of psychology by using his old and well-regarded foreign minister, Dr. Tran Van Do, to answer one question about peace negotiations, asking a representative of the leading political faction in the constituent assembly to answer one about a timetable for representative government, and inviting the correspondent of the Australian Communist Party newspaper, *The Tribune*, to ride back to Saigon with him in his plane to see conditions for himself.

January 27, 1967

A » This is the Australia Day weekend, and we are taking a holiday on Monday, January 30. Over the weekend we have been attending the thirty-third summer school of the Australian Institute of Political Science, which deals with "Communism in Asia: A Threat to Australia?" We have been surprised and impressed that a thousand people have paid $8.50 ($10 Canadian) to attend the three-day session. The first lecture, on "The Nature of Communist Regimes in Asia," was by Professor Robert Scalapino. He has

an encyclopedic U.S. post-grad grasp of the subject and the abil-
ity to organize it. Last night Dr. Goh Keng-swee, the Minister of
Defence of Singapore, whom I had known there, gave a talk titled
"The Nature and Appeals of Communism in Non-Communist
Asian Countries," which he illustrated from his own experience;
this morning we heard Professor Miller of the Australian National
University talk on Communist China's foreign policy; tonight we
hear a talk titled "Does Asian Communism Constitute a Threat to
Australia?"; and tomorrow there is a windup titled "Australia's
Policy Toward Asia: The Choices." Given the limitations imposed
by the numbers attending, the discussion has been quite good
and interesting.

February 5, 1967

A » I went down to Sydney Friday noon and returned Saturday
noon. On the way down I sat beside the Minister of Defence and
had a good chat. He drove me into town. I spent a little time at
our commercial counsellor's office and then went with him to call
on International Nickel Southern Explorations, where I got little
information. The main purpose of my trip was to greet Mr. Justice
Ivan C. Rand, who is heading an Ontario royal commission inquiry into labour disputes. He and his counsel, Mr. Pollock, will
spend a month in Australia looking into the Australian system of
conciliation and arbitration. Australia has had a system of en-
forced conciliation and awards for fifty years. Basic wages are set
by a government commission. It would be hard for one province
in Canada to adopt such a scheme, and even if Canada as a whole
were to do so, there would be questions of the effect of U.S.
labour settlements on our awards. Mr. Rand hopes to take home
some ideas. I gave a dinner for him that was attended by Leslie
Bury, the federal Minister of Labour and National Service.

February 13, 1967

A » The two important events in Australia this past week have
been the disastrous fire in Tasmania and the election of a new

leader of the Australian Labor Party. When it gets very hot and dry in Australia, forest fires seem to break out with little provocation. Tasmania was swept by fires over the past weekend, with over fifty lives lost and over six hundred homes burned. This is really shocking and has resulted in considerable help being offered from all states. As for the Australian Labor Party elections, Gough Whitlam, an able fifty-year-old lawyer, won over Jim Cairns, a left-winger. This is a good omen for the rebuilding of the ALP and the prospect of its providing an alternative to the present government. Whitlam is irrepressible: once he threw a glass of water in the face of the Minister of External Affairs, Paul Hasluck, right on the floor of Parliament.

We gave a dinner on Thursday in honour of François and Nina Brière. François Brière is the French ambassador, and he is retiring next month to teach at Monash University in Melbourne. In a toast I told the story about the students who were told to write an essay on the elephant. The German expounded on the engineering skill of the elephant in moving an enormous weight with little effort; the Englishman told how he shot the elephant and mounted its tusks; the Frenchman wrote on "l'éléphant et ses amours"; and the Pole wrote on "l'éléphant et la question Polonaise." I related this to the bilingualism and biculturalism question in Canada.

February 19, 1967

s » I will stick to the domestic scene this week, because it has permeated the whole house. All last weekend Arthur and I were aware of some bad smell in our bedroom, but kept thinking it was the damp weather, and a mould or such in the carpet. We tried airing the beds and everything movable. The smell got stronger, and Arthur moved downstairs to sleep better. I would wake up several times and spray Airwick around. Well, by Wednesday we could stand it no longer and decided it must be something dead. It was! There was a dead rat under the floor—under our bed. Of course it was not as simple as that to track it down. The wall-to-wall carpeting has been there for about twenty years, and under it was the weirdest assortment of bits and pieces of underfelt, and under that the old floor, and under that a sort of seaweed or grass used as insulation, which of course would appeal to rats as nest-building material. We have a contract with a pest control company, which comes and checks every four months. Evidently all they do is place boxes of poisoned bait under the roof in various places, and refill them each time. After eating this the rats are supposed to feel very thirsty and sick so that they want to rush outside to die. Well, evidently this one got mixed up in his directions and died under our floor. Once it was opened up, and even after we had located this one carcass—which took real prodding, because the company's usual theory is that "we can never find the body"—I felt there was still so much smell that there might be more. So we are sleeping downstairs for a week while the underfelt is replaced, and the insulation replaced with a more modern variety. Of course all this has needed emergency permission from Canada. We look forward to returning to a sweeter bedroom by next week.

February 26, 1967

A » The new Parliament, elected in the November 1966 elections, was opened on Tuesday, February 21, with the sort of ceremony we have in Canada. A new speaker (chairman) had been elected in advance, bringing to office a friend of ours, Bill Aston of Sydney, who had visited Canada for an Interparliamentary Union conference just before we came out to Australia. We went to the opening—Sheila in afternoon dress, gloves, and hat, and I in straight trousers and a short black jacket—at 3:00 p.m., and had fixed seats with other heads of mission in the Senate chamber. After the Governor General came in, the Gentleman Usher of the Black Rod went to summon the members of the House of Commons, who trooped in to hear the speech by the GG, which announces new government legislation, etc. Later we had tea in the courtyard, affording an opportunity to chat with MPs. On Thursday night there was a black-tie reception beginning at 9:00 p.m. I had a chat there with Frank Ford, who was Australian minister of defence in the early war years, then high commissioner to

Canada for six years, and is now retired, well over seventy years of age. We also chatted with various MPs from South Australia, where we are to visit in a fortnight.

The British Secretary of State for Commonwealth Relations, Mr. Herbert Bowden, visited Canberra this past week, and I went to a Press Club luncheon on Thursday at which he gave a workmanlike but unexciting talk on British relations with Australia, touching on defence, British entry into the European Common Market, immigration, investment, etc.

s » Arthur started off for a change. Now to continue my report on the tearing up of the bedroom from last week. I sure am glad I insisted that all the old seaweed insulation be taken out and replaced, the floor put back, new underfelt laid, and the carpet relaid on top. You will never guess how many rats, in various stages of decay, some recent, some old, were found under the floor—about fifteen in all! We will move back upstairs tomorrow. It has meant an upset week. Actually we were away Friday, Saturday, and today until 5:00 p.m., so escaped the finishing-up. We went to Merimbula on the South Coast. We motored the sixty miles to Bateman's Bay on the same road we used when we went to the coast before, then instead of turning north toward Sydney we went south, passing many of the famous beaches and holiday resorts, and ending up at one just about at the end of the string. All along that coast there are what are called lakes but are really just inlets filled with tidal water. They make much quieter places to fish or swim than out in the surf of the main ocean. The motel turned out to be fair. It was also a hotel with a bar that did most of the town's business, and we could have done without that, but luckily were on the side away from the noise. We went fishing twice, once by ourselves in a small boat with an inboard motor (Arthur had some luck), and early this morning deep-sea fishing with a man with a large boat. He took two ladies from the hotel as well. Even I had luck, so we have brought back about eight good-sized fish for the deep-freeze. Edith is delighted. Most are what are called flatheads. They have rather nasty-looking faces and are dirty brown in colour, but they're said to taste good.

March 5, 1967

s » This has been as busy a week as any we have had in Australia, because we have been out of town for two days in Melbourne and one day in Sydney, and had two royal visitors in town, which entailed social functions at odd hours of the day that had to be attended on the dot, plus our own paperwork and preparations, etc. For Princess Alexandra and her husband, Mr. Ogilvie, all the Commonwealth representatives plus many parliamentarians were invited to Government House for a reception. Diplomats were lined up on one side of the hall in precedence, and on the other side were all the members of the cabinet and their wives. Such a lot of rigmarole for an "unofficial" visit. It certainly is difficult to be "unofficial" when the press are on all sides and report each meeting and farewell and function in detail. However, I must say Alexandra was very poised and polite. She was outdone in charm by Prince Philip, Duke of Edinburgh, later in the week. He is out here to make plans for his study conference next year. Arthur went to the government reception for him at Parliament House. Again along with the other Commonwealth representatives we were included in a dinner for fifty at Government House. It is the biggest dinner by far that we have attended here. The Duke was very affable, pleasant, informal, and willing to talk. He was much thinner than I had imagined—he has a lean, boyish look.

Because the Governor General was busy with the Duke, we were asked to substitute for him at the official opening of the Castle Hill Agricultural Show. This is about twenty miles from Sydney. It was interesting to be part of this community agricultural show, which is used by many farmers as a testing ground before the big Royal Easter Show at Sydney. There were fine displays of cattle, horses, poultry, etc., and of things I know a little more about, like horticulture, art, photography, and dog-judging. The patron of the show is Mr. Vincent Fairfax, owner of *The Sydney Morning Herald*. His daughter, who is married to an External Affairs chap, has been in Canada, so we knew them slightly. He and his wife very kindly conducted us all around the show and then drove us to their home, and later to catch the plane to Canberra. Arthur's five- to ten-minute speech to open the event went very well—out in the centre of a big ring, facing all the animals instead of the people, who were around the edge of the showground listening by loudspeaker. It was hot, about 75 degrees.

A » Tuesday and Wednesday of this week we went to Melbourne. Tuesday evening we gave a reception at George's, the exclusive high-quality store, for the opening in their art gallery of a display of forty portraits by Yousuf Karsh, as part of a Pacific Photographic Fair. We had about 150 guests, including the Deputy Premier, Mr. Rylah, the Mayor of Melbourne, Mr. Beaurepaire, and others. Eric Westbrook, director of the Melbourne Art Gallery, gave a very good talk on the art of photography, and it remained to me to thank all concerned and do a little advertising. That evening Adrian and Gwen Gilbert took us out to a dinner at the Royal Victorian Automobile Club.

Next day I opened a display of sixteen National Film Board of Canada photographs in the Reserve Bank building. The manager, Gordon Menzies, gave a little reception beforehand and I gave a luncheon afterwards for art critics from the various papers and some of those who had been helpful. Both exhibits were successful. While in Melbourne Sheila recorded a twenty-minute interview with Lois Lathleen on radio station 3AW in which she covered the Karsh exhibits, Expo 67, the status of women in Canada, and Canadian education. We listened to it and I can say with pride that our girl came through very well!

March 11, 1967

S » The new term at the University started this week. I have enrolled in two adult education courses, knowing full well that we will be out of town for some of the lectures, and even when in town will often have conflicting engagements, but still hopeful that I will be able to attend enough to make it worthwhile. I'm continuing the Australian History course. Last term took us up to 1850, so this one continues from 1850 to 1901. Presumably next year he will go on to modern-day Australia. I am also taking a new course on Women in Australia. There are ten different lecturers. The first one, from the Department of Political Science, was excellent.

A » Thursday noon I had three professors from ANU in to meet and talk with two defence scientists from Ottawa, Drs. Koop and Eaton, about Australian views on nuclear weapons, and the proposals for a nuclear detection club and a nuclear non-proliferation treaty. We had just the sort of useful discussion that I like on such occasions, which so often get sidetracked into social trivia. Prof. Newstead is an expert on seismic detection arrays. Australia has one at Tennant Creek that can pick up earthquakes or significant nuclear blasts almost all over the world. The tremors are registered on IBM tape, and the idea of the nuclear detection club is to exchange tapes or data from tapes so that there will be an internationally verified record of earthquakes and nuclear explosions, and we will see if any cheating is going on. The other two, Arthur Burns and Bruce Miller, talked about Australian public attitudes toward national security, including the threat to Asia arising from Communist China's acquisition of a nuclear device.

April 2, 1967

A » Thursday I went down to Sydney for the afternoon for the opening of the Southeast Asia Commonwealth Cable (SEACOM), which extends from Cairns on the northeast coast of Australia around by sea to Madang on the north coast of New Guinea, then to Guam, Hong Kong, Jesselton, and Singapore. It is linked with the transpacific cable to Canada and from there by the transatlantic cable to London. The half-hour ceremony was conducted before a thousand guests in the ballroom of the Wentworth Hotel, with amplifiers carrying perfectly the voices of various prime ministers or acting P.M.s as they exchanged short remarks and quips. It was quite remarkable to get such clarity of reproduction.

April 9, 1967

S » We had the man who is taking two sheepdogs to Canada to

put on demonstrations at Expo in for dinner—and his friend from whom he got one of the dogs, and who is a judge at the current national sheepdog trials in Canberra. Saturday we watched the champions. Our Mr. Miller was fourth. Three sheep are let out in an area about the size of a football field, and the dog is released at the other end. On his master's word he starts off, and by always keeping behind the sheep, routes them through a real obstacle course. First he has to get them the whole length of the field into a circle, then around two flags in the centre of the field, then into a pen, and through it to a ramp like a loading platform on the far side, and next into a pen, where a gate is shut behind them—all in fifteen minutes. The winning dogs did it in twelve minutes or so, with about 92 points out of 100—very clever and cunning. Later they had a demonstration with twelve sheep, then with about twenty. That was much easier—they just follow the mob. It is too bad that they will be giving demonstrations in Canada only on Australia Day, June 6, because I think they would have an appeal all over Canada. Of course Australian laws on the entry of animals are so strict that Mr. Miller will have to sell the dogs in Canada. He hopes to get about $600 for them. Anyway, I hope the Canadian sheep they provide him are co-operative!

April 22, 1967

A » On Saturday, April 15, Sheila and I flew to Sydney, where Andrew met us with the car and we drove north 150 miles to Cessnock in the Hunter River Valley—inland from Newcastle on your maps. There we were given a civic welcome by the mayor and aldermen. I was able to point out that Canada is the second-best customer for Australian wines produced in the Hunter Valley, that Alcan Australia, a subsidiary of Alcan Aluminum of Montreal, is beginning to build a 30,000-ton alumina smelter nearby that will employ 350, and that a Canadian company had won a $60-million contract to install boilers in the Lyddell power plant, which is being built in the Valley. Over the weekend we attended a Beefsteak and Burgundy Society dinner between the great wooden maturing barrels in a winery and joined in judging the wines, and we had a barbecue lunch at another winery. I went down underground in a coal mine where I watched the operation of modern excavating machinery and listened apprehensively to the groaning and thudding of the rock as pressure changed with the removal of the coal seam. I spoke to a hundred or so at an Apex Club dinner. Tuesday we motored two hundred miles over the rugged Blue Mountains to Bathurst, which is on the edge of the great central plane, in sheep and wheat country. Here there was another civic luncheon and reception, and I spoke to 180 people at a Rotary Club dinner. Then another two-hundred-mile drive back through rolling sheep country to Canberra. It is good to get out and see the country in this way, but office work slips behind in the process.

The Australian Prime Minister's Visit to Canada,
June 4–8, 1967

These letters have mentioned preparations for Australian participation in Canada's 1967 Centennial Year celebrations, including the promotional visit of Honourable Judy LaMarsh, the design of the Australian pavilion for Expo 67 in Montreal, and the appointment of retired Air Marshal Sir Valston Hancock as Australian Commissioner General for the Exposition. But the most important event was the visit to Canada of Prime Minister Harold Holt from June 4 to June 8, 1967.

Sheila and I returned to Canada to assist in hosting Prime Minister Holt, Mrs. Holt, and the rest of his party during this state visit. We left Canberra on May 17, made a short visit to Fiji, and arrived in Vancouver on May 20. We stopped for a week in the Toronto area to visit my sisters and some people with special interests in Australia. On May 28 we flew on to Ottawa, where I was put on duty helping to ensure that the program for the Holts' visit was fine-tuned.

The Australian party arrived by R.C.A.F. aircraft at 4:25 p.m., Sunday, June 4, and was met at Ottawa Uplands R.C.A.F. base by the Coordinator for Visits of Heads of State Lieutenant-General R.W. Moncel. Prime Minister and Mrs. Holt were accompanied by a roster of senior Australian officials, including Sir John Bunting, Secretary of the Prime Minister's Department and Secretary to the Cabinet, Lady Bunting, Sir Lawrence McIntyre, Deputy Secretary of the Department of External Affairs, Peter Bailey, First Assistant Secretary of the Prime Minister's Department (and son of the Australian High Commissioner to Canada, Sir Kenneth Bailey), Bob Pritchett, Assistant Secretary in the Department of External Affairs, and other security and press personnel.

The Australian party was driven to the Government Guest House at 7 Rideau Gate, and then immediately to Parliament Hill for an official welcome with a Guard of Honour by Prime Minister L.B. Pearson. They then went to a reception at the residence of the Australian High Commissioner Sir Kenneth Bailey and Lady Bailey. That evening Prime Minister Pearson hosted an official dinner for Prime Minister Holt and party at the Country Club. Sheila and I were included in all these welcoming activities.

June 5 began with a call on the Mayor of Ottawa, Donald Reid. Then the Australian Prime Minister and party called on Prime Minister Pearson at the Centre Block of the Parliament Buildings for an hour of official talks, followed by a press conference at the National Press Building. This was followed by an official luncheon at Government House hosted by the Right Honourable Roland Michener, Governor-General of Canada, and Mrs. Michener. There had been a separate ladies' program in the morning for Mrs. Holt and party. It happened to be Sheila's forty-ninth birthday, which we did not mention publicly.

In the afternoon we went by government railway car to Montreal, where we were met by the Commissioner General for Visits of State 1967, Honourable Lionel Chevrier, and taken to the Queen Elizabeth Hotel. That evening Jean Drapeau, the colourful mayor of Montreal, gave a dinner for the Holts at City Hall.

On June 5 there was an official welcome at Place des Nations by the Commissioner General, Pierre Dupuy, and a brief visit to the Australian Pavilion at Expo 67. This was followed by a luncheon at the Restaurant Hélène de Champlain.

The morning of June 7 was focused on an extended visit to the Australian Pavilion. This was an imaginatively designed building with exhibits covering many aspects of the geography, history, and current life of Australia. I recall sinking into a high-backed armchair, which turned on a commentary on Australia. There were attractive young Australian officials in splendid modern uniforms. Outside the pavilion there were pens with Australian kangaroos and koalas and cages of brightly plumed exotic birds. We watched Australian sheep dogs rounding up sheep. Altogether a splendid show, very popular with all visitors to Expo 67.

In the afternoon we flew to Quebec City and went immediately to visit Laval University. In the late afternoon there was a reception at La Citadelle hosted by the Lieutenant-Governor, Honourable Hugues Lapointe. And in the evening the Government of Quebec hosted a dinner at the Hôtel du Gouvernement. Bill Pritchard and I had been trying en route to review a few short sentences of French for Mr. Holt to use. I recall him rising to say, "Malhereusement je ne parle pas bien la belle langue française parce que mon professeur était un Écossais." This brought forth a welcome clapping of hands. He then gave the rest of his speech in English, except for a final "Merci beaucoup."

The Australian party flew out of Ancienne-Lorette Airport for New York on June 8. Sheila and I were well satisfied with the success of the visit.

July 23, 1967

s » The Commercial Counsellor and Mrs. O'Neill leave tomorrow after three and a half years here. We had a farewell dinner in their honour Wednesday, and went to a cocktail party for them on Thursday. By the time people are leaving they know a group of friends well, so a party runs more easily and is more relaxed than with the unknowns of a welcoming party. We had six other receptions or dinners in the week—I mean to go out to, not given by us!

A » My principal outing for the week was a 150-mile flight Saturday morning over the Snowy Mountains to Corryong on the Victoria side, from which we took a bus to Khancoban. We lunched there and then went on for another half-hour to attend the official opening by the Prime Minister of the Murray 1 Power Station. There were fifteen hundred guests in attendance, because the station, with an output of 950,000 kW, is larger than all the other stations so far built in the Snowy Mountains scheme. Canadian General Electric supplied the transformers. You may recall that last May Sheila, Kenneth, and I toured the Snowy Mountains scheme for three days. Melting snows from this "roof of Australia" are caught and channelled through power stations that supply about twenty-five percent of the electricity for Victoria and New South Wales. Sale of the power will amortize the cost of the works. Off-peak cheap power is used to pump water running down east to the sea back through the range, where it ends up in the Murrumbidgee or the Murray and provides two million acre-feet of water for irrigation purposes. The whole scheme is taking twenty-five years to build and it will cost $800 million Australian ($1 billion Canadian). The opening show was well done, and the event marked a milestone in a great Australian achievement.

July 30, 1967

S » Another busy week. Either I have been out or we have had a dinner here every night, and the same holds this week until Friday. Monday I attended my history class at the University. Next week finishes the term-two course. My other night out without Arthur was for the annual meeting of the Pan Pacific and South East Asia Women's Association. Although I have been pleased to have had the experience of being on the executive and working closely with the group this past year, I decided I would not stand for office again this year because of our many absences from the city. As the elections draw closer I am very pleased I stayed out, in spite of all sorts of phone calls, entreaties, etc., from those wanting to nominate me again, because it developed into a real political campaign. Two factions, whose rivalry is based chiefly on religious differences, aspired to office, some nomination papers were lost, and others were not delivered until the day after the deadline, etc. However, I think the compromise executive they finally got at their meeting is pretty good. I have got a good insight into how women's clubs work here. What with the squabbling and the results that are hidden behind the scenes, they are comparable with what you find in Canada and other countries I have been in.

Tuesday night we had a dinner here in honour of the Minister for Education and Science, Senator Gorton, and Mrs. Gorton, as well as the new Indian High Commissioner and Mrs. Thomas—who are Christian, and so present no dietary problem. The Gortons were the Australian representatives at the coronation of the new King of Tonga last month. He was quite disillusioned by the trip, and the insistence on carrying on British formality, especially in dress, in the tropical heat.

August 6, 1967

A » Thursday afternoon and Friday I visited Queensland for the opening of the Queensland Alumina plant. I was just having my bag weighed in at the airport for the flight to Sydney and then Brisbane when U.S. Ambassador Ed Clark came over and invited me to ride with him and Mr. and Mrs. Edgar Kaiser in their private plane. We played bridge all the way. Three hundred government and business leaders were invited for the opening. There was a big dinner at Lennons Hotel in Brisbane Thursday night. Then on Friday morning we flew three hundred miles in chartered aircraft to Gladstone, a town of 12,000, where the Queensland Alumina plant has been built during the past three years at a cost of $150 million Australian to process 1.2 million tons of bauxite from Weipa on the Cape York Peninsula into 600,000 tons of alumina powder, which is the stuff that is later smelted electrolytically into aluminum. The plant is run by a consortium in which Kaiser takes 312,000 tons, Alcan Aluminum of Canada takes 120,000 tons, Pechiney of France takes 120,000 tons, and Conzinc Riotino of Australia takes 48,000 tons. The plant, one of the most modern in the world, uses the Bayer process of mixing bauxite with caustic soda at high temperatures to form a sodium illuminate, which precipitates on top of the mud or slurry. This cake is then calcined in huge heated cylinders to produce fine alumina powder. There are very modern facilities for loading the alumina aboard ships for smelters in Australia or overseas. The opening involved speeches by the Deputy Prime Minister, John McEwen, Premier Nicklin of Queensland, Edgar Kaiser, and Sir Maurice Mawby, our host. I returned to Canberra Friday night, but was glad to have made this reconnoitre of Queensland at the expense of Queensland Alumina, with its twenty-percent Canadian share.

September 24, 1967

A » Monday we had an important guest from Canada, Lorne Gray, president of Atomic Energy of Canada Ltd. He came out with a team to strengthen relations with the Australian Atomic Energy Commission and to impress upon the Australian federal and state authorities the capabilities that Canada has in the field of engineering and the construction of nuclear power reactors using natural uranium, which Australia mines. I took him to call on various people Monday and gave a lunch and a reception for him. This is one of those specialized fields in which diplomats try to acquire a minimum of knowledge that will at least compare with that of the non-expert Treasury official or the minister.

October 1, 1967

A » Tuesday and Wednesday we went to Sydney for the opening of the Canadian Government Travel Bureau office, at 40 Martin Place. On Tuesday I gave a lunch at the Union Club, of which I'm an honorary member, to enable Dan Wallace, the director of the CGTB in Ottawa, to meet Hon. E.A. Willis, the Minister for Tourism of New South Wales, Mr. N. McCusker, the Chairman of the Australian National Travel Association, and ten others. Then on Tuesday and Wednesday evenings I was official host at receptions, for about eighty each time, to mark the opening. Speeches were made. In addition we had a review of Canadian relations with Australia, which lasted half a day, and other meetings.

Wednesday night we went to the posh suburb of North Sydney, about fifteen miles out, to dine with the Bob Hutchinsons. He is manager of Kennecott Copper in the South Pacific and a Canadian. There were other Canadian and Australian mining and business people there for a very handsomely catered dinner.

After returning to Canberra Thursday morning, I took Dan Wallace to call on the federal minister in charge of tourist activities, Don Chipp. We spent about an hour talking to him, and I think can regard him as an ally in seeking lower transpacific air fares in order to promote tourism. Later I gave a lunch for Wallace so that he could meet members of the new Australian Tourist Commission.

Friday night and all day Saturday I attended a private invitational seminar at the Australian National University on the implications for Australia of the British announcement that it would withdraw defence forces from Southeast Asia by the mid-seventies. There were academics, journalists, and bureaucrats, all talking off the record in the most interesting way. I find it hard to believe that Australia can keep garrison forces in Malaysia after the Brits withdraw, but I get the impression that the Australian government wishes to wait until as many as possible of the variables become known and until public opinion is more formed.

October 15, 1967

A » We have just returned from a quick weekend trip to Adelaide, the capital of South Australia, some seven hundred air miles away. We left at noon on Friday and were compelled to spend an inordinate amount of time in the airport in Melbourne because the drivers of the Shell trucks for refuelling the aircraft suddenly went out on strike. Luckily I was able to use an office and work on my speech. We were transferred to another airline and got to Adelaide about 7:40 p.m. We rushed to the hotel, changed quickly, and got to our meeting about twenty minutes late. The event was the national conference of the various state branches of the Royal Commonwealth Society, which was followed by a seminar on Canada. There were about 110 there to hear an introduction by Senator Laught and to see our film, *Helicopter Canada*. Saturday morning we started at 8:45 with a seminar proper, attended by about eighty I would say. I was the first speaker, on "Canada and the Commonwealth." I tried to point to the milestones in development: first the white dominions became independent, then the Asian republics joined them, and, finally, in the last decade, the African countries have joined, with an emphasis on racial equality. I then went on to discuss the various ways Canada was active in Commonwealth affairs. This talk was followed by four discussion groups. Later, Professor David Corbett, a Canadian who is head of the Political Science Department at Flinders University, talked on "Canada and Australia." There was more discussion and a summing up. Then we headed out twenty miles to Hardy's McLaren Vale Winery, where we had a barbecue lunch, tasted wines, and inspected the works. This morning we stopped in to see Mrs. Harris, the well-intentioned, at times intriguing, but also offbeat vice-president and main force of the Australia-Canada Association of South Australia. We left at 11:00 a.m. and got back at 2:30 p.m.—much better than the trip down.

In our hand-written letters to Kenneth and Norah last weekend we reported visiting Sydney to lunch aboard HMCS *Yukon*, which was tied up alongside HMCS *St. Croix* in the naval base there. Then Sunday we travelled on to Melbourne, where I gave the opening address to seven hundred who were attending the National Jaycee Convention. On Monday Captain J.B. Young, Commander of the Second Escort Squadron, Commander I. Ker of the *Yukon*, and Commander Donald of the *St. Croix* came up here to pay their official calls. I took them to call on the Governor General, Lord Casey, and we got quite a good photo taken with him. In the evening we gave a reception for about seventy to meet them. We had the Chairman of the Chiefs of Staff, Sir John Wilton, the Chief of the General Staff, Lieutenant-General Sir Thomas Daly, and the Chief of the Naval Staff, Vice-Admiral Sir Alan McNichol; the rest were mainly naval officers and wives.

October 22, 1967

s » We have been receiving a stack of correspondence from a Mr. Lewis McGregor, first Australian Trade Representative in Canada, who is now retired in New York and is making a sentimental return trip to Canberra with his daughter, his wife, and his grandson, a lieutenant in the U.S. army—three generations headed by this eighty-two-year-old. He turned out to be a regular dynamo, and a very interesting talker. He was in Ottawa at the time of R.B. Bennett, and negotiated the first Canada-Australia trade agreement by walking up from the Château to the East Block in the mornings and chatting with him and then going to Dad's office to record what they had agreed on. He has the amazing ability to recall everything in complete detail, with all the interesting little tidbits, which was fascinating. He made quite a little speech after lunch to the group we had collected to meet him. His daughter told me he has written 1,800 pages of autobiography. Some at least of it would be interesting reading.

A » Wednesday night we attended a very pleasant dinner at David Anderson's. He used to be Australian ambassador in Vietnam and is now in charge of Southeast Asia. It is good to get into an Australian home. Thursday evening we went to the first in a series of lectures on Australian-American relations by Professor Bruce Miller. He spoke on problems of understanding, and made a first-class survey of the way U.S. society is organized today. Friday night we went in for about an hour to support an Australian-Canadian Society fundraising bingo, which attracted good crowds in the Monaro shopping mall. Then last night we had two young couples in for supper and took them to see a fairly good presentation of Shaw's *Arms and the Man*. One couple was our newly arrived Information Secretary, Cameron Jess, and his wife Linda. He comes from the Maritimes and she from Calgary. The other couple was the Keith Wades. He is a Canadian PhD student at ANU who has spent the last fifteen months collecting botanical specimens on 15,400-foot Mount Wilhelm in New Guinea. They lived at 11,300 feet, and he walked to the top at least once a week.

We gather it was a cloud-shrouded, damp, and cold existence, but he has some good materials for his thesis and some good stories.

The Australian government announced this week they were sending another 1,700 men to Vietnam, to bring the number there to over 8,000. This decision arose from promises made during the Senate election campaign. It was meant to be a demonstration of support for a firm U.S. policy, and it gives the Australian task force more flexibility and striking power. It uses up all Army forces, though, and leaves little flexibility to deal with other crises that may arise in Asia, and little money to spend on economic aid.

October 29, 1967

A » This week the Australian Minister for External Affairs reported to Parliament on the war in Vietnam, arguing that the "free world forces" were winning militarily and claiming that those who had advocated a cessation of the bombing of North Vietnam without a reciprocal gesture from Hanoi were simply encouraging the North Vietnamese to continue their pressure on the South. The vigorous views he expressed were markedly different from those expressed by our Mr. Paul Martin, who now advocates that the U.S. take the initiative in stopping the bombing of the North in order to test the willingness of the North Vietnamese to come to the conference table. Such differences add a certain interest to my job here.

Last Sunday evening we flew up to Newcastle, one hundred miles north of Sydney, for a solid two-day visit. Our hosts were the officers of the Newcastle Businessmen's Club, which I addressed Tuesday at lunch, with three hundred present. Our days were filled with a visit to the Art Gallery and Public Library, where we saw the commission given in 1804 to First Lieutenant C.A.F.N. Menzies to command and superintend the settlement of Newcastle County. We spoke at a girls' high school and also a primary school. We toured an electric light manufacturing plant, where we saw all the stages, from the blowing and moulding of the globes and tubes to the insertion of filaments, etc. Many of the girls were fifteen and sixteen years old, and they get $15 Australian a week. We also toured the great sprawling BHP steelworks, which produces 1.8 million tons of steel a year, and the State Dockyard, where they build 20,000-ton ships. One of the most interesting tours was through parts of the Technical College, where they run 120 different courses for trade apprentices. Because of the strong trade unions and the system of wage awards by an arbitrator, all would-be tradesmen have to serve a four-year apprenticeship, involving one day a week at Tech. We met again there our old friend from Malaya, Bill Carson, whose daughter Pamela was a friend of Norah. Although Newcastle is an industrial city sitting atop coal mines and is the busiest export port in Australia, it has good beaches, some pleasant residential areas, a new university, and some people we found very kind.

November 5, 1967

A » We returned at noon today, Sunday, from two days in Sydney. The purpose of the trip was to take part in a seminar on "Relations between Australia and Canada" arranged by the New South Wales branch of the Royal Commonwealth Society. This is one of those I.O.D.E.-type organizations made up of some old United Empire Loyalists together with a sprinkling of quite competent people in public life. Friday night there was a black-tie reception to open the seminar. The Hon. Eric Willis, Chief Secretary of the New South Wales government, spoke very effectively about visits he had made to Canada, the experiences he had had and impressions he had formed. Then on Saturday there was an all-day seminar, with four speakers, questions, discussion periods, etc. I was the last speaker and so took the leftovers of untreated subjects. The discussion was better than I expected. Most of it seemed to concentrate on the need for more human contact between Canadians and Australians through better information services, books, radio, TV, etc., and some schemes to subsidize travel. We had several Canadian participants, including Kenneth's friend David Glasgow, who is doing post-grad work in English at Sydney University.

November 19, 1967

A » An RCAF Yukon aircraft came in Tuesday morning with my old friend Air Marshal Ed Reyno aboard and a crew of some twenty-five. Ed is Chief of Personnel in the Canadian Armed Forces. I took him to call on the Chairman of the Chiefs of Staff, Lieutenant-General Sir John Wilton, and the Chief of the Air Staff, Air Marshal Sir Alister Murdoch, and then to a lunch with Canadians. In the afternoon he talked to the Strategic and Defence Study Centre at the University, and then dined with us and a stellar group, including the upcoming Minister for Social Services, Hon. Ian Sinclair, and his wife. Next day he talked to the RAAF Staff College, played golf with Wilton, Murdoch, and our Tom Read, and then talked to me for half the night.

December 26, 1967

S » I will leave the details of the Holt Memorial to Arthur. It is hard to realize all that has happened to Australia in the last week, since Mr. Holt was reported missing last Sunday. He was such a sport and an informal person that it was quite in keeping that he would think nothing of swimming in heavy surf—it was just his custom when relaxing at Portsea on weekends. All Canberra was stunned, and any function that government officials were to attend was cancelled, so we had a quiet but tense week. Wednesday we had Sir Kenneth and Lady Bailey in by themselves. They were back on leave, and he will likely return to Canada for another term as high commissioner in two months.

A » I think that President Johnson's decision to visit Australia to attend the memorial service for Mr. Holt precipitated a lot of other attendances. Britain did not wish it to look as though Australia had slipped completely into the American camp, so sent Prince Charles and P.M. Wilson. Most Asian nations were represented by heads of state or government. Mr. Pearson asked Mr. Laing to represent Canada, and he left at 7:10 Wednesday morning, arriving two hours late at 9:15 on Friday morning. By then things were running pretty close. However, the Australian government laid on a fast Mystere jet, which got us to Melbourne by 11:05. Then we had a 60-mph race into the city behind a motorcycle escort with sirens wailing to reach the church. Sixteen hundred attended the service, each sitting in his appointed place, with Mrs. Holt and family on one side at the front, and Prince Charles, the Governor General, and President Johnson on the other side. We sat between the U.S. Ambassador Ed Clark and Mrs. Clark and a television camera. The Anglican Dean of Melbourne gave quite a good eulogy, reminding Australians of the high purposes at which Mr. Holt had aimed. Afterwards we went to Government House for lunch. There the Laings called on Mrs. Holt briefly, and he and I had ten minutes with the Governor General as well as talks with various visitors. At our motel there was a brief visit from the Minister for National Development, David Fairbairn, and then the Laings went to bed.

FOUR

1968

January 7, 1968

s » After having landed last week in Melbourne, my elder brother, Herbert Skelton, and his wife Daisy have arrived in Canberra to continue their Australian holiday. We have decided to show them some of the nearby mountain scenery. You may remember that last New Year's we stayed at this VIP lodge in Kosciuszko State Park for four days. It is well equipped and beautifully situated, far from most other people but accessible to the park headquarters and the small village of Jindabyne for supplies, etc. We did several drives in the Park, and on two mornings Herbert and Arthur got up at 4:30 and went fishing, each time catching only one fish, but each a beauty, a rainbow trout of about two or three pounds, enough that we had a good meal—and in one case lunch the following day as well. Art went again this a.m. at the crack of dawn for another six hours, with no results—but then, other fishermen we saw were not having any better luck. Herb and Daisy saw three kangaroos close to the lodge and had a good view of two emus beside the road, and we saw hundreds of rabbits, especially about dusk.

A » During our stay at Waste Point Lodge we made a number of drives in Kosciuszko State Park. The first day we drove to the lower Snowy River Valley, a descent almost to sea level, down steep valleys with lovely views. There is a western cypress there that is unique in eastern Australia. All the original water of the Snowy is being impounded in the new artificial Lake Jindabyne, but with further water from lower tributaries it is still a respectable river in Australian terms. Another day we drove to the top of Mount Kosciuszko, 7,300 feet, and climbed to one of the remaining snowbanks. The alpine flowers above 6,000 feet were quite lovely. Still another day we took the Schlink Pass Road up over the top and then descended on the western side, where one gets a magnificent view of the soaring peaks, which they call the "China Wall." Another afternoon we drove thirty-five miles to the Lake Eucumbene Dam and had a ride out on the lake in a launch, courtesy of the Snowy Mountains Authority. So you see we kept fairly active in our holiday week. Last night it was cool enough for us to enjoy a log fire, while other days have been warm and sunny.

February 4, 1968

s » This has been quite a memorable week for Arthur and me, because we have been to the Independence celebrations of the tiny new country of Nauru, which is in the Pacific, 2,500 miles from Sydney and only thirty miles south of the equator. Until a couple of weeks ago I knew little about it except that it was under the trusteeship of Australia, and had phosphate. To fill you in on the background, it was discovered in 1798 by Captain Fearn, of Britain, who commanded a whaling ship, and it continued as a whaling port. In 1888 it was annexed by Germany, and in 1900 phosphate was discovered, and first worked in 1907. At Versailles, after the First War, Nauru became a British mandate. In 1920 the League of Nations gave the mandate jointly to the U.K., Australia, and New Zealand, with an administrator to be appointed by Australia. A board of commissioners known as the British Phosphate Commission was set up to work the phosphate deposits, with one commissioner from each of the three countries. During the Second War, Japan occupied the island and sent most of its inhabitants to concentration camps in the Caroline Islands. Australian forces reoccupied it in 1945, and civil administration was re-established. The January 31 date for Independence is of particular historic significance, because it marks the twenty-second anniversary of the islanders' return to their home from the Carolines. In 1947 the United Nations approved the trusteeship agreement, with Australia, New Zealand, and the U.K. having administering authority, but with Australia continuing on their behalf to exercise full powers of legislation, administration, and jurisdiction. The administrator, most recently Brigadier Leslie King, whom we knew in Japan and Korea days as a colonel in charge of the camp near Tokyo, is responsible to the Australian government through the Minister of State for Territories, at present Mr. Barnes, who was the chief guest at the Independence celebration.

The island is just eight square miles in area, and twelve miles in circumference. Two-thirds of it—all of the central plateau—is phosphate-bearing, with just a narrow coastal strip of coconut and pandanus palms. This means that they have to import just about everything they eat from Australia and New Zealand. Usually the ships that take the phosphate out even bring in the drinking water in bulk. At the present rate of extraction the reserves of phosphate will last another twenty-five years or so. All the royalties part is a little complicated, so I will leave Arthur to explain that, and the actual ceremonies. We certainly were dead tired from all the flying, but found it a fascinating trip. I'm quite prepared to go to any other independence celebration Canada wants a representative at! Sure were glad to get mail on our return—the first real batch since the start of the postal strike on January 9.

A » Under a trusteeship agreement with the United Nations the administering power is required to advance the people toward independence. The three administering powers really thought Nauru too small to be independent. After all, there were only three thousand Nauruans, with only eleven hundred on the electoral roll, and another equal number of contract labourers from Hong Kong and the Gilbert and Ellice Islands. They thought they should be satisfied with the local government council that was established a couple of years ago. But they reckoned without Chief

Hammer De Roburt, an Australia-educated nationalist. He and some of his associates felt that the declining phosphate asset of the island should belong to them and that they should get a world price for it, rather than subsidizing the agricultural industries of Australia and New Zealand. So they kicked up a fuss in the Trusteeship Council and, as a first step, were granted higher royalties for the phosphate. It is blended with sulphuric acid, which is made in Australia mainly from Canadian sulphur, to make superphosphate, a fertilizer. Then they set about pressing for ownership of the phosphate, and got an agreement some months ago by which title would pass to them in 1970, provided that they pay the $23 million estimated value of the capital works by then. In the meantime they will be paid $11 per ton for the 2,000,000 tons extracted each year. For their part they will have to pay about $5 per ton to dig, dry, and ship the phosphate, and all the costs of administering the island heretofore paid by the British Phosphate Commission. Still, they will be much better off than they were, and should be able to borrow the money they need to buy out the plant.

Sheila and I were specifically invited by Head Chief Hammer De Roburt because of the interest I have shown in the island, and because Canada is a senior Commonwealth country with a frontier on the Pacific. The Nauruan government chartered a DC-4 from Qantas to fly us up there. It took twelve hours actual flying time, plus a two-hour stopover in Honiara, Guadalcanal, in the British Solomon Islands Protectorate. We had been preceded by an RAAF C-130 that carried the RAAF band, another RAAF plane with the official party from the administering powers, a Fiji Airways plane, and a TAA press correspondents' plane. We got in at about 2:00 p.m. on January 30, having flown all the previous night from Sydney. We were greeted by dignitaries, including Mr. and Mrs. De Roburt, and had leis of frangipani put round our necks. Then we were whisked off to our quarters. We were fortunate enough to be put up at Nauru House, the number-one guest house of the British Phosphate Commission. Other guests there were Fiame Mataafa, the Prime Minister of Western Samoa, Mr. Carter, leader of the New Zealand delegation, Mr. Anderson,

Commissioner for the British-administered Gilbert and Ellice Islands, and their wives. We were lucky to get an air-conditioned room, because Nauru, being on the equator, was hot and sticky.

In the evening we went to a reception given by the retiring Administrator, Brigadier Leslie King. There we drank a toast to the Queen and watched the flags of the three administering powers lowered at sunset for the last time. Later we went to a Chinese New Year celebration as guests of the Chinese community and watched some pretty corny Chinese opera and a livelier Lion Dance before refreshments were served. Then on to an open-air church service—Roman Catholic and Protestant—followed by a splendid display of fireworks for forty-five minutes or so. By then we were well into January 31, Independence Day.

Independence Day began with a private meeting of the Legislative Assembly, at which they elected a five-member Council of State, or Executive, to rule the country until the constitution is finally settled and a president is chosen, sometime in the next five months. Nauru is to have an essentially British type of government, with the prime minister also occupying the position of president and head of state. Mr. Hammer De Roburt was elected chairman of the Council of State. At ten o'clock there was an outdoor ceremony at which Mr. Barnes read the Governor General's proclamation of the independence of Nauru and a message of good wishes from the Queen. Then the Nauruan flag was hoisted. It has a medium blue field to represent the sea, a yellow stripe horizontally across the middle to represent the equator, and a yellow twelve-pointed star to represent the districts of the island. Then selected guests went into the Legislative Assembly, and some were invited to take seats on the Assembly floor. These ten were invited to speak briefly. I read out a message of good wishes from Prime Minister Pearson. Later, gifts were presented to the Council of State in a series of private calls. I presented an album of Canadian Centennial photographs, and am recommending an addition to their public library.

Mr. Marston, manager of the British Phosphate Commission, and Mrs. Marston then gave a buffet luncheon for about 180 of the principal guests. I was amused by one incident. We had been told that the principal fish caught around Nauru were tuna, or bonito, and flying fish. I was dissecting a long Australian barramundi fish at the buffet table when the Japanese Ambassador came up and said to the New Zealand Phosphate Commissioner, "Is this a frying fish?"—by which he meant "flying fish." Mr. Tennant replied, "No, I think it's been grilled."

In the afternoon we were amused by some Nauruan games. People from the north and south of the island were divided into two teams. There was a local form of wrestling, in which the first man of each pair to throw his opponent wins. Then there was a lengthy preparation for a form of Nauruan cricket. A pitch was ruled out in the sand with much ritual and argument. The receiving side lined up nine men to cover their court, as in a volleyball game. Then, from fifteen yards away, the other team hit a wooden ball covered with woven palm leaf with the open palm of the hand. The aim was to get the ball into the receiving team's court without it being caught. Throughout there was much heckling by women fans and all sorts of little victory jigs danced by those who achieved success. Finally there was a girls' game, like softball, in which a woven palm leaf ball was hit with the open hand, and about six bases were run instead of four. In the evening there was an all-island barbecue, where about two thousand people consumed a ton and a half of steak, a ton of chops, and a ton of sausages. Later there was a good variety show, with dancing and singing to local instruments. It was particularly interesting to see the variety of dances performed by the Nauruans (a mixture of Polynesians, Micronesians, and Melanesians), Gilbert Islanders (Micronesians), and Ellice Islanders (Polynesians). The RAAF Band wound up the concert.

On our last day we spent the morning touring the phosphate works. The phosphate consists of fossilized marine animal and plant deposits from pinnacles of coral, originally in the current trough in the ocean, that were lifted above the surface as a result of some sub-oceanic upheaval. The phosphate, in the form of either hard yellow stone or yellowish brown soil, is in layers eight to forty feet deep between those pinnacles of coral. It is dug out by tracked cranes with bucket jaws on the ends of cables. When the process is finished the coral pinnacles look like so many closely packed stalagmites. When the phosphate is first removed these pinnacles are yellow, but later they turn a dark grey. The plateau portion of the island was not used by the Nauruans, but naturally they are concerned about its rehabilitation. This would cost a lot of money, and probably wouldn't be worth it. The general feeling is that they would be better advised to invest the $400 million they would earn in more productive enterprises.

Nauru has the population of a small town, and is the size of a medium Australian sheep property. But it is rich with phosphate, which should give it an investment fund of $400 million by about 1995, when the phosphate is mined out, and it has a proud and independent-minded people. Good luck to them.

March 3, 1968

A » During this last week I have been trying to catch up on office work, as I leave this coming weekend for ten days in New Guinea, and we have thirty-five members of the National Defence College of Canada arriving on Wednesday morning. I have to make a speech to them, talk to Rotary in Port Moresby, and talk on French Canada in Adelaide on my return. You will have seen where former senator John Gorton was elected to the House of Representatives in the Higgins by-election in order to make himself eligible to become prime minister, and has named his new ministry. Although there are no changes in major portfolios, he has given the Northern Territory, which may become a seventh state eventually, to the Minister for the Interior, and has changed the name of the Department of Territories to "Department of External Territories." He has appointed a new minister, Bill Wentworth, to be Minister of Aboriginal Affairs and Social Services, and has made some other minor shifts.

March 10, 1968

s » We were pleased that for the first time the Canadian National Defence College has included Australia in its tour for senior staff types. There were thirty-five officers on the tour, mostly Canadian Armed Forces officers at the colonel level, as well as some U.S., some British, and a sprinkling of executive-level people from other government departments—Trade, Immigration, Transport, External, and Mounted Police. External usually has one member on the directing staff—this time it was George Grande, our recent high commissioner to Ceylon—and one member as a student. The tour leader was General Carpenter, a most outspoken person who has a hundred and one ideas. They had two days of seminars and meetings with Australian officials—one day basically with the Army, one day at the University, and lunch at Parliament House and ANU. We held a big reception at the office for 120 people (we had invited about 160) and arranged afterwards that all the members of the course be taken on to private dinners in small groups, where they would have a chance to talk with Australians. We took the four tour leaders, and had the new Minister of the Navy, the Chief of the General Staff, the Secretary of Defence, the secretary of the department that looks after New Guinea, etc. We also had the Canadians Alfred and Harriet Rive, now retired, who were in Canberra as tourists—but as he was at one time External member on the directing staff, they fitted in very well. Because Edith had done the preparations for the cocktail party, we held a dinner in the private dining room of the Commonwealth Club—the first time we have used that venue. Had Canadian salmon first, and then fillet, and a real Australian dessert, passion fruit pavlova, which is meringue filled with whipped cream and passion fruit.

March 31, 1968

s » We just got back from Adelaide Monday night. We had three days at the Festival, where we saw the Barranggay Folk Dance Troupe from the Philippines, an excellent troupe, on a very confining stage. Adelaide hopes that by the time of its next festival, two years from now, it will have a large new hall and more adequate facilities. We also saw a Spanish dancer, Lucero Tena, who did wonders with castanet and guitar accompaniment. We were most impressed with the eighty musicians of the South Australia Symphony Orchestra, who put on an all-Gershwin program in a hall for 2,500 people. All in all the musical attractions of the Festival were of a higher class than the dramatic ones, but the two plays we saw were good: *The Recruiting Officer*, a comedy by George Farquhar written in 1703, and one commissioned by the Festival called *The Lotus Eaters*, by Patricia Hooker, an Australian now living in London, about the unrest among wharf workers in Queensland. It was an amusing satire on the demands of the labourers, through their unions, to get mosquito nets, nets with smaller holes, better lights for loading, special compensation for the weather, special pay for handling wet cargo, etc. Given that one of the reasons Herbert and Daisy's ship was late was that "it was too hot to work" in Melbourne, there was a lot of truth in the piece. However, the message was hammered home a bit too hard.

We also enjoyed our two non-Festival days in Adelaide. Because of the 19-to-19 results in the state elections there, the Governor was needed in Adelaide, so we substituted for him at the opening of the National Trust branch at Naracoorte, which is 180 miles southeast. We flew in a small Cessna plane. About two hundred people were gathered at the old schoolhouse, which has been turned into the new headquarters. There is a bronze plaque on the front saying, "opened by Mr. A.R. Menzies, Canadian High Commissioner," so there, at least, Arthur has a more tangible memento for posterity than for most of his speeches. We were also tendered a very nice civic lunch—and another speech from Art. The president of the local trust there is on the executive of the Canadian-Australian Association of Adelaide, which was why we got the interesting assignment. Sunday we had a relaxing time with David and Pat Corbett. He is professor of political science at Flinders University, and on Monday Art addressed the Political Science Club there.

Tuesday evening, March 26, I went to hear the foreign affairs debate in Parliament. Mr. Hasluck gave a sober "soldier on" statement on Vietnam, talked of the British withdrawal from east of Suez and its implications for Australia, and then discussed the Nuclear Non-proliferation Treaty, which Australia has not yet agreed to sign. He was roundly criticized by the Leader of the Opposition, Gough Whitlam, who argued for Australia to use its influence with the U.S.A. to stop the bombing of North Vietnam in the hope of getting negotiations started.

April 7, 1968

s » I have just been telephoned by the communicator on duty at the office, who told me that Trudeau has won and will be our new prime minister. This is one time that we wish there had been a transmission by satellite of all the voting—it would have brought us in touch with the excitement in Canada. This last week we have seen excellent programs from both Japan and the U.S. by satellite, as clear as could be.

We try to keep in touch with the young Canadians who are around. There is no compulsion for Canadians to register at the office, and the University here is very unorganized about its records and reluctant to give addresses, so we are never too sure until the last minute just how many will turn up. In order to have a clear idea when we were finished just who was who, we planned two small cocktail parties this week, one on Thursday and one on Friday, and had in the end thirty-two at one and thirty-one at the other. Most are from ANU, out here for one or two or three years doing some sort of graduate work or research. Most are married, and quite enthusiastic about the help with housing and the other arrangements that are made for them here, much more than in most parts of the world. We also had some office people and the new executive of the Australian-Canadian Association in Canberra. The atmosphere at such a reception is quite different from that at the diplomatic and political ones we attend so often. For most of these young people it is a real event to arrange for a sitter and go out for an evening, and many have not met any other Canadians since coming here—which we think is very good, we like them to mix in with the Australians; but once in a while they obviously enjoy being identified as Canadians.

A » I'm adding my piece of this letter at noon on Monday, because it was getting on toward 11:00 p.m. when I got in last night and I was tired. I left before seven on Saturday morning with Eric Conybeare, a Canadian petroleum geologist at the Australian National University, Gojko Sekulovski, the Yugoslav Ambassador, and Sir Leonard Huxley, just retired from being Vice-Chancellor of ANU. We motored two and a half hours to Anglers Reach on Lake Eucumbene in the Snowy Mountains. There we got a pleasant A-frame cabin and settled in. We got two motorboats and went off fishing. Sir Leonard came with me. He had never fished before so I lent him gear and offered guidance. This was sufficiently good that he caught the most fish, and the two biggest. I caught three three- to four-pound trout. The scenery was lovely and the outing relaxing, but with sun, wind, early hours, and too much tea and drink it was rather exhausting.

Last Thursday and Friday we had a De Havilland of Canada turboprop short-takeoff-and-landing (STOL) aircraft here to be shown to Australian servicemen and ministers as a potential replacement for their piston-engine Caribou. They dropped freight by parachute in the drop zone, took people up for rides, etc. It is a remarkable performer and the Aussies are interested.

April 21, 1968

s » We have just got word of the new Canadian cabinet, and that Sharp is our new minister. A great many Australians will be a little wiser about Trudeau now, because there was a half-hour program about him on TV last night, Saturday, at top viewing time, and it was repeated today. It shows his popularity during his campaign and gives a commentary by himself about his rise and his views on art, books, etc. Certainly is different.

A » The Economic Commission for Asia and the Far East has been meeting in Canberra since Wednesday morning. There are some 360 people involved, with twenty-nine member delegations and a number of observer delegations. I was designated head of the Canadian observer delegation, made up of my officers plus Arthur Wright from our embassy in Bangkok, where the headquarters of ECAFE is located. The main topics include a review of the economic situation in the area, planning, the Asian Institute of Economic Development, the Asian Development Bank, trade, industry, transport, the Asian Highway, statistics, the Mekong River Development, population planning, etc. There are a lot of speeches, including mine, and private talks in receptions and lunches, etc. It goes on until April 30.

Friday I attended a ceremony marking the unveiling of a bronze memorial, a replica of one originally put up in Port Said and destroyed in 1956, in honour of the Anzac Desert Mounted Corps, which fought in the Sinai in 1916–18.

Another military event was a Beating the Retreat ceremony at the Royal Military College, Duntroon. We were senior guests, so had the honour of sitting through a rainstorm. Afterwards they played the 1812 Overture by Tchaikovsky, which musically describes the defeat and ends with the ringing of church bells and the firing of cannon—real twenty-five pounders.

April 28, 1968

A » Inche Mohamed bin Baba, the Malaysian High Commissioner, and his wife Puan Halimahton have been here since August 1966 and are scheduled to leave early in May. He was deputy secretary of Defence and later secretary for Rural Development when we went to Malaya in 1958. His wife was one of the first women in the Malayan parliament. So we have had a special bond with them. We gave a dinner in their honour on Tuesday, April 23.

Two Canadians have visited me at the office this week. Miss Rae Chittick was Director of Nursing Training at McGill and is now making a W.H.O. survey of nursing training in Australia. She said that the academic and post-grad side was poor, but the problem is how to suggest improvements without offending people. The other Canadian was a Mrs. Lyn (Richard) Harrington, 12 Castle View Avenue, Toronto, who is here to gather material for two books, one on the River Murray and one on the Chaffey brothers (George and W.B.), who came from Canada in the 1890s to found the irrigation settlements at Mildura and Renmark on the Murray. Her husband illustrates her books.

April 25 is ANZAC Day, commemorating the landing of Australian and New Zealand troops at Gallipoli in 1915. This is the major Australian war remembrance ceremony of the year, and we had beautiful autumn weather for it. We took Canadian Army Standardization Officer Major Ken Reeves and Mrs. Reeves with us.

May 19, 1968

S » Canberra has had a real influx of state visitors this past week. Haile Selassie was here for a couple of days. Arthur went to a large lunch, with three hundred guests, in the Parliament Buildings, given by the government. The Emperor made his speech in Amharic and had a translator, although he does speak French and English. He's more at home in French, Arthur found. Then the Duke of Edinburgh arrived to open the third Duke of Edinburgh Study Conference here. There are about three hundred delegates from Commonwealth countries. The Canadian delegation of thirty-five people is the third-largest, after the Australians and the British. They are all young executives—business and trade and labour union leader types—and they come from across Canada. They must be between twenty-five and forty-five years of age. The only Canadian we knew was Chris Young, editor of *The Ottawa Citizen* and a good friend of ours, so we had him in for supper before our big reception for the rest. We had about seventy people here on Friday night, the thirty-five Canadian delegates and others connected with the conference, etc. They seemed a bright, interested group. After the briefing and formal speeches here they break up into groups of twelve to tour the country for a couple of weeks, and re-assemble in Melbourne for the conclusions.

While in Canberra the Duke also opened the new Forestry Building at ANU, in which there is cedar panelling from Canada in the upstairs foyer and Douglas fir beams in the upstairs labs, donated by the government and B.C. lumber producers. We gave a lunch Thursday for the lumber companies' representative, who came up from Sydney, and his wife. It is a handsome building, and Arthur has worked hard since our arrival here to make the arrangements for this Canadian contribution. Also, we were fortunate to have the opportunity to go to the formal dinner in honour of the Duke at Government House for all Commonwealth high commissioners. He certainly strikes you as a bright and "with it" person, very informal in the way he conducts the Study Conference or chats with people, but very apt and perceptive in his observations, which he expresses clearly and well. It was a welcome change from some of the stuffy and wordy declarations some British visitors make here, and the repetitious speeches of the U.N. meetings here last month.

This weekend, from Saturday to Thursday, we have Mark Stiles with us, the nineteen-year-old son of the former Canadian trade commissioner in Sydney, who stayed at a boarding school here, and Bob Richards, a fellow sixth-form pal of his, an Australian from Sydney. I have been doing a certain amount of sightseeing with them while Art is preparing speeches for this week.

A » The Canadian Deputy Minister of Energy, Mines, and Resources, Claude Isbister, and Mrs. Isbister, along with a Dr. Crosby, arrived at noon today direct from Ottawa, thirty-two hours after leaving home. They're here for a fortnight's visit to look into Australian arrangements for the administration of offshore gas and oil. In Canada the question of whether the federal or provincial government owns these resources was referred to the Supreme Court. Here the federal and state governments entered a political deal to divide the royalties and let the states administer the arrangement. At first it was hailed as a wise shortcut, but recently the federal government has been criticized for giving away too much and permitting the Esso-BHP producer to make too much money at the expense of the gas and oil consumer. We have a full program planned, including drinks tonight and a dinner tomorrow night.

May 25, 1968

s » We have had two major dinners here this week, with fourteen on Monday for Dr. Crosby and Dr. and Mrs. Isbister to meet officials of the Department of National Development and the Attorney General's Department and to discuss offshore oil rights, and twelve on Friday in honour of Paul Hasluck, the Minister of External Affairs, and Mrs. Hasluck. We have had the Minister to dinner a couple of times before, but Mrs. Hasluck usually stays in their constituency in Perth, West Australia, so this was the first time that we have had her as well. Both went well. As the entrée course we featured mushrooms (collected a couple of weeks ago) in pancakes, a specialty of Edith's.

We left after lunch on Thursday and drove 117 miles to Cootamundra, where Arthur gave the high school closing speech. It was listed on the program as an "occasional address"; that seems a rather offhand way of referring to the major performer if you ask me. Anyway, Arthur cracked a few jokes for the children and had the audience of about six hundred listening for fifteen or twenty minutes. It was a well-run show. Beforehand we had dinner with the principal and his wife, and the deputy and his wife. It was all friendly, but it was in a really chilly Australian house— positively freezing in the dining room, where we ate. And it was cold and raining outside. When we drove back the following morning the weather was a little better.

A » Australia has not been feeling so forlorn recently, because of the spate of overseas visitors. Mrs. Indira (I saw "India" in one paper) Gandhi, Prime Minister of India, has been here for a five-day formal visit. We were invited to an overcrowded reception at the Indian High Commission and to a government luncheon. The Prime Minister and the Leader of the Opposition welcomed Mrs. Gandhi and she replied with a written text that carefully balanced the success so far achieved in India with the tasks that lie ahead. She bluntly criticized the Nuclear Non-proliferation Treaty for failing to provide her country with adequate protection against the Chinese nuclear threat.

Wednesday afternoon I flew up to Brisbane to talk to about two hundred people at the annual general meeting of the Victoria League for Commonwealth Friendship. I spoke on "Canada and the Commonwealth," trying to identify what the Commonwealth means to Canadians and suggesting ways of revitalizing the association. It was perhaps a little too heavy for the audience, as I noticed some of the older ladies nodding off. Before the meeting two couples gave me a very nice dinner. I left to return at 7:15 the next morning.

Mr. Gorton and his wife left for a brief visit to the United States this weekend. He hopes to get some indication from President Johnson and the various presidential candidates about their willingness to continue to contribute to security in Southeast Asia after the end of the Vietnam War. Australia will be taking part in five-power talks in Malaysia on June 10 to discuss future security arrangements there, and I suppose it would be helpful to get an inkling of U.S. ideas, although I doubt if Mr. Gorton can really expect much hard information.

June 2, 1968

A » Friday afternoon we drove 150 miles northwest to Canowindra (pronounced as if the "i" wasn't there), where we checked into the Bluejacket Motel. We were to have been met by the Rector of All Saints Anglican Church, Reverend Hart, but at 8:00 p.m. we had to go looking for him. Eventually we found the manse, and met various clergy from the surrounding area and Mr. and Mrs. Doug Newton (she is a Canadian war bride, and is the one who got us involved). Then we repaired to the Town Hall, where some six hundred had assembled to watch me receive seven pretty sixteen- and seventeen-year-old debutantes and make some short remarks of an allegedly humorous nature. Then there was dancing and supper. We escaped at 12:00 midnight. Next morning we visited a local property, then drove the ninety miles to Parkes to visit the famous radio telescope, the most sensitive, next to Jodrell Bank, in the Commonwealth. There is a great dish that looks like a big radar-sensing device, which catches radio signals from outer space and reflects them into one receiving point, where they are then unscrambled and interpreted by astronomers such as Jasper Wall, a young Canadian PhD student now using the equipment for his research. We got back about 5:45 Saturday afternoon, after a long but interesting drive through country turned a lush green by recent autumn rains.

June 9, 1968

A » Mr. Jahn, a minister of state in the German Foreign Ministry and a Social Democrat associate of Willy Brandt, visited Australia this last week. I went to a luncheon at the German embassy attended by NATO ambassadors and various senior Australian officials. In the evening we went to a reception there as well.

Prime Minister John Gorton arrived back from the U.S.A. last Monday. He was well received by President Johnson, saw Humphrey, and talked on the phone to Nixon. He reported that he had brought back a sense of assurance that the U.S.A. would continue to maintain its interest in Southeast Asia after the Vietnam commitment had been terminated. On Wednesday he left for a visit to Vietnam, Malaysia, Singapore, and Indonesia. These trips will give him a broad view of the most immediate Australian interest. He is the sort of man who wants to figure things out for himself and not be pushed around too much by the bureaucratic machine. He seems to have some of Mr. Diefenbaker's feelings for extemporaneous speech, which tends to alarm officials, who always like to keep government spokesmen to a text.

I stayed up for an hour from 11:30 to 12:30 last night listening to and watching by satellite the TV broadcast of Bobby Kennedy's funeral at St. Patrick's Cathedral in New York. What a tragedy this second assassination has been. One cannot help thinking that some of the risks would be reduced if there was a much stricter control of firearms in the U.S.A., and in Canada too.

On Wednesday Harry Horne and Kevin Osmond, our commercial counsellors from Sydney and Melbourne, came up for the day, and we talked about Canadian interests in Australia.

June 23, 1968

A » Thursday noon I went to a National Press Club luncheon, where Prime Minister Gorton reported on his trip to Southeast

Asia. He spoke directly, but without embellishment, for about twenty to twenty-five minutes, mainly about the security situation in Vietnam, Malaysia, and Singapore as it affects Australia. Afterwards he answered questions for forty-five minutes very competently. It is said to have been one of his better public efforts since coming to office. The following day I lunched with our old friend Harold Cox of *The Melbourne Herald* and considered the possibilities of an early federal election here. The redrawing of electoral boundaries should be through before the end of the year. Here federal elections must be held every three years, but are not due until March 1970.

June 30, 1968

s » We seem to be participating in a long and varied celebration of Canada's hundred and first birthday. Art and I went to Sydney to be guests of honour at the Canada Ball there Friday night. Although the Canadian Club in Sydney was only recently revived, they now have a large membership, and mustered three hundred people for a ball at the Chevron Hotel, complete with a full-course dinner that featured New Brunswick clam chowder and roast baron of beef (that is supposed to be a Canadian term, but I've yet to find out exactly what it means; anyway, it was a good roast), and the committee had worked hard to get wonderful donations for door prizes and raffles—like a plane trip to Canberra for two, or a magnum-size bottle of Seagram's or Hiram Walker's. Art had to propose the toast to Canada and make a five-minute speech on Trudeau. He did very well and people were enthusiastic. Trudeau obviously has supporters here as well as in Canada.

a » I'm going to add something to Sheila's account of our visit to Sydney. The lady got three dresses and two purses, so had a reasonably successful outing herself. For my part, I called on Alcan Aluminum, one of the big Canadian investments here, which is producing about 25,000 tons of aluminum products and building a smelter near Newcastle, and owns a share of Queensland Alumina, which processes bauxite into the powdered form from which alumina is smelted. I also visited International Nickel Southern Explorations, which is prospecting for nickel in several places in Australia, and in the Solomon Islands, New Caledonia, and Indonesia. I took Paddy Laine, their local manager, to lunch. I also spent time visiting our new immigration office, our tourist office, and our trade office. Saturday morning I too shopped. I bought a new white vest for my evening tails suit and spent most of the rest of my time in bookshops.

Last Wednesday we went to a buffet supper at the home of Kieran and Bernice Desmond. He has been the External Affairs representative in Nauru for six months, and had President Hammer De Roburt and other Nauruans and friends in. The President is here to try to negotiate a better price for Nauru phosphate, which I gather he didn't get.

July 7, 1968

s » Norah passed her driver's test on July 1. She feels confident, and drives well, even in traffic, which stood her in good stead, because at 7:15 a.m. she and I took off for the 410-mile trip to Melbourne, and she insisted on driving more than half the time—and all of the time in the traffic of Melbourne, a city of two million. It took all our combined wits to read the maps and to be in the right lane, and we went on many a detour. By making two trial runs the night we arrived, we got to the Dog Training Centre on time Thursday morning. I left Norah outside and went to the city by bus so she could get to her interview. The big city is a real challenge. I hope Norah enjoys it.

a » Our new counsellor, Allan Roger, and his wife Gene arrived on Tuesday night. He is thirty-nine, and has served in a number of posts. They have four boys. The oldest, who is fifteen, is on a scholarship at Fettes College in Scotland. We had them in for supper last night and find them enthusiastic about the job here.

July 14, 1968

a » Wednesday I had eight at the Commonwealth Club to meet

136

Professor Edward McWhinney, the director of the Institute of Air and Space Law at McGill. He is an able young Australian-born lawyer who is very articulate in a number of fields, including federalism and international law. We had also been to a dinner given for him by the dean of the ANU Law School, Professor Jack Richardson, who spent last year at McGill. Friday I went to a lunch for him and various External Affairs officers. He gave a useful post-election commentary on what Canadians expect from a triumphant Trudeau.

August 11, 1968

s » We have had a very busy month, because we've had a variety of Canadian visitors, along with the usual. We gave quite a reception to welcome Sir Valston and Lady Hancock back to Australia. He was the commissioner general of the Australian Pavilion at Expo. He is retired now and will live in Western Australia, where he has a brother with many mining interests, but they were in Canberra for one week to look up old friends, en route to Queensland, where they will have several weeks of holiday in the sun. Many of the people who were part of the Expo 67 team are now members of the Expo 70 team for Osaka: the same young architect from public works designed the Australian pavilion for Osaka; the Number Two from Hancock's team is the Number Two for the Japanese one, and has already made several trips to Japan. It is interesting to see the differences between communicating to an Asian audience and to a North American one.

We have also had quite a group of Canadian doctors: H.D. Dalgliesh, the head of the Canadian Medical Association, Arthur F.W. Peart, the executive secretary, and others. This Commonwealth medical conference was a small show, however, compared to the Commonwealth universities group that we are busy preparing for now. On Friday, August 16, we will have between eighty and a hundred at the chancery for a sit-down buffet supper. We have never coped with this many for a meal before, just for receptions, so it takes some squeezing of people in, rounding up of tables, cleaning up of the basement, etc. Everyone is very helpful and co-operative, but things like postal strikes do not help planning.

A » The long Canadian university summer vacation provides a good opportunity for Canadian academics to travel abroad, and this seems much more possible these days with the help of Canada Council grants. We have had a number of able and congenial Canadians here: Professor Donald Watts of Queen's, who is an expert on federalism, gave a number of lectures; Professor Ed McWhinney, professor of law at McGill and born in Australia, made a particularly favourable public impression; Assistant Professor Lorne Kavic of Simon Fraser University, who used to work in my division in Ottawa, and is gathering material for a book on Canada and the Pacific; Professor Earle Birney, the distinguished Canadian poet, who gave a reading here about which I was unnecessarily apprehensive, because he turned out to be a droll and human raconteur of the circumstances of his poems, and read them well. We had a function for him, attended by all the literati of the Australian Capital Territory. Several others are attending a conference on contemporary Commonwealth literature in Brisbane, including my old soccer mate Des Pacey, now head of the English Department at UNB, whom we hope to see this week.

August 18, 1968

S » This past week has been our busiest in Australia, I think. I was down in Melbourne and Geelong Monday and Tuesday staying with Norah, and gave a speech to about 125 women of the Australian-Canadian-American Women's Club, formed shortly after the war to give war brides a chance to make friends, and now a very worthwhile charity-raising venture—they gave the first heart machine to Geelong Hospital by putting in a grant of $3,000 that the government equalled. I was pleased to have the opportunity to go with Norah and her date to the class party put on by the graduating class of the Dogs for the Blind. There were eight pupils in this class. Each training period is one month, and Norah has followed it right through. They had two trainers, one of whom was a skilled harmonica player and organized quite a concert.

The Commonwealth Universities Congress occupied us the rest of the week. All the chancellors, vice-chancellors, and presidents were invited to Canberra for two days. This meant about twenty-two Canadian heads and, in the majority of cases, their wives. Actually the one who got the most publicity was Sister Alice Michael Wallace of Mount St. Vincent College in Nova Scotia, because she was the only woman, and also because she is quite "with it"—she wears a very sensible short habit with a turtleneck shirt inside and a rather smart cap arrangement. We went to a dinner for two hundred university people Thursday night.

Friday night we had our big function at the office, for which we have been preparing for several weeks. We had eighty-eight sitting down to dinner in the end. It required a lot of work by a lot of people to get the basement all organized to hold enough chairs, tables, etc., and look half decent. Edith did an excellent job of cooking and preparing the meats, and I had the same caterer I had on July 1 for cold things, salads, etc. All the Canadians were most appreciative, and Arthur made a good short speech, to which Dr. Leddy, Assistant Deputy Minister of Education for Ontario, gave an amusing reply. I was able to get a really good assortment of Western Australian flowers, and each table had an unusual arrangement. We have a few bits and pieces to return and clean up still, but we are pleased with the response to our efforts.

A » Saturday afternoon we flew down to Sydney to attend the official opening of the Commonwealth Universities Congress in the Great Hall of Sydney University. The hall was built in 1854–57 and is an impressive Gothic-style stone building. The Governor General, Lord Casey, gave the opening address with his usual vigour and personal involvement in the subject. He is quite wonderful for man of seventy-eight. Afterwards we met more of the Canadians at a reception. There are seventy-seven Canadian university professors attending, and with wives the number would be about 120. Today, Sunday, we had invited two Ottawa professors and their wives out for lunch, but their plane from Canada was five hours late so we missed them. However, we did see Philip and Jinny Slyfield and young Christopher off at the airport. They have been on our staff for three and a half years and are returning to Ottawa.

Another big event of the past week was the opening of the $8-million National Library building, run by our neighbour, Harold White. It is a beautiful building on the shores of the lake, and very well designed and decorated.

September 8, 1968

s » Norah left for Sydney at 7:50 this morning. She found it easier to get up early than she sometimes does, because two Canberra girls she knows were going on the same flight, and all three of them would have a while on the ship *Monterey* in Sydney today before Norah takes her Pan Am plane this afternoon to Fiji, where she connects with the Canadian Pacific flight to Honolulu that originates in New Zealand; then she has the day there and again flies all night from Honolulu to Toronto non-stop, a new service.

We were pleased to have the opportunity to see something of Norah during the week we cruised on the Murray River in the paddle steamer the *Coonawarra* (which means black swan). We drove back from the river via Melbourne and left Norah there for a few days to see all her friends. All in all we think she has had a pretty happy summer in Australia, because of her interesting job and her pleasant friends in both Melbourne and Canberra. She registers at Ottawa U. on September 16.

Our holiday turned out even better than we had expected. We did not know anyone who had made the river trip, so were not too sure from the Tourist Bureau handout what to expect. Now that we've been so satisfied and pleased, I am sure others from Canberra will follow. There is infinite variety to the river—some high cliffs, some low-lying areas, some towns settled for a long time and now almost abandoned because there is no longer such dependence on the river for transport, all the scenery lovely and green because of the recent rain and good weather, unlike the drought we last saw in that area. We motored about 750 miles to

Murray Bridge, then did about 250 miles on the boat, then a farther drive of about 900 miles, stopping one night in Melbourne
with Norah and one at Eden, a small fishing centre on the South
Coast. Arthur and I found the drive back on dirt roads rather than
the main highway very pleasant, and did not mind that we could
not make the time on the winding roads. The week away was a
real break, and it was more relaxing because we were treated as
ordinary tourists, not diplomats.

A » This past week we have had a visit from the Honourable Stan-
ley Randall, Ontario's Minister for Trade and Development. I had
heard he was quite a publicity-seeker. I was able to persuade him
to give some books from Ontario to the National Library rather
than plant a tree. This went very well. We gave a reception for him
to meet about sixty local people, and he was very appreciative of
our efforts. He presented Sheila with a trillium pin and me with
cufflinks with the Ontario coat of arms—paid for by your taxes,
of course.

Paul Davoud, Vice-President, Sales, of De Havilland of
Toronto, was out here during the week to present a proposition
to the Australians on the turbine-engine De Havilland Buffalo,
to replace the piston-engine Caribou the Australians are now
flying. We were able to give him some help. Also we have a
Canadian naval captain on the British Imperial Defence College
course.

Friday I attended the installation of Dr. Coombs, former governor of the Reserve Bank of Australia, as Chancellor of the Australian National University. He gave a thoughtful speech in which
he spoke of the need for two-way communication between students and staff, and for the University to stand far enough apart
from the establishment to offer objective criticism.

September 15, 1968

A » Mr. Barnes submitted a five-year development plan for Papua
and New Guinea, to cost Australia $1 billion over the five-year pe-
riod. It is a good study.

September 22, 1968

s » This has been my week of Australian ballet. As soon as I
saw that the Australian Ballet Company was coming to Canberra I booked six seats for the girls from the office, after a
lunch here at Saturday noon, and also four seats at the same
performance for Edith, Mrs. Jansen (Andrew's wife, who does
our washing, ironing, and cleaning), Nettie de Fries (the wait-
ress who most often serves for us), and Mrs. Van Schieeven
(the janitress at the office). All these are very pleasant, quiet
women for whom I like to do something besides the usual
Christmas present and for whom the four-dollar seats are far
beyond their reach. Then we also ordered six tickets for a second program, which we will see tomorrow night with four
friends after an early dinner here. What I hadn't bargained for
was that we would be invited by the Company as guests for the
opening night, along with about fifty special guests. Naturally
we weren't going to turn that down, so I saw the same program
Friday night and again Saturday. I enjoyed it both times, especially the Sun Music ballet, which has been specially written for
them by Sir Robert Helpmann. You have to admire his original-
ity and imagination in creating this very modern ballet, and
that of the other Australian, Peter Sculthorpe, who wrote the
music, which uses sounds like the rustling of grass, the squeak-
ing of brakes, vibrations, and recordings of people humming
and chanting two or three syllables as a refrain along with the
orchestra. It fits in so well with the dancing that although it
bothers you in the first two sections, by the final three sections
you are not aware of it. The five parts are called "Soil," "Mi-
rage," "Growth," "Energy," and "Destruction." "Energy" featured beach boys with two huge rubber balls, all very athletic
and full of movement. The young ballerina picked for the lead
is admirably suited: her gymnastics and lithesomeness are fantastic, as is her dancing ability. To balance this new ballet, they
opened with the traditional *Swan Lake*, Act Two, and ended
with a very beautifully costumed Imperial Ballet, to
Tchaikovsky's *Piano Concerto Number 2 in G Major*.

A » President and Mrs. Park of Korea, with four ministers, officials, and press, arrived at the beginning of the week for a four-day visit. We attended a reception for heads of diplomatic missions at Government House, and I attended a parliamentary luncheon for them. I also talked to officials and wrote a report. Australia and Korea both have troops in Vietnam, and Australia gave Korea 10,000 tons of wheat because of their drought. There was a promise of a cultural agreement.

The major wheat exporters, Canada, U.S.A., Argentina, the E.E.C., and Australia, met here this week to discuss export prices under the International Grains Agreement. We had Jack Moran, Deputy Minister of Trade and Commerce, Bill McNamara, chairman of the Canadian Wheat Board, Esmond Jarvis, Assistant Deputy Minister of Agriculture, and three others here. The talks were tough, as there is a surplus of wheat in the world, but they hammered out an understanding. On Friday we had bilateral trade talks with the Australians all day, reviewing problems such as the price of Australian canned peaches in Canada and talking about a review of our trade agreement. This was very useful. The party left on Friday evening.

September 29, 1968

A » Each time I take off on a trip it triggers me to try to clean up the messes of paper that I accumulate from week to week. I have taken the weekend to clean up and have had my secretary in this Sunday afternoon for more dictation. I'm in fair shape now for the trip.

In terms of Canadian-Australian relations, the most significant news this week is that Right Honourable Paul Hasluck, Minister for External Affairs, and Sir James Plimsoll, Secretary of the Department of External Affairs, are visiting Canada from September 26 to October 2, with a couple of days in Ottawa (at which time I hope Plim will leave a small radio for Norah), two days in the Northwest Territories, and two days in Toronto. We hope all goes well and that we get a little feedback in the Australian press.

Monday night we took the Peter Baileys (he's the son of the Australian high commissioner in Ottawa), Judith Dexter (whose husband was away in Queensland for the Council on Aboriginal Affairs), and our Nick Etheridge to see the Australian Ballet in *La Fille Mal Gardée*. It didn't provide the variety we had on Friday, but it was sweet and well performed, with a pony cart onstage pulled by a diminutive Shetland pony.

The Melbourne paper carried an External Affairs ad for secretary-typists that said, "Applicants should be medically fit for overseas service and be under 40 years of age (50 years eight months for sex-service women)." Salary, of course, according to experience.

October 27, 1968

A » I am writing my report on our visit to the Northern Territory now. In many ways the problems there are similar to those of our Northwest Territories, although ours are cold and theirs hot and dry. First, the area is big, so air transportation is essential. Second, both are thinly populated. Third, each has native populations whose advancement poses special challenges. Fourth, each has mineral resources that will help to supply employment and revenue. Fifth, each has a legislative assembly that is not fully responsible, because the federal government must subsidize administration and development. I found it interesting to talk to the Administrator and the heads of departments, and to visit Aboriginal settlements, schools, and mines.

November 24, 1968

A » I spent November 18 and 19 in Adelaide, primarily to present 350 volumes on Canada to the University of Adelaide Library. The Vice-Chancellor, Professor G.M. Badger, made a nice speech, and I replied, with television cameras grinding. Our books were well displayed. The University of Adelaide is the only university with a course (half-term) on Canadian literature. The Barr Smith Library has about 2,000 books on Canada, but

I am glad to say that our presentation didn't duplicate many. During my trip I explored the possibility of showing our Canadian Patterns Exhibit at various sites, and concluded in favour of David Jones, a department store. I also called on the Mayor and the Premier of South Australia, and had a rather winey lunch with the general manager of the Australian Wine Board, Harry Palmer, and the manager of Orlando's Winery, Syd Gramp. They made a great fuss when I squeezed a lemon over my oysters with my right hand, and insisted that I should wash my hands—otherwise the lemon oil would affect the bouquet of the wine.

Thomas Bata, chief executive of the Bata Shoe organization, with seventy-nine factories in seventy countries producing 200 million pairs of shoes a year, the most in the world, was in town Wednesday. I gave a lunch for him, and Sheila gave one for Mrs. B., and then I took him to call on Mr. McEwen, the Minister for Trade and Industry and Deputy Prime Minister. They were very pleasant Canadian guests.

December 1, 1968

A » This past week we have been concentrating on last-minute preparations for our Canadian Patterns Exhibit, which is being assembled in the St. John Priory Hall for its Australian premiere tomorrow night. I recorded a ten-minute radio interview and a five-minute TV interview to help advertise the show.

As you all probably know, Canada is one of the leading designers of nuclear power stations that use natural uranium. As the Australians mine some uranium and would prefer not to send it abroad for processing, there is a fair prospect that when they decide to build a plant here they will adopt the Canadian design. I lunched on Monday with the Secretary of the Department of National Development, Bill Boswell, to discuss the subject.

December 8, 1968

S » This has been the Week that Was: probably our busiest in

Canberra. The Canadian Patterns Exhibit opened officially on Monday night. We were fortunate to get a cabinet minister, the Honourable Peter Nixon, Minister of the Interior, who is responsible for the capital, to do the official ceremony and make a nice little speech. Arthur presented him and his wife with one of the National Film Board pictures, which we had just got framed, to mark the occasion. We had nearly two hundred at this opening ceremony. We served drinks and they toured the exhibit. It provided good publicity, as we had all the heads of missions and top government officials, and of course art and culture group presidents. Then the following day it was open to the public from 9:00 a.m. to 5:00 p.m., and in the evening we were on hand for the second, much larger reception—about two hundred at 6:00 p.m., two hundred at 7:00 p.m., and two hundred at 8:00 p.m. They were invited by the other officers in the office and paid for by them, but the invitations were issued in our name. Many people stayed much longer than expected, so the groups tended to overlap, and the exhibit was so crowded that you could not really see it all easily, but again it was good publicity, and all those who were most interested returned sometime later in the week with other members of their families to see it more at their leisure. All the notices they sent out to school principals paid off, and during the week that it has been open nearly 4,000 school children have toured it. This is the final week of school, and most have finished exams and are at loose ends, so it was a welcome break for many teachers. Some children were well behaved and learned quite a bit from their tour; some were not and probably didn't profit much! All the TV screens kept going off and on, so we have had to hire an audiovisual technician from Melbourne to be on the job full-time. He will likely travel with the exhibit in other capital cities, because if the TV screens go off, half the impact of the exhibit is lost. The office staff had a very busy time last weekend setting up the exhibit, and they all, plus many from the Australian-Canadian Association, have been on a roster to act as guides for it through the week. This weekend it has to be taken down and packed away—many more hours of work for everyone.

On top of the Canadian Patterns Exhibit, and in connection with it, we had our annual staff conference here on Thursday and Friday so that the officers from Melbourne and Sydney could see the setup. Altogether there were eighteen officers and twelve wives from the three centres. Many of the Canberra juniors had not met the people from Sydney and Melbourne, so it was a good opportunity for all of us to get acquainted. We had all sorts of social events, and the men had meetings at the office all day. We had a ladies' lunch at Stapletons' on Thursday, then all had drinks here and dinner up at the Carousel Restaurant that night. It seems a real expense for us to wine and dine thirty up there, but once a year it is appreciated. Then on Friday we went to the Rogers' for buffet lunch, played tennis on their court in the p.m., and went to the Weisers' for another pleasant buffet in the evening.

On Saturday, Freeman Tovell, who now has the title of Director General of Personnel, arrived from Ottawa on a tour of most Far East and Pacific posts. He will be here till Wednesday. We had him for dinner Saturday night, and had an expedition in the country with him today. Art is back at the office now (Sunday night), so I've typed all of this letter.

December 15, 1968

A » Tuesday afternoon we drove to Goulbourn, sixty miles away in the direction of Sydney, where I was asked to speak at the closing ceremony for the local high school. After changing at a motel, we had dinner with the principal of the school, Mr. Chattaway, Mrs. Chattaway, and the chairman of the Parents and Citizens Committee before going on to the school. There were about 550 parents and students there for the annual report, the prizes, and—luckiest of all—my twenty-minute speech. Afterwards we went to the principal's for a late-night supper. Next morning the Parents and Citizens chairman, Mr. Travis, took us to visit his Sirdar knitting-wool spinning-mill, which employs about a hundred, mainly women. Girls leaving school at sixteen get $15 a week. This rises to $30 a week by age twenty-one. After that we drove out to a big sheep and cattle property called Springfield, established about 1832. The present owner, and descendant of the founder, Mrs. I. Maple-Brown, received us most hospitably, gave us lunch, and showed us about her old home and garden. She has a museum in an upstairs wing with old rifles and pistols used to hold the Bush Rangers at bay one hundred years ago, many items of old clothing, and many household items. We drove another fifty miles to Gunning, where I spoke to 360 at Speech Night in Gunning Central School, had supper, and then drove back to Canberra, arriving about 1:00 a.m. In a sense, teachers and parents in these country towns are discouraged by the lack of local employment for those going on for a higher education, because they almost inevitably move to Canberra or Sydney.

FIVE

1969

February 2, 1969

A » This week we have had a five-man Canadian defence equipment production team here to tell the Australians what we can produce in Canada and to discuss potential areas of joint research, development, and production. I took the leader of the team to call on the secretary of the Department of Defence, and I also gave a lunch. We have sold electronic equipment and Caribou aircraft here.

February 9, 1969

s » Although this is not for public broadcast, we were very pleased that Arthur received a letter this week from Marcel Cadieux, Undersecretary of State for External Affairs, saying that because Art was doing such a good job here our term would be extended. We think this is a very good post. There is much to do here, and the job is much more satisfying than those in many other places would be, so we are pleased to have this official word that we may stay on. Theoretically our three and a half years would have been up in May, so we were not sure whether Norah would get another trip out here, but now we know that she can definitely plan to come. Who knows ... we may even be here to see the new residence built! They talk of calling tenders at the end of this month. I'll believe it when I see it!

Every day in February until today it has been over 90 degrees. The heat is beginning to wear people down—they're tired out from having to water their gardens. So thank goodness we woke up today to nice gentle rain, even if it meant there was none of the usual tennis on Sunday at 8:30 with the Martins. The weather has also been more conducive to my working on the speech I have to give at the Cowra Quota Club tomorrow night. They originally asked Arthur to speak, but as he is busy, he suggested me. I'll motor the 125 miles there tomorrow afternoon. Then at the end of the week we are going for a week's leave at Ulladulla. Our mail will be sent on. We will return on Sunday the 23rd, because we expect Ronnie MacDonell, our high commissioner in New Zealand, as a house guest then. Edith will be away for more than two weeks, because she has won a trip to Perth to represent the ACT bowlers in a national competition, and has been looking forward to this big trip and big holiday all year.

A » This has been a busy week at the office, with consultations on Canadian China policy and a number of other subjects. I took a new contact, Dr. Garrod, out to lunch this week. He is responsible for science policy in the Department of Education and Science. Canada, with its Science Council and Science Secretariat, is rather ahead of Australia in making an inventory of its research and development activity and in pointing directions for new development. But our problems are roughly similar to those of Australia, and there is room for more systematically planned co-operation in the broad field of science.

March 1, 1969

S » Arthur is still busy working on his speech for the church program called "A Pleasant Sunday Afternoon," which is held in a Melbourne Methodist Church each week at 3:00 p.m., with an audience. It is broadcast live to listeners all over New South Wales and Victoria. Evidently it is something of a tradition and an institution in Melbourne, and has had many famous speakers, so it's something of an honour. We will also be in Melbourne Monday at

10:30 a.m. for the opening in Myers Department Store of the Canadian Patterns Exhibit, which we showed in Canberra just before Christmas. It will be a rushed trip, because we must be back here for a dinner in honour of the president of De Havilland Aircraft of Canada and Mrs. Boggs on Monday night.

March 9, 1969

s » The "Pleasant Sunday Afternoon" church program in Melbourne went well. Arthur's twenty-minute speech was fine; he read it, in order to keep within the limits. The other chief performers on the program were two singers from the Elizabethan Opera Company in Melbourne, in connection with their Moomba Festival. Both were excellent. The audience in the church was mostly "oldies," as they are called here (i.e., the over-60s) but the radio audience is the important part. The red light to mark the end of the time on the air came on exactly as the soloist finished, and then the congregation sang one more hymn, which was not on the air. This Sunday they will have a special feature, the 600-voice Billy Graham choir, because he will be in Melbourne this coming week.

The Australian Department of External Affairs has a larger than usual class of new recruits (called "cadets" while they are still probationary) this year. As an experiment they are sending each of them to another country's office to see how it is run. So a three-day seminar has been going on this week for these young chaps —and one girl. Arthur has lectured to them twice, and we went to a cocktail party at Nick Etheridge's one evening where we enjoyed chatting and answering all their questions. Only four are married, out of about thirty. They now say that they know more of how the Canadian government and all its various departments work than about their own, so I guess the seminar was a success.

March 24, 1969

s » We have had such a busy week it seems hard to believe it was just last weekend that we went to Melbourne. Sunday afternoon we were given a conducted tour by the director of the Melbourne Arts Centre, which was finished last July. It is the most handsome building, inside and out, that we have seen in Australia. It incorporates all the latest modern techniques, so it doesn't feel like an old-fashioned museum. It has escalators and a variety of flooring—carpet, lino, and wood—so you don't get weary of walking. It is designed around three inner courtyards, so there are no long galleries you have to backtrack through. The lighting is excellent, mostly from two angled windows that look out onto the courtyard. Reference material for each area is stored in an accessible space just behind the display section instead of in a remote cellar where only a few scholars would ever be permitted to see it. The entrance charge is twenty cents, and that certainly pays off. There were hundreds of teenagers, whole families, and of course lots of arty older types, just streaming through. They have had more than a million visitors since opening. Art was most impressed with the cases displaying Chinese and Middle Eastern treasures, beautifully lit from underneath, while I was pleased to see their collection of Australian paintings. Anyone who is in Melbourne can certainly pass many interesting hours there, and they have plans to add a theatre and concert complex that will rival the Sydney Opera House.

We were very pleased with the setup of the Canadian Patterns Exhibit in the new hall of the Royal Commonwealth Society. It was infinitely better than in the Myers Store, where it had been in the two previous weeks, and where it was lost on the toy department floor and had little advertising. It will be easier to take schoolchildren to this venue as well. The Minister of Education for Victoria opened it, and Arthur made a little speech.

A » During our Melbourne visit we visited Victoria's third university, La Trobe, which was started only two and a half years ago and now has three thousand students. The Vice-Chancellor, Dr. David Myers, was Dean of Engineering at UBC for ten years and is well disposed to our attempts to facilitate the sharing of common research interests between Canadian and Australian universities.

We toured Menzies College (named after the former prime minister) and met those on the staff who either were Canadians or had Canadian connections.

Back in Canberra, we had a visit on Wednesday from Geoffrey Massey, the architect of our new residence. We talked over the plans during lunch. The tenders are to be opened this coming Friday, and construction should begin in a couple of months. We find we will be located between the UAR and Israeli embassies, so we may need anti-ballistic missile protection.

March 30, 1969

A » Brian Marson, the Asian representative of Canadian University Service Overseas, visited Canberra on Wednesday and I took him to call on the Secretary of the Department of External Territories, because I would like to see CUSO sending some Canadian volunteers to New Guinea. I am hopeful something will be worked out in time.

When tenders were opened Friday for building the new residence the lowest one was thirty percent over the limit approved by Treasury Board, so I foresee a long—if not indefinite—delay in construction.

Friday I flew to Sydney, then by chartered plane one hundred miles north to Kurri Kurri, where Alcan is building a 40,000-ton aluminum smelter, to be completed in November. Work is going well, and I was much impressed with the standard of engineering design and supervision, and with the contract work.

April 7, 1969

A » Mr. Gorton's visit to Canada from April 2 to 4 was overshadowed in the press here by his visit to Washington, which included fifty-one minutes with President Nixon, and which turned out to be more successful than was thought possible. Particular attention was given to a dispute over freight rates on wheat under the International Grains Agreement. Mr. and Mrs. Gorton returned to Sydney Easter Sunday morning and are taking a few days leave.

I hope to get reports on the visit from Ottawa and from the Secretary for External Affairs, Sir James Plimsoll.

April 13, 1969

A » I suppose that my most noteworthy activity of the week concerned a day-and-a-half visit to Canberra by Maurice Strong, president of CIDA (Canadian International Development Agency), and one of his officers, Charles Greenwood, before they went on to the Asian Development Bank meeting in Sydney. I met them Tuesday noon and took them directly to a luncheon that the Deputy Secretary of External Affairs was giving. They made various calls, including one on the aid people in External and one on External Territories. I gave a luncheon to enable them to meet some of the professors at the Australian National University. As a result of the visit I made considerable progress in persuading Strong that Canada should undertake a modest economic aid scheme in the South Pacific, including Papua and New Guinea. This is a project I have been pushing since I visited New Guinea nearly three years ago, and have been turned down several times. But, if at first you don't succeed, try, try again. And that is what we are to be permitted to do.

April 20, 1969

S » This certainly has been a busy week. When I realize how much Arthur especially has been on the run, I marvel the more at how Mr. Pearson, who will be seventy-two next week, has stood up to it all and been able to perform at such a high intellectual peak all through it. Last Sunday night Art worked at the office right up till the last minute. Next morning we got to the airport just as the plane was being boarded for Sydney so that he would be on hand bright and early to meet Pearson and his party (Bert Hart, formerly with External, now with the World Bank Development Commission, Mr. Harrison and Professor Silcock, also of that organization, and Miss Perron, who has been secretary to Mr. Pearson and before that to Mr. St. Laurent), who were due to arrive from Singapore at 7:05 a.m. They came in an hour earlier, at 6:05, but had to wait in Sydney for a press conference and for the VIP flight that had been scheduled to arrive in Canberra at 8:40 a.m. Luckily Art had been alerted in time.

Mr. Pearson was a guest of the Australian government when here, but his hosts were the Australian Institute of International Affairs and the Australian National University, where he held seminars in connection with his current work with the World Bank, surveying and reporting on the present state of development assistance. He stayed at University House, and Vice-Chancellor Sir John Crawford was really his host, so it was not like an official visit of someone still in politics. This meant we did not have to have a big reception. We told all the people wanting to meet him that they could get tickets for his public lecture if they wanted to see or hear him. Instead, we had a dinner for twelve here on Monday night. We were pleased to get the leader of the Country Party, Deputy Prime Minister and Minister of Trade and Industry Mr. McEwen, and his wife to come. We had not known until just the last week whether Mrs. Pearson was going to be here with Mr. Pearson, so we were not sure whether it would be stag or with women. It ended up with seven men and five women. We also had Dr. Coombs from Sydney, head of the Reserve Bank and Chancellor of ANU, and Mrs. Coombs, Sir William Hudson, ex-commissioner of the Snowy Mountains scheme, and Lady Hudson, Sir James Plimsoll, the permanent head of the Department of External Affairs, and Allan and Gene Roger of our office, who have worked hard with us on the preparations for the visit. I was so relieved to have Edith on hand for this important dinner. I think the menu (clear beef soup, cold Canadian salmon salad, fillet of beef with mushrooms, potato croquettes, Chinese peas and carrots, and Canadian mix angel cakes and fresh raspberries from our own garden with whipped cream) suited all. Also I was lucky with flowers. The florist had a poor selection, and we had nothing unusual in the garden—though I used our nice roses for the table. But I got some huge yellow dahlias about four inches across from a friend of Edith's, which I combined with brown dried Australian cones and palm leaves in the hall to make a really effective arrangement, if I say so myself —but at a cost, because I jabbed my middle finger badly under the nail with the needle holder. I was too busy Monday to do much for it, and it didn't show, but on Tuesday I had to get an anti-tetanus shot and antibiotics. It has taken most of the week to tame down. I'm lucky that there was so much rain at the beginning of the week. Tennis was cancelled. The visiting Canadians thought that all the sunny weather we talked about was a myth, though they have it now. It's still cold, though, and of course by Canadian standards it's cold in the houses here.

On Tuesday Mr. Pearson visited seminars at the University and had a private dinner with the Governor General and Lady Casey, just the three of them. Wednesday in the pouring rain we had him to the chancery to meet the staff. He then went outdoors to plant a Canadian maple tree beside the ones Sir Robert and Dame Pattie Menzies planted when the office was opened. He went to a Cabinet lunch and gave press and TV interviews and a big public lecture at ANU. Every seat was taken, which pleased us. Good discussion and questions afterwards. On Thursday there were all-day seminars at ANU. On Friday Art left with him for Melbourne to call on Sir Robert Menzies and address an Institute of International Affairs lunch. Then they flew to Cooma and a weekend in the Snowy Mountains, relaxing and talking to various people brought here for that purpose, such as David Hay, Administrator of Papua New Guinea, who used to be Australian high commissioner in Ottawa. I'm having five for supper here tonight with Alison Hay. At one time we were to go to the Snowies too, but it was changed to a stag. Oh yes—I had a ladies' lunch for Miss Perron here on Friday.

A » When introducing Mr. Pearson to the staff, I referred to my trip around the world with him to attend the conference of Commonwealth Foreign Ministers in Colombo, Ceylon, in January 1950. Mr. Pearson asked, "Can you tell me last night's hockey score between the Toronto Maple Leafs and the Montreal Canadiens?" I confessed I didn't know, but perhaps one of our communicators had got it over the wire from Ottawa. Mr. Pearson cracked, "You're no darn good as a Canadian high commissioner if you don't keep up with the hockey scores." This got a good laugh from the staff.

April 27, 1969

A » I am just in from meeting the Canadian Minister of Industry, Trade and Commerce, Honourable Jean-Luc Pepin. He is an affable 44-year-old who is easy to get on with. I went down to Sydney last evening and we returned this morning by Mystere jet. He rests today, with a visit to a sheep property, a quiet supper at the Weisers', and a briefing, but then he has three busy days in Canberra, Sydney, and Melbourne. I go round with him, then on to Rockhampton in northern Queensland to make a speech.

During his busy schedule in Canberra Mr. Pearson asked me to take him to the great War Memorial to visit the underground War Museum. He stood for a long time looking at three graphic dioramas of the ANZAC and Newfoundland Regiment attacks on Gallipoli in the First World War. He then turned and said to me, "I carried a bedpan with the University of Toronto Field Hospital Unit in the assault on Gallipoli. I was so distressed by the sight of badly wounded soldiers and those suffering from dysentery that I resolved to seek a transfer to the RAF, where at least I wouldn't see the effects of our strafing." We then left quietly.

Mr. Pearson left for Tokyo last Monday night. After his round of meetings here I took him to Melbourne to call on Sir Robert Menzies, with whom he reminisced about earlier Commonwealth meetings and other international events. He talked at a luncheon meeting and then we went off to the Snowy Mountains, where he enjoyed a quiet weekend of relaxation. We visited a famous stud ram property called Hazeldean, owned by Jim Litchfield, and went fishing. David Hay, the Administrator of the Territory of Papua New Guinea, came up for an evening and talked about the problems of development there. He knew Mr. Pearson from having been high commissioner in Ottawa. Mr. Pearson was a wonderful guest.

May 4, 1969

s » Everyone seemed pleased with Jean-Luc Pepin's visit in Canberra last Sunday and Monday. He is a pleasant, amiable, clever, refreshing person with a nice sense of humour. He said he was coming here before Trudeau like John the Baptist, only he was Jean-Luc the Baptist! He spoke to the National Press Club luncheon Monday. He had worked with Arthur and the trade officials here and the two high-powered ones who came with him, Andy Kniewasser of Expo fame and Nixon, who was here as commercial counsellor five years ago, and he had a prepared text, which was handed out to the reporters who were present. However, he made it much more personal by really just taking the headings and speaking in his own way and with his own style and his own vocabulary, which added charm. He had meetings with the Minister of Trade for a couple of hours, with the Minister of National Development, and with the Prime Minister, and he was at a Cabinet lunch. At our reception in the evening, held at the chancery, he was very affable and attentive with all the two hundred guests. Afterwards Mr. McEwen, the Deputy Prime Minister and Minister of Trade, had a stag dinner for sixteen of them. Arthur has been with him the rest of his visit here, accompanying him to Sydney and Melbourne.

Art did come back to Canberra for the middle part of Wednesday to be here for the official installation of the new Governor General, Sir Paul Hasluck. The ceremony of taking the oath of office was administered by the Chief Justice and took place in the Senate. It was a very short affair, only about ten minutes, but of course there was lots of colour, with uniforms, and judges, and diplomats. I felt our seats were too good (they were in the second row on the floor of the House), whereas some poor senators were not there at all. There was a big reception afterwards. Hasluck will do a good job—though I don't agree with the idea of appointing a politician.

May 11, 1969

A » Fortunately this has been a quiet weekend for us, so I've been able to get caught up on some of the reading material that had accumulated during the Pearson and Pepin visits.

First of all, let me refer again to these visits. I found Mr. Pearson as charming and interested in all about him as ever. I had a long talk with him about the future of Canada. Of course as one of the principal architects of "co-operative federalism"—perhaps its principal architect—he had a point of view to maintain, but I found his comments reassuring. And if Mr. Pepin is a sample of the new French-Canadian leadership, then I was well satisfied that reason and a good sense of compromise will prevail.

Last Thursday, after Mr. Pepin and his party left for New Zealand, I flew 1,000 miles north to Rockhampton, Queensland, on the Tropic of Capricorn, to give the opening address to 350 attending the Southern Queensland and Northern Rivers Zone of the Australian Jaycees. We import alumina from the Queensland Alumina refinery at Gladstone, eighty miles southeast, for use at Kitimat, B.C. International Nickel is in partnership with BHP (Broken Hill Proprietary, the largest mining company in Australia) in prospecting for nickel sixty miles north. Also, pineapple, which we import canned, comes from Yeppoon on the coast. So I was able to point to local connections. The Jaycees engage in community service and self-improvement, such as public speaking. Besides the conference I visited a local flour mill and the big open-cut Mount Morgan gold and copper mine, and saw over a couple of properties.

Since returning we have had a visit from Mr. Frank Davies, Director of the Defence Research Telecommunications Establishment at Shirley Bay, near Ottawa. I have known him since the last war. We had a small dinner for him, after which he gave an illustrated talk on the Canadian Alouette satellites, and also on problems of communication in the Arctic.

Friday evening we went to a dinner at the Rogers' for Sir Percy and Lady Spender. Recently retired as president of the World Court, he was minister for External Affairs at the time of the first Colombo Conference of Commonwealth Foreign Ministers in January 1950, and nearly gave his name to the Colombo Plan. He is still a lively old geezer and a great talker.

May 19, 1969

s » This is being written on Monday evening, because we have been away for a very busy weekend in South Australia. We left a half-day early to go via Sydney so that we could go to the David Jones Store there, which is putting on our Canadian Patterns Exhibit and running many other Canadian features along with those of many other countries in connection with an international fair. We were especially interested to see Mr. Joanasie Salamonie, a Canadian Eskimo carver they brought out to give demonstrations in the store. He had with him a large collection of Eskimo soapstone carvings to sell. We took him out to early dinner before the train to Adelaide, along with Terry Jones of our Sydney office. Mr. Salamonie comes from Frobisher Bay, where he runs the co-op store. After this promotional job he will tour in South Australia under the auspices of the Department of Aborigines Affairs, to talk to groups of Aborigines on reservations, demonstrate his carving, and perhaps interest the people on one station in using a type of green rock that is now wasted, except for very choice green bits that are sent to Hong Kong. It will be a small but interesting sociological experiment in the meeting of two native cultures.

The main purpose of our trip to South Australia was for Arthur to open a National Film Board display of Canadian pictures in the Naracoorte Art Gallery, which shares the building that bears Art's name on a plaque as the official opener. It was opened two years ago. Of course that means a speech. Arthur did some research to dig up connections between South Australian art and Canada, and found some. On the same evening we gave a showing of Canadian films. Sixty people turned out—pretty good for a small centre like that, where most people have to drive in to town from their properties.

To get to this place we had to fly from Adelaide to Mount Gambier. We were met there by our host, Richard Lawson, who drove us back the ninety miles via several interesting stops. Lawson is the son of a wealthy landowner who runs a huge property. The parents were away, so we stayed in their mansion while the son and his expectant wife were in their cottage next door. The house was built in 1868 and is huge, with about eight big bed-rooms upstairs and beautiful furnishings. But they have no ser-vants nowadays, and only electric heaters (I was glad I had taken my heating pad to warm the bed). It was an interesting weekend. We saw firsthand how a big landowner lives, and we visited agri-cultural research stations and looked at sheep, crops, etc. You could hear Arthur holding forth, asking questions about the eco-nomics of growing vineyards or running so many sheep to the acre, etc.

This morning we started at the crack of dawn and returned by car to Mount Gambier and by plane from there to Melbourne and then on to Canberra. There is a partial transport strike that made for delays, but so far it has not affected planes, just other forms of transportation. Art went straight to the office and now is at a stag reception for a Mr. Legge of the Toronto Workers' Compensation Board, for whom we are giving a lunch tomorrow. He'll sure be tired when he returns here.

Norah and her friend Sonja Kekkonen left Canada May 17, and arrive here June 1.

May 26, 1969

s » We had an interesting weekend trip to Armidale, New Eng-land, in the northern part of New South Wales, close to the Queensland border. We were there under the joint auspices of the Arts Council and the Apex Clubs. There was a showing of Cana-dian films for schoolchildren, and a second one in the evening, sponsored by the Arts Council with a grant from the Canadian high commission. Both were held in the hall of the University of New England. Arthur gave a little speech beforehand and there was a reception of "arty" types after. In between films we had an interesting trip to a property just recently bought by an English-man and his Rhodesian wife who—luckier than most—were able to get their money out of Rhodesia and set up farming again. They obviously had lots of money. With the help of a Sydney architect, they have made a most attractive open-style house using Aus-tralian woods and the brown and beige basalt rock that is found in that area. The rock is piled up in huge walls all around the house to give a courtyard effect. I don't know when I've seen a house that fitted in so well with the brown and beige background that the rather dry grass and the gum trees produce. It almost melted into the background, yet it was rugged and individual.

A » One of our expeditions from Armidale was an hour's flight in a Piper Comanche four-seater aircraft that gave us a wonderful view of the New England tableland. This is an area about 200 miles wide that begins 125 miles north of Sydney, extends up to the Queensland border, and lies between a narrow coastal strip and the western plains. This plateau land is about 3,000 feet in elevation and has some good grazing land. Twenty years ago Armidale was represented by a strong New South Wales Minister of Education named Drummond, who got a Teachers College built in his constituency, and then the University of New England. We visited both. Professor Zelman Cowan, the Vice-Chancellor of the University of New England, had us to lunch; Professor Hardy, head of the English Department, who had taught at the University of Toronto, took us about the grounds and buildings.

I gave a talk on "Canada and Australia" to the international relations dinner of the Apex Club, attended by about 120, including the Minister of Public Works of New South Wales, Mr. David Hughes.

Last Wednesday we gave a buffet here for about twenty-five to meet a group of a half-dozen Australian parliamentarians who will be going to Canada for a three-week official visit. The government sends two such groups abroad each year, and this is the first time that one has gone to Canada. They begin in Vancouver on June 8.

June 15, 1969

A » We arrived in Broken Hill about 1:30 p.m. on June 11. A rich strike of silver, lead, and zinc was found there in 1883, the same year that the nickel-copper strike was made at Sudbury. Hence this town of 30,000 that has grown in the salt bush-sprinkled semi-desert area of western New South Wales. The Barrier Industrial Council was formed there in the 1920s to prevent internecine warfare between the trade unions, and it has gained renown. We visited the Flying Doctor Base, and Sheila talked on the School of the Air to children in an area of the outback of over half a million square miles. I went 2,600 feet underground in one of the mines, down to the eighteenth level, and clambered up and around to see the drilling and hauling of ore. I spoke to sixty at an Apex dinner, while Sheila spoke to about fifty women at a general meeting. We also went out to a water reservoir scheme on the Darling River, sixty miles to the west. We were received with much warmth of hospitality by all we met there, and the visit gave us a better idea of the far west of New South Wales.

June 22, 1969

s » Wednesday Norah and Sonja took off in the Datsun, which had just had its 600-mile checkup. They plan to go via the East Coast to Brisbane and up into Queensland to get some sun at Hayman Island, a coral island, then cut inland across the outback of Queensland and into the Northern Territory to visit Sue Tait, who used to work for Qantas here and is now on a cattle station beyond Mount Isa. There they will be joined by Pam Stuart, daughter of the Singapore high commissioner here, an outgoing friend of Norah's and Sue's, and another girl Pam invited, a Venezuelan who is visiting her sister, the wife of the Spanish ambassador — just to add a touch of the unknown. Norah and Sonja had the car almost full when they left, as they had borrowed a tent and sleeping bags, etc., to cut down on expenses. They expect to be at least a month, but their plans are rather flexible, and we'll know more from their progress reports from time to time. Even Canadians don't realize the vast stretches of long driving across desert sand that is involved in getting around this vast continent. The last ten days have been miserable and cold and rainy over just about all of eastern Australia, so I hope at least they are out of that belt by now.

A » The Five-Power Defence Conference was held here Thursday and Friday, June 19 and 20, to put an official ministerial stamp on arrangements made by officials during the past year. Racial strife in Malaysia cast a bit of a shadow, as did Australia's reluctance to commit itself to the defence of East Malaysia (Sabah and Sarawak). I have yet to get the information on which to base a report. I hope to have it on Monday before leaving for Melbourne, where I am to talk to the United Services Institute on "Canadian Defence Policy."

June 29, 1969

s » When we are abroad, the celebration of Canada's birthday involves us deeply on several fronts. On Friday night the officers of the High Commission held an Eskimo *kaget* (that means a carve-in!) at the National Library. Allan and Gene Roger did a lot of work setting up the Eskimo carvings that David Jones, the big store, had brought out here in connection with their international fair. Joanasie Salamonie, the Eskimo from Frobisher Bay we met in Sydney last month, was in Canberra this week, and was the shy star of the evening. He talked for about five minutes about his people and then answered questions from the 250 in the audience. Before that, slides of the Arctic were shown in the small intimate theatre in the basement of the handsome new National Library building, then Art welcomed people in a short speech, then we had *Kenojuak*, the National Film Board picture, then Salamonie talked, then we had *Living Stone*, the film about carving. Afterwards, while people looked at the exhibit outside in the foyer, drinks were served. It was a change and it was well received. The exhibit will remain there ten days for the public to view, but the Eskimo returned to Canada this weekend.

Since we saw him in Sydney Mr. Salamonie has visited and talked to Aborigines on reserves in South Australia, where he found the green rock too hard to carve with the simple chisels used on Canadian Arctic soapstone. He was taken out by some Aborigines in a truck to hunt rabbits. Art asked him how he got along with the Aborigines. He replied, "Them fellows don't talk much. I don't either. But by and by we begin to think together."

A » This past Tuesday I went down to Melbourne for a day and a night. I visited our commercial office, which is to move to new accommodation on July 24, had lunch with Creighton Burns of *The Melbourne Age*, and then in the afternoon called at the Nauru office. In the evening I had dinner with the executive of the United Service Institution and then addressed about a hundred serving and retired officers on "Canada's Defence Policy." I talked for forty-five minutes, and was then questioned for an hour and a half about unification, relations with the U.S.A., our policies in the Pacific, and so on.

July 13, 1969

s » We left for Brisbane last Sunday at 1:00 p.m. and after changing at Sydney arrived there at 5:30. We had a brief bite to eat after chatting to Dr. Groves, a zoologist who is the president of the Australian-Canadian Association there, and Mrs. Hilliard, the secretary, and got some inkling of the fireworks and jealousies to expect at the meeting that night, sponsored by the Royal Commonwealth Society. We also heard from the information chap from our office, Cameron Jess, who was in town to set up the Canadian Patterns Exhibit there. Not as many fireworks at the meeting as we had been led to expect; not as many Canadians either. Art gave a short talk on Canada since Trudeau took over, and there was a program of Canadian films, new ones I'd not seen before. On Monday Art called on the Premier, and we went to the new Teachers College, where Art gave a very good forty-five-minute talk on Canada to the student teachers there — which he felt was a much more worthwhile audience than the old biddies at the meeting the night before! At 2:30 p.m. the Queensland Premier opened the Canadian Patterns Exhibit in the big David Jones Department Store, where it will be for two weeks. They are already booked up with school tours for every a.m. and p.m.

When we accepted the invitation by the Rural Youth Clubs of New South Wales to open the Thirteenth Annual Conference at Tamworth, part of the idea was that on the map Tamworth looks so close to Brisbane, but because they're in different states and not on the main airline, in the end we discovered that the quickest way was to fly from Brisbane all the way back to Sydney and then fly from Sydney to Tamworth, repeating most of the trip on just a slight angle!

A » We were very hospitably looked after during our two and a half days in Tamworth. On our first day we were taken by Ray Walsh, the chairman of the Peel-Cunningham Shire Council, to visit an irrigation farm on the Liverpool Plains, near Breeza. This region has rich black volcanic soil, very different from that in much of Australia. In the afternoon we toured the Peel Valley. On July 9 I officially opened the Rural Youth Club conference with a twenty-minute speech. By calling myself an agricultural ignoramus and following that by three farm jokes, I got a good hearing. Well, we listened to speeches and debates, saw cooking contests, etc. Major awards, including overseas trips, are given to those completing successful farm or homemaking projects. Several visit Canada. There was a dinner in the evening, at which I spoke briefly, and a ball. On our final day we visited an agricultural high school. I spoke to four hundred senior students at Tamworth High, and we visited the local agricultural research station and a hybrid wheat-breeding venture. We had magnificent winter weather for the visit, 40 to 65 degrees. It was a good outing.

July 27, 1969

s » Last week I wrote each of you longhand from the motel in Mildura. We had arrived there late Friday night after a long delay in Melbourne because of engine trouble in the plane, and were met by the local MP and invited to his home for coffee. We find this typical of Australian hospitality in country towns. You get invited inside people's homes much more than you do in the capital cities, where there is more formality. Both Saturday and Sunday were easy days, just touring the area with people interested in showing us around and telling us something of the citrus and grape industry, or rather the dried fruit industry. Although this is a very bad year for dried fruit, they will keep up the amount sent to Canada, because we and New Zealand are their biggest markets. They will have to cut back on their other more recent and diverse markets. We especially enjoyed our day with the John Gordons. He is chairman of the Dried Fruits Board, and we have been to their home each of the three times we have been in Mildura. Saturday evening we felt we were made rather an exhibition: we had to sit right up at the front beside the speaker and the chairman of the Mildura Historical Society for a lecture by an owner of a military museum who talked for an hour and a quarter on "The Eureka Stockade," an early skirmish in the Ballarat area between the miners of gold and the authorities, which signalled the beginning of democratic action in Australia. Arthur kept pinching himself to stay awake, and although we saw many in the audience in front of us nodding off, we kept giving each other dirty looks to keep attentive to the lecturer. After that he showed slides for twenty minutes. Wow!

On Monday, because of the moon landing, the schools were given permission to give their pupils a holiday, and many did. This competition for their attention, which we quite understood, cut badly into attendance at the two school showings of Canadian films. There were about 150 at each instead of the 400-each that were planned for. There was better attendance at the adult showing in the evening. In between, at 5:00 p.m., about ninety prominent local citizens were at a reception at the mayor's. They even have a Canadian flag flying from the City Hall in our honour! Arthur made a good twenty-minute speech. All in all Mildura is quite an attractive cultural oasis, as well as an irrigation centre.

A » Graham and Joan McInnes arrived late Thursday as our house guests. Graham is at present Canadian ambassador to UNESCO in Paris, and on leave, but he has deep roots in Australia, having been brought up in Melbourne, and it is the setting and story of his life there that is described in his two books, *The Road to Gundagai* and *Humping My Bluey*. His mother, Angela Thirkell, also a writer, divorced his father when he and his brother were

167

very young and took them to Australia. Graham married Joan, a fellow student at the University of Melbourne, and as recently as 1967 wrote *Finding a Father*, about his becoming a Canadian. He has great power of almost total recall of scenes, smells, and events, so was quite nostalgic upon his return to Australia. Joan had not been here for thirty years, and had never been in Canberra, so we had a busy and exhausting three days with them here, with all sorts of literary and poetic and publishing connections whom we don't entertain very often. We gave two small lunches, one here and one at the Commonwealth Club, and one large reception for them. We also had a morning at a property in the country with them. They were pleasant and considerate guests.

August 3, 1969

A » I have been asked to return to Ottawa on temporary duty for two months to co-ordinate submissions from government departments and draft a policy paper on Canadian interests in Asia and the Pacific and on the options open to the government over the next ten years, for submission to ministers as part of the government's review of Canadian foreign policy. Although a date hasn't been set, I expect to leave about the end of August and travel by way of a number of Asian capitals, to arrive in Ottawa for meetings commencing September 15. Sheila will fly back separately and meet me in Ottawa. We expect to return to Canberra by the end of November.

I am pleased to have been asked to conduct this review of Canadian policy in the Pacific, as it indicates that management continues to think that I have a contribution to make. Naturally I am much interested in the subject and glad to be given the responsibility, while remaining high commissioner to Australia. Incidentally—and this is quite unrelated to the special assignment—I have been given another promotion, to FSO-9, just one step below the top rank, which has about four positions in it.

We will keep you informed about our plans as they develop. We look forward to seeing relatives in Canada.

s » I preferred that Arthur break this big news to you. My return trip will be paid for as home leave, which was due us after three and a half years in this post. From the point of view of timing it is not the best, in that we have just had Norah out here, but it is a good time of year to return to Canada, and we are very pleased, because it means that we will return for at least a full year or more here. Arthur broke the news to the officers on Friday and I to Edith, etc. She will just stay on in the house as she does when we are on trips away from here.

August 17, 1969

s » This has been a very busy week, because of the visit of the Duke and Duchess of Kent to Australia en route to Port Moresby to open the third Pacific Games, and our leaving for Perth on the same day as the luncheon for the Duke and Duchess with the ten high commissioners. Originally we had planned to have about ten days in Western Australia, but because of Art's assignment in Ottawa we cut it short to just three days, to cover the bare essentials, and not go outside Perth. The object of the visit was to be on hand at David Jones Department Store for the official opening of the Canadian Patterns Exhibit by the Governor of Western Australia, Sir Douglas Kendrew. The exhibit will be there for the next two weeks. Art took the opportunity to call on the Acting Premier, the Minister of Education, the Minister of National Development, and several mining contacts with Canadian interests. Also he addressed a Rotary Club, and I went off with a Country Women's Association state treasurer to address a branch meeting in Perth, and later to attend a luncheon and speak to their state executive. They have a handsome new three-storey headquarters, partly rented out as offices, and seem as flourishing as in any other state.

Sir Valston Hancock, Australian Commissioner at Expo 67, comes from Perth. He has a brother there who is very involved in mining development, and we went to his office to see a new film made about him called *Dig a Million, Make a Million*. It was a fabulous story of the iron in the Hammersley Range. Also we had a pleasant dinner with the Hancocks.

The second day there we had a tour around the campus of the University of Western Australia. Quite a number of new buildings have been built in the three years since we were last in Perth, mostly in an architectural style that's in keeping with the attractive sandstone buildings they had before. The University has just 7,000 students and, because of its proximity to Singapore, etc., more Asians than any other Australian university. In the evening we attended a reception held in our honour by the Royal Commonwealth Society. Arthur made a good speech there. Next morning we had a pleasant tour by car of the Swan and Conning River area with Val Hancock's sister. Perth has a much more progressive and spacious air than most Australian cities.

August 24, 1969

s » D-Day (departure day) is fast approaching for Art. He leaves Tuesday, August 26 for Djakarta, then on August 29 flies to Singapore, on August 30 to Kuala Lumpur (he will be there over a Merdeka weekend), September 2 to Bangkok, September 4 to Phnom Penh, September 5 to Saigon, September 8 to Hong Kong, September 11 to Tokyo, and Saturday, September 13, to Vancouver. I will have left Sydney Saturday night, and if planes are on time we will have a short night's sleep in a Vancouver hotel and will go on together to Edmonton on Sunday, September 14, stopping for two and a half hours there to see Aunt Margaret Judge, Arthur's father's sister, who has maintained the Menzies family ties over the years. We arrive in Ottawa on Sunday night. Art is to report for his new assignment on Monday, September 15, the beginning of another fearful rush for two months!

A very nice dinner was given in Arthur's honour by Minister of the Interior Peter Nixon in the Parliamentary restaurant, attended by all the people who went to Canada recently on a parliamentary delegation and were evidently well received, and therefore well disposed to Arthur for all the arrangements he had made. It is always nice when a group is appreciative. The Speaker and another group will be visiting Ottawa in September before we arrive.

Kenneth is in the process of changing from L.S.E. to Essex University for this next academic year, because the tutor at L.S.E. was not really competent to advise on his thesis. He has been busy clearing the details with the Canada Council and trying to find accommodation near Essex. Just about the whole group of them are moving to Essex. It has a very good reputation in sociology, it seems.

August 26, 1969 · aboard Qantas Boeing 707 from Sydney to Djakarta

A » On quite a number of trips I have had the ambition to write a diary, but each time I seem to have given way to the weaknesses of the flesh. However, I'll start another one and see if I can maintain it.

As you know, the origin of this trip was a request from the Undersecretary, Marcel Cadieux, that I should return to Ottawa on temporary duty to co-ordinate interdepartmental submissions and write the chapter of the Canadian government's review of foreign policy relating to the Pacific and Asia. I have been authorized to travel back to Ottawa by way of a number of Pacific Rim capitals. Sheila will fly direct via Honolulu to join me in Vancouver on September 13, and we will go together to Ottawa on September 14. I am to begin work September 15.

Canberra had the look of spring as I left. Last evening, at a farewell reception for the Argentine Ambassador at the residence of the Philippine Ambassador and Dean of the Diplomatic Corps, the Korean Ambassador, Dong-Whan Lee, said to me, "The water flower are nice now." I replied that my water lilies had shown no sign of emerging from winter rest. It was only after an exchange of puzzled glances that I grasped that he was talking about wattle, Australia's bright yellow early-spring-flowering shrub-tree that adds so much delightful colour to the landscape at this time of year. The prunus (plum) adds gaiety to Canberra streets and gardens, and there are many spring-flowering bulbs out. This is that season of 40s by night and high 50s by day (without bush flies) that is most enjoyable in Canberra. By the time we return at the end of November it will be high spring.

August 29, 1969 · *Djakarta to Singapore*

A » This entry is beginning while we are awaiting takeoff from Djakarta aboard a very comfortable Japan Airlines DC-8.

August 29, 1969 · *Djakarta*

The contrast between August 1969 and November 1965, when we visited Djakarta shortly after the October coup, is enormous. Then the city was dirty, there were troops bivouacked in parks, and there was a curfew after 8:00 p.m. There was an air of uncertainty as to whether President Sukarno had been really dumped or might regain power. This time the vigorous general who governs Djakarta has cleaned the place up a lot. Lights festoon some monuments from the August 17 national day. There is a lot of traffic. From my round of talks with earnest and able young Indonesian planners and with diplomats such as the Australian, Dutch, and U.S.A. ambassadors, I got the sense that all are pleased with the sensible and determined way the Suharto government is setting about trying to rehabilitate the economy to the levels of the 1950s, when it began to deteriorate under Sukarno. Of course there are many problems to be overcome, but they are being faced squarely. I hope that we can increase our aid.

September 2, 1969 · *Kuala Lumpur to Bangkok*

A » We are about to take off on the hour-and-three-quarters flight to Bangkok on a Japan Airlines DC-8 similar to the one we flew in from Djakarta to Singapore.

In the day I had in Singapore I had a talk with the Foreign Minister, Mr. Rajaratnam, and a very pleasant dinner with interesting guests at the remodelled residence of our Acting High Commissioner, Milton Blackwood, who is also Commercial Counsellor. Other appointments fell through, so I spent some time roaming the city: Change Alley, C.K. Tang's, etc. I bought a few little items, but baggage weight and time precluded more. Singapore looks much the same as in 1965 and 1961, except for the many more good hotels intended to cater to the international tourist trade, the new blocks of residential flats, and the new Jurong industrial area. Because of the withdrawal of British forces east of Suez by 1971, a good number of Singapore employees are being let out, and this has caused about ten-percent unemployment.

The Singapore government is doing all it can to attract industry, including textile plants, services to the travel industry, tourism, and the usual entrepôt trade with Malaysia and Indonesia. The overseas Chinese, or, as they now prefer to be called, Singapore citizens, are shrewd and hard-working, and I am sure they will make out. We do a fair trade there, and are giving some aid in establishing a technical high school.

September 2, 1969 · *Kuala Lumpur*

A » I arrived here on Saturday morning, August 30, and it looked much as Sheila and I saw it on our November 1965 visit. I was met by the First Secretary and Acting High Commissioner, Glen Shortliffe, of Edmonton, and stayed at his Canadian government-owned house on Jalan Langgak, right on the golf course. It is a good house in a fine location. They have two boys, Scott and Newton, who, at two and three and a half, are very active little fellows indeed. They were most hospitable over the Merdeka weekend and entertained me well. Glen is a dynamic, able chap and good company. I hope to speak to his parents in Edmonton.

On the Saturday morning I was immediately embarked on a round of calls, accompanied by Shortliffe and Inche (Mr.) Mustapha, who returned recently from being Malaysian counsellor in Canberra. I called in succession on Tun Dr. Ismail, Minister of Home Affairs, Tun Razak, Deputy Prime Minister, and Tun Tan Siew-sin, former minister of finance and leader of the Malaysian Chinese Association, and I lunched with Inche Khir Johari, the Minister of Commerce and Industry. On Monday morning I had an hour each with Tan Sri Kadir, head of the civil service, and Tan Sri Ghazali, Permanent Secretary of the Ministry of Foreign Affairs. In addition, I talked to our officers and had a stag dinner with the Australian, New Zealand, British, and American heads of mission. I spent a fair time writing up notes, and had a swim at the golf club in the same setup as we used to use ten years ago. All the Malaysians I saw I had known well before, so I had as good sessions as I could hope for. Oh yes—I also attended a reception by the Agong (the Sultan of Trengganu) for the twelfth anniversary of Merdeka. I had known the Agong before, as I had Tunku and several others I met there.

May 13, the day of the communal riots, is uppermost in everyone's minds. There is relatively little evidence of the fires, but there are many police about. There is a curfew between 2:00 and 4:00 a.m., but most people are off the streets by 9:00 or 10:00 p.m. As described to me, the Alliance government had become a bit self-satisfied; in fact, interracial tension was building up, and economic dissatisfaction. The Malays claim that in the original bargain set out in the constitution, one and a half million Chinese were made immediately eligible for citizenship. In return, the Malay language was to be recognized as the national language, and Malays were to be helped to catch up economically with the advanced Chinese. The younger Chinese forgot about this and wanted full equality, or abolition of Malay privilege, and no insistence on the Malay language. The younger Malays felt that by studying in Malay they lost economic opportunity, and they resented the Chinese monopoly of the economy. Restoration of interracial co-operation will take time, and probably provisions entrenching Malay privilege. Meanwhile, the Malays control power in the army, the police, and the government—but I'm sure they wish to be fair and return to intercommunal co-operation.

September 3, 1969 · *Bangkok*

A » I arrived here at 11:15 p.m. yesterday and was met by my old friend Bubs Britton, who was commercial counsellor with us in Japan from 1950 to 1953 and is just about to retire at age 66 as Canada's first ambassador to Thailand. We drove to the Erawan Hotel, where I have stayed several times before, and then on to his recently rented residence for lunch with Mary. Access to the

residence, which is in a big Chinese-owned compound, is not too
elegant, but the house is lovely, all air-conditioned and with fine
accommodation for living and entertaining. They gave a reception
in the evening for me to meet some people, including Leonard
Unger, the U.S. Ambassador, whom I've known, P.K. Bannerjee,
the Indian Ambassador, who was in Ottawa twenty years ago, and
others. I've called on Thai and ECAFE (Economic Commission
for Asia and the Far East) officials, and had a good lunch talk with
working-level diplomats and long talks with our own officers.
They have done well in getting established in two years. I'm
pleased with the setup and the connections with Thais and international organizations.

November 16, 1969 · *Ottawa*

s » I have always known that my dear husband had a great capacity for hard work, but I must say I admire the persistent way he
has kept at this difficult report over the past two months. Apart
from the two early weekends away to visit Herb and Daisy and
Marion and Frances and their families, he has been relentlessly
pursuing the material needed, writing up the various sections,
and directing his two assistants to press on for more or to check
details and rewrite sections, morning, noon, and night. Obviously
he can't relax the pace yet, but he is now beginning to see the
home stretch.

Although we would have liked to get away by next weekend, it
just doesn't seem realistic in view of all the administrative and
Australian business Art also has to attend to while in Ottawa, and
to which he can't turn until his mind is free of the report. Therefore, in order to make planning easier and to give some warning
to Kenneth and Janet along the way, we now plan to leave Ottawa
on Monday morning, November 30, arriving in London that
night. So this week we will start getting reservations on that basis.
We will still be back in Canberra in time to get turned around for
the staff conference of all Canadian personnel in Canberra on December 11 and 12, and, according to present reservations, we will
take off on December 18 for New Zealand and what I hope is a bit

more relaxing holiday for Arthur for ten days. Such a great deal has happened in Australia in our absence—an election, a contest for the leadership of the Liberal Party, naval visits—that it will take us a while to grasp all of these developments and events.

November 30, 1969 · *en route from Montreal*

A » We are on our way back to Australia after two and a half months in Canada; it's three months since I left August 26 for Djakarta and other Asian capitals on my way home.

The preparation of my paper on "Canada and the Pacific," one of the studies making up the "Review of Canadian Foreign Policy," involved a lot of co-ordination of material relating to Canadian interests in the Pacific, from Japan to Australia, and from trade promotion to cultural relations. I benefited from updating my knowledge and also from learning something of the style of the new Trudeau administration. Of course there were the added dividends of catching up with friends and relatives, so that we feel we have really put ourselves back in touch with Canada and its affairs after four years away.

December 4, 1969 · *Malaga, Spain*

A » Our six-hour Air Canada trip across the Atlantic was uneventful. We were surprised to find snow on the ground when we arrived in England. We moved through passport control and customs very easily, got one of those high-backed cabs, and made our way to the Cumberland Hotel, Marble Arch. Kenneth arrived as he said he would at 9:30 Monday morning and took his mother shopping while I went to talk for an hour to Arnold Smith, Secretary-General of the Commonwealth, mainly about the emerging territories in the South Pacific. Then Sheila, Ken, and I went to Grosvenor Square for lunch and much natter about the Department, with Louis Rogers, our Deputy High Commissioner, and his wife June. After lunch, I went to Australia House and called on Bill Boswell, Acting High Commissioner, whom I knew well in Canberra as secretary of the Department of National Development, and Bill Pritchett, Deputy High Commissioner representing External Affairs.

About 4:30 p.m. Sheila, Ken, and I joined forces at the Cumberland, took our bags by cab to Liverpool Street Station, and spent two hours going to Frinton-on-Sea, Essex, northeast-by-east of London, past Colchester. Frinton is a genteel upper-middle-class seaside resort and retiring place with very attractive homes. Five Canadians and one Turk share a big house. We ate at about 9:30 and chatted until midnight. It was cold and bleak, so that even with a hot-water bottle Sheila did not sleep well. Next day Ken took us by bus (a half-hour trip) to Essex University, a new university whose current enrolment is 1,400, but is expected to rise to 10,000 by 1975. It is in the country, about three miles from Colchester. The students are as unconventional in hairstyle and dress as at any Canadian university. We looked over the buildings and then went to Colchester, visited the old Norman castle, now a museum, and returned to Frinton by train. Another late dinner and late talk. Then up at 7:30 Wednesday, December 3, to return to London. Ken accompanied us to the West London Air Terminal.

It was wonderful to see Kenneth again after a gap of two and a half years, to see his setup, meet his friends, visit his university, and mainly talk about his thesis and his future plans. We can now visualize his environment better.

Wednesday noon we flew to Madrid and took a connecting flight to Malaga on the south coast of Spain. There Janet Skelton, the widow of Sheila's brother Alexander Skelton, was waiting for us. We came to the Hotel California, where Janet was staying, and where Madame Garcia made us feel most welcome.

Today, December 4, the sun was shining in a clear blue sky and the temperature was around 60 degrees. We rented a little Simca 1000 drive-yourself car and started out about 10:30, driving back through Malaga and westward toward Gibraltar. The Costa del Sol has gained considerable recent popularity, so that many eight- to fifteen-storey apartment buildings are being put up to cater for winter and summer visitors, many of whom want to get away from the cold or the clouds that enshroud Western Europe in winter.

We drove out through Malaga (population 400,000) to Torre-molinos, Fuengirola, and Marbella to San Pedro de Alcantara. I got pinched there for going through a red light I didn't see; I was fined a hundred pesetas ($1.60) on the spot. We stopped to take stock and to have lunch. Janet and I had a paella, a dish of saffron rice with oysters, shellfish, shrimp, chicken, etc., all stewed together. Then we drove back to Los Boliches and visited Janet's flat, which is quite charming, in a big complex of apartment buildings around a swimming pool half a mile from the sea. We had done some shopping before and left at about 5:00 p.m. to return to Malaga.

We have breakfast at 6:45 a.m. tomorrow and fly at 8:00 to Madrid, where we stay much of the day, lunch with Gerry Hardy, our ambassador, and his wife Thérèse, and fly on to Rome in the evening.

We are very glad to have seen Janet's setup. She is well located and comfortable, if a bit on her own.

December 6, 1969 · *Rome*

A » We had a good day in Madrid yesterday. We were met at the airport by a young third secretary, Kerry Campbell, and driven to the embassy residence, a big old mansion that belonged to a Spanish marquis. We were cordially received by Gerry and Thérèse Hardy, who moved to Madrid just three months ago from London, where he was deputy high commissioner. After a cup of tea we went off to tour the Royal Palace, an enormous place of 1,200 rooms built in 1738. We started, somewhat inadvertently, on a two-hour tour through the vast apartments, a dining room seating 140, the throne room, etc. The marble floors, the wall adornments, the chandeliers, the ceiling paintings, the furniture, and the fancy clocks were quite amazing. One felt a sense of recent habitation, because Alphonso XIII was just ousted by Franco in 1931, and the latter still uses the palace on state occasions. We saw some very fine collections of tapestries going back to the fifteenth century, paintings by Spanish and European masters, and a vault containing the Spanish crown jewels. The palace was chilly, which did not help Sheila's cold.

We had a pleasant lunch and chat with Gerry and Thérèse Hardy at the residence, then went off to visit the Prado, a great art gallery. We hired a guide who could speak French to give us a quick one-hour selective tour. They have some wonderful paintings, rooms full of Goya, Velasquez, Rubens, Van Dyck, Titian, and others. We saw a lot of paintings that were done as the basis for some of the tapestries we had seen hanging in the palace.

Later we went to look at a department store and shops. Madrid is a big sophisticated city of three million people. Shops are open 9:00 to 1:00 and 4:30 to 8:30. There is a long siesta. Dinners are at 10:00 or 11:00 p.m. The traffic moved very slowly to the airport road. We came on to Rome by Ethiopian Airlines.

As we came into the city we passed the Forum, the Colosseum, the monument to Victor Emmanuel, the Quirinal Palace, etc. We have not been out this morning, as we wanted to rest before our long flight to Singapore, which leaves 3:00 p.m. Saturday and arrives 12 noon Sunday.

December 14, 1969

A » We had twenty officers attending the annual staff meeting this year. We seem to have a very good group of officers here now, well qualified and keen and personable. In the next year we hope to sell a nuclear reactor to Australia worth $100 million, take part in the Captain Cook Bicentenary Celebrations, and, in May, have a visit from Prime Minister Trudeau.

SIX

1970

January 11, 1970

s » I will try to start the New Year right by getting back to the weekend carbon-copy letter system. What with our trip to Canada and then our holiday in New Zealand it seems quite a while since we were in a routine here. I must say it is taking some time to get our heads above the piles of work, correspondence, and essentials that have accumulated here in our absence.

Anyway, we should come back at full steam, because the time in New Zealand was really a holiday. We were there as tourists, not officials, and it was pleasant for a change not to be on a schedule, and not to have to make speeches. It's a rainy climate, but we were most fortunate to have had good weather all the time except for two days—Christmas Day in Wellington it rained and blew a bad storm, and the last day at Te Anau we had to take a bus 110 miles to Queenstown to catch our plane, because there was fog from the lake at Te Anau. Otherwise it was good summer weather, and because it has been cold and raining in Canberra it was a good time to be away.

The day we got back—Monday the 5th, at 12:30—was also the day that house guests, Mr. and Mrs. Jim Miller from the Canadian International Development Agency, arrived. He worked in the External Aid office when Arthur filled in there for six months after Malaya, and is now head of their Project Development and Coordination Division. His wife, Joyce, is an Australian, originally from Leeton, then Sydney, and in the twenty years they have been married she has been fortunate enough to get back to Australia eight times. (They have been lucky in the stock market, and have no children.) We knew them fairly well before, but of course now that we have had them stay with us for three days we are much better acquainted, and enjoyed them.

A » When we were in Canberra for nine days before Christmas I didn't really have time to get caught up. Now Allan Roger is away looking after the Canadian Patterns Exhibit at Surfers Paradise for three weeks so I've got extra work to do here as well as trying to keep in touch with what is happening to my report back in Canada. It has been sent out to government departments and posts abroad for comments, and I hope it will stir up some constructive discussion. That's its purpose. I am to go back to Canada in February or March for discussion with business and academic groups. The dates for the various meetings have not yet been decided in Ottawa so I can't plan my trip yet.

Jim Miller's visit to Canberra gave us another occasion to talk with the Australians about our respective procedures in giving development assistance in Southeast Asia. He had two full days of talks here and I took part in some of them. We also gave a dinner for officials.

February 1, 1970

S » I will type the weekend letter this time, because I want to have the study tidy for the men to use tonight after the dinner for former Canadian Minister of National Defence Paul Hellyer. Arthur has gone fishing up at Lake Eucumbene for the weekend and will return before the dinner, but with not too much time to spare if I know him. Harry Horne, our commercial counsellor from Sydney, is one of the other six men on this expedition, but he is staying up with the main party and returning late tonight. He will sleep here and return to Sydney tomorrow. We are only going to have a small group for dinner, including the Minister for Defence and Mrs. Frazier, the permanent Secretary of External Affairs, Sir James Plimsoll, who has just been appointed Australian ambassador to Washington, and Sir Ken Bailey, former Australian high commissioner in Ottawa, and Lady Bailey. We are having a turkey that Edith won at bowling last weekend and I bought from her.

We went to a big reception in honour of Australia Day given by Mr. McMahon, the new Minister of External Affairs, and his wife. If they had been certain of the weather it would have been held outdoors in the courtyard of Parliament House, but with clouds threatening rain, they moved indoors—and it was stifling hot!

Thursday night we gave a dinner in honour of the Whites, the National Librarian and his wife, who live just across the road from us. He was knighted in the last honours list, and although they had received congratulations from around the world, I think we were the only ones who gave a dinner in their honour, and that tickled them. Art made a little speech, and Sir Harold replied at length. He was in a reminiscing mood, and spoke of his dream of the new National Library building here, and of the various Canadian high commissioners who had been their neighbours. (Just yesterday I was catching up reading old issues of *The Ottawa Journal* and read of the death of Colin Fraser Elliott in December at the age of eighty-one. He was here after Chile, and was a good friend of Mom and Dad.) Oh yes—after Harold's speech, Elizabeth made a little speech too—and no, I did not feel called upon to continue....

February 8, 1970

A » I have now made the reservations for my return flight to Canada. I will leave February 21, spend three days in Fiji to talk to people about the impending Independence there, and arrive in Vancouver Tuesday night, February 24. I am to address a closed meeting of the Canadian Exporters Association there on the 25th or 26th, and for the weekend I'll go on to a seminar in Victoria run by the Canadian Institute of International Affairs. Then I'll head east to Ottawa, but my timetable is not set yet. I have no fixed time of return, but it should be toward the end of March. When more definite plans develop I'll let you know.

Evan and Do Gill, our predecessors here from 1962 to 1965, have been here for a week. He works for a mining company with a property in Western Australia. We gave a dinner for them Thursday night.

Honourable Paul Hellyer, who as minister of National Defence unified the Canadian Armed Forces, was minister of Transport from 1967 to 1969, and resigned from the Cabinet because he thought the federal government should assume more responsibility for housing, visited Canberra Sunday and Monday. Our dinner for him last Sunday night went well, and I kept him busy all day Monday, with a lunch at noon. We found him agreeable, modest, and intelligent.

A select committee from the New Guinea House of Assembly has been here for talks with the government. They would like greater ministerial responsibility in Port Moresby and control over the forty-five percent of their expenditures that they raise in taxes there. I met them in a reception; some of them I had met before, up there.

February 15, 1970

s » What a week of visitors! I spent all Tuesday escorting General and Mrs. Clark around the sights of Canberra. He commanded the Canadian troops at Vimy Ridge so is in his 80s now, but he's very spry. He was also once an MP, and head of the Canadian Bar Association, so even though they were here as tourists and he didn't bother to get in touch with us until they were right in Canberra, one cannot disregard people like that. On Friday I did the same tour, only more, for Mr. and Mrs. Leonard Walker. He's president of the Bank of Montreal. If I'm ever out of a job I will apply to a travel or tourist guide agency.

February 20, 1970

a » I lunched during the week with E.E. Payne, first assistant secretary in the Department of the Interior in charge of government and social affairs in the Northern Territory. He had spent three weeks in the Canadian North and was struck by the similarity in the problems, although the climate differs.

February 21, 1970 · *en route from Sydney to Fiji by CPAir*

A » I must begin by apologizing for being so badly organized before departure that I didn't allow a suitable amount of time for leave-taking. Then the ten-minute advance on the scheduled departure time came as a bit of a shock.

Harry and Pat Horne were at the International Terminal in Sydney. We talked about Prime Minister Trudeau's visit, trade, etc., then they had to leave for a dinner.

Eric Birdsall, the CPAir manager in Sydney, had signalled my plans, so I have been well treated on board.

February 24, 1970 · *Nadi, Fiji*

A » I'm back at the Mocambo in Nadi awaiting my Qantas plane for Honolulu. I've had a busy but useful two days of talks.

I made a series of calls on the Chief Minister, the Governor, the opposition leader, businessmen, etc. I visited the Legislative Council and had tea with Mr. Speaker. The Chief Minister gave a reception for me to meet his cabinet, and Bob Birch, the Australian Commissioner, gave a lunch. Also, Mr. Adu of Ghana, the Deputy Secretary-General of the Commonwealth, was visiting, and we had dinner together last night and a good chat.

This afternoon I visited the University of the South Pacific. It is just beginning its third year and has 462 students, including seventy-five from the South Pacific islands. They are in some old RNZAF buildings and haven't too much money. I'd like to see us give them some help. Kenneth's friend Dr. Ron Crocombe is there teaching Pacific History.

February 26, 1970 · *Hotel Vancouver*

A » I arrived in Vancouver yesterday, and this evening I was picked up and taken to the Vancouver Club, where about thirty men had assembled, organized by Hon. J.V. Clyne of MacMillan Bloedel. We had drinks and a nice dinner. I talked for about half an hour. Then they questioned me and I got some expression of views from them. Everyone expressed surprise at the extent of my knowledge of Pacific affairs and seemed genuinely appreciative.

February 28, 1970 · *Victoria, British Columbia*

A » We have finished a day and a half of seminar. There are about thirty attending, including, from External, the Minister, Honourable Mitchell Sharp, Collins, Seaborn, Brett, Larry Smith, and Ken Williamson, representatives of several other departments, academics, and businessmen. The group has been small enough to permit considerable free interchange of views. My paper has fared well so far.

The weather has been fine and mild, up to 50 degrees during the day, with crocuses, daffodils, cherry blossoms, and a few rhododendrons. We have been staying at the Empress Hotel, with all its charm and too little time to enjoy it. Our meetings are half an hour away at Royal Roads. There is a lovely Japanese garden there that I recalled from my 1964 visit.

March 1, 1970 · *Vancouver*

A » I'm writing this letter in the Vancouver airport at 12:30 noon, awaiting a connecting flight to Toronto and Ottawa. It is still lovely weather here, with a temperature of about 50 degrees, bright sun, and lots of spring flowers. Indications are it will be cold in the East, so I will have my rubbers and overcoat on.

I think that the conference or seminar went well. There were not enough businessmen and too many civil servants. The academics were not too impressive. David Corbett did well; so did Kavic (who used to work for me in Far East Division, later married an Australian, and is now an academic). We had our windup session this morning, and were able to get quite useful expressions of views on the options. I am delighted that the Minister was present throughout to hear views and take such an active part in discussions.

I understand that the requirement now is for a thirty-page publishable summary to go with Geoff Murray's overall review of Canadian foreign policy. In addition I will try to get as many thoughts into Prime Minister Trudeau's speeches in Australia as I can.

March 1, 1970

s » Wednesday evening I was the speaker at the first meeting this year of the Pan Pacific and South East Asia Women's Association. About fifty or sixty attended, which is about twice their usual number, so I was pleased. The meeting part dragged on, then I spoke on Canada for about twenty minutes, mostly background about Trudeau because of interest in his coming visit to Australia. Then we had two films—or we should have. Actually the projector played up, and the chap from the office who was the projectionist had to rush back to the office for another machine. We had tea in the interval instead of at the end, which worked out all right. I must say I prefer talking in small centres outside Canberra where I do not know people in the audience, rather than looking down at all sorts of people I recognize and who are much more accomplished speakers than I am. At least that is over for another year. I spoke to them the first year I was here, when I was on the committee. Friday morning the PPSEAWA had a small coffee party to meet an interesting visitor, Faletua Taualofa, the wife of the secretary-general of the South Pacific Commission, Afioga Afoafouvale Misimoa, from Western Samoa. She is twenty-nine and he is seventy. It was her first time outside Samoa and New Caledonia. As I am supposed to have a good memory I was given the job of introducing her to the members as they came in—just those first two names, I never could have learned the rest! She was very charming, and made a little thank-you speech for the flowers she was given that was most sincere and well-spoken, with a few tears! Of course I told her about Kenneth's three months with the South Pacific Commission. I had a big surprise this morning when I walked into an exhibition of Sabah and Sarawak photographs put on by a friend of ours, and the lady handing out programs said, "You are Mrs. Menzies. I taught Kenneth in Kuala Lumpur." She was a Mrs. Daroesman. Talk about a good memory for her pupils!

March 2, 1970 · *Ottawa*

A » It is 11:40 p.m. I've just come in from a dinner that Mr. Sharp gave for the Foreign Minister of Thailand, Thanat Khoman, at 7 Rideau Gate. The atmosphere was nice, and there was a good dinner, contributed to by Mrs. Blair. Sharp was hung up in a cabinet meeting and so was fifteen minutes late, but we managed to delay the Thai Foreign Minister. After dinner there was a good talk about Thailand in Southeast Asia, half in English and half in French—I put my foot into it by referring to the *demi-monde de neutralisme.* André Bissonnette drove me home. He has his troubles, inherited from Marcel Cadieux and not yet taken over by Paul Tremblay, regarding Quebec representation at one of these educational conferences.

March 5, 1970 · *Ottawa*

A » I'm starting this note to you while waiting for my train to start for Montreal, where I am to speak at noon at the Queen Elizabeth Hotel to about ninety at a luncheon meeting of the Canadian Export Association.

We had freezing sleet yesterday afternoon, which made the homeward trek treacherous. A couple of inches of wet snow fell overnight. There are still great piles of snow about and most streets have three inches of ice on the sidewalks. It isn't too cold, about 25 or 30 degrees, but it's not melting yet.

March 10, 1970 · *Ottawa*

A » Had a useful talk with Dr. Lorne Gray, President of AECL, regarding the nuclear reactor. As a result I will lunch with key deputy ministers next Tuesday to discuss a submission to Cabinet. I'm preparing a separate paper.

Sharp accepted all my Fiji recommendations, so there will be some extra drafting.

March 15, 1970 · *Toronto airport*

A » I had a good long weekend in Toronto and with family in Burlington and Lucknow, and am now en route back to Ottawa. I flew down Thursday afternoon, registered at the Royal York, and showered and changed in time to make the Toronto Club at 6:30. About thirty senior officers and companies interested in Australia were assembled. After dinner I talked for half an hour and then the discussion went on until 11:30. It was a good session and I think I did well.

Friday morning I was picked up by a Gerry O'Sullivan of AECL and driven out to Pickering to see the four 500 MW nuclear power reactors being built there for Ontario Hydro. It is a tremendous place, with enormously complicated engineering and electrical work. I am humbled in a place like that by the foresight that must be exercised by the design engineers. It was useful to see the plant and get the rundown to help in our job in Australia.

I had lunch with John Holmes, then went to the museum, where James Hsü is making good progress in his work on Father's collection of ancient Chinese oracle bones. He expects to have a volume of rubbings ready for publication by December and a book of interpretative comments, etc., in the next few months. I was well pleased.

March 19, 1970 · *Ottawa*

A » My paper is coming on rather better now than before; problems now relate more to form in relation to other parts of Prime Minister Trudeau's foreign policy review project, and what things the Minister wants to go firm on. The Minister wants the material over Easter. I hope to be finished in time to return over Easter weekend. I can't say more now, as I just have to get the report finished and cleared in the Department before that.

later:

I hope to circulate the first draft of my paper to about ten people in the Department tomorrow so that they can look at it over the weekend. I hope to have a revised edition about ready by Wednesday or Thursday, and then escape. However, much will depend on reactions from management, because this paper presents recommendations, not options. I stuck my neck out in the hope that at least some of the recommendations will be accepted by political masters wishing to create a new image for themselves in the Pacific. If I get some accepted I'll feel elated, and that the work has been worth it; if not ... well, I tried.

March 23, 1970 · *Ottawa*

A » I finished a draft of my report and circulated it to about a dozen in the Department on Friday afternoon. I wasn't entirely satisfied, but I wanted to finish up. Ed Ritchie said it was a good paper and made only minor drafting clarifications. I spent Saturday p.m. going over it with Ralph Collins, and we did some rearranging of sections that I think was useful. I'm expecting their comments today. I hope to finish up by Wednesday, as the Minister wants it Friday.

March 30, 1970

S » Hurrah, three cheers, and a hiccup—Arthur got back safe and sound at 12:30 today. He is looking well, is now catching up on a bit of lost sleep, and says he will be happy to go to the Thai Ballet tonight. It certainly is good to have him back after five weeks and two days away. Actually I had expected him at 3:00 p.m., so was surprised to receive a phone call from the airport at 12:15 saying he was on a plane due in fifteen minutes. Without changing from slacks, etc., I made it by the back roads just in time. I am so glad he did not dally around Sydney for the scheduled flight.

A » My return by way of Mexico was a great success, with a night and a chatty breakfast with the Canadian Ambassador and Mrs. Saul Rae in Mexico City and two full days with my brother-in-law Herbert Skelton and Daisy at their winter home on Lake Chapala. The weather was gorgeous and the flowers superb and the whole stay very relaxing. We drove to visit local villages and to the far side of the lake, saw Good Friday services in the local church, and spent half a day in Guadalajara with its lovely old cathedral, Spanish-style government buildings, colourful Libertad market, and modern stores and office buildings and hotels. After Herb and Daisy dropped me at the airport I was able to catch an earlier plane to Acapulco and spent three hours wandering about the Waikiki Beach-type resort with its enormous hotels. The flight to Sydney by Qantas took sixteen hours plus time on the ground in Tahiti and Fiji. Naturally I'm glad to be back to sunny Canberra.

April 5, 1970

A » I was relieved and pleased to learn from Ottawa on Thursday that the Minister "had reacted very favourably" to my report on "Canada and the Pacific," and directed that it be distributed to other ministers for early discussion in Cabinet. So that is one hurdle negotiated.

Saturday Sheila and I went with Ron and Claire Stapledon to the Yass Show, about forty miles away. There are a couple of hundred such country shows in New South Wales alone. This one had riding events, cattle and sheep judging, fleece judging, fruit, vegetable, and cooking displays, a dog show with over four hundred entries, a bird show, Highland dancing, marching girls, etc. We were received by the president and had lunch. Afterwards I officially opened the show with a short speech, which didn't carry well because of echo from the loudspeakers. We spent the afternoon looking at the exhibits. It was a lovely sunny day!

April 14, 1970

s » Monday, Tuesday, and Wednesday last week we were in Gipps-
land, an area in Victoria along the Bass Strait, about one hundred
miles east of Melbourne. This is the constituency of Peter Nixon,
the Country Party member who is in the cabinet as Minister of the
Interior. It is primarily a dairy farming area, and he owns a large
farm there. His office had made the program arrangements for us
in connection with the local Rotary Clubs of Sale and Traralgon,
two of the chief towns. We were met in Melbourne by a Commonwealth car and driver, so we got a good idea of the area as we drove
out—and then we came back by a different, more scenic route. The
country looked much greener than around Canberra, and in parts
has irrigation farming, which makes it very valuable. Arthur had to
give short speeches at civic receptions in the two towns, and he was
the major speaker at the Rotary International Night dinner. The
audience was more sophisticated than they often are. They seemed
to be interested in Canada, and asked good questions. We had a
good tour of various industries in the area—the Esso gas and oil
works, where some Canadians are conducting a training program,
a State Electricity works based on brown coal, of which there is a
vast deposit mined in an open pit nearby, a large Australian Paper
Mill, which makes paper from a combination of pine and eucalyptus, and a large farm property. Art also had a half-day in our trade
office in Melbourne on our way home, and I had a half-day to shop
in Melbourne—I bought a new dress for one of the umpteen functions during the visits of the Queen and Trudeau.

We were back only two days before we left on Saturday for the
Sydney trip. On arrival in the p.m. we visited the display devoted
to Captain Cook in the Mitchell Library. This bicentenary of
Cook's landing has made every Australian man, woman, child,
and every conceivable organization Cook-conscious, and all sorts
of exhibitions and memorials are planned in his honour. This
spurt of interest in the past is a similar to the one we had in
Canada during our centenary year and Expo. Then when you add
the Queen's visit to Australia, it means that things everywhere are
decorated, spruced up with new buildings, or refurbished. All in

all things look really attractive, especially if there is sunshine and good weather. Saturday evening we went to the Hornes' for drinks with the members of an Ontario trade mission, and then on to the Sydney Golf Club for a dinner in honour of Dr. Malcolm Brown, chairman of the Canadian Medical Research Council (he went to Queen's with me), and Mrs. Brown. He is in Australia to give some lectures. The guests were mostly medical people we did not know. Sunday we were very interested to drive up to Concord, on the Parramatta highway, for the Centenary Mass at St. Mary's Concord, which was celebrated out on the oval in the centre of town in 80-degree temperature. Several thousand parishioners were present. There was a cardinal, many archbishops and bishops, all sorts of lesser religious dignitaries, choirs, politicians such as Mr. Whitlam, Leader of the Opposition, whose constituency is next door, and local government officials. We were special guests of honour, because the Canadian exiles from the Papineau Rebellion in Lower Canada who were shipped out to Australia had served their time in that area, and Mass had been celebrated for them on the oval in 1840, so that the early church there had connections with them before the St. Mary's church was built. Thanks to the Archives in Canada and the National Library here, an exhibit of historical documents and pictures related to the Canadian rebels had been set up in the church hall. It was really as a result of Arthur's initiative that our participation in this event was arranged, and, what's more, he has been able to have an expedition to this area included in Mr. Trudeau's rushed itinerary. Mr. Trudeau will unveil a plaque in memory of the Canadian exiles when he's out here next month.

April 19, 1970

s » This week was climaxed by a buffet-style dinner at the office last night in honour of the Canadian delegates and their wives who have been attending the Combined Orthopaedic Conference (Australia, New Zealand, U.K., U.S.A., Canada, and South Africa), the opening of which we attended in Sydney last weekend. As always it was very difficult to get definite information on the plans of delegates until the very last minute. We had twenty-three Canadians, six Americans, another dozen Australian doctors and delegates, and a dozen people from our Canadian office. I had small tables for six set up in the basement of the chancery, enough for fifty-four, but the actual count was forty-nine. Edith had put a lot of work into the preparation of hot dishes as well as cold salads and warm apple pie and cheese. Oh yes—and a cup of chicken soup upstairs first. What's troublesome is not so much the preparation, it is the transporting of every piece of equipment and cutlery, and the borrowing and returning of everything from the office. Anyway, Arthur made a speech of about ten minutes on the work of the high commission that was well received, and Dr. F.P. Dewar of Toronto, the leader of the Canadian delegation, responded.

A » At the office we have been paying special attention to Dick Guthrie and his efforts to persuade the Australian Navy to buy UACL gas turbine engines worth $50 million for their new destroyers. We have heard that Rolls-Royce has got the nod, but have left no stone unturned in our effort to push the Canadian product. On Tuesday, Weiser gave a lunch that featured Mr. Killen, the Minister for the Navy, and on Thursday Magee gave a reception for officials.

Sheila and I gave a lunch on Friday for Dr. and Mrs. Malcolm Brown; he is chairman of the Canadian Medical Research Council, and is out here to talk to his Australian opposite numbers. He told me that we spend over six times as much as the Australians on medical research. Wednesday evening we went to a dinner given by Sir John Crawford, Vice-Chancellor of the Australian National University, and Lady Crawford.

I think I have told you that we are trying hard to sell a nuclear power reactor to Australia. On Monday Dr. Archie Aiken, general manager of Nuclear Power Marketing for Atomic Energy of Canada, was in town, and I gave a lunch for him and officers of the Prime Minister's department. We had a long afternoon of discussions afterwards. This is a subject that will be discussed during our Prime Minister's visit.

Wednesday evening we attended a dinner given by Senator and

Mrs. Gordon Davidson of South Australia, whom we have known quite well for some time. Afterwards I went into the House of Representatives to hear the Prime Minister make his announcement about the withdrawal of one battalion of Australian troops from Vietnam, in keeping with President Nixon's announcement of the withdrawal of 150,000 over the next twelve months.

Last Monday evening, while Sheila went dutifully to French, I went to a piano duet concert at the German embassy—very good.

April 26, 1970

s » We are just in from the British government's official handing over of the carillon tower and bells to the Australian people. The Queen unveiled a plaque commemorating the fiftieth anniversary of the founding of Canberra in 1913. (Things take a little time to materialize here.) The carillon is on the tiny island in Lake Burley Griffin. The only trouble was that we were seated in the shade, and a bitter wind was blowing off the lake. Yesterday afternoon in glorious sunshine and not so much wind there was a more spectacular event, also focused on the tiny lake: the Queen pushed a button that activated a device modelled on a Swiss one in Geneva that can send a jet of water 450 feet in the air. There was a host of little sailboats with coloured sails all around, and the spray from the jet made a rainbow that was very effective. All this is Canberra's memorial in honour of the bicentenary of Captain Cook. Because it was a Saturday, and because Anzac Day is a public holiday, there was a splendid turnout of an estimated ten thousand Canberra people, on stands specially built for the occasion. I must commend the speeches at both yesterday's and today's functions: none was more than three minutes. At the War Memorial in the morning, wreaths were laid by the Queen and Philip, by the Prime Minister and the New Zealand High Commissioner (jointly, as is the custom, to mark the Anzac tradition), and by the other high commissioners. We have never seen half as large a turnout in any of the other four Anzac services we have attended since coming here.

To go back to the beginning of the Queen's visit to Canberra:

she arrived Thursday p.m., and, as had been her poor luck on her arrival in several other Australian cities, the usual good weather broke, and it was most uncertain during the day—not bad enough to call off the ceremonies, but worsening rapidly in the hour before arrival, so that we were sitting on open stands at the airfield with raincoats and umbrellas, all rather a sorry sight. But the Queen is a good public relations person: she went and spoke to the crowd all along the ramparts in spite of the weather. That night at Parliament House there was a glittering reception for 850 people, the men mostly in white ties and all the women in long formal evening dress. Next day we had a good opportunity to see the Queen, Philip, and Princess Anne, because the ten high commissioners were received at Government House at noon, and the men were photographed with her before she met the rest of the diplomatic corps. Of course our most intimate contact with them will be tomorrow, when the ten high commissioners give a joint lunch for them at the New Zealander's. We are leaving for our rehearsal for that in a few minutes. Quite a week to be struggling to find time to fit in Canadian income tax forms as well.

A » Various representatives of the Australian territories have been brought in for the Queen's visit. Friday Sheila and I went to a reception for these people given by the secretary of the Department of External Territories. We had a lunch on Friday for David Hay, Administrator of the Territory of Papua and New Guinea, and his wife Allison. We have known them for twenty years.

On Friday, Mr. Albert Henry, the Premier of the Cook Islands, a New Zealand dependency, came to call and gave me some idea of how Islanders feel about the need for a forum to discuss political relations. That night we took the Barrie Dexters to see the Ballet of the South Pacific, which combined austere, serious Australian Aboriginal dances with gay Cook Island Maori dances.

May 3, 1970

S » Canberra weather fluctuates between glorious fall days and, when there is a wind, rather nasty, cold, bitter days. Two weeks ago, we were able to convince all the orthopaedic surgeons that this was the most ideal place on earth, but then last weekend, with the Queen in the city, things were really grim—either raining most of the time, or threatening to rain, or cold. And, women being women, it was comical, especially at the royal garden party of 3,500 people at Government House, to see some really shivering in floppy straw garden-party hats and silk and satin ensembles, while those in fur coats (of which I have never seen a wider range in Canberra before) and the odd maxi coat or dashing woollen pantsuit, were really comfortable. At the Duntroon Military College parade in the morning, at which the Queen presented new colours to the College, I wore my lined Canadian snow boots and got by with them easily.

Of course the event we were most concerned with in the Royal Tour was the lunch given by the ten high commissioners at the home of the senior one, who is from New Zealand. Ten flagpoles were erected in front, and the ten national flags flew outside for that one day only. All went smoothly. We ate at two tables. I was beside Prime Minister Gorton and Art beside Mrs. G. (they were the only Australians present). We had a simple menu of avocado pear, a chicken pie with a flaky crust and a sort of soufflé sauce and tomatoes and asparagus, and then a fresh pineapple ring on cake as dessert. I wore my purple (the royal colour) and green Thai silk check that I got for our national day last year.

This weekend again has been excellent fall weather. We were fortunate to have an expedition in the country. (Actually, with Trudeau preparations on his plate Art is very busy, but there was little choice.) Mr. and Mrs. Litchfield, who entertained Mr. Pearson when he was here, are going abroad this month, and insisted that we come before they left; they also invited the Mexican ambassador and his wife. So we drove the seventy miles up toward the Snowy Mountains, past Cooma, to visit their property, a mere 12,000 acres, including a prize merino stud place and some cattle as well. They have the money to maintain the whole place well. We saw rams with wonderful fleece being prepared for the Melbourne show, and some ewes too, and were shown around the wool shed, etc. We enjoyed a lovely lunch out on their patio, which is topped with a trellis of ornamental grapevine, still a lovely red, and some green leaves of wisteria that must be pretty at a different time of year.

Back here, in the evening, we attended the sixteenth national Eisteddfod, because for the first time the local Australian-Canadian Association of Canberra offered a prize for a choir singing one Canadian and one Australian folk song. A committee spurred on by Allan and Gene Roger went to a lot of trouble to get the Canadian music and make it available to the schools, etc., and also to design a unique trophy that incorporates an Eskimo carving the ACA bought. Eight choirs were entered, most consisting of about fifty high school pupils, and all but one of which was from the immediate Canberra area. The winning choir was from a suburb of Sydney. Their standard was very high, and their renderings of whichever of the three Canadian songs they chose—"The Canadian Boat Song," "Alouette," or "A Frog He Would a-Wooing Go"—were really most impressive. It was a good venture. Art—up on the stage along with the president of the ACA and Gene Roger—presented the prizes before a packed hall, with people in the aisles and the balcony.

May 10, 1970

s » Arthur has been frightfully busy with the Trudeau visit preparations, as you can imagine. We have had all sorts of crises and problems, which will be amusing in retrospect—after a few months—but are not very amusing now. He is at the office this Sunday morning, but will take enough time off this afternoon to play some tennis with the New Zealand High Commissioner and his wife. Arthur is going to fly to New Zealand to meet the Trudeau party in Christchurch and fly back on the plane with them to Australia, though he will not be stopping off in Brisbane, where Trudeau will get off for a private holiday weekend of scuba diving on the Barrier Reef with Mr. Gorton and a select few, but will continue on with the main planeload of officials to Sydney, and back here for a dinner for officials on Saturday, then back to Sydney next Sunday to meet Trudeau again and begin the official part of the visit on Monday morning.

Also, Art is going on the plane to Darwin next Wednesday with the Prime Minister's party and will stay on for a while in the Northern Territory.

May 16, 1970

s » I will type the weekend letter a day early so that Arthur can see it before he takes off again tomorrow for Sydney. He got back last evening from the flight to New Zealand to meet the Trudeau party and immediately went with the other Canadian officials to their hotel and then out to the Carousel Restaurant for dinner. Today, Saturday, they started a round of meetings with Australian officials at 8:30 a.m. They will end with a stag dinner tonight for twelve: Canadians Gordon Robertson, Clerk of the Privy Council and Secretary to Cabinet; Ed Ritchie, Under-Secretary of State for External Affairs; Dr. Lorne Gray, President of Atomic Energy of Canada; Allan Roger; and Art, and Australians such as Ken Bailey, former High Commissioner to Canada; David McNicol, present High Commissioner to Canada; Sir Arthur Tange, Secretary of the Department of Defence; and Sir John Bunting, Secretary of the Cabinet, etc. etc.

Tomorrow, Sunday, we will take Gordon Robertson and Ed Ritchie for a morning drive around Canberra and go to the Rogers' for lunch before they board a plane at three for Sydney.

There was a lot of unexpected drama yesterday, because the Gorton Government had an unexpected vote of confidence brought against it on its handling of offshore mining rights, so Mr. Gorton could not fly to Brisbane for the weekend on the Barrier Reef and talks with Trudeau (Mrs. Gorton did go). After twelve hours of debate, the Government rallied enough support to achieve a majority of six. The best-laid plans of mice and men do not take into account such unforeseen political crises. You should see the eight pages of instructions I have just received headed "Order of Arrangements Arrival at Canberra Airport." If I don't know when to stand at point A and move to point B and shake hands with Gorton or Trudeau and get into car number 3 at

1.37 minutes, etc., it will not be the officials' fault. The preparation that goes into one of these tours is fantastic.

Besides the tree-planting ceremony by Mr. Trudeau at the office, which affords us the chance to get some of the Canadians involved, he will be on the property for just forty-five minutes, and in the building only thirty minutes of that, so you can see how quick it will all be. We are now having drinks and a snack here at the residence on Tuesday night, before the big government reception at Parliament House, at which they expect between eight hundred and a thousand. We were allowed to suggest the names of a few Canadians from Sydney and Melbourne who might be included in the reception, so felt we ought to entertain these out-of-towners and at least give them a chance to meet Canadian officials, even if their chances of meeting Trudeau are slim. We could not organize this until yesterday, because no one knew until then who was going to the small dinner the Prime Minister is giving before the reception.

I have just been to the florist to get the flowers I ordered. From our own garden we have enough floribunda roses for the dinner table tonight, but I now also have a tall vase with maple leaves—nice and red still, though most on the trees have turned brown and withered. They are Japanese maples, not Canadian as I had a month ago, but at least they add colour, and then I have seven large white mums and three bright red gladioli—Canadian colours—arranged in my pottery boat. We will use them here, on Monday at the office, and then back here on Tuesday—so I'll get my money's worth!

May 20, 1970 · *Darwin*

A » This is written at 10:20 p.m. The trip was uneventful. We had very good briefing portfolios, prepared according to Bob Swift's directions. However, many in the party were beginning to think ahead to Malaysia. I'm not sure how well Mr. Nixon held Mr. Trudeau's attention. The tour here was perfunctory. I'm sure Mr. Chaney, Administrator of the Northern Territory, meant well, but we saw nothing of real interest. It was a refuelling stop only.

All aboard said they appreciated our efforts. I'm glad we didn't try to overwrite the briefs.

Ritchie told me there was no proposal up yet about our next posting. He said we should plan on 6–9–12 months. He couldn't be more precise. I'm satisfied that we rate well.

I leave at 8:30 a.m. to visit the Aboriginal settlement and the bauxite operation at Gove. I have a ticket but no details.

May 24, 1970

s » You can imagine how excited and delighted I was to receive at breakfast this morning the following telegram from Norah: "RE-SULTS TODAY LOVE NORAH MENZIES B.A. BENE PROBATUS."

As she has done better each year in college and has been getting very good results all this year, we were never worried, and are delighted for her that now she has earned the piece of paper that means such a milestone in life. This achievement will mean much for future happiness. When we look back now and see how she has matured, socially and academically, her choice of the University of Ottawa seems to have been a good one.

Said Norah begins a summer job May 25 at the Ottawa General Hospital as a social worker while the regular one has an operation. In these days when students have difficulty finding worthwhile summer jobs she was fortunate to have gotten such a challenging one. As you know, she has been accepted at the University of British Columbia (again her choosing) to do graduate work in social work in September. We're very proud of her.

Trudeau came, saw, was seen, and, more importantly, spoke and was listened to, and made a great impact on Australia in his five days here, especially the two and a half official days in Canberra, where he had the maximum press and TV coverage imaginable. The Australian Broadcasting Corporation carried live both his speech at the National Press Club, which had the greatest turnout in its history, about three hundred people—and they have had such figures as Sir Robert Menzies, Agnew, Prince Philip, President Ky, etc., speaking to them—and also his speech at a parliamentary luncheon for four hundred given by Gorton and the government, with all House representatives and their wives, senators and their wives, and other important officials, including all heads of diplomatic missions.

Tuesday evening he was exposed to the largest crowd—although no speech was involved—at the large government reception for about eight hundred people at Parliament House, which turned into quite a swinging ball, with two bands, one just returned from Expo 70. He stayed right until 1:15, dancing.

On the more serious side, I think Arthur was pleased with the Prime Minister's meeting with the Australian cabinet and Gorton. It was unfortunate that there was a political crisis last weekend and that Gorton did not dare to leave in case there was a non-confidence vote, so he could not make it to the Barrier Reef. But at least Mr. Trudeau had a restful change up there, and in a trip to six countries that is very necessary.

Arthur took advantage of the opportunity to get a lift in Mr. Trudeau's plane to the Northern Territory, where it made a fuelling stop in Darwin before flying on to Kuala Lumpur. He will return to Canberra this Wednesday, May 27. Shortly afterwards, on Friday, we take off together for Nelson Bay for a weekend planned by the local Rotary and Apex clubs. Therefore if you do not get a letter from me next weekend, it will likely be for one or both of two reasons: the impending postal strike in Canada, and my skipping the weekend here.

A » Sheila has reported on the social and public angles of Prime Minister Trudeau's visit to Australia. I thought I might take advantage of my position as a member of the very strong delegation of senior Canadian officials accompanying the Prime Minister to comment on the similarities and differences in perspective between Canada and Australia that were discussed at both the prime-ministerial and the senior official talks. There is a real bond between these two old dominions, and it extends to our relations around the world. But there are also differences, which arise from our distinct geographic locations and the priorities that drive our respective foreign and domestic policies.

I was asked to fly to Christchurch in the South Island of New

Zealand to join the Trudeau party and brief the Prime Minister on the points of agreement and disagreement between Canada and Australia. My views were respected, as the Canadian cabinet had just approved my paper, "Canada and the Pacific," part of Prime Minister Trudeau's review of Canadian foreign policy.

Mr. Trudeau was in good spirits, having just returned from an expedition into the snow-clad New Zealand Alps. He greeted me warmly, recalling our various meetings in the East Block of Parliament in Ottawa. He wanted to re-read the briefings in his large confidential briefing book on the major issues to be discussed, and he also wanted to review the proposed texts of his public statements, so he had only a short time to ask me a few questions.

I told him that Canada's growing interest in the Pacific, which he had spoken about in New Zealand, was very much appreciated in Australia. Canada, as a north Pacific country, looked primarily to Japan and China and Korea. We had been prepared to enter the war against Japan when the atomic bombs were dropped on Hiroshima and Nagasaki. We had been joint members of the Commonwealth Division in the Korean War. Now, seventeen years after the end of the Korean War, the Australians supported the American policy of containment of Communist China, and wanted to protect the status of the Nationalist Government on Taiwan as the representative of China on the Security Council. Although the People's Republic of China was being lashed by the Great Cultural Revolution, I thought that Mr. Trudeau was right to open talks in Stockholm on recognition and the establishment of diplomatic relations, in order to bring Communist China into the comity of nations. I told Mr. Trudeau he would have to tough it out with the Aussies, although, admittedly, the opposition Labor Party supported the Canadian view.

We also have a different position on Vietnam and the whole of Indochina. Canada accepted a role in 1954 on the International Commissions for Supervision and Control in Vietnam, to try to bring a peaceful end to hostilities. Although we were only partially successful, we did achieve a ceasefire and an exchange of prisoners of war, and arranged to have Roman Catholics moved from North to South Vietnam. Now, sixteen years after the ceasefire, the Americans have replaced the French in Vietnam, and Australia has felt constrained to send eight thousand troops to support the Americans. The Australians think that the International Supervisory Commissions should do more to stop Ho Chi Minh's forces. But the Geneva Agreements of 1954 would have to be amended to give the Commissions more real power. Again, Mr. Trudeau should stick to the Canadian approach.

Mr. Trudeau was getting restless, so I said quite briefly that Canada and Australia face similar tariff problems as a result of Britain's entry into the European Common Market. Canada and Australia also need to consult regularly on exports of minerals and agricultural products to Japan to ensure that we are not being played off against each other. Also, we have a nuclear power system to sell to the Australians.

Well, I had held Prime Minister Trudeau's attention for thirty minutes, and feel that I was fortunate to have done so. He went on to read his confidential briefing book and his proposed speech texts.

We left Christchurch at twelve noon on May 15 and arrived in Brisbane, Queensland, at 3:40 p.m. Mr. Trudeau was met there by Mrs. Gorton, Prime Minister Gorton having been held up by a close vote in the House. The Minister of the Army, Andrew Peacock, was a co-host. They flew to Rockhampton in an RAAF BAC 111 for a private scuba diving holiday on the Great Barrier Reef on the 75-foot cruiser *Coralita*, with three Australian experts as backup.

A Canadian air transport flew the rest of the officials and newsmen on to Sydney. Prime Minister Gorton offered the newsmen a trip to Melbourne as his guests in an RAAF aircraft. The main party of senior Canadian officials returned with me to Canberra, where Sheila and I entertained them at dinner at the Carousel Restaurant on Red Hill. On Saturday May 16, senior officials began their meeting at 8:30 a.m. We ended the day with a stag dinner of twelve at our residence.

On Sunday afternoon, May 17, I went with senior Canadian officials to Sydney, where we stayed at the Wentworth Hotel. Mr.

Trudeau also flew to Sydney from his scuba diving experience on the Great Barrier Reef. He too was staying at the Wentworth Hotel, and we agreed to meet for dinner. Partway through dinner Mr. Trudeau excused himself to go to the bathroom, and disappeared into the night. The Australian security authorities had been dodged, and they blamed me for not keeping control of him. The next morning the front page of the *Daily Telegraph* in Sydney was dominated by a large photograph of Mr. Trudeau dancing with Bobo Faulkner, the stunning moderator of a late-night television show. The photo was taken in the Taboo nightclub in King's Cross, the centre of Sydney nightlife. It showed the Prime Minister wearing a brightly patterned open-neck shirt and beads. The *Daily Mirror* described him as a "daring, dashing, jet-set heartthrob."

Next morning, Monday May 18, we were up early to be ferried in an Australian Navy launch up Sydney Harbour to Cabarita Park, where Prime Minister Trudeau unveiled a plaque on a stone cairn to mark the 130th anniversary of the landing of fifty-eight French-speaking exiles from the uprising in Lower Canada led by Louis-Joseph Papineau. They were incarcerated in the nearby Longbottom Stockade for two years before being released on ticket-of-leave, and eventually pardoned and allowed to return to Canada. As a result of the uprisings led by Papineau and William Lyon Mackenzie, Lord Durham was sent out to Canada to investigate and make his famous report on the North American colonies, in which he recommended the granting of responsible government. When this was extended to Canada it was also extended to the Australian colonies, so that out of these times of colonial unrest we saw steady progress to self-government, and eventual independence.

After returning to Sydney airport, we boarded the Canadian Forces aircraft at 11:00 a.m. for the forty-minute flight to the Canberra airport, where there were official arrival ceremonies, after which there was a National Press Club lunch, at which Mr. Trudeau talked about the responsibilities of the Canadian and Australian governments to develop their vast territories in an ecologically responsible way. After the Press Club lunch Mr. Trudeau went to the Australian National University for a very popular teach-in with graduate students. From 4:45 to 5:30 he visited the Canadian Chancery, where he planted a Japanese maple, which would be more suited to the Canberra climate than one from home. He had time for a jog before going to a white tie dinner at Government House.

On Tuesday May 19 Mr. Trudeau laid a wreath at the National War Memorial, and then attended a Parliamentary lunch, at which he spoke of our common traditions of government, and supported the prospect of further exchanges of officials, teachers, and university professors. That night there was a big reception at Parliament House.

On May 20 there was a ceremonial departure ceremony at the airport before the Canadian Forces transport plane took off for Darwin in the Northern Territory. I went along for the ride.

Altogether Prime Minister Trudeau made a strong impression with his trendiness and his clear and independent thinking, which appealed especially to young Australians.

Canadian Interests in the South Pacific

Prime Minister Trudeau, in his speech to a parliamentary luncheon on May 19, made specific reference to the Canadian government's plan to begin providing development aid to the South Pacific through a Canadian International Development Agency grant to the University of the South Pacific in Fiji. This was a result of my lobbying, so I took the opportunity of an invitation to speak to the Foreign Affairs subcommittee on the South Pacific to repeat the Prime Minister's statement and then to lay out some of my thinking on the development of Canadian relations with the five million people who live in the South Pacific, a scattered community of growing interest to Western Canada. (A.M. 2008)

Mr. Chairman:

I assume that you have invited me to speak to your subcommittee on the South Pacific because of Prime Minister Trudeau's expression of increased Canadian interest in the South Pacific at the Parliamentary Luncheon in Canberra on May 19. He said,

> I am happy to repeat today what I announced in Wellington last week: that Canada is extending its aid program to the South Pacific. We are offering to the new University of the South Pacific in Fiji an assistance package comprising scholarships, teaching assistance, and a modest amount of equipment. I wish to announce this afternoon that Canada will assist as well certain voluntary agency programs in Papua and New Guinea, will make several scholarships available under the Commonwealth Scholarship Plan in these areas, and will make a gift of books to each of the universities in Fiji and in Papua.

Our Prime Minister was referring to a Canadian International Development Agency grant of $250,000 Canadian over two years to the University of the South Pacific in Fiji to be allocated to scholarships similar to those provided by Australia to students from the various island territories of the South Pacific, provision of some teaching assistance, and a modest amount of research and teaching equipment.

Up to the time of this announcement by Prime Minister Trudeau on his Pacific tour, Canada had expressed no direct interest in the South Pacific. Rather our interests were focused in the North Atlantic and in our relations with the United States, our great neighbour to the south. Now Canada, under Prime Minister Trudeau, intends to give greater attention to the Pacific area as a whole. In the past we have had many connections in missionary work, in trade, in fisheries, in civil aviation with the countries of the North Pacific, particularly Japan. It is only recently that we have begun to look in a more systematic way to the South Pacific.

Of course Canada has had some direct interests in the South Pacific. For instance, the B.C. Sugar Refinery has taken about 20 percent of Fiji sugar production since the early 1920s. We have also sold to Fiji Canadian timber products and paper, canned fish, and other commodities of this kind. The Commonwealth Pacific cable from Vancouver to Auckland and Sydney has a way station in Fiji. Canadian Pacific Airlines planes stop at Nadi in Fiji and there has been a growing interest in tourism in Fiji as well as investment in this fast-growing sector of the Fiji economy. In the territory of Papua and New Guinea, Placer Development Company of Vancouver, British Columbia, took an interest prior to World War II in the dredging of alluvial gold in the Bulolo-Wau area. After the war Placer invested half of its income in the Commonwealth New Guinea Timbers mill in Bulolo, which produces plywood from the famous klinkii pine. Noranda Mining Corporation has an interest in copper deposits in Misima Island, off the eastern toe of Papua. Canadian Superior Oil is a member of the consortium drilling for oil and gas in the Gulf of Papua. We have had strong missionary interests in the territory: the Montfort Catholic Mission in the Western District of Papua, Lutheran missionaries in the Western Highlands and others at the Summer Institute of Linguistics at Ukarumpa, near Kainantu in the Eastern Highlands. In New Caledonia the International Nickel Company has entered into a consortium with French interests in COFIMPAC to develop a large low-grade lateritic nickel ore body. Patino Mining Corporation has entered into a joint venture with La Société Le Nickel. We have a score of Brothers of the Sacred Heart teaching in the Colony. In the British Solomon Islands Protectorate, International Nickel Company has been examining lateritic nickel deposits on Santa Isabel Island. This, then, is a brief summary of some of the Canadian interests that have been accumulating in the South Pacific, but have not been expressed in positive terms until our Prime Minister spoke in Wellington and again in Canberra.

In addition to the announcements made by Prime Minister Trudeau during his visits to Wellington and Canberra, there are certain other Canadian aid programs in the South Pacific that I might mention here. Firstly, in Suva, Fiji, the Canadian International Development Agency has agreed to provide matching funds to assist the YWCA of Canada to contribute to the building of a new YWCA Centre in the downtown area of Suva. Similarly, in the territory of Papua and New Guinea the Canadian International Development Agency will assist the Canadian YMCA in a joint venture with the

Australian YMCA in the construction and staffing of a YMCA Youth Centre at Mount Hagen in the Western Highlands. Then, the Canadian University Service Overseas, which is supported about 80 percent by CIDA funds, is sending ten volunteers to Papua and New Guinea at the beginning of September. I think it is important that in this way young Canadians will get to know young Papuans and New Guineans during the important final years before the Territory moves toward independence. I am particularly pleased that one of the first six indigenous graduates of the University of Papua and New Guinea, Mr. Rabbie Namaliu, will be going to the University of Victoria in British Columbia to take a post-graduate MA degree on a Canadian Commonwealth Scholarship prior to returning to the Territory to teach history in a local high school. Finally, I might mention that the Canadian government has agreed to offer the services of a bilingual expert on planned program budgeting for the South Pacific Commission Technical Meeting on Co-ordination of Economic Development. A Professor Gagnon from Laval University will be coming out to attend this conference in August. This indicates that, where desired, the Canadian International Development Agency will be prepared to provide bilingual experts to assist in development projects in the South Pacific area.

Canada also has an indirect interest in the political and economic development of the South Pacific. Canada is one of the active members of the Commonwealth of Nations, a member of the United Nations, a Pacific country, an associate of Australia, New Zealand, and Britain, a bilingual country, a member of the Colombo Plan, a contributor to the Asian Development Bank, an observer at ECAFE, and last year it sent an observer to the South Pacific Conference. I think that, with all these international relationships that have a bearing on the Pacific area, we have a basis on which to ask some searching questions concerning future relationships in the South Pacific. Although Canada should not be expected to take a lead, I think it appropriate to ask whether the existing international organizations in the South Pacific area provide adequate forums for discussion of trade, political development, and economic development in the area. From our point of view we would like to know through what international organizational channels we should develop our relationships with the South Pacific countries and territories.

Perhaps the first question one might ask is: What is the relevance of the Commonwealth of Nations to the South Pacific? Could the Commonwealth have a special regional relationship in the South Pacific such as exists between the members of the Commonwealth in the Caribbean? In 1966, for instance, the Commonwealth Caribbean countries had a special meeting with Canada to review their development plans and the part Canada might be prepared to play.

Another question is: Does the South Pacific Commission and the South Pacific Conference provide a suitable forum for a) political association and b) development consultation? Can these existing agreements for consultation be broadened to meet the requirements of the emerging territories of the South Pacific?

Another interesting question is this: Should the Colombo Plan be broadened to take in the South Pacific? When I was in Fiji at the end of February, the Chief Minister, Ratu Sir Kamisese Mara, indicated that he was thinking of applying for membership in the Colombo Plan in order to fill the gap in provision of technical services to Fiji after the end of the period of British colonial responsibility. I wonder whether it is wise to submerge the relatively small and manageable development problems in the South Pacific islands in the much greater development problems of the countries of South and Southeast Asia with their vast populations?

Another question that arises is: Should ECAFE be broadened to embrace the South Pacific islands and territories? As you probably know, Fiji and Western Samoa are both Associate Members of ECAFE. In this way they are enabled to obtain access to the Asian Development Bank. At the most recent meeting of ECAFE the Territory of Papua and New Guinea was admitted as an Associate Member; again, this provides the Territory of Papua and New Guinea with access to the Asian Development Bank. I have been wondering whether it might not be desirable to consider a section of the Asian Development Bank, possibly with designated special funds, to deal with problems of the South Pacific on a regional committee basis.

All of these international organizations could be extended to cover the South Pacific. What we need to ask ourselves is: What is the desirable international relationship, the desirable organizational structure for the South Pacific islands to meet the requirements of the 1970s and 1980s? Australia's interests in the South Pacific are direct and considerable. She has a responsibility to be ready to respond to the wishes of the South Pacific islanders. Canada is an interested, if not so directly involved, observer of the changing South Pacific scene.

June 7, 1970

A » Nelson Bay is about one hundred miles north of Sydney and twenty-five miles north of Newcastle on an inlet called Port Stephens. We had a good weekend there under the guidance of an oyster farmer, Warren Dienar, who took us to inspect his oyster leases and explained in detail the process of catching spawn, bringing oysters to maturity, and marketing them in the big cities. We also enjoyed a trip around the bay, tennis, and general relaxation. I talked to a dinner meeting of over eighty on Monday night.

June 15, 1970

A » During this past week I have been engaged in some further research on the administration of Papua New Guinea, the Northern Territory, and Aborigines, at the request of our own Department of Indian Affairs and Northern Development. In the Territory of PNG it seems likely that there will be a division of the budget, with a fixed grant for ordinary expenditures and all responsibility passed to elected members; Australia will then take over the allowances of expatriates and also make a development grant. This will transfer a good deal of responsibility to the elected representatives without granting full and internal self-government. In the Northern Territory there is a demand for more state-type authority, but because only twenty percent of the budget is

raised there, there is reluctance on the part of the federal government to grant it.

I spoke to a subcommittee on the South Pacific of the Foreign
Affairs Committee of Parliament about ten days ago. Last week I
was invited to have dinner with the members.

June 21, 1970

A » Wednesday night of this past week Sheila and I motored the
sixty miles to Goulburn, where I was guest speaker at the annual
meeting of the Breeders of British Sheep. I made sure they understood that I was an agricultural ignoramus. I said that I was
one of those people who think that you feed iron pills to sheep to
get steel wool. I talked on agriculture in Australia and Canada,
and referred to the recent embargo on Australian mutton shipments to Canada as a result of the poor inspection system here. It
was a homely evening.

Thursday I had one Canadian and two Australian history professors for lunch to talk about ways to further academic exchange
between Canadian and Australian universities. There is a growing
awareness here that Canada, in light of its history as a British settlement colony, as a frontier society, and as a nation influenced in
its development by the U.S.A. and the U.K., has much in common with Australia.

Today, Sunday, we went with the Australian Capital Territory
National Parks Society to look at waterfowl, parrots, etc., at Lake
George.

June 28, 1970

S » We have just been away for twenty-four hours. We left at 4:00
p.m. Saturday for Melbourne, arrived by 5:15, went to the hotel
right away and changed to evening clothes, were taken by Kevin
Osmond, our commercial counsellor there, out to their place, had
a short visit with him and Winifred, who is just over shingles, and
went on with them to the annual Dominion Day dinner and
dance of the Canada Club of Melbourne. Usually Melbourne has

had their dance on the same day as the July 1 celebrations, so we have had to be on hand here in Canberra. But because they held it on the weekend this time, we thought that, rather than go to Sydney's Canada Club celebration, which we have attended for the last three years, we would go to Melbourne this year in order to be fair—and also because Trudeau appeared in Sydney but not in Melbourne, which naturally did not please Melbourne. Anyway, it was a very pleasant function of its kind. Arthur had to make a little speech. He prepared a light one, with lots of jokes, as that is what seems to be required on such a festive occasion. However, it was eleven o'clock by the time he was called upon to speak, and so, sensing the mood of the party very accurately, he gave an amusing speech, but not the one he prepared. It hit just the right note. Everyone said it was the highlight of the evening, and I agree. This morning we were picked up by the young administrative officer there, Peter Oldham, and his wife Margaret, who have just recently been cross-posted from New Zealand to Melbourne. They are a talented couple. They have built their own harpsichord, which she plays, and he plays a flute. She also teaches mentally retarded children, having trained in that field in Ontario. They drove us to the two o'clock plane after a pleasant light lunch.

Art will tell you about the External Affairs cadets. Thursday afternoon I had the wives and the three female officers in the course for tea and informal discussion with our External Affairs wives. The Canadians told of their experiences and helped answer the questions that all the new officers and their wives worry about —entertaining, packing, children, education abroad—and seemed glad to get our slant on things. They are an attractive, well-educated group of young girls.

A » This is the second year that we've had about twenty Australian External Affairs cadets in to see how a middle-sized mission works. We give lectures the first day, and then they divide into two groups for the next two days and we have questions and answers, seminar-fashion. This lot included the first two Papua New Guinea cadets. One of them, Leo Morgan, had known Kenneth when he worked in Port Moresby.

Friday I went to a lunch at the University for Professor Arens from the University of Toronto, an authority on criminology. I found it interesting to hear the Australian lawyers saying that they thought that Canadian legal precedents were more relevant to their situation than the British cases usually cited.

July 4, 1970

s » I will start this on Saturday night, because Art has gone to the office to clear up papers, and tomorrow we have a busy day, with the Australian-Canadian Association barbecue, tea at Miss Hall's to see her new house, and then a farewell cocktail party for a newspaperman who is returning to Adelaide.

Thank goodness the week of the year with the most entertaining is over. Our Canada Day reception was better than usual this year, we think, because we had a focal point. You will remember that the Australian-Canadian Association sponsored a class in the National Eisteddfod in which choirs were to sing one Australian and one Canadian song. It was won by a choir from Castle Hill, near Sydney, and in May we invited them to come to sing two songs when Trudeau planted the tree out in front of the office and we had a small reception for him. Well, for this larger reception (about three hundred people came, out of the six hundred-plus who were invited, which is just about the same number as the last two years and so represents a great holding of the line and resisting of the temptation to add, since we have been here longer now and know more and more people) we invited the choir that to us seemed to have the most pep—or its leader did, a very attractive young girl named Mrs. Bonham—and it was from Melrose High School here in Canberra. Actually she had two choirs at the festival, one of boys and one of girls, but as our space in the chancery, where we have to hold the reception, is limited (they stood on the stairs to sing), we asked her to make it a smaller one. So we had sixty children, about one-third of them boys. They gave a nine-minute performance of two Australian songs, a swing version of "Waltzing Matilda" and "Kookaburra," and two Canadian ones, "Land of the Silver Birch" and "Alouette," excellently rendered.

(Given that Commonwealth countries do not exchange toasts on their national days as non-Commonwealth countries do, we seem to have started something, because at the American national day reception three days later, besides the toast they had some women sing "America.") As the Stapletons are leaving early next month, they invited all forty people from the office back to their house for a buffet supper after our reception. This meant that people were encouraged to get moving out of ours earlier than they sometimes do, which suited us! We left the Stapletons' at about 10:30 p.m., but we gather that it went on with music and dancing, etc., until the wee small hours. So most had a Canada Day to remember.

A » Tuesday evening the other nine Commonwealth high commissioners and their wives give a joint dinner at the Commonwealth Club for our departing New Zealand friends, Luke and Anita Haslett, who are retiring after six years here. He was a wealthy Liberal Party man in New Zealand who left office work to the professionals, but established remarkably intimate personal relations with Australian cabinet ministers. Anita has a peppy and engaging personality. I gave the speech and Sheila and I organized the dinner as the next most senior.

July 11, 1970

A » One of my projects has been to try to stir up some Canadian interest in Papua and New Guinea, the largest remaining dependent territory of the Commonwealth. Prime Minister Gorton has been in the Territory this past week and announced the transfer of quite a bit of authority to the elected ministerial members and the Administrator's Executive Council, including spending funds once approved, and raising local taxes. On Friday the first Canadian University Service Overseas representative, Fred Harland, arrived in Port Moresby to initiate a program I have been pushing. There should be eight to ten there in a couple of months. I am very pleased! I will be giving more than three hundred Canadian books to the University of Papua and New Guinea when I'm in Port Moresby.

PHOTOGRAPHS

Sheila and Arthur Menzies.

Arthur, Sheila, and the Canadian High Commissioner's residence, 32 Mugga Way, Canberra.

Edith Dorn, cook and caterer at the Canadian High Commission.

Allan Roger, Political Counsellor at the Canadian High Commission, and Gene Roger.

Otto Lang, Canadian Minister of Manpower and Immigration
(third from left), chats before dinner with R.E. Armstrong,
Secretary of the Department of Immigration (left), Arthur, and
A.J. Forbes, Minister for Immigration (right), while on an official
visit to Australia, November 1971.

FACING PAGE
ABOVE: Arthur presents his letter of introduction to Australian
Prime Minister Robert Menzies, October 1965.

BELOW: As Canada's first High Commissioner to Fiji, Arthur
presents his letter of introduction to the country's first Prime
Minister, the Honourable Ratu Sir Kamisese Mara, on
Independence Day, October 1970.

Judy LaMarsh, Canadian Secretary of State, enjoys the company of a koala bear in the Taronga Park Zoo, Sydney, while Arthur looks on, July 1966. Below, Arthur tries in vain to capture the attention of a busy Canadian beaver at the Melbourne Zoo, May 1966.

FACING PAGE
ABOVE: Arthur offers a treat to a koala bear at the Taronga Park Zoo, Sydney.

BELOW: Arthur, Sheila, Kenneth, and Norah arrive at Rockhampton, Queensland, after a tour of the New Hebrides, the Solomon Islands, and Papua New Guinea, August 1966.

Arthur greets Lester B. Pearson during a visit in April 1969 as head of the World Bank's Commission on International Development, known as the Pearson Commission.

FACING PAGE
Arthur shows Pearson where to plant a Canadian maple tree at the Canadian High Commission office on a rainy day in April 1969.

Arthur examines a model of the Australian Pavilion at Expo 67 with Prime Minister Harold Holt and Sir Valston Hancock, who oversaw Australia's participation in the Exposition.

FACING PAGE
Arthur admires a bronze plaque on the new National Trust branch at Naracoorte, South Australia, that says, "opened by Mr. A.R. Menzies, Canadian High Commissioner," March 1968.

Arthur and Sheila join Ralph Hunt, Australia's Minister of the Interior, in greeting Jean and Aline Chrétien upon their arrival in Canberra, April 1971.

FACING PAGE
Minister of Indian Affairs and Northern Development Jean Chrétien with his catch, a forty-two-pound barramundi, March 1971.

Arthur and Sheila visit the Australian Highland Club and Burns
Club to toast "the immortal memory of Robert Burns," January
1966.

FACING PAGE
Royal visits to Australia by the Queen Mother (April 1966, top)
and by Queen Elizabeth II and Prince Philip (April 1970).

Arthur and Sheila, along with many others, enjoy the state visit of Prime Minister Pierre Elliot Trudeau, May 1970.

Arthur R. Menzies, High Commissioner to Australia.

FACING PAGE
Sheila standing before the screen, made by Australian artist
Alison Willis, that was presented to Mr. and Mrs. Menzies by the
diplomatic corps on the occasion of their departure from
Australia, July 1972.

Arthur on Black Mountain, at the lookout over Lake Burley Griffin, Canberra, December 1968.

July 26, 1970 · *Honiara, Solomon Islands*

A » This has been our fourth visit to the Solomon Islands. We came through in August 1966 with Kenneth and Norah and spent about twenty-four hours here. Then in January 1968 we stopped for two hours or so en route to and returning from the Nauru Independence ceremonies. With three and a half days this time we have been able to get a much fuller impression.

We are fortunate to have been guests at the centrally air-conditioned new residence of the British High Commissioner for the Western Pacific, Sir Michael Gass, a bachelor who has served in the Gold Coast (now Ghana), here for six years as chief secretary, four years as chief secretary in Hong Kong, and now back here for eighteen months as high commissioner. He has been full of information about the Protectorate, and has provided a car, a program, and a swimming pool. An ADC, Flight Lieutenant Williker, has been most attentive. A big reception was held to enable us to meet local people.

The Solomons are a string of islands running between New Guinea and the New Hebrides for a distance of about nine hundred miles. There are six main islands, whose names, such as that of Guadalcanal, were made famous in the Second World War. They are about 11,500 square miles in area, and their population, mainly Melanesian, is about 150,000.

Copra (dried coconut meat) represents 80 percent of exports, with timber second in importance. Friday we flew by small plane to Yandina in the Russell Islands to visit Lever's Pacific Plantations, and were driven around in a Land Rover in teeming rain to see the hot-air drying process, experiments in crossing yellow Malayan dwarf coconuts with Rennell tall types, means of keeping down undergrowth, etc.—all very scientific. A young English manager, Jay Walton, and his attractive wife were enthusiastic, and they imparted this enthusiasm to their visitors. Their accountant is a Canadian from Trail, B.C.

The Protectorate is trying a new experiment in government. They used to have a legislative council of the usual British type. Now they have seventeen elected and nine official members in a governing council, which passes all legislation. The main work is done in five committees, all of which have elected majorities. About 55 percent of the recurrent budget comes from Britain, as well as the salaries of three hundred expatriate staff and $5 million in development grants. We attended a session of the governing council and listened to debate on two bills.

We visited the Geological Survey department and learned about feasibility studies made by International Nickel on Santa Isabel Island, which established a low-grade 1.3-percent nickel ore body. The question is whether it is worth developing. There is also a good bauxite deposit on another island. At the Forestry Department we learned about the logging of some 7,000,000 cubic feet for shipment to Japan, and the problems of replanting. We visited the general hospital and then the Technical Institute, where tradesmen are trained, and finally went for a drive in the country.

The British are trying to speed the political and economic development of the islands. An increasing number of bright young people are ready to play their part, or preparing to do so. The islands are not overpopulated, so future prospects seem reasonable.

We were supposed to leave at 7:00 a.m. on Sunday the 25th, but we got word the night before that our plane had been delayed in Kieta and wouldn't arrive until 10:00 a.m. So we got up and went to the Anglican Cathedral with Sir Michael Gass. It is a new building with completely open sides to let the breeze through, and some fine mother-of-pearl inlay work decorating the chancel. About four hundred attended and took communion, all clean and neatly dressed.

On our flight by DC-3 west to Bougainville we got a fine view of the New Georgia Islands group and the Blanche Channel, where the coral formations make the water a radiant turquoise. We stopped at Munda, where fine woodcarving is done, then flew across a narrow strait to the Australian territory of Bougainville, landing at Kieta on the southeast coast.

August 30, 1970

A » Professors Ted English of Carleton and Saffarian of Toronto came up to Canberra following an academic conference in Sydney on Pacific Trade and Development, so I gave a lunch for them and we had some good discussion. Wednesday I gave a lunch for Dr. Lorne Gray, President of Atomic Energy of Canada Ltd., at which he met Mr. Bott, the Secretary of the Department of National Development. AECL is bidding on the supply of a nuclear power reactor here.

Thursday I went down to Sydney at noon and called on my visa (immigration) office and commercial office to meet my new consular officer, John Sims. In the evening I attended a dinner at the Union Club given by AECL for their Australian opposites. Next day I tripped around the offices of Placer Development, Kennecott Copper, and Alcan to review recent developments, and lunched in the revolving forty-sixth-floor restaurant of the Australia Square Building, with the most wonderful views of Sydney Harbour.

Although it is not yet announced, I am to be dually accredited as Canadian High Commissioner to Fiji after Independence on October 10, so Sheila and I will go up with our Minister of Justice Honourable John Turner and his wife to the Independence ceremonies from October 8 to 14. Some of this flows from the report I wrote in Ottawa after my visit at the end of February.

September 6, 1970

A » I went to Sydney on Tuesday, mainly to meet and talk to ten Canadian CUSO co-operants who had just arrived from Canada on their way to New Guinea. I was well pleased with the impression they gave as clean-cut intelligent young Canadians of twenty-two to twenty-five (except for an art instructor aged fifty-six). I talked for a few minutes on Australian-Canadian relations, the South Pacific, and New Guinea, then we chatted for another fifty minutes. They will be spread all over the Territory.

Thursday another interesting group arrived from Canada. This is a four-man French-Canadian private TV team called Via Le Monde Canada Inc. The leader, M. Bertolino, and a M. Boucher came up to talk to the information officers of the Department of External Territories. I had the group in for lunch and again for dinner. While alone we talked in French the whole time, as they felt more at home that way. They have a contract with the CBC to do a one-hour colour film on New Guinea, and are going to concentrate on the Western District and the Montfort Catholic mission. They will stay for three to four months, so they plan a study in depth, as well as other smaller pieces. I am delighted of course to have this publicity given to one of my favourite subjects.

Another day I had lunch with John Ballard, the First Assistant Secretary in External Territories, responsible for political and social matters in New Guinea. He gave me a good exposé of current problems.

September 12, 1970

A » We have been busy at the office this past week making arrangements for the visit of the Canadian delegation to the Commonwealth Parliamentary Association, planning the program for the Minister of Justice, Honourable John Turner, and preparing for the unveiling of a memorial to exiles from Upper Canada on September 30 by Honourable Douglas Harkness, former Conservative Minister of Defence. Sheila and I are to go to Hobart for the ceremony and Sheila has been doing some good historical research for speeches. Also, there have been preparations for the Fiji Independence ceremonies on October 10.

Sir John Crawford, Vice-Chancellor of the Australian National University, has agreed to serve on the board of governors of the International Development Research Centre of Canada, which is to spend $30 million over five years doing research into problems of developing countries. I lunched with him on Tuesday to give him my ideas on the subject and also to put to him some of my ideas on the need for academic exchange between Canadian and Australian universities.

September 27, 1970

A » It is a lovely warm sunny Saturday afternoon. We will be going to play tennis at three. I've been to the office this morning to get a little caught up. There is a lot to be done—preparation for the Commonwealth Parliamentary Association meeting, including draft speeches and programs, our program for the Tasmania visit, for which we leave Monday afternoon, a program and briefing material for Honourable John Turner, who arrives in Sydney tomorrow, a program and briefing for our joint visit to Fiji with the Turners, and the program for our subsequent tour of the Fiji Islands, New Hebrides, and New Caledonia. With so many balls in the air we'll probably fail to catch them all. I'm especially pleased that Mr. Bernard Pilon, a French-speaking MP, has agreed to visit New Guinea after the conference, and I am making up a program that will enable him to see various Canadian interests.

Jack Richardson, Dean of Law at ANU, gave a lunch Wednesday at which I was able to talk with the secretary of the Attorney General's department about legal matters to be discussed by his minister and our Mr. Turner. Jack spent a year at McGill so is well disposed toward Canada.

October 4, 1970

s » Our three-day trip to Tasmania for the unveiling of a plaque on a memorial to the ninety-eight English-speaking Canadian exiles from the 1837 rebellion who were sent to Van Diemen's Land (Tasmania) for four to seven years was a really worthwhile expedition. The state government and the city of Hobart had co-operated and planned very well, and the ceremony was a success. The site they chose for the stone memorial is ideal. It's in a beautiful spot at Sandy Cove Beach, where the exiles landed, now a popular swimming place, not far out but accessible to all. The day of the ceremony was bright and sunny, and about eighty people turned out at 10:00 a.m. The Deputy Premier made the first speech, then the Deputy Mayor of Hobart. The Canadian official who did the unveiling was the Honourable Douglas Harkness, former Minister of National Defence, who is one of the delegates in Australia to the Commonwealth Parliamentary Association conference. He spoke well, using the draft speech we had given to him. We found both Mr. and Mrs. Harkness very pleasant, competent, and considerate VIPs to be with for the few days. Arthur and I then acted as hosts to the assembled guests at "morning tea" in a very pleasant hotel that looks out directly onto the memorial and the park, and was therefore just a one-minute walk from the stone. There were press and TV on hand, so the Canadian exiles will now be remembered on many tourist tours of Hobart. The day before was full, what with touring by car with the Harknesses in the Huon Valley, outside of Hobart, famous for apple and fruit growing. It would be about two weeks before the blossoms were out there, because it is so far south, but the countryside looked very green. The Premier, Mr. Bethune, gave a very elaborate dinner for just twelve in the local hotel. I've never seen such a spread. The meal went on for more than three hours. We also visited the museum and art gallery to see displays related to the convict period in Tasmanian history. The previous day the CPA delegates who were on tour in Tasmania had visited Port Arthur, the site of the chief prison. Arthur and I have now been to Tasmania twice, but have not yet been to that part.*

The Menzies family had a close connection with those Upper Canadian exiles who ended up in Tasmania after participating in the 1837–38 rebellion, led by William Lyon Mackenzie. My great-grandfather, Robert Menzies, had come to Canada in 1832 from Chapel Hill, Logie Almond, Perthshire, Scotland, on the invitation of a maternal uncle. This uncle had no children, so he named Robert as his heir. When the uncle died, however, Robert was cheated out of his inheritance by a deceitful lawyer. The legal battle that ensued is recorded in the files of the court at Milton. Needless to say, Robert lost the case, and he blamed his loss on the corruption of the "Family Compact," which ruled Upper Canada, and against which Mackenzie's rebellion was directed. Robert was left with a piece of stony land on the upper section of the Appleby Line, about three miles southeast of Campbellville. Limestone Creek runs through the property, so it was called Little Creek Farm. Great-Grandfather Robert built a little cabin on the farm, and later replaced it with a fine big farmhouse that remained in the family until 1976.

After William Lyon Mackenzie and his followers were unsuccessful in their attack on Toronto, they retreated to the United States to regroup. On 14 December 1837, he led his "Patriot Army" from Buffalo and occupied Navy Island, in the Niagara River above Niagara Falls, planning to use it as a launching site for an attack on the British regulars and Canadian militia on the north side of the Niagara River. At that time ships from England carrying immigrants and supplies could not sail beyond Montreal and the Long Sault Rapids, so they would be transferred to smaller boats to sail through Lake Ontario to the foot of the Niagara Gorge. From there a portage by carts would carry them around Niagara Falls. The British had constructed a dockyard on Navy Island, and in the years from 1761 to 1764 they built the first decked vessels to sail the upper lakes, a fleet that proved essential in the suppression of Pontiac's uprising of 1763–64. From that time until Mackenzie's occupation Navy Island lay undisturbed.

My great-grandfather, as a member of Mackenzie's "Patriot Army," was ready to take part in the attack when a messenger informed him that his wife had given birth to a baby boy, my grandfather, David (1837–1929). Robert immediately took off for Little Creek Farm. The British regulars and the Canadian militia had prepared substantial defences, so in the face of a seemingly hopeless situation Mackenzie and his followers abandoned Navy Island on 14 January 1838. Eventually ninety-two of Mackenzie's followers were exiled to Tasmania. Perhaps if my grandfather had chosen a different birthdate Robert Menzies might have been one of them. (A.M. 2008)

The sixteenth Commonwealth Parliamentary Association conference has dominated the rest of the week in Canberra. We met the Honourable John Turner, Minister of Justice and Attorney General, and Mrs. Turner Thursday morning. He is the leader of the thirty Canadians, counting wives, who have come for the meeting. High commissioners resident here are included in many of the ceremonial and social events connected with the conference, and we were also at the official opening Friday morning by the Governor General, Sir Paul Hasluck. We held a cocktail party at the office Thursday night to give the Canadian delegates an opportunity to meet the seventy-eight Canadian graduate students, their wives, and the professors from Canada who are here at the Australian National University. There are some from each Canadian province, so they enjoyed talking to their MPs and getting some recent Canadian news. We had 150 people altogether. The next night we had a dinner at the house in honour of Mr. and Mrs. Turner and their Australian counterparts, the Attorney General and Mrs. Hughes, the Solicitor General and Mrs. Ellicott, and professors and experts on law. There were fourteen of us, and discussion was good. Mr. Turner is a very articulate and clever speaker. At noon that day he spoke particularly well to the students of the law faculty at ANU, in a light, informal, but very pertinent way. His mimicry of John Diefenbaker was superb! Last night we went to Minister of Defence and Mrs. Fraser's for a dinner for the Turners and other CPA delegates. Fraser and Turner were students together at Oxford. There was a lively group of Australian guests, mostly moneyed property people from around Canberra.

The Turners, like Mr. Trudeau, like their sport and exercise and relaxation, and are keen tennis players, so we have included some of that between sessions of the conference. Tomorrow we have a joint reception with the other nine high commissioners at a large hotel for all conference delegates, and afterwards we have twenty to dinner at the Club. Our main guests at that time will be the two provincial premiers, Mr. Campbell from PEI and Mr. Strom from Alberta, and, on the Australian side, Mr. Frank Ford, who was prime minister of Australia for a short time and is a former high commissioner to Canada, now in his eighties, but very interested in talking and meeting such people. Tuesday morning at the house I am having all the wives of delegates for tea and talk and a demonstration of Aboriginal art by Greta Daly. What a week!

November 1, 1970

s » We just got back last night, right on schedule, from our twenty-three-day trip to Fiji, the New Hebrides, and New Caledonia. Of course the main reason for the trip was to be present at the Fiji Independence ceremonies on October 10, and for Arthur to present his letter of accreditation as Canadian high commissioner in Fiji, signed by Prime Minister Trudeau, to the new Fiji Prime Minister, Ratu Mara. The diplomatic corps in Fiji is small, and mostly nonresident. We called on or entertained all our colleagues. The Indians gave a dinner for us. The Fijians had made very complete preparations for all the ceremonies related to Independence: the lowering of the flag for the last time, the raising of the new flag, the all-island night of dancing by every community in Fiji—Fijian, Indian, Tongan, Maori, Nauruan, Cook Islanders, Wallace Islanders, Gilbert and Ellis Islanders, etc.—and also choirs and singing groups, chiefly from the Fijian and Indian communities. We were fortunate to be included in the lunch at Government House in honour of Prince Charles, and also at the banquet given in an official *burre* (a Fiji-style bungalow) built in the yard of the prime minister for future cabinet meetings and official entertaining. The Minister of Justice, John Turner, the chief Canadian delegate, and Mrs. Turner were there for the first two days of festivities, but left Saturday p.m. to return to Canada. In some ways the second part of our Fiji visit, our tour after the official ceremonies to the less touristy, off-the-beaten-track parts was even more interesting. We spent most of the two days driving from Suva to Nandi on the main island instead of flying as usual, and then four and a half days touring on two outer islands to Lombasa, Savusavu, and Taveuni. The district officer in each place arranged very good programs for us, and considering that each place had also coped with Prince Charles just two days before, they sure were busy. But everything looked its best, just as it had been presented to Charles! We had two days back in Fiji to get straightened out and do calls and paperwork.

On Wednesday, October 21, we left for the New Hebrides, the condominium jointly administered by the British and the French. It struck us as a ridiculous setup when we were there four years ago and seems just as much so today, although there have been some infinitesimal improvements. The French lycée now teaches English, and the English secondary school French, but none of either is taught in the other's elementary schools, and the duplication of hospitals, police, co-operatives, and such still continues. Naturally we spent half our time officially with the British and half with the French, and had a big reception in our honour hosted by them jointly, but on Sunday, an unofficial day, we went again to British Resident Commissioner and Mrs. Allen's for a quiet lunch.

Our French in the New Hebrides was pretty halting, but by the time we completed the next week in the wholly French surroundings of New Caledonia it began to pick up. I must say I found it a real strain to have to go out to dinner and talk nothing but French for three and a half hours at a stretch. Instead of sleeping that night I was still translating, thinking of all the bright things that I should have said in French! Arthur had two full days, up at 5:15 a.m. to catch early planes, flying to see International Nickel and other Canadian mining sites.

To finish our stay there we went for one night to the Isle of Pines, a lovely island and hotel, to swim, etc., with a Canadian couple from International Nickel.

December 6, 1970

s » The highlight of the week was the trip Arthur and I made to Sydney for the audience Pope Paul VI gave especially for the diplomatic corps. Neither the dean of the corps, Sir Charles Johnston, nor the number two, the Greek ambassador, was going to Sydney, so Arthur was the top diplomat going, and on his shoulders fell the honour of making the speech of greeting to the Pope on behalf of the corps, and then to introduce each one to him in turn. We were all assembled at the Apostolic Delegation in North Sydney between 4:30 and 5:00 for the audience at five o'clock. There were representatives of thirty-seven out of the fifty countries represented in Australia. Most sent their ambassador, or top representative, a few a consul from Sydney. We were quite a mixture—Catholics, many other Protestants, Muslims, and agnostics-Communists. Arthur had to prepare his short speech with great delicacy so as not to offend any of the beliefs represented in the corps. The Pope replied in a written speech that he read in French, and then added a bit ad lib. Then each couple was presented in turn, and he was most generous in talking a couple of minutes with each and presenting a medal to each couple. We were most impressed that during this part of the performance, which lasted about twenty minutes, he spoke fluently in English, Italian, Spanish, and German as well as French. He certainly went out of his way to be diplomatic and pleasant. Most women were in dark-coloured afternoon dresses with sleeves, and either mantillas or small hats. Afterwards there was another special audience in the same place for leaders of Catholic Action. That evening a huge Mass was celebrated in the big Sydney Racecourse, at which a quarter of a million turned up. Altogether he celebrated three large well-attended Masses during his four-day stay in Sydney. We did not stay for the Mass, but went to supper at the home of one of the young officers in our Sydney office, who drove us to the airport to catch the 9:30 p.m. jet back to Canberra. It made a different, memorable day, and having the added responsibility of representing the corps was interesting.

Fiji Independence
(submitted by A.R. Menzies and published, with minor modifications, in External Affairs, *December 1970)*

On October 10, 1970, H.R.H. the Prince of Wales, in a ceremony in Albert Park, Suva, handed the Constitutional Instruments of Independence to Ratu Sir Kamisese Mara, first Prime Minister of independent Fiji. The occasion was the ninety-sixth anniversary of the Cession of Fiji by the High Chiefs to Queen Victoria. Fiji's new sky-blue flag with the Union Jack next the staff and the Fiji coat of arms in the fly was then hoisted, and the Fiji Military Force in their colourful red tunics and white *sulus* fired a *feu-de-joie* while a battery of field guns fired a 21-gun salute.

Fiji's Independence celebrations combined the precision of parades by the Fiji Military Force and Band with traditional Fijian and Indian ceremonies. High Fijian Chiefs in traditional grass skirts and tapa-cloth cloaks sat on mats to prepare a special drink from Yaqona root in a ceremonial three-legged wooden *tanoa* bowl to welcome Prince Charles. A mountain of fourteen thousand yams and *dalo* roots, one hundred nineteen freshly slaughtered pigs, and twenty-three great sea turtles from the fourteen provinces were presented to him. Regional welcome dances, called *mekes*, were performed by lines of grass-skirted Fijian warriors, chanting and brandishing spears. These were followed by Indian dancers and drummers.

Twenty thousand people watched the Independence celebrations, including representatives from about thirty countries and South Pacific territories. Canada was represented by the Minister of Justice, Honourable John Turner, and Mrs. Turner and the Canadian High Commissioner to Australia and Mrs. Arthur Menzies.

On the afternoon of Independence Day, Honourable John Turner presented to the Prime Minister Canada's Independence gift, a painting by British Columbia artist E.J. Hughes entitled *Mill Bay*. He also handed over copies of the report of the Commission on Bilingualism and Biculturalism in Canada, in which the Fijian Prime Minister had expressed an interest. Mr. Menzies presented to the Prime Minister a letter of introduction signed by Prime Minister Trudeau in which Mr. Menzies was designated to serve concurrently as Canadian High Commissioner to Fiji, while retaining his residence in Canberra.

Fiji consists of 844 volcanic and coral islands, about one hundred of them inhabited, with a total area of 7,055 square miles. The two main islands are Viti Levu (4,010 square miles) and Vanua Levu (2,137 square miles). Viti Levu, which includes the capital, Suva (population 55,000), and the international airport, Nadi, has more than seventy percent of the population. Suva is 3,000 miles southwest of Honolulu, 2,000 miles northeast of Sydney, and 1,300 miles north of Auckland.

The Fijians are Melanesian in origin, with an admixture of Polynesian. Abel Tasman sighted the Fiji islands in 1644. In 1774 Captain Cook anchored off one of the islands. After the mutiny on the

Bounty, Lieutenant Bligh charted many of the Fiji islands as he made his way through them by launch to the Dutch East Indies. In the nineteenth century the search for sandalwood and, later, *bêche-de-mer* (edible sea slugs) brought adventurers and firearms. In 1830 a small European trading community was established at Levuka and in 1835 missionaries arrived. Fighting between the Fijian tribes kept the island in a disturbed condition until on October 10, 1874 the Fijian High Chiefs led by Cakobau ceded the islands to Queen Victoria in order to ensure peace and the rule of law.

During the 1870s Indian labourers were introduced into Fiji to work on the sugar plantations. On the expiry of their ten-year contracts many remained. By 1917, when the indenture system was abolished, 63,000 had been brought in, of whom only one-third had sought repatriation. Today, the total population of 520,000 is 50 percent of Indian origin, 42 percent Fijian, and the rest of mixed race.

Early constitutional development in Fiji featured the maintenance of a balance in the Legislative Council between Fijians, Indians, and Europeans. At a constitutional conference in London in 1965 there was a difference of views between the Indians, who wanted a common electoral roll, and the Fijians and Europeans, who favoured a roll that distinguished among the racial groups. A partial compromise was made that involved a combination of communal and cross-voting systems, which did not satisfy the predominantly Indian Federation Party, led by Dr. A.D. Patel. A boycott of the Legislative Council by the Federation Party and subsequent inter-racial tension over by-elections in 1968 led party leaders to the realization that a new effort was required to find a basis for inter-party understanding. After the death of Dr. Patel in October 1968, Mr. S.M. Koya was chosen as leader of the National Federation Party and successfully pursued the talks with Ratu Mara. On January 17, 1970, Ratu Mara and Mr. Koya issued a joint statement saying, "Inter-party discussions have led to the point where it is agreed Fiji should proceed to Dominion status ... as soon as possible without fresh elections being held beforehand."

At the second Constitutional Conference in London, from April 20 to May 5, 1970, it was agreed that Fiji should seek independence on October 10, the ninety-sixth anniversary of Cession. The

Constitution provides for maintenance of traditional ties with the British Crown, a Governor-General, an appointed Senate, a fifty-two-member House of Representatives with continuation during the first post-independence elections of the communal and cross-voting system and subsequent appointment of a Royal Commission to make recommendations. Thus differences over electoral procedures were submerged in order to make progress on early independence.

In his Independence Day broadcast the new Prime Minister said, "We are a community of many races, with different cultures, customs and languages, but the things that unite us far outnumber those on which we differ.... Above all, there is our fixed determination to build a strong, united Fiji, rich in its diversity and tempered with tolerance, goodwill and understanding."

On becoming independent, Fiji indicated its intention to remain a member of the Commonwealth of Nations. On October 14 Fiji became the 127th member of the United Nations. Addressing the General Assembly on October 24, the Prime Minister expressed the hope that, so far as it was authorized by its friends and neighbours, Fiji hoped to act as a representative and interpreter of the peoples of the South Pacific. The South Pacific Conference and Commission had met in Suva just before Independence, and Fiji was expected to become an influential full member. It could be expected to change from being an associate to a full member of the Economic Commission for Asia and the Far East, and the Asian Development Bank. Initially, Fiji will have only three diplomatic missions abroad: in London, in Canberra, and at the United Nations.

Fiji's economy has been based largely on sugar and coconuts, the production of which does not grow quickly enough, because of quotas and low world prices, to support the population growth. Fortunately there has been a recent rapid growth in tourism, with substantial investment in tourist hotels. Further diversification into timber, mining, and light industry is also taking place.

Canada's relations with Fiji extend back to the last century, when the Vancouver Sugar Company developed properties at Navua in Viti Levu and on Taveuni. These were sold sixty years ago, but the British Columbia Sugar Refinery has continued to buy about one-fifth of the Fiji sugar crop since then. In 1969 Canada bought some 72,000 tons of Fiji sugar, worth $5.5 million. Canada has shipped to Fiji about $1 million per year worth of goods such as timber, paper, and canned fish. Canadian Pacific Airlines has been stopping in Nadi en route to Sydney and Auckland for twenty-five years. The Commonwealth Pacific Cable from Vancouver to Auckland and Sydney has a way station at Suva. Many Canadian travellers stop in Fiji en route to or from the South Pacific.

About 1,300 immigrants have entered Canada from Fiji during the past four years.

When Prime Minister Trudeau made his tour of the Pacific Rim countries in May 1970, he announced that Canada intended to extend its international development co-operation to the South Pacific. Specifically, he announced a grant of $250,000 over a two-year period to the University of the South Pacific in Fiji for scholarships, equipment, and some teaching staff. Canada has also made a grant of $100,000 to supplement contributions by the Canadian YWCA to the Suva YWCA building project. Two Fijians are at present studying in Canada under Commonwealth Scholarships. Canada is also providing assistance to Fiji under the Commonwealth Programme for Technical Cooperation. In these ways, Canadians take satisfaction in their associations with their new Commonwealth neighbour in the Pacific.

SEVEN

1971

January 5, 1971

s » There is a postal strike on in New South Wales at present, but everyone hopes it will be short, so I must not use it as an excuse to put off any longer our first typewritten letter of 1971.

Since we last wrote we have celebrated Christmas with two dinners, one on Christmas Eve with the Roger family. They have a regular ritual that includes touches from their various postings around the world, starting with *glögg* (mulled wine served with raisins and almonds), a custom from Finland, their last post. There are Christmas decorations in each and every room of the house—little tiny carved figures, an Advent candle ring, embroidered placemats. I never saw such a collection. There was a lovely turkey dinner with the four boys and another young couple, and then the reading of the Christmas story from the Bible and the recitation of "The Night Before Christmas," then the opening of one gift—only one. They spend all Christmas morning opening the rest one at a time, unbothered about preparing a big meal.

On Christmas Day we had a second turkey here with Edith, and topped it off with a raspberry pavlova, using the last of the first crop of our raspberries. Edith won a fancy pavlova (meringue to you Canadians who do not know the Australian dessert) dish, which has the recipe on it and which can go in the oven, so we were trying it out for the first time.

Our phone call to Norah was the only one we had been able to book for Christmas Day, but we were pleased that it and the other two later, to Frances and Marion, both in Burlington, and to Kenneth, which we received up in Kosciuszko, all came through clearly, right at the times arranged—a great improvement over some attempts.

On Boxing Day we left for the VIP lodge up in Kosciuszko State Park, where we have spent New Year's three times since coming to Australia, and thoroughly enjoyed the change, even if it was decidedly cooler than other years, with more rain. Luckily the weather was best for the first part, when we had as our guests Colonel Geoff Corry, his wife Eleanor, and four children, Donald, 16, Leslie, a girl of 14, Patricia, 12, and John, 7. They are living in a motel until they move to a house in mid-January. Geoff is the new Canadian Armed Forces adviser. All Australian wildlife are new to them, and we were delighted when three kangaroos came into the field next to us one day as we were driving. The children had marvellous views, and went right out as soon as possible to feed them bread and crackers from their hands. We couldn't possibly have put on a better show. We had the Corrys half the time, and afterwards enjoyed a quieter time by ourselves.

I can now say that I am definitely over the shingles and can do absolutely everything. Art and I played tennis on a nearby court almost every day, between rainstorms. We went fishing on Lake Jindabyne once, and Arthur caught a beautiful brown trout of more than six pounds, the biggest fish he has ever caught. He also caught five other very good-sized fish from the shore near the Lodge, some brown, some rainbow trout. We froze them all, and Edith was delighted when we returned with them.

January 10, 1971

s » Our first day back from holidays we went to Sydney to take part in a very sad occasion. Harry Horne, our commercial counsellor there, and his wife Pat had a little ten-year-old boy who was mentally handicapped and rather stunted in growth. Two days before Christmas he was rushed to hospital for something altogether unrelated to that. Appendicitis was suspected, but it turned out not to be the trouble. Just after the operation his heart stopped for seven minutes and did irreparable damage to his brain. He entered a coma that he never came out of, and died New Year's Day. The funeral was in the Roman Catholic church near their home, and burial was in a Sydney cemetery. It was very hard on both Pat and Harry. Pat's whole life has been centred on Bernie, and very restricted because of him. Their other children are both older—at college, one of them married—whereas Bernie was always around. We were the only out-of-town people for the funeral, but thought it the least we could do. We left at 7:15 a.m. and returned at 2:00 p.m. the same day.

The 28th Congress of Orientalists is taking place in Canberra from January 6 to 11. It is a huge undertaking. At first they expected about 800 delegates, but have ended up with 1,400. There are about 200 from Japan, 200 from India, 200 from the U.S.A., and 24 from Canada. Most of the Canadians are professors, from Montreal, Toronto, Calgary, Vancouver, and Victoria. Many are of Indian or Chinese origin, most of them now Canadian citizens. Of course, because of the subject Arthur also knew several of the American scholars. We went to the opening, where Sir Paul Hasluck gave a very thoughtful speech. He wasn't afraid to raise such questions as whether their emphasis should be only on the classical aspects of culture, or on the more contemporary study of Asia as well, and the difference between the terms Asian and Oriental. There was a reception at the Australian National University afterwards. Because it is holiday time at the University, the delegates are mostly billeted in the halls of residence. We went to the opening of an exhibition at the National Library of items of interest to Orientalists from museums and private collections all over Australia, a worthwhile collection and well displayed. In many ways the Australians are pleased to host this group for the first time, and to show that their universities and scholars are of a calibre to run such a show, provide leaders for seminars, etc. After much rushing around, we rounded up twenty of the Canadian delegates and had about twenty other people to meet them at a reception here on Friday night. We were fortunate that it was at a time when we could be outside on the patio, which is reasonably cool.

January 17, 1971

s » All day Monday from nine to five I attended a seminar held in conjunction with the Orientalists conference but open to teachers and others, on Teaching Asian Languages in Australian Schools. They had four excellent speakers in the morning: the director of the Department of Indonesian at ANU, a Sydney school inspector who is largely instrumental for introducing Japanese in the few schools that teach it, the head of a crash course in Chinese now on at the Canberra College of Advanced Education, and a schoolteacher from Melbourne. In the afternoon (the temperature was near 100, so my poor old brain was not at its best) we split up into seminars. Mine discussed obstacles in the way of teaching Asian languages. That evening we had quite a mixture here for dinner —a Fiji high-school teacher and his wife and three children, aged 22, 12, and 10, and one of the Canadian professors still around from the Orientalists conference, whom Art wanted to talk to about academic exchange. He had been in Fiji several times, and had done some digging for archaeological pottery, etc., in the New Hebrides, so they fitted together better than we had expected.

January 24, 1971

s » This week I was interviewed by a woman from the Australian Broadcasting Corporation for a program "for their Pacific service, not for Australia," on the subject of diplomats in Canberra. One question she asked was, "And what about planning for entertaining?" I said there were two kinds: for one, everything was worked out very carefully in advance, with great attention to the guest list, etc.; the other just cropped up. Well, we had a dinner of the first sort this week for General Turcot, commander of the Mobile Command. It was under his direction that all the Army's activity against the FLQ was carried out, and he gave a very interesting account of it. With him we had Lieutenant-General Sir Thomas

Daly, the ex-head of the Duntroon Defence College, who knew Turcot, and Lady Daly; an army colonel just back from commanding in Vietnam; and our own Armed Forces adviser, Colonel Corry. Earlier we had been to a reception at the Corrys'—they had moved into their fully furnished new house on Monday and the party was on Wednesday, so it took some organizing.

A » We have been following the Commonwealth Prime Ministers Conference in Singapore closely. One gets the impression that Heath, Gorton, and the East Africans were playing to home audiences more than they were trying to solve problems. Gorton and Trudeau lunched together, but we've not had a report yet.

This next fortnight will be crowded, with a premiers' meeting here at which all will be looking for money from the federal government, the retirement of Sir John McEwen, long-time Deputy Prime Minister and leader of the Country Party in the governing coalition, and his replacement by a newly elected leader, probably Doug Anthony, and probably some measures to stem inflation, which is gaining uncomfortable momentum. That's quite a bit of activity for midsummer, when most would like to be away at the beach.

January 31, 1971

S » Poor Australia! Ever since we have been here we have been aware of the terrific droughts it suffers, and on rare occasions the flash floods. It has seemed a case of too little water most of the time, but occasionally too much. Earlier, this phenomenon had always been associated with some other part of the country, but this week it hit Canberra—with tragic consequences. Canberra is supposed to be a "planned" city, benefiting from all the most modern engineering knowledge, with things like runoff and drains prepared scientifically, so understandably there is now a great deal of criticism.

The heavy rains started in an ordinary way at about 7:30 Tuesday evening, while we were at a reception given in honour of Australia Day by the Minister of Foreign Affairs and Mrs. McMahon, just back from the conference in Singapore. It was held in the main dining areas of Parliament House rather than out in the courtyard as planned, because rain showers had been forecast. It was about 90 degrees and really hot and sticky, as it had been for several days—really uncomfortable tropical weather. Well, the break came at about eight o'clock, with a humdinger of an electrical storm and a real deluge. It was such a downpour that when Andrew drove us home with the Rankins, visibility was almost nil. Later that evening we were without lights for a couple of hours, but it wasn't until the next morning that we read that on one of the new roads a tiny stream had overflowed the drains, and in half an hour the water was ten feet deep. A rushing torrent swirled cars around so that by 8:45 one car was washed away, and shortly afterwards another, and hundreds were stranded. Seven people were missing—four children from one family. All sorts of police squads and helicopters and volunteers have been searching all week, and although two bodies were found after one day, the last two were only found yesterday, Saturday, five days later—and upstream instead of downstream, such must have been the eddying around. And all this in the midst of a big city, or within its boundaries. What a tragedy!

We had Bruce and Mona Rankin, our Canadian consul general from New York and his wife, here as house guests from Monday afternoon until Wednesday afternoon. He started off in our Department of Trade and Commerce as a trade commissioner, and now is one of the people who have been doing the report on the integration of the various government departments abroad, which will begin to come into effect on April 1 this year. Her parents are Canadian but have lived in Sydney for ages, and Bruce and Mona were out here on a holiday for the parents' fiftieth wedding anniversary. The Rankins had been married in Sydney when Bruce was posted in Australia twenty years ago. They are interesting, well informed, and not afraid to speak their views, so we enjoyed our talks. We had about twenty-five people in for a small reception with them the first night—friends whom they suggested—and then with one other couple up to the Carousel Restaurant on Red Hill afterwards. On Tuesday Frank and Ellen Weiser took them to lunch while we went with eight other heads of mission to a sticky, hot, truly diplomatic lunch at a *cher collègue*'s.

February 7, 1971

s » The past week has been about our very busiest ever in Canberra, because most of the time we had two very important Canadian groups here. The National Defence College from Kingston included Australia on their annual tour. We had a similar group here two years ago. Thirty-seven came on the Pacific tour—on a Canadian plane this time—led by Admiral Davies, and besides army, navy and air force people at about colonel level there were also representatives from several other civil service departments, such as Manpower, Trade and Commerce, Immigration, and External Affairs, and besides the one External "student" we also have an External Affairs officer at senior level on the directing staff, this time Paul Malone, who served here in Canberra at the beginning of his career and married an Australian girl who is related to the new leader of the Country Party, Douglas Anthony, who was just sworn in as the new leader and deputy prime minister during the week. The NDC people had made one stop in Australia, at Alice Springs, where they had been met by Allan Roger and our Armed Forces adviser, Colonel Corry. Arthur, of course, was with them for their briefings and lectures by all the various Australian people here, and Tuesday night we gave a large reception in their honour at the office for about 150. Then afterwards, the Rogers, Corrys, and Weisers each gave a dinner for them and their Australian counterparts. We took in two of the dinners.

In addition, we had a reception for the twenty-man Canadian delegation to the fifth Commonwealth Education Conference, which opened in Canberra on Wednesday for a two-week session. Friday noon we held a lunch here for Arnold Smith, the Secretary-General of the Commonwealth, and his wife (he is a fellow officer from External, on loan to the secretariat), at which we had, among others, Davidson Dunton, the leader of the Canadian delegation

236

to the conference, and Monsieur Garneau, deputy director of universities of Canada. It was a memorable lunch, because for the second time in two weeks Canberra had a cloudburst—right at noon hour this time—with terrific flash flooding. No lives were lost, as there were on Australia Day, but there were many blocked drains and the like. Even at our place we stuffed bath towels between the screen door and the side door to keep the water out. And the main bridges were closed, so all our guests had to detour to get here and arrived half drowned, the last of them at half past one. But at three o'clock, by which time they had all left, the sun was shining brightly and we could laugh about the whole affair. Neither car belonging to the two waitresses would start, and by the time the NBMA truck came around to fix them it was five o'-clock.

We had seats for the opening of the conference, and Arthur is an official delegate, but he hasn't time to attend any of the seminar sessions. We have taken in social events: receptions by the University and one at Parliament House given by the Minister of Education. Although education is a state affair here, as in Canada, they are ahead of us in that they also have a Commonwealth Education Department, and it does the co-ordinating work during a conference like this.

Last night we were the only diplomats at a very pleasant wedding between an Australian girl who had been an air hostess on Qantas and a Canadian chap from Edmonton, whose parents had flown out from Canada for it. It was rather incongruous that all his friends and relatives from Canada had been able to get here, but because of the terrific floods in Australia nine very close relatives of the mother of the bride were stranded about a hundred miles from Canberra, where there had been a washout on the road. The ceremony was at 7:30 p.m. in the Church of England church, and then they took over the complete restaurant on the top of Red Hill (it was the first time we have seen such an occasion held there). There was a sit-down dinner for 100 guests—minus the nine stuck in the flood. The speeches were amusing and everything was well planned. We were among the first to leave, at 1:30 a.m.

February 14, 1971

s » I remember that Valentine's Day was the day of the seven-inch snow in Tokyo, so I guess that February is the month for abnormal weather around the world. It was interesting to get Marion's report written in Wingham Hospital about the extraordinary blizzards in Western Ontario. When the Gordons left here they gave us the most appropriate gift we have yet received from house guests: a rain gauge. It's a gadget that you put up outside to record the amount of rainfall. Here it is registered in "points" (there are a hundred points in one inch). We have had the February average already in the first half of this month, and January was nearly three times as wet as any other January on record in Canberra.

Monday I gave a ladies' lunch for the wives of the two Canadian delegates to the Commonwealth Education Conference, Mrs. Chiasson of Nova Scotia and Mrs. Bergstrom, wife of the Deputy Minister of Education for Saskatchewan, who fitted in well with my guest Miss Kay Russell, who was with us for two days as part of a nine-month round-the-world tour all by herself after retiring from thirty-seven years of teaching—all at Sudbury High School. She was in the French department when I taught there. She has a fantastic memory for the places she has visited. Next she was going on a cruise to Africa, and we spent a lot of time in a torrential rainstorm after lunch getting her visa for Ghana, picking up extra passport pictures, etc., and sightseeing with the other two ladies. Between that day's soaking and the next I had a sore throat and laryngitis for the rest of the week, and although I couldn't let up then, I've let up a bit this weekend and am feeling better— also probably because I have had three very powerful injections of protamine sulfate to give me pep in the legs after the shingles; I am to get another two this week.

One of the nicest Australian couples we know, John and Dorothy Gordon from the Murray irrigation area, near Mildura, came to stay with us Tuesday, Wednesday, and Thursday. John is chairman of the Dried Fruits Board and was here for the Outlook in Agriculture Conference, at which agricultural people give their views to the government. Dorothy was in Canberra for the first

238

time in five years, so there was much of interest to show her that was new to her.

While Art and John went to the conference opening Dorothy and I went to the Repertory Theatre production of *The Physicists*, by Friederich Dürrenmatt, the same person who wrote *The Visit*, which you may have seen as a movie. It begins like a conventional crime drama with a corpse on the stage, but the criminals involved are all inmates of a mental institution run by a brilliant hunchbacked German woman doctor. They are far from innocent idiots, and put across very well the message that the deadliest of sins is to escape from responsibility—and what a great responsibility scientists and physicists have.

Wednesday noon we had the Gordons for lunch with friends of theirs at the Commonwealth Club, and in the evening had a dinner here in their honour. Also with us were the president of the Australian Wine Board, who runs Seppelt's Vineyard, one of the biggest wineries, and the secretary of the Wine Board. They were in town as hosts at a wine tasting, and they will be looking after our ten Canadian liquor commissioners, who will be among our next guests. It's a never-ending stream, especially now that it is Canadian winter! Again there were floods in Canberra, which made planning and getting around difficult, but the dinner went well. The ground is so absorbent that next morning Art was able to have his early tennis lesson, though the court where I usually play was washed away and has to have major repair work done on it.

All the wet weather has produced a dividend, which pleases Art especially: there's a fantastic crop of mushrooms springing up in people's lawns and in sheep paddocks. So yesterday, Saturday, we phoned Dr. and Mrs. Davy, friends of ours who live out near Bungendore and have pastures where mushrooms grow, and asked if we could come and pick some. We got about five buckets full, and last night we helped Edith prepare them for the freezer and for dinner tomorrow night for the Bank of Montreal president.

February 21, 1971

A » I have been asked on short notice to return to Ottawa to be chairman of the Senior Officers Promotion Board from March 15 to 19, and to stay a few days afterwards for consultation. Although this comes at an awkward time in terms of work here and preparation for the visits of the Minister of Indian Affairs and Northern Development, Mr. Chrétien, and the Chief of the Defence Staff, General Sharp, I have decided to go, as I find it useful to maintain contact with management. I will be leaving Canberra on the afternoon of March 9, spend three days in Fiji, and arrive in Vancouver on Saturday, March 13. I'm looking forward to seeing Norah there and I'm asking her to arrange accommodation. I leave for Ottawa Sunday. I will try to get down to see Marion and Frances and families on the weekend of March 20 and 21, and I leave for Australia on March 25, eventually getting back here on March 27. It will all be a rush, but that's life. It's good I'm still thought about for jobs. It will give me a chance to talk about Australian business and to snoop about what may be in store for us.

The Commonwealth Education Conference ended this past week. It did not make the headlines, as the Commonwealth Prime Ministers Conference in Singapore did, because there were no political differences. The conference is held only once every three years. Our representatives found the developing countries more mature and less grasping for aid, and yet quietly convinced that the Commonwealth serves a useful purpose. I found it interesting to hear two French-Canadians say that they had found the Commonwealth worthwhile for the first time. I had some very useful talks with members of the Canadian delegation.

February 27, 1971

s » Last weekend we wrote you about Arthur's quick trip to Canada. All the first part of that schedule still stands. Now, however, he has been able to arrange to return via London so that he will be able to see Kenneth for a few hours, instead of returning as he went, by way of the Pacific. It will mean a very tiring trip, but he hopes that by breaking it for one night on the ground in Singapore for a night's sleep, and still having two night's flying, he will not be too dead tired for the frightfully busy week he will

have here on his return with General Sharp and Minister Chrétien. We are both really delighted that as a sideline to the trip
home he will now be able to see both Norah and Kenneth for a
very modest extra fare. It certainly seems worthwhile.

In view of this killer schedule and the fact that he has so
much on his plate before he leaves and that we have been committed for months to go to South Australia next weekend to open
an agricultural show near Adelaide, we have both really tried this
week to cut down on social activities and get our colds better.
Arthur went to the doctor on Monday and got antibiotics and I
went Tuesday, and we are both definitely much better from a
week's dose.

We have been to an interesting concert on the Canberra Caril-
lion this afternoon, put on by the Canadian Dominion Carillonneur, Robert Donnell, jointly with the Australian Carillionist, John
Gordon. They do not pronounce carillon the same way we do,
and, as you notice, do not even refer to the professional performer
by the same word. Donnell was brought out by the Australian
Council for the Arts after a suggestion made by Trudeau when he
was here last year. Again tomorrow, Sunday, he will perform a
solo concert for three-quarters of an hour. The carillon is on a
small island in Lake Burley Griffin that is connected by a small
bridge to the mainland, and there is a small park surrounding the
carillon tower. It's a lovely setting, and a pleasant spot on a good
sunny day like today. Most people sit in their cars and listen with
their doors open. Others wander, or sit on the grass on the island.
We were taken up in the tower to see the keyboard, but listened
outside under the trees. On Monday we are giving a reception in
honour of Donnell for the Arts Council and other musical people.
He will be in Sydney for concerts during the week and will return
to Canberra next weekend. He will train two trainee carillionists,
then go to New Zealand and home.

It makes quite a contrast with the earlier visitors we had this
week—the liquor commissioners, representing the ten provincial
liquor commissions of Canada. We had about forty at a reception
for them. Edith had to go to Yass to finish playing in a bowling
competition she had entered, which, because of rain, had run on

longer than expected, but she had prepared the reception before, and returned here just in time. And she won her competition.

March 7, 1971

s » Because of the very short notice given Arthur before his trip back to Canada he has been terribly busy this past week. The preparations for the visits of General Sharp and Mr. Chrétien involved a lot of work on programs, and although Art is very concerned to get these things settled and prepared before he leaves, other people are not stirred the same way. One thing I am very glad about is that both of us have finally shaken our colds.

On Friday we left at 8:00 a.m. for Adelaide via Melbourne and arrived by 10:30 a.m.—very quick connections. Arthur had been invited a long time ago by the federal member of Parliament for the area of Tanunda, the centre of the Barossa Valley, where seventy percent of Australian wine for export is produced. Tanunda is forty-five miles from Adelaide. Mr. Giles, the MP, had worked out a very good program for him, with lots of public relations work. There were interviews at the radio station right after our arrival, and then Art spoke to a businessmen's club luncheon of about sixty-five. He called on the Premier, etc., in the afternoon. In the evening we both went to the staff centre at Flinders University for a dinner meeting of the Australian-Canadian Association. This organization has been reconstituted and revitalized recently in South Australia. Some very attractive and dynamic Canadians and Australians were there. Arthur spoke for about fifteen minutes, and after the dinner there was a social time, and two young people put on a musical program. One played the piano beautifully and the other, a refreshingly young and attractive girl, sang an operatic selection.

Saturday we left at ten o'clock with the Commonwealth car and driver to motor to Tanunda. We went via the park where they have set up the Canadian totem pole—a gift of the B.C. timber merchants—that Arthur had presented to the city of Adelaide on his last trip, which I had never seen before. The temperature was 96 degrees and the countryside looked very, very dry and brown. However, the sunshine is good for producing the grapes and the wine that this area is famous for. The picking of grapes will begin next week. We had a police escort into the show ground, and inspected all the exhibits in the large new show building. It was certainly one of the best country shows we have seen in Australia. The exhibits were of a high standard and beautifully arranged. The fruit and vegetables were gorgeous. The flower display was outstanding too, both the individual blooms entered in all the classes—the dahlias, the gladioli, etc.—and in the displays and competitions of floral art. There were many arrangements with fresh flowers, many with dried, and some were a combination of the two. The display of wines was interesting too. From that building we went out to the show ring, and Arthur was called upon to open the show. He made about a ten- or fifteen-minute speech that was well received. He talked about Canada's being the chief customer for their wine and dried fruits. Then we went to the official opening of the new building by the Minister of Agriculture of South Australia. There was an official luncheon for about forty people, which started about 1:30 and went on until 3:00, with at least ten different people giving speeches: the president of the show, the secretary, all the MPs, state and federal, the shire president, and visiting representatives from other shires and towns. It was really quite a talk-feast—all in 96-degree heat, and of course with lots of the wine and other products of their valley. We were presented with five bottles of different varieties, which we packed in my hat box to bring home safely! After the lengthy lunch we watched the grand parade of animals, chiefly Guernsey cattle and horses, and then some sheep-shearing, before driving back to Adelaide. In the evening we went to a club for a very good dinner with the same MP and the federal Minister of Aboriginal Affairs, Mr. Wentworth, who was in town for another assignment that same weekend. He is a very controversial person and a great talker, so we had a good discussion. Returned this morning in time for the carillon, and a reception for the Canadian carillonneur at the Rogers'. Then Art went to the office.

March 13, 1971 · *Nausori Airport, Fiji*

A » Darling Sheila: I have neglected writing to report my

progress, but I've really been kept on the go with appointments the whole time. Now I have a little time to fill in at the airport because I foolishly didn't check, and on arrival found that my flight had left at 12:00 noon rather than the 1:00 p.m. on my schedule. There is another at 2:30 p.m., which, if we are on time, will just catch my 4:15 flight from Suva to Honolulu and Vancouver.

There has evidently been much rain here recently, and it washed out part of Prince Philip's program. The weather improved for me, so that while there have been showers, I've not got wet between appointments.

The prime minister's office prepared a very good program for me, with calls on five cabinet ministers, a visit to the YWCA, where they are still digging the foundations, a visit to the South Pacific Commission's Community Education Centre, where teachers and social workers are given a home economics course, and a visit to the University of the South Pacific, where I met ten students on Canada scholarships from all over the South Pacific. I dined the first night with Mrs. Kannangara, a Ceylonese statistician supported by Canadian Commonwealth Technical Co-operation funds, lunched with a U.S. consul, Bob Skiff, dined with the Indian High Commissioner, lunched at the University of the South Pacific with Aikman, and dined with Robert Sanders. All this gave me a chance to follow up in informal discussion points that had been raised in my interviews. The visit has been useful and I think I've accomplished as much as I could hope to in three and a half days.

Jim Boutilier, a Canadian history professor teaching at USP, came in for a drink. He and his wife had travelled very widely in three months. He reported that the university hiring market in Canada is dismal for history professors. He visited sixteen universities and got an offer only from R.M.C.

I picked up a little touch of sore throat again, perhaps because of changing from air-conditioning to humid heat, combined with getting insufficient sleep. I'll be all right.

I haven't had time to write up my notes so will try to do so now and on the plane. I'll mail this in Nadi.

March 14, 1971

s » This has been the most exciting week politically since we have been in Australia. And once started it became more and more complex, as old animosities came out to divide the party. On Monday the Minister of National Defence, Malcolm Fraser, resigned because the Prime Minister went around him to people in the army, and that made public many cabinet differences about defence policy with respect to Vietnam and the handling of troops in New Guinea. You may remember a similar crisis in Gorton's cabinet when Trudeau was in Australia; at that time another minister, Mr. Fairbairn, resigned because of differences over offshore rights. That led to a close contest for the leadership of the party, but it blew over. This time the Liberal Party had a vote on leadership, and the result was 33 to 33, with Gorton casting the deciding vote against himself rather than have five members of the party cross the floor and force the Government out. Then Mr. McMahon was voted in as the new leader of the Liberal Party and hence the prime minister. This could only happen now because the former leader of the Country Party, John McEwen, who had said he would not serve under McMahon as prime minister, retired in January; Doug Anthony, the new leader of the Country Party, which was the other part of the coalition government, has no such reservations. By Wednesday the most surprising thing of all happened. Gorton decided that he would run for deputy leader of the Liberal Party— against Fraser and one other—and won, so that the prime minister and the number two in the party have now just changed places. To add to the incredible, McMahon asked Gorton what portfolio he wanted, and Gorton said defence—which all the trouble started about—so he will be sallying forth for an inspection trip to Vietnam soon, a trip that Fraser postponed last Sunday. Of course the personal repercussions of such an upset are immense in a small city like Canberra. Everyone is touchy, and until the new cabinet and major changes of secretaries, etc., are announced, terrible lobbying is going on. It looks as if we'll have a new foreign minister to succeed McMahon. He's Mr. Fairbairn, who has been just a backbencher since he resigned last year.

You can well imagine that it is not the easiest time to be planning the visit of the Defence chief, General Sharp, or of a cabinet minister. There was one change in the department corresponding to the one Mr. Chrétien has when Anthony moved up and Mr. Hunt became minister, but with the new cabinet there may be more changes, so no one wants to make a decision on anything. Why anyone wants to be a politician in these days of cruel press and instant publicity and behind-the-scenes lobbying I can't understand.

While all these shenanigans were going on, Arthur was in the last furious whirl to get work wound up before his takeoff for Sydney and Fiji on Tuesday p.m. It was an exciting time to have to leave, but of course he will have enough on his plate to occupy him fully in Fiji and then Canada, and then back here. He will return in time to a less passionate, more sober Canberra. Just now it is still nuts: you don't like to leave the radio or TV in case you miss the latest juicy accusation or piece of dirty linen. How all this will affect the elections that will likely be called in 1972 is the big question.

Yesterday I had a ladies' luncheon for twelve in honour of Mary O'Flaherty, one of the communicators at the office, who is returning to Canada. Mostly young friends of hers. Saturday is the day that suits office girls best. Although that meant cutting out one day of bowling for Edith, I was glad she won $29 on the horses and, the night before, $20 on bingo, so she hasn't had too bad a weekend after all. Andrew, our chauffeur, is out of hospital, and is so restless to be back at work that he has been on most of this week, although the doctor said to rest another week.

March 14, 1971 · *en route from Vancouver to Toronto*

A » Darling Sheila: My all-too-brief visit to Vancouver is at an end. I hugged and kissed our girl goodbye at the airport a little while ago. That is another brief contact, too, too quickly over. I had a moist eye as I turned to go.

I'm afraid I wasn't at my best. When I wrote you that postcard at 1:00 a.m. in Honolulu I remarked whimsically but prophetically about seeing the dawn over Diamond Head. They had trouble with the plane's hydraulic system and eventually, at 4:00 a.m., took us to the Holiday Inn, where we were booked in (without baggage) to nice rooms. I showered and lay down for an hour and a half. They got us up at 6:15, and the plane eventually left at 7:30, six hours late, getting into Vancouver at 2:30 p.m. instead of 8:50 a.m.

With so little sleep my sore throat worsened.

Norah was there at the airport to meet me, looking wonderful in a hand-me-down orange ski parka and white slacks. We drove in her Volkswagen, with its cracked front window on the passenger side. We went first to call on the Forbeses, who had been invited for lunch, which, of course, had had to be cancelled. Norah had prepared a cream cheese cake with a graham cracker shell, which was delicious. We talked for an hour, had tea, and inspected the crocuses and other flowers that were peeking through. Both seemed well and pleased with our visit. They asked about you. Their only daughter, Louise, now 48 and married to an engineer, Norman Willis, is in Seoul, Korea, where her husband is building an electric power plant in which Caltex has an interest.

We then drove out to Burnaby, a very long way out—a half-hour by car from downtown and twenty-five minutes from UBC. The house is an old wooden one. The girls have the upstairs and the Kuipers (pronounced Coopers) the downstairs. They have good space: a large living room, a separate kitchen-eating room, a storage and sewing room, and two bedrooms. They share a good basement, with washer and dryer. Norah has an enormous bed that occupies much of her room—with a sheepskin rug on top. She had her room well cleaned for me, and indeed the whole apartment looked much, much better than her last.

Tessie, Norah's beloved sheltie, is really blind, but moves well in the area she knows, and Norah is evidently much devoted to the dog. Corry the cat, a robust-looking black and white monster, gets on well with Tessie.

Val Medlock (22) and Gillian Boyd (21) are both pleasant-looking girls. Both have $400 secretarial jobs and Val has just bought a car for $300 to save the long bus trip. They evidently plan to move into a modern West End apartment soon. Norah plans to stay put, and I told her we would pay the extra rent. If she is still there in the fall a classmate will move in with her.

Eddie Langevin still doesn't have a job other than working a couple of days a week for his uncle's moving firm when they need extra help. Evidently he feels that he has come closer to getting a job recently, but he must be quite discouraged. He still gives a good impression as a sincere, gentlemanly chap. They are devoted to each other.

I had an hour's rest after unpacking, and then at 7:00 p.m. Norah, Ed, Val, Gil, Konrad and Allison Kuiper, and I went downtown to the Nanking Chinese restaurant, where we had a good North China dinner, replete with Peking duck. Kon and Allison, who are from New Zealand, are very pleasant, and good talkers. She teaches English at a community college and he does some teaching while he works on his PhD Norah wore a crimson slack suit with white lapels and her Mexican sarape and looked very well in it. She hasn't lost weight, but says she keeps very well. I tried to maintain a cheerful front and keep up the chatter despite a sore throat.

I went to bed at 10:30 with a couple of sleeping pills and did-n't get up until 10:00. After breakfast I toured the flat and the garden and watched Tessie do her obedience tricks. Then it was time to drive to the airport to catch a flight at 1:25, as the one I had been booked on didn't go through to Ottawa.

It was all too too brief, and I'm afraid I wasn't as bright and vivacious and able to use every moment as I would have wished. I needed you.

Norah says she manages on our remittances but withdraws capital for extras. She hasn't touched any of the money with the trust company; she says that if she took the interest she'd spend it. I told her to let us know if she needs more.

This plane is packed with quite a number of Chinese immigrants, most of whom speak no English. I have an old and a young Cantonese beside me. The young one knows some Mandarin; neither speaks any English. I'm supposed to get to Ottawa about 10:00 p.m.

Vancouver was sunny for the first time in a couple of weeks

when I arrived, and about 40 degrees. It rained overnight and lightly in the morning.

Well, I've tried to give you an account of my visit with Norah. I know that I haven't managed well. I tried to convey our joint interest and love. We have an attractive, affectionate, maturing daughter of whom we can be very proud.

March 15, 1971 · *Ottawa*

A » Dearest Sheila: Your letter number one, dated March 14, talking about the change of prime minister in Australia, was awaiting my return to the hotel this evening. There has been a mild turn here, with temperatures in the high thirties and streets awash with slop.

I am chairman of a board concerned with promotions from FSO-7 to -8. There are forty-six competing for five possible promotions. Others on the board are Saul Rae, Russell of the Public Service Commission, Tom Burns of Industry Trade and Commerce, and Blouin (who won't sit until Wednesday). Fred Bild is secretary. We got through about fifteen ratings this afternoon. As we were in organizational meetings all morning I didn't get a chance to accomplish any of my own business. I'm getting to bed early tonight to try to lick my cold.

March 16, 1971 · *Ottawa*

A » I'm in the Auberge—formerly the cafeteria—of the Château, penning this letter at 8:00 p.m. while waiting for an order of roast pork at $2.40.

I visited CIDA this morning and got the impression that I still have a lot of missionary work to do to persuade people of the worth of the South Pacific as an aid objective. I'm to have a couple more sessions there.

I lunched with Andy Ross, now more white-haired than ever, who has been preparing for a posting to Chile. He talked about his experiences working for the Interdepartmental Committee on External Relations. Rather unsettling.

We have been once through the list of names. The reports at FSO-7 level are *very* sketchy and a good deal of one's own knowledge must be introduced. I must say that more system is desirable!

Saul Rae lives just down the hall. I had a drink in his room with Jennifer, who has a five-month-old daughter. The Raes have been six months in Mexico and have no knowledge of a move.

I see Ed Ritchie, the Under-Secretary, on Friday and hope to have some indication then of any future plans.

I'm still going strong; cold pretty much under control.

March 18, 1971 · *Ottawa*

A » Ralph Collins told me yesterday—for my private information —that he has been nominated as ambassador to China and expects to leave in late May after settling his mother and his family. He has mixed feelings and hopes not to stay too long.

I see Ed Ritchie tomorrow. Couldn't get anything out of Martin, who said Ritchie would probably wish to "keep his options open," which might mean our staying put a year. Ralph said I was one possibility to succeed him. So there you have it.

Last night I had Bishop Deschamps of the Montfort Mission in Papua in for dinner and a talk. He'll be here till June. He must wait until May for the central R.C. organization to review all outstanding applications for aid.

March 19, 1971 · *Ottawa*

A » This is just a brief note to let you know I'm still battling on.

Yesterday I met with Doug Wilson of Property Management and concurred in his recommendation that 32 Mugga Way be reconstructed at a convenient time and that we abandon the other, Turrana Street site because of costs.

Then I talked to twenty representatives of departments about minerals and uranium in Australia.

I lunched with Mr. Nichol, the Australian High Commissioner, and will attend a dinner there Monday for Chrétien. Margaret will go out on General Sharp's plane. Nothing new there.

We finished our promotion board yesterday afternoon.

Today I go to CIDA at nine, Ed Ritchie at 11:30, and lunch with Don Cornett.

March 19, 1971 · *Ottawa {11:30 p.m.}*

A » Before turning in I thought I would send you a few lines.

Ed Ritchie was not prepared to comment on future moves now. He said things might clarify further in three months. He said Ralph hoped to be in China only one year, so that was a possibility. Also mentioned Japan and a return to Ottawa. So nothing is clear. Don't mention the possibilities. He was very affable; said we had done well and that I would get a worthwhile assignment.

March 21, 1971, Toronto airport

A » Darling Sheila: I've had my weekend with the family and am now waiting for the 10:55 a.m. plane to Australia. I got into Toronto at 9:30 a.m. and by 10:30 I was at the museum, where Mr. James Hsü was waiting for me. They are getting ready to publish a 290-page volume of photos of rubbings of bone fragments. Hsü also has another volume on the incisions on the back and some monographs. On the whole I think that we are at last getting the work into its final phase. Hsü is staying on for two years as a PhD candidate, but not at the expense of the Menzies fund.

Then I went to see John Holmes, who is well and asked after you, and talked for an hour or so.

I caught a 1:00 p.m. express bus that got me to Burlington at 2:00 p.m. Had a good gab with my sister Frances and Ervin Newcombe, with Gordon popping in from time to time. Frances is working and enjoying it and looks well.

March 21, 1971

s » Prime Minister McMahon is to announce his new cabinet tonight at 10:00, so they will be sworn in at Government House Monday morning. One way the reporters speculate who is in the new ministry is by finding out who will arrive in Canberra tonight to be on hand in the morning—but this does not help them calculate what portfolio each will have. The rumours of the past week have been very interesting, and the strong tips for the top jobs are quite different from what they were one week ago, when Gorton was just out. Said Defence Minister Gorton is off in Vietnam this weekend, but will be back in a few days. He was sworn in last week. Dame Annabella Rankin, who was minister for housing, has been appointed high commissioner to New Zealand. It is good that a woman has made it to the top in the diplomatic field here, but I'm sorry that it was not one of the Foreign Affairs career women who made it first. There is not likely to be a woman in the new cabinet, since, as in Canada, there are very few in Parliament.

I am very pleased with the three lectures I have attended so far in the Australian National University evening course called The Three Arts, taught by Mrs. Nancy Parker, a local Canberra painter. She has travelled widely, has a marvellous collection of slides, and is very resourceful about getting films and other aids to illustrate her talks. The basic theory is that architecture, painting, and sculpture energize each other, and she is showing the links between those modes of expression, especially during the last hundred years. There are about twenty of us enrolled in the three-term course (most of us pay for one term at a time so that we can stop if we must after one term). My trouble will be of course that we will often have other commitments or be out of town on Monday nights from eight to ten. However, I am lucky even then, because one of my best friends here, Jess Keehn, is also taking the course, so will bring me up to date.

March 25, 1971 · *en route from London to Singapore*

A » On my way back to Australia from a ten-day visit to Canada I stopped in London for five hours in order to see Kenneth. He met me at Heathrow Airport about 11:30 this morning, looking a bit like Scott of the Antarctic, with a thick nut-brown beard and moustache, but hair of normal length behind a fast-receding hairline. He wears dark black-rimmed spectacles. He had suede boots, blue jeans, a red turtleneck sweater, and my old heavy black leather short coat. He carried a soiled knapsack of books on his back with straps over both shoulders, a convenience for motorcycle riding.

We rode in by airport bus for an hour to the city terminal, then took a train from Victoria Station (which serves the south) for about twenty minutes to Streatham, which is on the South Road to Brighton (the A23). It is a pleasant area of respectable shops and older homes. Kenneth's rented house at 35 Woodbourne Avenue is part of a varied row, with a small front garden where the crocuses and snowdrops are out. The house itself is of genteel First World War vintage, fully furnished at £100 a month, of which Kenneth pays £20 (Canadian $50) for a fine big third-storey room with a big window that gives good daylight. Each of the five occupants puts in the equivalent of one dollar a day for food, intended to cover breakfast and dinner (four nights) and fish and chips (three nights). They take turns cooking.

Kenneth goes down to Essex University at Colchester about once a week. He also uses the London School of Economics library. He works for the most part at home. He has completed four and a half out of eight chapters of his thesis. He hopes to complete the first draft by October or November of this year, leaving time for revision, final typing, and submission in April or May 1972 and an oral exam in June. Herminio Martins, the Portuguese professor who has been supervising his thesis, is going to Oxford in October this year, but Kenneth thinks that he will remain as his external examiner.

Kenneth has had an informal feeler about teaching at Essex this fall. This would defer his PhD for two or three years. He is unclear about the opportunities for sociologists at Canadian universities. I urged him to finish his PhD now while he is at it. He is inclined that way too. He is particularly interested in the theoretical aspects of the Parsonian theory, which is over my head.

We talked about his life, his recreation, family affairs, etc. It was good to get caught up. He is a serious young man, obviously widely read, but with a natural courtesy. It was all too short a visit. We took a forty-five-minute taxi ride back out to Heathrow, and by 4:30 it was time for me to enter the boarding system. The visit was too short, as was my visit with Norah; but better short than not at all.

March 28, 1971

s » Hurrah! Hurrah! Hurrah! I am so pleased to have Arthur back home again safe and sound after his around-the-world trip. The plane had been about an hour late getting into Sydney from Singapore, so he missed his flight to Canberra. Allan and Gene Roger were with me at the airport to meet him, and our disappointment that Art was not on the intended flight was somewhat diminished, because we witnessed one of the most moving meetings I have ever seen. A little old lady in her seventies, I'd say about four feet high, shrivelled up and slightly hunched with age, from Yugoslavia or Greece (everyone on the plane said she had spoken no English, and all eyes were on her), was met by a son and, after a dramatic moment when she was quite swept off her feet, crying with happiness, by other relatives. Gene and I both had tears in our eyes just seeing them. Anyway, we went back into town but were on hand for the next flight two hours later, and delighted to see Arthur. We had a bowl of soup, and after he unpacked a little bit he crawled into bed, where I have orders to leave him until about 6:30 p.m., when we'll have a bite of supper and he'll survey some of the umpteen hundred urgent, most immediate important, confidential, etc., matters piled up on his desk.

April 18, 1971

s » It was three weeks ago today that I last typed a letter with carbons for everyone. As you know, we left for Sydney with Minister of Indian Affairs and Northern Development Chrétien and Madame Chrétien on Saturday, April 3. We had a busy day there, with lunch at a restaurant overlooking the harbour, a cruise on the harbour, and a visit to a small nature reserve, after which we went to the Royal Easter Show (rather like Toronto's Royal Winter Fair), where most of the Canadian party saw a polo game for the first time.

Sunday we left for Darwin in the large Canadian Armed Forces plane that had brought the Chrétien party and General Lipton's party out to New Zealand and Australia. The Chrétiens stayed with the Administrator of the Northern Territory and Mrs. Chaney at Government House, as did we, and the rest of the party stayed at a Darwin hotel. I think they got the best of the deal, because they had air-conditioned rooms and a swimming pool, whereas our room had just a fan and no pool in the 96-degree weather. The Chrétiens had the one air-conditioned room, but a storm blew out the power at Government House, so it didn't work the first night! There was a very strong and interesting delegation with the Minister: four members of parliament, including the full-blooded Indian from Kamloops who defeated Davie Fulton. By far the most colourful of the party was George Manuel, president of the Indian Brotherhood of Canada. He had brought his great blue feathered headdress and a large "talking stick," which he used as a ventriloquist's prop, like Edgar Bergen and Charlie McCarthy. He would address the talking stick, and then, casting his voice in a different tone, would produce a response that seemed to come from the stick. He was very jovial, and delighted to put on a little dance and chant or song at every stop we made. You can imagine how this broke the ice, and it went over very well in the Aboriginal settlements and missions we visited. For the next four days we visited places in the Northern Territory to observe contrasts and parallels with the problems of the Canadian Northwest Territories and the Yukon (one of the others in our party was the Commissioner of the Yukon). Arthur and the Minister and the Administrator also got a trip in a small plane to a fishing spot one night and slept there after catching about three hundred pounds of fish in one hour!—including a thirty-two-pound one by Chrétien!! We visited three Aboriginal settlements, Maningrida, the one near Gove, the big mining town, and one on Groote Eylandt, near the manganese mine, where we had spent a weekend once before and where we got our best bark paintings. We found the Minister and all the party pleasant, and interested in all they saw. We returned to Darwin Thursday afternoon to connect with the Canadian plane again and went in it that night to

Brisbane. The official party took off for Tahiti and then Canada on Good Friday morning.

After seeing them off at Brisbane Airport Arthur and I picked up the drive-yourself car we had reserved and took off southward via Surfers Paradise on the coast, then turned inland up into the McPherson Range of mountains to Lamington National Park, where we had a reservation for Easter weekend at Binna Burra Lodge. This turned out to be a very pleasant spot. For the weekend it was filled to overflowing with all sorts of families and young people, all with one thing in common, a love of the outdoors and a desire to hike in the park. Every morning at breakfast a sheet was circulated outlining the program for the day, with suggested walks of different grades: beginning, at about three or four miles; medium, seven or eight miles; and for the experienced ones, twelve to fifteen miles. Sometimes they have two- or three-day walks too. A guide goes along on the advanced walks. But the trails in the woods are well marked and lots of the trees are labelled and identified, as in Algonquin Park in Canada, so you can wander along at your own pace. It is rain-forest country with very thick vegetation, tropical trees such as palms, jungle vines intertwining with huge specimens of eucalyptus, and ash and mahogany and Morton Bay fig. We had never seen such fantastic growth. It was a delight to walk in the cool shade of the great cover. Each day we took a picnic lunch and the "Billy" supplied by the lodge, and cooked our noonday meal at one of the prescribed fireplaces along the routes. Although my feet were weary each day, we thoroughly enjoyed the change—and it was quite a shock to go back to the busy world of Canberra!

Northern Territory of Australia Visited by Canadian Delegation: A Report to the House Committee on Foreign Affairs

Although the tropical heat of Australia's Northern Territory contrasts markedly with the arctic climate of Canada's Yukon and Northwest Territories, a delegation of Canadian members of Parliament and officials led by the Minister of Indian Affairs and Northern Development, Honourable Jean Chrétien, found during a week's visit, from April 2 to April 9, 1971, that many direct comparisons can be made—with respect to constitutional status, mining development, and the advancement of native peoples.

In Canberra Mr. Chrétien had discussions with the Honourable Ralph Hunt, Minister for the Interior, who is responsible for the Northern Territory, and the Honourable William Wentworth, Minister of State for Social Services and minister in charge of Aboriginal affairs. He learned that the constitutional status of Aborigines in Australia differs from that of Indians and Eskimos in Canada, who, under the British North America Act, are a responsibility of the federal government. In Australia, responsibility for Aborigines had rested with the states, except in the federally administered Northern Territory, until a constitutional amendment was passed in 1966 giving concurrent and, if necessary, overriding power to the federal government. The Council for Aboriginal Affairs and the Office of Aboriginal Affairs, which report to Mr. Wentworth, are responsible for developing broad policies for Aborigines, endeavouring to secure uniform nondiscriminatory treatment of Aborigines in the states, and providing additional financial assistance and loans for Aboriginal enterprises.

Arriving in Darwin, the capital of the 520,000-square-mile Northern Territory, on April 4, the party was met by the Administrator, His Honour Mr. Fred Chaney, D.F.C., who was to be its host during the tour of the Northern Territory. First, there was an afternoon drive around the modern city of Darwin, which has a population of 32,000, out of a total of 69,000 in the Territory. Most of the houses are up on cement piers, which give better access to the breeze in the seven months of "the dry," and shelter for laundry and playing space for children in the five months of "the wet." Solar heaters, looking like skylights on the roofs of houses, supply hot water. Among Darwin's fine modern buildings is the new Civic Centre, where the Canadian delegation was received by the mayor and councillors.

A visit to the Legislative Council for the Northern Territory permitted comparisons to be drawn with the powers and procedures of the Yukon and Northwest Territories councils. There are eleven elected and six official members of the Legislative Council, whose responsibility is to make ordinances for the peace, order, and good government of the Northern Territory, subject to review by the Administrator and the Governor General on behalf of the federal government. All questions relating to land and Aborigines must be referred to Canberra. Not satisfied with a purely legislative role, the elected members of the Legislative Council are pressing for more state-type powers of self-government, in order to have a say on financial matters. Expenditures on state-type matters cost $82 million in 1969–70, whereas only $12 million was raised in the Territory. In Canada the comparable ratio in 1969–70 for the Northwest Territories was $92 million spent against $19 million earned and, for the Yukon, $32 million spent against $12 million earned. In both Australia and Canada the federal governments are reluctant to hand over financial authority to territorial councils, which raise such a small proportion of local revenues against substantial expenditures.

On April 6 the party flew to Maningrida Aboriginal Settlement, on the coast 230 miles east of Darwin. Here they were met by the superintendent and elected councillors, who serve in an advisory role and represent the 1,300 Aborigines of the Settlement. A concert was given in the schoolyard with songs by the children and Aboriginal dances by some schoolboys; then a group of men in corroboree body paint and decorations performed "the butterfly dance," accompanied by sonorous tones. Mr. George Manuel then put on his gorgeous blue feathered headdress, took out his "talking stick," and entertained the Aborigines with Indian songs and dances.

The party stopped for the night at Gove, 175 miles east of Maningrida, where Nabalco Pty. Ltd., a consortium of Swiss and Australian interests, is spending $300 million to develop a bauxite mine, which will export 2,000,000 tons of bauxite a year, and an alumina plant with a capacity of 1,000,000 tons. A large work force is employed at this remote site, which must be supplied by sea or air, as there are no connecting roads. A modern townsite is being built for an initial population of 5,000.

The Canadian delegation also visited the nearby Methodist Mission Settlement, where some 600 members of the Yirrkala Aboriginal tribes live. These tribes had lodged a claim in the High Court of the Northern Territory for recognition of their title over the land on which the Nabalco bauxite and alumina project is being built. No treaties were signed with the Aborigines during the settlement of Australia, and no Aboriginal claims to land ownership have been recognized yet. In conversation with the Canadian visitors to Yirrkala, councillors showed an interest in Canadian practice regarding Indian land titles. The elders also indicated their uneasiness over the extent to which this industrial project would affect their traditional ways. The Canadian party was able to see at first hand the problems arising from the advent of modern technological society in what had heretofore been the remote and inaccessible Arnhemland Aboriginal Reserve.

Although Aboriginal land rights have not been legally recognized, the Northern Territory administration has taken a number of practical measures to assist Aborigines. Half of the 2.5-percent mining royalty is paid into an Aboriginal Benefits Trust Fund, administered by an Aboriginal board and used for their own economic and social development projects. A condition of mining leases on reserves is that 25 percent of employment should be offered to Aborigines. There are joint ventures that give Aborigines an equity interest in mining exploration projects.

The Canadian party made its last stop at Groote Eylandt, an island in the Gulf of Carpentaria, where they saw a manganese mine and a prawn-freezing factory. Here they visited the Angurugu Aboriginal Mission, where members took a special interest in the pre-school classes for three- to five-year-old Aboriginal children. The guided play at the pre-school helps the child to become familiar at an early age with shapes and techniques that are not part of the Aboriginal way of life, but about which the Western school system assumes knowledge.

In all three Aboriginal settlements, the Canadian delegation had the opportunity to see Aboriginal art, such as bark paintings, woodcarvings, and basketwork. They left with an appreciation of the cultural traditions that Aborigines wish to preserve. They had been made aware of the continuing tasks facing the Northern Territory administration in integrating Aborigines into the Western economy and society while preserving their cultural identity.

April 25, 1971

s » You all know something about precedence in the diplomatic corps. Everything is counted from the date on which the ambassador or high commissioner presents his letter of credentials. In our case, for Australia, this was November 15, 1965. As of this week, because of seniority, Arthur has become the dean of the diplomatic corps. For more than five years the Philippine Ambassador was the dean, and as they had a large, gracious, well-equipped house, well suited for all sorts of large parties for welcoming diplomats or bidding them farewell, and as the Philippines does not have a terrific amount of business here and the Ambassador liked to devote his time to ceremonial and protocol, during all the early part of our time here there was no problem. When Ezpeleta left, at the end of last year, Sir Charles Johnston, the British High Commissioner, stepped up to his place, though he knew unofficially at the time that he would only be here a short time longer. He left at the beginning of April. Next in line was the Greek, Mr. Tsamissis, but his is a one-man diplomatic office here, and he said he just could not take on such a big job (it needs administrative and other support, which he does not have), so he started agitating to get his government to move him, and has succeeded. So he was passed over—he only gave the departing reception for Sir Charles Johnston—and the mantle has fallen on Arthur.

The chief chore of being dean is to provide the farewell reception for each departing head of mission. As our house is much too small to hold such events without taking all the furniture out—and then of course it would not be suitable—we hold these farewells at the office chancery, where we have always held our national day reception and any large affair for over eighty guests. We can handle about fifty or sixty maximum at the house. The diplomatic corps in Canberra now numbers close to fifty, so with wives that means up to a possible one hundred. Actually only about forty of those are resident full-time here, so usually it is closer to eighty at a farewell. If the head of mission cannot go, he designates someone else from his office. The corps pays jointly for the reception and for the gift for the departing colleague, usually a silver salver with people's signatures on it, or a silver cigar box, but any equivalent gift worth around $200 is acceptable. At the time of the presentation a speech is made, usually extolling the fine work the ambassador has done in Australia. This is done by the dean, and it varies according to the calibre of the dean. Under Ezpeleta it was often rather feeble, under Sir Charles a very high standard of polish and appropriateness was set, and now under Arthur of course I say the best has been reached—but naturally it requires time and thought to prepare such a speech. The speech usually lasts just about five minutes, then a representative of the government makes a short speech seconding the dean, and the departing colleague makes a rather longer speech—depending on his nature. Under Ezpeleta farewells lasted from 5:00 to 8:00 p.m., then were cut to 6:00 to 7:30; under Charles Johnston they lasted from 6:00 to 7:00 p.m. or from 11:30 a.m. to 12:30 p.m. We are sticking to the 6:00 to 7:00 idea.

The chief advantage to being dean is that you represent the corps at the arrival and departure of all heads of states, and at entertainments for such VIPs. This means that you have quite a bit more contact with people like Governor General and Lady Hasluck, Prime Minister and Mrs. McMahon, and other cabinet ministers and parliamentarians.

This week, therefore, this new honour involved us deeply in the twenty-four-hour state visit of the King and Queen of Nepal. We were at the airport twenty-one-gun salute, etc., then the whole diplomatic corps was received at Government House at four o'clock in the afternoon to meet Their Majesties, and in the evening we were back again for the white-tie dinner. We'll get to be real quick-change artists, and will have a use for all our finery—our morning coats, etc.

May 2, 1971

s » There was to have been a state visit here this week by the Prime Minister of Fiji, Ratu Mara, and, being accredited to Fiji, we were looking forward to it. However, at the last minute it was called off, because he did not want to leave the country during the serious dock strike there. Most events, such as the parliamentary lunch and the Fijian high commission reception, were cancelled, but a dinner at Government House went on, with the chief guest changed. There was no Fiji P.M., no Australian P.M. or leader of the opposition—so to our surprise, as dean of the corps, we ended up being the number-one guest! It is a funny world.

This has been the week our Canadian minister of Energy, Mines, and Resources arrived in Australia. Mr. Greene is accompanied by a strong team of six: Mr. Austin, deputy minister of EMR, Dr. Lorne Gray, president of Atomic Energy of Canada, Mr. Drolet, assistant deputy minister of EMR, Mr. Schwarzmann, assistant deputy minister of Trade and Commerce, Mr. Runnalls, and Mr. Golab, also from EMR. Arthur has been up to his neck in work and meetings. Wednesday, the day of arrival, there was a stag dinner for twelve Canadians here at the house, a working meeting to plan the details of the program for the next ten days. They all had their briefcases and briefs, etc. Thursday they had their meetings with Australian government departments, and we held a reception for about ninety people in honour of Mr. Greene at the office. Then the Rogers and the Weisers entertained about twenty each for buffet dinners afterwards. We went with the Minister to the Weisers. Friday they had more meetings, lunch, a stag hosted by Australian cabinet minister Swartz, etc., and early Saturday morning six of them, including Arthur, left for a two-day trip to the Snowy Mountains hydroelectric scheme, part of the time touring it, part just driving. It was supposed to be a relaxing weekend, but actually it was rather tiring I'd say. They came in from Cooma by plane this afternoon and had fifteen minutes at Canberra airport to connect with the flight for Melbourne, where they will be for two days, then on to Sydney for three days. Art will return after

Mr. Greene leaves, likely on Friday night or Saturday. It's a great life—full of interest if you don't weaken!

You may remember that about a month ago there was rain on the day of the Australian diplomatic tennis tournament, in which I had entered the mixed doubles. They only have mixed doubles and men's doubles. Anyway, it was rescheduled for this weekend, which turned out to have much better weather, although yesterday was rather windy, and I have a wind-burned face from a full day of sun and wind. Fortunately this time I drew a fairly good partner, an Australian Navy captain who hasn't played much recently but is basically a good player. This helped, and we ended up the winners on our court—meaning we beat the other five couples there—and so were in the quarterfinals today. Luck was with us this morning, for we pulled a bye and so got to the semifinals (that is the way I like to play), but our good fortune didn't last beyond that. We lost 5 to 8 against a chap from the British high commission and an Australian Foreign Affairs wife with whom I play regularly. As I put my name down originally in the tournament to prove to myself that I was over shingles and could enter it, I was very pleased to get that far. Of course this is in the second division of the tournament; all the best players are in the top division.

The Australian-Canadian Society presents a prize for a class in the National Eisteddfod. It started just last year, and we had the winning choirs sing for Trudeau and for our national day. Well this was the second competition. Arthur should have presented a prize but of course was away with Mr. Greene, so Allan Roger did, and I was there with Allan and Gene. We were disappointed that only five choirs entered this time, but their singing of first one Canadian and then one Australian song was of a very high standard. Again, a high school from Sydney won the first award, an Eskimo carving mounted on a piece of Australian wood, plus $30 for books; the second prize is also $30.

May 9, 1971

A » I think that the visit of the Canadian Minister of Energy, Mines and Resources and his team of officials can be counted a real success. The team worked and talked and worked and talked the whole time, so that there was a feeling of accomplishment at the end. In Canberra there were two full days of talks with officials at round-table sessions as well as discussions with ministers. Then over the weekend we spent two days touring in the Snowy Mountains, seeing something of the hydro projects there. In Melbourne we had meetings with the two mining giants, Conzinc Rio Tinto Australia (CRA) and the Broken Hill Proprietary (BHP), with Victoria state ministers and officials, and with bankers, and had a dinner with the Mining Industry Council. Then on to Sydney for three days of meetings with the Reserve (Central) Bank, with the AMP Society (Australia's largest insurance company, which does a lot of investing), and with a group of Canadians engaged in mining. The Minister also talked to the annual meeting of state ministers of mines and their deputies. Altogether he seemed pleased with the arrangements and outcome, so I guess that the Honourable J.J. Greene can now be counted as a friend.

May 16, 1971

A » This is a very special day for us because we talked by telephone with Norah for an hour and ten minutes after her 22nd birthday. Our connection was good and enabled us to hear about the way she celebrated the day, her presents, how Tessie has been mending since her fall, and Norah's new job as a social work counsellor at the hospital.

Some time ago I accepted speaking engagements in Crookwell, eighty-five miles north, and Oberon, another hundred miles north of that. We planned to spend a couple of days leave in between. Then we had the visits of Canadian ministers and a lot of business that might otherwise have provided an excuse for a delay. Despite business, we took off on Wednesday afternoon and motored two and a half hours to Crookwell, which is at an altitude of about 3,000 feet, and north of Goulburn. The latter part of the way was over slippery dirt roads, as there had been quite a bit of rain. We just had time to change at the motel when we were picked up and taken to a civic reception that we had not been told about in advance. This was one of those typical Australian occasions when "a few words" are spoken in welcome (meaning a fifteen-minute inventory of the fine points of Crookwell), to be followed by a suitably appreciative response from the guest. Then we were taken to see the new Anglican church, done in a simple A-frame design for economy but very well conceived and finished with local woods. The Apex Club International Relations Dinner at which I spoke was held in the Anglican church hall, with about eighty attending. I spoke for thirty minutes, answered questions for fifteen minutes, and then showed a film called *Trans-Canada Journey.*

Thursday morning it began to clear, and we went out to inspect some of the local potato farms, although it was too wet for them to be harvesting. We learned that potatoes can be left in the ground for six months, until they begin to sprout, so this gives the farmers and graders plenty of time. We visited a grading and packing shed. Then we went on to an apple orchard, whose owner is an Apex member. We had lunch there and looked at their storage and sorting and packing shed. I should also have mentioned a brief tour of the Crookwell high school and a visit to the public school, where I talked for a while to the children.

From Crookwell we drove a hundred miles north to the Jenolan Caves, where Sheila has been trying to entice me for the past three years. These are a series of limestone caves, first discovered in 1838, when they were a hideaway for a bushranger, and they were developed over the ensuing years so that today there is a fine hotel, and nine caves have paths and steps and electric lights and guides to take tours through. We saw just three of the caves. Each one took one and a half to two hours to go through, with corridors, cement stairs, iron ladders, etc. Lights have been strategically located to show up the various formations of stalactites, stalagmites, fossils, pools of water, and so forth. Some of the larger chambers are most impressive. We also enjoyed our walks, seeing and feeding the possums and rock wallabies, and getting two long nights' sleep.

Saturday noon we drove on to Oberon, at 3,700 feet, near the top of the Great Dividing Range, 113 miles west of Sydney. After booking into our hotel we were taken by two Apex Club members to visit the local Pyneboard Factory, where they make a flake board from the thinnings of 200,000 acres of local pine plantations. We then went on to visit a Dorset sheep stud farm, where we had tea. In the evening I spoke to about eighty at a dinner at the new RSL club, including the local MP, the mayor, etc., and showed a film.

Today, Sunday, we motored back about three hundred miles, by way of Katoomba, which is the big resort centre of the Blue Mountains west of Sydney. Katoomba is atop a great limestone ridge with steep thousand-foot cliffs dropping away on all sides.

May 23, 1971

s » About twice a year Arthur manages to get off for a weekend of fishing. I am pleased that he has managed it now, before it is altogether too cold. He went with the same three men he has gone with several times before: Eric Conybeare, the organizer of the expedition and a Canadian geology professor at ANU; Sir Leonard Huxley, ex-vice-chancellor of ANU; and the secretary of the University. As they like to fish after sunset, Art warned me not to expect them until late this evening. They left Friday noon and are staying at a cottage near Lake Eucumbene, where they will rent boats. Here's hoping they catch something!

When we returned from our trip last weekend we were distressed to find that Peter Hayden (made Sir Peter just last year), the Secretary of the Department of Immigration, had died of a heart attack Saturday. His wife, née Naomi Slater of Ottawa, met him in Washington when he was in Australian External Affairs. He was high commissioner to India and to New Zealand before changing departments to become permanent head of Immigration ten years ago. Because of their jobs and the Canadian connection we got to know them very well. No one in Canberra had such a fund of stories and anecdotes as Peter—usually throwing light on some Australian political figure—and no one told a story better, or got more kick out of it himself in the telling. He had just played nine holes of golf and won a competition, and although his doctor had warned him about playing more than nine, he had done so well that he continued, and was back in the clubhouse having a drink when he collapsed. The saddest part is that their elder daughter is to be married this Wednesday, and Naomi's sister-in-law, from Whitby, Ontario, had just arrived that day to be on hand for the wedding. By coincidence, her husband, Naomi's brother, had dropped dead when Naomi had visited her, so that each has been through a similar shock. It must be a great help to Naomi to have her here. Now she feels that because her sister-in-law is only here for three weeks, she ought to carry on and help her to see something of Australia. So I was more than surprised that she went ahead with the small ladies' lunch two days after the funeral, that she had arranged earlier for her sister-in-law, and she told me that they would still come here for a coffee party I had arranged, three days after. It all seemed a little forced and strained to me, but as that was the way she wanted to handle it, naturally I went ahead. Also yesterday I drove Naomi and this Mrs. Dyson Slater out to a friend's place in the country. Julie's wedding now will be a small house event for just about forty people instead of a larger reception at the golf club.

Entertaining this week, as is usual now, was a mixture of our duty as dean of the corps (for example, a welcoming lunch for the new French Ambassador and his wife, who seemed eager and prepared to talk English, in spite of—or perhaps because of—our repeated attempts to talk French, which is a great change from their two predecessors here; then a dinner for a mixture of diplomats and Australians), and a small reception in honour of the two Canadian delegates to the Commonwealth Association of Architects; one was Roy Sellers, the Dean of Architecture at the University of Manitoba, and the other a Mr. Davies, from Vancouver, and each had his wife along.

We have started planning to be in Fiji again, for about ten days beginning Saturday, June 5. When Art had to go to Canada for the promotions board meeting he just had three days in Fiji en route, and he found he could not get nearly everything done he wanted to. Naturally I will be interested to see the changes since I was there for Independence six months ago.

May 30, 1971

s » Another busy week behind us, but not as busy as this next one will be, because we must get things cleaned up before we take off on Saturday, June 5, for ten days in Fiji. We will return to Canberra on Wednesday, June 16. The office will forward our mail.

This was our week for the Pakistanis; both occasions were farewells, in our capacity as dean of the diplomatic corps and as a fellow high commissioner. Thus on Tuesday we had a dinner here for them with other high commissioners from Malaysia, U.K., and New Zealand, as well as an Australian Foreign Affairs representative. It went well, chiefly because of the bubbly effusive nature of the Malaysian, Donald Stephens, who is a roly-poly sort of individual who always exudes goodwill along with his cigar smoke. Friday at the office we had seventy-eight people turn up for the diplomatic corps farewell. For the first time since he has been foreign minister, Mr. Bury attended and made the supporting speech on behalf of the government, after Arthur's speech. Art has set a very high standard in the farewell speeches he has made so far. It is not easy to say something appropriate and different each time, but so far he has excelled.

He had an even more difficult place to speak in on Thursday night, a sort of foyer restaurant at the theatre in Melbourne, where the Australian premiere of the Canadian film, *Goin' Down the Road*, had been held. The 31-year-old Canadian director, Donald Shebib, has made a good, realistic, natural film about two young chaps who leave Nova Scotia in a 1960 Cadillac bound for the big-city life of Toronto, only to discover the problems of jobs and money in a strange new world. The acting was very good, and altogether we thought it was well done, and a credit to the Canadian film industry. Of course the test will be how long it stays in Melbourne, then in Sydney. Evidently it ran well in some American cities, but not in all Canadian cities. Have any of you seen it? Before the film we had dinner with Kevin Osmond and his wife Winifred (he is our commercial counsellor in Melbourne) and the Gilberts (he is the previous Canadian trade representative, and has retired in Melbourne).

The kind of invitation that we are always happy to receive is for dinner in an Australian house for just a small group, without the fuss of waiters and such and without a lot of other diplomats, so that we get the feeling we are being entertained as friends, not as the Canadian high commissioner. This week for a change we were at two such dinners, the first with an ex-Foreign Affairs couple, now in Defence, and the second with a Trade couple—the wife and I belong to several of the same groups. In each case the family helped, and the whole atmosphere was much more informal and pleasant than the usual fancy spread we go to.

It has rained both yesterday and today, so we have not been able to play our usual weekend tennis, nor has Edith been able to do her usual weekend bowling. Allan and Gene Roger have moved into the new house that the Canadian government has just bought for the political counsellor at this post. We have just been over to see it, and it's a very handsome house, spacious and well located, and (what will no doubt please the majority of its future occupants) with a swimming pool and a very pleasant outdoor entertaining area with a well-screened garden behind it. Both it and the new house bought for the economic counsellor are newer and larger houses than ours—but of course the ultimate plan now is to rebuild and enlarge this house rather than build on the other site, which has been held in readiness for so many years. As long as we are here we are quite prepared to have the smaller place and not have any of the upset and delay and frustration of having building going on around us. We think Gene and Allan are very good-natured about this, their third major move since they have come here.

Oh yes—I forgot to tell you that last weekend we had the two largest fish Arthur caught, nice brown trout, baked as the entrée for the dinner for the Pakistanis. We will have the other four smaller ones in some shape or form for the dinner we're to have this week for the Singapore High Commissioner. Everyone is suitably impressed with the skill of the fisherman.

June 19, 1971

A » Our principal news this week is that we have been authorized to return to Canada for the visit there of the Prime Minister of Fiji, the Honourable Ratu Sir Kamisese Mara, and Adi Lady Lala Mara during the last week of July, and we will take some home leave afterwards.

Our visit to Fiji was a good and useful one. We had four days first in the Western Division, around Nadi, with a visit to Castaway Island, a sugar mill and forestry project at Lautoka, a sawmill in the Nausori Highlands, tobacco curing sheds, and a real Fiji village *yaqona* ceremony and lunch. We had three and a half working days and two and a half days of holiday on the Suva side. I had a string of appointments with officials, the University of the South Pacific, etc. We visited the Fiji School of Agriculture and the Navuso Agricultural School. We also went to the South Pacific Commission Community Education Training Centre, where we had photos taken in connection with a gift of $30,000 I got for them from the B.C. government. We now have a Canadian marine biologist, Professor Lindsey, at the University, and an architect, Mr. Peter Zubas, with the Public Works Department.

Our visit coincided with the Queen's birthday celebrations, so we attended a parade by the Royal Fiji Military Forces in Albert Park similar to the one for Independence. This time the field was partly covered with pools of rainwater, and it was amusing to see the soldiers slosh through them. We had seen the RFMF Band off for a tour of B.C. while in Nadi, so the police band provided the music. There was a Gurkha company there as well that marched at the double quick. In the afternoon we attended a garden party at Government House, and in the evening a black-tie dinner at the British High Commissioner's, attended by Governor General and Lady Foster.

We enjoyed two weekend outings, one to Deuba, about twenty-five miles along the coast from Suva, where we swam and lunched with two British couples working in Foreign Affairs. The other day we went with the Vice-Chancellor of the University, Colin Aikman, his family, and friends out by boat to an island, where I spent an hour and a half floating with mask and snorkel looking at beautiful coral formations and the most gorgeous tropical fish. Got sunburnt.

I was able to make progress on arrangements for the P.M.'s visit to Canada and on quite a number of other matters, so feel that the visit was worthwhile.

June 27, 1971

s » When we were in Crookwell for Arthur to give a speech to Apex about a month ago, we also visited the studio of Mrs. Allison Willis, a painter I had heard about. This is the type of Australiana that one doesn't often see done, and she is a master at it. We were so impressed that we said we would arrange for her to give a demonstration to some of our friends if she came to Canberra. Well, she came this week, and with her came her agent, a Mrs. Bassingthwaighte, who sells her paintings in a store in Crookwell and also has appeared with her on two TV programs explaining her work. While Mrs. W. paints, Mrs. B. explains the process and answers questions.

We had invited about sixty people, the maximum who would be able to see in the basement of the office. Most were diplomats who are interested in looking for some sort of craft or art form that is a little different to take back home when they leave Australia. Mrs. Willis collects the bark of the tea tree, found chiefly in coastal areas in Queensland and in northern New South Wales. This is placed in very thin strips, and builds up the landscape of her picture. To represent a gum tree she will tear off several strips or layers of bark and build up the trunk so that it has a three-dimensional look. The sky is painted with watercolour, and if there is a pond it may be painted or may be represented by bark and painted over. Most of her scenes are rural—a few gum trees, perhaps a sheep or a cow or an Aborigine fishing. To make the foliage of the gum trees she uses light green lichen, and for some of the grasses she uses seaweed. She demonstrated by making one picture about twelve inches wide, and finished it in close to one hour. It was fascinating to watch the growth of the picture, as more bark or lichen or moss or seaweed or tiny root was added to build up into a very realistic natural country scene. Afterwards we served coffee and drinks and people wandered around and looked at the collection of about forty works of hers that we had arranged around the room with well-placed spotlights to highlight them. Mrs. Willis must have been pleased, for altogether between that night and the next morning she sold twenty-nine pictures, some small, just about three by six inches, some a couple of feet across, and one at least four feet across. We had the two of them stay with us one night. Mrs. Willis is a very unusual dedicated artistic type, probably because of her Seventh Day Adventist faith, and a strict vegetarian. Tea would be too stimulating, so she drank juice!

Other years we have celebrated Canada Day by taking in a dance, alternating between Sydney and Melbourne. This year it so works out that we will celebrate the day at three dances. This weekend we have been to Melbourne for a function at the Trak Centre very nicely arranged by the Melbourne Canada Club for about two hundred people. Arthur was in fine fettle for the "few remarks" he was called upon to make; he gave an amusing speech most suitable for the occasion, and later led in the singing of "Alouette," with variations, which was a great success. This week we will have our large reception at the chancery on July 1 from 6:00 to 7:30 p.m., then go to the dance arranged by the Canberra Australian-Canadian Association for 8:30. We expect close to two hundred there again. Next weekend we will complete the trio with a similar do in Sydney. Such patriotism!

We have absolutely no more news about our trip to Canada with the Fiji Prime Minister. As with most such official tours I am sure all the decisions will be made in the last few hectic days; meanwhile we are still planning to leave Canberra on July 14 and leave Fiji for Canada July 17. Our days are numbered to do a great deal of work. Poor Arthur is up to his neck.

Canberra had its coldest recorded day this past week. You will laugh when we tell you it was "7.8 on the grass." They often announce the weather here in that way: in summer if they mean in the shade they say "under the tea tree," and in winter if they want to stress that it's right on the ground where the frost is they say so many degrees "on the grass." Of course in places like the Snowy Mountains they would have snow, but we've seen none here yet this winter.

July 4, 1971

s » As I mentioned in last week's letter, we celebrated Canada's 104th birthday in three cities this year. July 1 is also the date of the birth of the Colombo Plan, and although we have not been aware of much celebration to mark the first nineteen anniversaries, on the twentieth the Foreign Minister gave a reception in its honour. As a result, many of the government and diplomatic officials who were at our 6:00-to-7:30 reception left a bit early to work that one in before it ended at eight o'clock. To balance these, many of the people who were going to the Canada Day ball came to our reception on the late side so that they could go straight on to the ball. So the crowd was pretty well spaced out. Although I have checked the list for the number of the 427 who accepted who were actually there, some other officers in the office have not yet. Unless we are one hundred percent sure we do not count a person. After our five years here, we know the vast majority ourselves. Edith did a yeoman job of preparing food. This year we concentrated on larger numbers of fewer items in order to simplify preparation. She had the trays attractively arranged, and lots of both hot and cold canapés. We had eighteen waiters and waitresses helping.

The atmosphere at the ball, in the Park Royal Hotel, was very nice. They ended up with 150, a good mixture of young and old, Canadian and Australian, and they had a nice buffet supper. It went on till 1:00 a.m.—and as we were at the head table with the president, we didn't dare leave early.

The Canada Day ball in Sydney, which we went down to yesterday and returned from today, was not so large. It is strange that in a huge city like Sydney, where they say there are over five thousand Canadians, the club has never been strong. I think that distances are just too great for people to come in often from the suburbs for functions in the centre. However, the eighty they had at an Aquatic Club had a good time. The decorations there were more elaborate than those at any of the other celebrations. Two of the women had made a super totem pole of Styrofoam, and for each couple a tiny igloo of Styrofoam with a flag on it, lots of red and white posters, banners, and Canadian and Australian flags, a favour of tiny perfume for each lady and miniature whisky for each man, and lots of spot dances with lovely prizes.

We returned to perfectly glorious weather here in Canberra, so rather than bother with lunch we went and played two sets of tennis for the only time we could get the court booked. Although the radio says it is only 57 degrees it feels like 60-plus because there is no wind. Everywhere we have been travelling we have been just ahead of the South African rugby team, which is running into a great many demonstrations against apartheid. It is a little ironic that this same weekend is the one on which the Australian Aboriginal girl, Evonne Goolagong, has done so well in tennis at Wimbledon. It will be a great victory for Aborigines all over Australia.

On Friday I had tea with the first woman graduate from the University of Papua and New Guinea. Actually she had studied at the East-West Centre for part of her course, but she finished in Port Moresby last year. She is married to an Australian who now teaches at the University, and she does research there. She was in Australia on a speaking tour to raise interest and money for the women's residence at the University.

July 10, 1971

s » I am typing the weekend letter on Saturday instead of Sunday because once we have the dinner over tonight I can get suitcases, etc., out for packing and start to pack away our valuables, which we always place in the office while we're away for a long time. Normally we try not to entertain on weekends, because we know how Edith enjoys her bowling then, and also we like others not to involve us on weekends. But there was no alternative this time: the Indian High Commissioner and his wife are doing a lot of farewell calls outside of Canberra in other states, so this was the only time possible. As we had had a dinner for the Pakistan and the Singapore high commissioners recently when they left, feelings might be hurt if we didn't do the same for our Indian friends. Besides, they live next door to us, and she knows our every move! With them we are having Sir Arthur and Lady Tange (he used to be the Australian high commissioner in India, and is now the Secretary of the Department of Defence), Dick and Birgit Woolcott (he is the only Australian around who has been a head of post in Africa—and the Indians are going to Zambia next), Professor and Mrs. Basham (he is an Australian married to an Indian and is head of South East Asian Studies at the University here), Lady Hayden, widow of Peter Hayden, the former high commissioner in India, who died fairly recently (this is her first dinner out since his death, but as a Canadian she feels at home with us), and, to even things, the bachelor Belgian Ambassador. We have the diplomatic corps farewell for the Indians on Monday at the office. If someone leaves during our two-month absence, the acting dean of the corps will be the Danish Ambassador, but it will still be held in our chancery.

Thursday I had a ladies' lunch in honour of the receptionist at the office, Jeanette Groeneveld, who is getting married next Saturday. She has been at the office nearly three years, so we wanted to do something for her. This is her second engagement, but this one is called Mr. Wright, so I trust it will go through. She will continue to work after a three-week honeymoon in Fiji, the popular place for Australians to go now to escape winter.

To return to Canada all we needed was smallpox vaccinations. However, in order to ensure we can travel through Asia when we return from seeing Kenneth in London, we had cholera and typhoid shots this week as well, both in one needle. Our reactions could have been worse. We need another booster in Canada in twenty-eight days.

For about five years, the second Friday in July has been celebrated as National Aborigines Day. This year the committees have planned much more extensive celebrations than previously: films, competitions, and exhibits. I went to the opening of a rock-painting exhibit, with facsimiles of drawings in caves in the Northern Territory. Because of the current tour of Australia by an all-white South African rugby team, and all sorts of bans and boycotts and demonstrations in connection with the tour, anything done for black Australians gets much more attention than usual. We will have left Canberra before the Springboks play here, but a Maori has been picked to play on the Canberra side, so that will add interest and demonstrations for sure.

We really do not know much more detail about our trip home. Arthur now does not need to go to Ottawa before Ratu Mara arrives in Vancouver on July 24, but he has to go over to Victoria to make arrangements, likely on Wednesday July 21. There is also to be an Australian ship in Vancouver that week that we expect to get involved with. We have all sorts of mail going to Norah's, and will straighten our program out when we get there. We now think that Norah is coming with us on our tour of the Yukon. It is a part of our country we are anxious to visit, and although flying is expensive we may not have as convenient an opportunity again. This means we will give the time to really seeing something there, and we'll have to cut down on our time in Ottawa.

September 1, 1971

A » In June 1971 I received a telex from the Department of External Affairs in Ottawa saying that Premier W.A.C. Bennett of British Columbia had invited the Prime Minister of Fiji, Ratu Sir Kamisese Mara and his wife Adi Lady Lala Mara to visit British Columbia to mark the two-hundredth anniversary of Captain James Cook's exploration of Vancouver Island and its geographical environment. I was instructed to invite the Fiji Prime Minister to visit Ottawa first in accordance with Canadian practice. Sheila and I were to meet the Fiji Prime Minister and his party and take part in the Ottawa program.

In due course it was agreed that the Fiji party would visit Ottawa from July 24 to July 27. This left us ample time to plan to take some leave in Canada before and after the Fiji Prime Minister's visit.

En route to Vancouver we stopped in Fiji to review with officials the details of the official visit to Ottawa. We also called on Prime Minister Ratu Sir Kamisese Mara and Sheila had tea with Adi Lady Lala. In Vancouver we stayed with Norah and her partner Ed and got fully caught up with their lives. I made a side trip to Victoria to review with officials their plans for the visiting Fijians. I was glad to hear that the band of the Royal Fiji Regiment, with their red tunics and white Sulu pants, would be coming to British Columbia and performing in several cities. I also called on Premier Bennett. He showed me the draft of his proposed speech at a welcoming dinner for the Fiji Prime Minister. I was able to make a number of suggestions for changes in the text, which pleased Mr. Bennett.

The R.C.A.F. provided a Viscount aircraft to pick up the Fiji party in Vancouver. Sheila and I were their hosts on the trip to Ottawa. The Honourable Mitchell Sharp, Secretary of State for External Affairs, met the Fiji Prime Minister and Adi Lady Lala at the R.C.A.F.'s Uplands headquarters.

The program in Ottawa followed the usual routine: a formal call on Prime Minister Trudeau at his office in the Parliament Buildings, an official dinner, calls on the Secretary of State for External Affairs Honourable Mitchell Sharp, on the Minister of Industry, Trade and Commerce Honourable Jean-Luc Pépin, the Minister of National Defence Honourable Donald Macdonald, and the Speaker of the House of Commons, the Honourable Lucien Lamoureux. Sheila was involved in the program for Adi Lady Lala, including a call on Mrs. Margaret Trudeau at 7 Rideau Gate. I recall a very pleasant evening hosted by Mr. Sharp listening to a symphony concert at the National Arts Centre.

Sheila and I accompanied the Fiji party out to Victoria to begin their British Columbia program. We stayed long enough to join the party on a tour of Vancouver Harbour on a launch belonging to the B.C. Sugar Refinery, which gets a substantial amount of its raw sugar from Fiji.

When planning our trip back to Canada we had learned from the Canadian Pacific Air agent in Sydney that we could make a deviation from the shortest route for a modest increment in the direct air fare paid by External Affairs. James Smith, the Commissioner of the Canadian Northwest Territories, who had accompanied the Minister of Indian Affairs and Northern Development, Honourable Jean Chrétien, in his visit to Australia in April 1971 to exchange views with the Australian Government on the common challenges faced by Australia and Canada in administering their internally dependent territories, had said to me that if I ever had the opportunity to visit the Canadian Northwest Territories he would be pleased to host me and my wife in his capital, White-horse. So we booked a circuitous flight from Vancouver to Ottawa via Whitehorse. Jim Smith received us hospitably and I had a good working session with him, reviewing the administrative challenges he faced in comparison with what he had seen in the Northern Territory of Australia. We enjoyed an evening cruise on the Yukon River aboard the MV *Schatka*, and were flown to Alligator Lake by float plane to fish for lake trout. After leaving White-horse we stopped for an afternoon and evening at Hay River, at the source of the Mackenzie River, which plays such an important part in the life of the Northwest Territories.

After reporting to the Department of External Affairs in Ottawa, Sheila and I visited my two older sisters, Marion Hummel and Frances Newcombe, at their summer cottages north of Muskoka, and Sheila's brother, Herbert Skelton, and his wife Daisy at their cottage in the Eastern Townships of Quebec. En route back to Australia we were able to visit our son Kenneth, who was doing post-graduate studies in England, and we made stops in Israel and Bali.

This trip to Canada for the visit of the Prime Minister of Fiji and home leave made a good break in our nearly seven-year tour in Australia and the South Pacific.

September 19, 1971

A » Well, here we are back at the weekly letter routine on a beautiful Canberra spring weekend. My assignment is to tell you something about our trip back to Australia—about our visit to England, Israel, and Indonesia.

After brother Herbert and Daisy Skelton left us at the Montreal airport, following a happily relaxing weekend with them at Lake Memphramagog, we got caught up in the problems we have encountered before of administering one of the big jumbo jets. We were told that the computer had a malfunction in Toronto, so the plane was delayed. When we did get aboard they found they had too many passengers, so they had to offload four, although they left their baggage on. We sat in a row directly behind one of the bulkheads, which gave us the privilege of watching the after-dinner movie at a distance of thirty-six inches, from 1:30 to 3:30 a.m., even though, in order to try to get some sleep, we didn't take earphones.

We got to London three hours late, but Kenneth was there to meet us. We went by bus and taxi to his house, which has a nice garden and is quite spacious. Ken turned over his third-floor room to us. That first night we took him and his housemates to a good presentation of *Hamlet*. Next day I made calls at the Australian, Canadian, and Fijian offices and the Commonwealth Secretariat, and we had lunch with Arnold and Eve Smith in their picture-filled flat near Marlborough House. That evening we saw another play, *Kean*, by Jean-Paul Sartre, about an actor who didn't know when he was acting and when he was himself. On Saturday Sheila and I went to the art gallery, shopped, and then met Ken for a film on drugs called *Taking Off*. In between we had time to get reacquainted with his housemates, including Jan Maher, who was in Russia for a year, and to talk to Ken about his thesis and future plans. We are very happy to have had catching-up visits with both Norah and Kenneth.

On Sunday, September 5, we flew to Tel Aviv, where my old friend McGaughey is ambassador and met us near midnight. Monday we took off with their car and their Christian Arab chauffeur, Joseph, to drive the one and a half hours to Jerusalem. We drove through busy streets in the suburbs of Tel Aviv, then out on a fine highway that winds up over the hills to Jerusalem. On the way one crosses the demarcation lines that were observed prior to 1967. Our first stop in Jerusalem was at the New Hebrew University, with its modernistic buildings. Looking across the valley one sees old tenements, and row on row of modern apartment buildings. Then we saw the new parliament buildings, or Knesset, before going to the King David Hotel for conveniences. We then went into the old city at the Jaffa Gate, where David's Citadel is located. Then on to the Zion Gate by car after picking up an Armenian guide, George Kaplanian, who has a brother in Vancouver. Here we visited King David's tomb and the site of the Upper Room. From near this location we got a good view of the Mount of Olives, with its rather unattractive recent addition, the Hilton Hotel; the Mount of Offence; Mount Scopus, where the UN Observer Group has its headquarters; the Pool of Siloam; and the Valley of Hinnom. Then we walked down to the Wailing Wall, still divided between men's and women's sections, took pictures of a visiting synagogue group reading their Old Testament on a big scroll, and I put on a black cardboard skullcap as a mark of respect. Next we entered the big courtyard of the El Aqsa Mosque and the Mosque of Omar, or the Dome of the Rock. You may recall that a couple of years ago a mentally unbalanced Australian set fire to and burned a quarter of the El Aqsa Mosque, so visitors are carefully inspected. The Mosque of Omar is particularly beautiful, with some of the finest mosaics in the world. Behind this is the site of the Roman Praetorium and the beginning of the Via Dolorosa. This winds through the ancient market area, with narrow cobbled streets, porters carrying great loads on their backs, donkeys, and lively street hawkers—all very colourful. We ended our visit to old Jerusalem by doing some shopping in the bazaar. I forgot to report that our windup visit was to the Church of the Holy Sepulchre, which is undergoing an extensive renovation that will take several years. However, the visit to the Holy Sepulchre itself brought back memories for me of the Ceremony of the Holy Fire, which I saw as a boy of thirteen. In this ceremony the Patriarch enters the searched tomb, and then later passes out fire to light the lamps of believers. We also visited, outside the wall, General Gordon's Garden of Gethsemane and the Church of St. Peter in Gallicantu.

Joseph then drove us to Bethlehem, where we visited the Church of the Nativity and walked about the streets to soak up the atmosphere. We returned to the McGaugheys' residence in Tel Aviv well after dark. After a cleanup we had a quiet supper and talked till late at night about Israeli affairs as seen by Canadians.

Next day we took off at 8:00 a.m. for the Lake of Galilee, a drive of something over two hours by good roads. We came at the lake from the south end, where the Jordan River runs out, and looked across to the Golan Heights, where the Syrians used to have artillery that fired on the Israeli kibbutzim. Then up along the lake to Tiberias, where we stopped to look at some of the old buildings and the boats moored by the shore. Then back by way of Nazareth, still a predominantly Christian town but with many new Israeli apartment blocks. From the hills we drove back down onto the plain of Jezreel and so back to Tel Aviv for lunch, and word that our plane was delayed. Indeed it was so delayed that we could anticipate missing our connection in Bangkok, so we made alternative bookings.

After a bit of a rest we packed and drove in to Tel Aviv, a big modern city with many fine buildings, to visit our embassy chancery and meet the staff. Then the McGaugheys drove us down to the shore of the Mediterranean Sea and along to the neighbouring city of Jaffa, with its old mosque, fortress, and bazaars. We got to the airport about 5:00 p.m., but didn't take off until 7:00 — by Trans World Airways.

I'm very glad we made this short visit to Israel. The Palestine I remember from our previous visit, in 1929, when we stayed some months while Father took part in the archaeological excavation, was an ancient land of Christian and Muslim Arabs tending their flocks and working their fields by traditional means. Palestine was then a British mandate and the Jewish settlements were still unobtrusive. Today one sees the results of the vigour of the European Jews (Ashkenazi), as compared with the Oriental or Asian Jews (Sephardi), combined with heavy Zionist investment and gifts from overseas. There are modern roads, fine new buildings, tractors plowing up the plains to plant wheat and cotton, irrigation schemes to spray water on the citrus orchards, etc. There is tremendous change. And yet the old city of Jerusalem, the holy places, and the various denominations of religious men and women who attend them remain quite unchanged by the modernization about them.

Our American TWA flight was like a transcontinental trip on a poorly maintained Greyhound bus. We had to stop in Bombay at about 4:30 a.m. and got into Bangkok at noon. After an hour's wait there we boarded a German Lufthansa plane, which was clean and had excellent service. With a stop in Singapore this got us to Djakarta at 7:00 p.m. instead of our anticipated 12:30.

We were met at the airport by Tom Delworth, who has had about a year in Indonesia as ambassador, and his new bride Pamela. We were taken to the residence and had a good chat over a quiet dinner. Sleeping in an air-conditioned room after a night on the plane was much appreciated. Next day Tom took me to visit Colonel Nurnathias, who succeeded Brigadier Supardjo as director of the Asian and Pacific Bureau in the Foreign Ministry. Then we went out to look at staff houses and visit the chancery and meet staff. Sheila went with Pamela to the museum. After lunch Til Purnell, whom we had known in Kuala Lumpur ten years ago, took Sheila and me to visit a batik factory, where we watched the elaborate process of drawing or stamping designs, painting in hot wax, dyeing, washing, restamping, rewaxing, re-washing, and so on. It is a painstaking business, where women are paid about $.65 a day and have their kids playing about them on the mud floor. Tom then took us for a drive around town to see the many new buildings that have been going up since I last visited Djakarta, in August 1969, en route home for the Pacific study. It is evident that the Suharto military-technocratic government has succeeded in turning the corner from the rampant inflation and corruption of the Sukarno era, and that there is greatly increased confidence. The Delworths gave a nice dinner, which was attended by some old friends such as Ambassador and Mrs. Palar, whom we knew in Ottawa fifteen years ago, General and Mrs. Kosasih (he was the ambassador in Canberra, and is now commandant of the National Defence Academy), the Purnells, and a couple of Canadians.

We left for Bali at 10:00 a.m. Friday, September 10, by a modern DC-9 of Garuda Indonesian Airways, a far cry from the old DC-3s that provided such spasmodic service before. We got in to Den Pasar about 12:30 noon and there were met by a guide, Mr. Ngourah, from Natour, with a flowery salutation: "I have come to meet Your Excellencies and to place my humble services at your disposal. Although my English is not so good I hope you will excuse me." So we went in his taxi to the Sindhu Beach Hotel—no great shakes, but with an air conditioner in our bedroom. We had two very full days touring the craft shops and temples of Bali and watching their dances. We had been there with Kenneth and Norah in 1960. There is a big international hotel now, the Bali Beach, and more art shops, but the life of the two and a half million Balinese seems to have changed little. They continue to be Hindus in an otherwise largely Muslim Indonesia. They live a life of ritual, dance, and worship closely related to the temples of their village communities and the rotation of the seasons in their beautifully terraced rice fields. There is a great charm about their rhythm of life. All seemed to be involved. The men break off work for a while in the heat of the day to repair to one of the pavilions in the village temple to train their fighting cocks, because some blood must be let by cockfighting as a sacrifice in the temples before important ceremonies. Other men gather in the evening to practise their orchestras of gongs, as old men and women teach young girls the intricate steps of the dance. There are only three cinemas in Den Pasar and none elsewhere in the island, so the old entertainments serve the people.

We visited shops where stone figures were being carved from limestone in the likeness of gods and mythical beings such as the Garuda. We saw fine filigree work in silver being done by painstaking men. Much weaving is done, and a lot of wood-carving. There is traditional and modern painting. We saw several dance performances, including part of the International Ramayana Festival, in which India, Malaysia, Thailand, and Indonesia are taking part. It was a busy two and a half days, but I enjoyed every moment of it, even if it was hot and humid.

We left Den Pasar about 11:30 p.m. Sunday, September 12, in a Qantas plane filled to the brim with Australia-bound immigrants. We were surrounded by Maltese who were far too excited to sleep. We got to Sydney at 8:30 a.m., and after a considerable wait arrived in Canberra about 12:30 noon, where we were met by the Rogers, the Shapiros (he is our new commercial counsellor), Lieutenant-Colonel and Eleanor Corry, and our driver, Andrew.

It was a long two months of travel, but satisfying. We are glad to settle back to our Canberra routine again.

September 20, 1971

s » Arthur did such a super job of reporting at length about our return trip that when he finished on Sunday night it was too late to continue with the typewriter. This Monday morning I will bring you up to date briefly on our first week's activities since returning.

Before we left Canberra mid-July there had been sixteen days with frost each morning, and evidently while we were away it was cold and windy and there was very little of the rain needed for gardens. Certainly as we flew in over Sydney it looked very brown after the lush green of Bali, and as we continued to Canberra we saw all the dry beige, tan, and burnt colours that we had not seen since we left Australia. Here in Canberra, thanks to the watering of gardens, everything is really looking very spring-like. Two things are out together—wattles, and fruit tree blooms—which means a profusion of all shades of lemon yellow, saffron yellow, and buttercup yellow in the different types of wattles, and white, pale pink, and deep pink and red in the various fruit trees: apple, plum, quince, and peach. It makes Canberra one of the most attractive cities we have seen in all our travels. In our own garden we have daffodils, narcissus, and hyacinths in bloom as well as shrubs, and are enjoying lettuce fresh from the vegetable garden, and still some of last year's spinach, and fresh rhubarb. We popped in for a few minutes on Saturday to see the annual spring bulbs show—daffodils and narcissus, and gorgeous camellias, a most attractive tree that does very well here either in pots around one's patio or in trees or hedges. When I think of the price of a camellia corsage in Canada I revel in the wealth of pickable flowers we have here.

Naturally we are back to some of our diplomatic activities. For example, we had the new Indian High Commissioner, Mr. Krishnamurti, and Mrs. Krishnamurti for lunch instead of just a call. As they are also our next-door neighbours, we are pleased that this new representative seems like a better-informed and more interesting political type than his predecessor. I am taking her to the library today. We also were invited—as dean of the corps, not as representatives of Canada, as there were only a few diplomats present—to the opening of the new Thai embassy residence. As is usually the fate of the person who has done most of the planning and work involved in a building of such importance, the present ambassador leaves October 1 and so will never live in it himself! It combines the traditional Thai temple roof with a quite modern interior. Although all the carved teak furniture that was ordered has not yet arrived, some lovely heavy Thai silk curtains are already in place. One special feature of the house is a separate suite to be available for the Thai prince, who will be a student at the military college here next year. He will use it when on holiday, etc. He was the one selected to do the official opening, because he is in Australia this year as well, doing his final year of high school to get his certificate and his English to the standard that he can enter Duntroon Military College in the new year. He is just eighteen or nineteen and very handsome, so was a popular choice for the ceremony—though I was disappointed that he just read his speech. Because it would have been too difficult to put gold on the roof in this country, they compromised and painted all the inside ceilings gold. It is mostly a rough cement stucco texture, so it does not turn out anything like the elegant real gold leaf that we had in the embassy in Japan. This fits the modern house better though. All the carpets are also a soft gold colour.

We have also been to one black-tie dinner, hosted by New Zealand. The leader of the opposition was there too.

September 26, 1971

s » We have just had an outing today with the Australian-Canadian Association—actually as guests of the Canberra Gem Association. We went to a place about twenty-five miles from Canberra to search for fossiliferous limestone and marble. It turned out that there was only one other representative from the ACA, the vice-president, who had three young girls, aged about seven, eight, and ten years. They had spent yesterday sewing up little "gem bags," cotton bags about the size used for marbles, and obviously expected that a gem society would be looking for gemstones. The people from the gem society, all of them old hands, turned up with plastic buckets, pickaxes, rock chisels, rock hammers, and sacks to put their finds in. They hacked off large and small pieces to take home "to polish." Perhaps that process would improve the uninteresting bits of rock we saw. We heard one say, "I have enough now for all my Christmas presents," so obviously we just don't have the seeing eye. Anyway, it was a pleasant day to be outdoors. From the place where we had to leave the cars and put all heavy equipment into two utility vehicles, to the creek bed, where the main chipping and hammering went on, was a good two-mile walk, downhill and up. As we had come for the outing, not the gems, we were happy. The dry Australian countryside looked very different from the green Canadian summer fields we had seen a short while before.

Last Wednesday we had our first diplomatic reception as dean of the corps since returning to Canberra, to say farewell to the Thai Ambassador and Mrs. Buncheon. He is a very quiet and sincere man who has been here more than four years and is now retiring. She is even quieter, but a friend of mine because she had had to leave ten cats in Thailand and a gibbon monkey in Malaysia, their last posting before Australia, so she has been lonesome for them all the time here—and all ten cats have died in the interval. She is taking back to Thailand a small loquat tree that she has grown from the stone in one of the fruits from our garden that I gave her last year. Obviously Thai customs people are not as strict about fruit as Australian ones are about animals! We were pleased that on short notice, because of the comings and goings of Australian cabinet ministers, the Minister of Defence and Mrs. Fairbairn came out. He gave the speech on behalf of the Australian government to support the initial speech Art had to make on behalf of the diplomatic corps.

October 24, 1971

s » Arthur left late afternoon Wednesday for Fiji. The chief purpose of his trip was to meet Neil Everend, director of planning for Asia in the Canadian International Development Agency, who was on a world tour and found this a convenient time to be in Fiji. They hope to set up plans for co-operation with the University of the South Pacific for the next couple of years. Also Art will meet with John McRae, head of nongovernmental organizations in CIDA, to review his discussions in Papua, New Guinea, and New Hebrides, and to review the progress of the YWCA building in Suva. He also hopes to arrange for a presentation of Canadian books to the University, so you see what a busy time he will have, with a night of travelling thrown in at each end, plus the heat. I guess this is just one of the corollaries of dual accreditation—having to be busy and in demand in two places nearly at once.

October 30, 1971

s » We will be leaving at noon tomorrow for Sydney for the 41st American Society of Travel Agents World Congress—and in this case "American" covers Canada. Because there are representatives of both federal agencies and provincial agencies, including people like Mme. Marie-Claire Kirkland-Casgrain, Minister of Tourism in Quebec, we want to be on hand. Arthur is to read a message from Prime Minister Trudeau at the opening on Monday morning.

As dean of the diplomatic corps we have been involved this week in the first official visit to Australia of Sir Arthur Porritt, the Governor General of New Zealand, and Lady Porritt. He was born in New Zealand, and left at an early age to be mostly in England, and she is English, but at least one can say he is their first New Zealand-born governor general. He was surgeon consultant to the Queen before this job, and was president of the British Empire Games, plus a Rhodes Scholar, like our Roland Michener, so all in all has a pretty good background, and certainly was very pleasant in all we had to do with them. We met them several times, the first of which was the official ceremony of welcome at the airport, on a very windy day. The hats of several of the guards of honour blew off as they were being inspected. Then Wednesday night we went to a white-tie dinner in their honour at Government House, where they were staying with Sir Paul and Lady Hasluck, who are just back from Tehran. Prime Minister McMahon had left that day for his trip to the States and England, so the top government representative was the Acting Prime Minister, Doug Anthony. Art and I sat beside his wife Margot at dinner. What a meal! Green almond soup, fish roll-ups, fillet and vegetables, an ice cream bombe, then tiny cheese puffs, then fresh pineapple. Poor Arthur was tired, having been up most of the night flying back from Fiji. Next morning we were on hand again at Government House, he decked out in chancery jacket and I in hat and gloves, for a short half-hour reception of all heads of diplomatic missions. Some wear their national dress on such occasions, and the Cambodian, Finnish, and Norwegian ladies looked almost as colourful as the usual sari-clad ones. Straight after the lunch we were invited in a private capacity—just as friends, not as dean of the corps—to a private lunch for just eighteen that New Zealand High Commissioner Jim Yendell and his wife Dora held at their residence. All the other guests were New Zealanders, either from their staff here, or outstanding New Zealanders living and working in Canberra, like the deputy chancellor of the Australian National University and his ninety-year-old mother, who is a truly remarkable bright alert person and doesn't look or act over seventy, and the former head of the Snowy Mountains scheme and Lady Hudson. Our fifth and last time with them here in Canberra was to say farewell this morning, a perfectly glorious day at the airport, in contrast to their windy Wellington-like arrival. We will see them again in Melbourne at the Cup this coming Tuesday, so will really be old pals by that time.

Friday we had the new Maltese High Commissioner in for lunch. He is a most unusual case, because although Maltese he moved to Sydney seventeen years ago and has been very active there as a businessman and labour leader. Now he is the official representative of Malta, but still counts as a resident in Australia, and claims he has the right to vote and to carry on his Labor Party activities—after hours!

November 7, 1971

s » As mentioned in last week's letter, Art and I left Sunday noon for Sydney to be on hand for the Canadian delegation's "kick-off" dinner for the American Society of Travel Agents Conference. There were 150 out from Canada, so they took over a whole restaurant that is not usually open on Sunday and held it there. French's Tavern had a very pleasant atmosphere, and served the best meal I have had in a restaurant. It was a great choice. There were three items for each course, and all were served piping hot. For me the best was a "meringue pancake," a pancake with a custard filling, served hot like a bombe Alaska with the meringue on the top. After all the feasting it was nearly 10:30 before the speakers of the evening were called upon. Arthur spoke well—not too seriously because of the hour and the setting, but very suitably for a group of travel agents from all over Canada, most of them in Australia for the first time. He was followed by Madame Kirkland-Casgrain, the Minister of Tourism in Quebec and leader of the Canadian delegation. She speaks well in both English and French, and her presence and manner are both quite charming. At the opening of the conference before the 3,000 delegates in the Sydney Town Hall the following morning, Art read a statement from Prime Minister Trudeau. The Governor General made a good speech, witty and original.

Then we left for the festivities in Melbourne for the Melbourne Cup. Cup Day is a holiday in Victoria—and it might just as well be in all of Australia, because all serious work stops for the afternoon, TV sets are in all offices, and there are sweeps and bets everywhere. On the eve of the Cup we went to Government House for a reception by Governor Delacombe of Victoria and Lady Delacombe. As dean of the corps it was Arthur's duty once more to introduce all the members of the corps who are on hand from Canberra to the New Zealand Governor General, chief guest at the Cup, and the Governor of New South Wales. There were sixteen heads of mission down from Canberra, and I got a kick out of quizzing Art in the car all the way to Government House as to the exact names and titles of our dear colleagues—for example, the chargé d'affaires of Laos and Mme. Vensagphay. On Tuesday, Cup Day, the weather was glorious—in the high seventies in the sun, but cool in the shade of the stands, where we were sitting.

Five years ago when we attended the Cup, Art bought a grey top hat—*de rigueur*—so had some use of it, with morning suit, for a second time. I wore a blue khersonese silk that Art had bought in Singapore last year and I had had Mrs. Christie make up, with a little pleated ruffle at the bottom and on the sleeves.

It is all quite a pageant, and the fine calibre of all the horses, not just the winners, is outstanding. The favourite did not win, but having taken Edith's advice I had put a bet on the second and third horses, so came out of the day with the great sum of $2.85 ahead. In the evening we took our commercial counsellor and his wife, Kevin and Winifred Osmond, out to dinner.

November 14, 1971

s » It is amazing to think that tomorrow, November 15, we will have been in Australia for six years—about double what we expected when we came. How little one knows ahead in Canadian diplomatic life. Arthur is away on a fishing trip this weekend with three men, Eric Conybeare, a Canadian professor from the University who now lives here, Sir Leonard Huxley, ex-vice-chancellor of ANU, now retired, and Harry Horne, our commercial counsellor from Sydney, who came up on the noon flight Friday and will return first thing Monday morning. It is now 8:00 p.m. and there's no sign of them, but Art said that with daylight saving time having just been introduced they would be able to be out on Lake Eucumbene till quite late, then to get their supper and pack up and motor back will take two and a half hours, so not to expect them until midnight. It has been pouring rain here today and, like last weekend, miserable weather except for the day they set off, so I hope they have not caught colds, just lots of fish.

Wednesday night we had another buffet cocktail party, chiefly for parliamentarians. We had a good turnout: three cabinet ministers, several ambassadors, press, and some Canadians—thirty-four altogether. All the chairs in the house were squeezed into the dining room, living room, and study so that people could sit.

A group of us visited a mentally retarded children's home this week, and had a very interesting morning watching the twenty-six children. We presented them with an electric train set. The greatest surprise for me was that they sang all the words of "O Canada," which they had learned for a Commonwealth Day concert last year. Because I was so touched by this I returned for a second time to take them posters, pins, and other Canadian materials.

November 28, 1971

s » We have been making some effort to get Christmas letters and cards off. When the snow is blowing outside and one can set up a card table in front of a fireplace one is more in the mood for it. Here I have the cold, if nothing else—the same bally one, dragging on. I have been out of circulation most of the week, just on hand for the most important day, Thursday, when we had a visit of just twenty-four hours by the Minister of Manpower and Immigration—also the minister responsible for the Wheat Board—Otto Lang, Adrian, his wife, Mr. Jarvis, Assistant Deputy Minister of Agriculture, and an executive assistant, Mr. Clark. We could not have had a nicer ministerial visit. A young thirty-nine-year-old cabinet minister comes across well in this country, and his wife is very attractive: courteous, grateful, and pleasant, much more outspoken than he but in a very likeable way. To look at her svelte figure and carefree manner one would never at first imagine she had seven children or serious political interests—as she has.

We had lunch here so that the Langs could meet senior staff, the Rogers and the Shapiros, and Jack Richardson, dean of the law school, and his wife. Mr. Lang had just been at the law school talking to students from all the law schools in Australia, who just happened to be having a meeting here. (Before politics, Lang had taught law.) In the evening there was a dinner at Parliament House for the men, which I will leave to Art, and I had a ladies' dinner at the Commonwealth Club. (Two functions here in one day is apt to be too, too much for Edith.) There were just eight of us, and it went very easily.

Art is out in the garden reading the Sunday papers. I am now up out of bed and will take our lunch out there on trays. We are very fortunate this year that the fly season has not yet started. If it stays this free of flies, we will be able to use the outdoors much more for entertaining, which would be nice.

A » I, too, found the Langs very agreeable visitors. Talk with the ministers was about immigration policies, as we are the biggest immigrant-receiving countries in the world. Mr. Lang talked to the press in terms that could not offend the Australians, although newspapermen tried to get him to say that Australia wouldn't get a sale of wheat to China unless she recognized Peking, as Canada did.

After the Langs left on Friday morning to spend a weekend at a beach resort near Sydney, I carried on to Melbourne. I had lunch there with Bruce Grant, the able political commentator of *The Age*, and then went out to see my friend Trevor Pyman at the Department of Civil Aviation about an application by CP Air to have two flights a week to Sydney from Vancouver. Then Peter and Margaret Oldham drove me out to Latrobe University, where I made a presentation of some two hundred books on Canada at a little ceremony in the library. I made the point that in the field of literature comparisons have been drawn only since 1962, and that Graham McInnis had written his accounts of life in Australia in the 1920s beginning with *The Road to Gundagai* in 1965. Afterwards I had dinner with Vice-Chancellor and Mrs. David Myers. He was dean of engineering at UBC for five years and has two sons and seven grandchildren in Canada. It was a pleasant evening, and I was sorry Sheila's cold prevented her from coming.

December 5, 1971

s » I don't know how many times one has to repeat something to make it a "tradition," but I guess by now we have a tradition here in Canberra of celebrating Arthur's birthday with his twin (same age), David Hay, who is now Secretary of the Department of Territories, before was administrator of PNG, and at one time was high commissioner to Canada; on two occasions there has been a triplet present as well, Lindsay Brand, but he is in Washington with the International Monetary Fund, so they remembered him with just a telegram this year. One other couple has been to each of the preceding dinners, the Stuart Jamiesons, also from External Affairs, now retired, and this year two different couples, whom the Hays suggested and we know well, the Huxleys (Sir Leonard goes fishing with Art, and Molly is a very articulate person), and Sir Thomas and Lady Daly (he has just retired as chief of the general staff, and was a controversial figure in the Gorton political days). Oh yes—and another of the couples, Sir John and Lady Bunting—Jack and Peg—were with the Holts on the trip to Canada, so are long-time friends of ours. This time Jack was dead beat because he was just back from a trip with Mr. McMahon. Dinner went well—some fish from Arthur's last expedition we had been saving for this special occasion, roast fillet of beef, our first Chinese peas from the garden, and two birthday cakes—one angel, one chocolate—ice cream, and strawberries. The Hays brought champagne. David went into hospital the next day for an operation for varicose veins and is still there, poor soul.

There were four young chaps from Vancouver here who were connected with the YMCA and had been up looking at the project the Vancouver Y is assisting in Mount Hagen, New Guinea. They stayed in Canberra one night; two of them were billeted with the Rogers and two with us, and they and Allan and Art had a good session over dinner.

Although I got out of the Penguin Christmas party Wednesday night because I was still fighting the dregs of the cold, I did not have the nerve to ask them to find a substitute for the speech I had promised to give at the last meeting of the year, on Friday, so I spoke for ten minutes on the topic of the month, for which I chose Christmas in Canada. There were three other speakers. It is good discipline to have to prepare such a speech for the rostrum critic, but quite a strain too. The day before, I heard a very good speech at the View Club by a professor from the Australian National University on the future of New Guinea. He kept the one hundred women fascinated for the full thirty minutes he spoke, and another fifteen when he answered questions.

A » This has been one of those valuable catching-up weeks for me at the office, as this next week we are to have our annual staff meeting, which will occupy, effectively, three days. There was a series of national days, including those for Yugoslavia and Thailand, a reception at the home of the chief of protocol, Bob Birch, and a meal at the Indonesian embassy for Sultan Hamengku Buwono of Djogjakarta, Minister for Economic Affairs in the Indonesian government, who was here for the establishment of the Australian Indonesian Business Co-operation Committee. I also attended a men's lunch at the Ghana high commission for a number of cabinet ministers. Played tennis yesterday and today and benefited from the exercise.

As part of the understanding with the Royal Ontario Museum regarding disposition of Father's effects, I have written a foreword this week to a book that will be published in Taiwan, reproducing the rubbings of some 3,000 oracle bone fragments that Father had that were lost in China and whose rubbings have not yet been published. This is to add to the reference material available to scholars of the ancient writing of the Shang dynasty, which existed from 1300 to 1039 B.C.

December 12, 1971

S » This is the Week that Was: we have had the annual staff conference. It all went well, we think, but it sure is a busy, hectic time. I just hope some dope doesn't make a suggestion that it be biannual! I'd collapse! To review: the first couple of years we were here it was a two-day meeting for all Canadian officer personnel, and as many wives as could come. They usually arrived from Sydney and Melbourne Thursday morning on early planes and there were meetings Thursday and Friday; some would return that evening, others stayed until Saturday. A total of about thirty people were involved. We did our entertaining by having a cocktail party here and then taking everyone up to Carousel Restaurant on Red Hill. Soon, however, the information people added a day of their own for meetings on the Wednesday before the others came in, so it became a three-day conference. Last year the number was up to forty, and included a CUSO representative from New Guinea and a National Film Board representative from India who covers this area. We decided it was too expensive to take so many out, so had a buffet dinner here. With the great emphasis this year on integration of all government departments, and as we have a military attaché here, called an "Armed Forces adviser," we decided to include the other Canadian military officers in Australia, which meant six more, four from a flying base in South Australia and two from an officers training centre in Queensland —and five of them were married and brought their wives. People started arriving on Monday, and both the military and the information people held meetings on the Wednesday, and ninety-nine percent of the people stayed over until Saturday this time. Some have even stayed longer, because six of the men, including Arthur and Allan Roger, have gone fishing up at Lake Eucumbene. They left Saturday morning and will return sometime after midnight tonight. Harry Horne will spend the night here and return to Sydney in the morning. Two others are also out of town. More wanted to go on the expedition, but the cottage will only hold six.

You cannot count on Canberra weather at this time of year. Last Monday it was 65 degrees, and Tuesday's high was 62 degrees. However, after bad rain all day Wednesday and Thursday morning, it cleared and warmed up enough that we were able to have the drinks outside under the willow tree on the patio, and this certainly relieved the congestion of having fifty here for the buffet dinner. I had taken down the bed in the end bedroom, and tried to fix it up as the sitting room, so we had people there, in the study, and in the living room and dining room. On Friday we were even luckier with the weather, and were able to be outside around the Rogers' pool for a Chinese food lunch, and there were varied sports—tennis, volleyball, and croquet—for those who were energetic (and didn't have to work, as Art did, of course). Again in the evening we were able to be outdoors part-time at Ben and Tillie Shapiro's. Oh yes—Eleanor and Geoff Corry had a cocktail party on Wednesday, and on Thursday noon while the men ate sandwiches at the office in the midst of their meetings, the women had lunch at MacKinnons' and held a meeting afterwards and then went to the office to get better acquainted with the information facilities and films and such that are available there.

As a result of these various meetings and social events we are really now pretty well acquainted with all the Canadian personnel in Australia, and it must make for smoother working during the year. It is an attractive group of young, well-adjusted people—good representatives abroad. Oh yes—I took nine of the wives for a three-hour sightseeing tour of Canberra on Friday morning.

Today I went by myself to the Canadian-Australian annual Christmas children's party, which takes the form of an outdoor barbecue on the shores of Lake Burley Griffin. There were umpteen other organizations also holding Christmas parties outdoors, but we had a good spot, and we had pony rides and races for the children, and raffles, etc., for the adults. There were about fifty children, mostly under ten, and about thirty adults. I have spent the rest of the day putting things back to normal in the house and doing up children's presents in preparation for the office party this week.

December 19, 1971

s » On Wednesday we had our annual Christmas staff and children's party at the office. Many features were the same as other years we have been here. The children were dressed in their best, and their parents were casually dressed. They arrived at 5:30 p.m. And we had Canadian films in the basement of the chancery, this year just a half-hour program—featuring Terra Nova National Park in Newfoundland, Canadian Indian dances, the Feux Follets, and a short cartoon about two birds that exchange their feathers for the foliage of a tree and then change back again. We had invited ninety-nine to the party; things grow each year, but with some on holidays already (for example, our administrative officer, Derek MacKinnon, his wife, and three children have taken off to motor across Australia to Perth and back in three weeks), some of the young secretaries with more interesting pursuits, and some sick, about eighty accepted. Our menu, which has always proved popular, and manageable in the large numbers in a confined space, was the same: sandwiches, hotdogs, hot mince tarts, ice cream, and drinks, soft and hard.

We had one innovation this year, though. I had seen a picture in the paper of a young pop group called The Young Sounds, composed of kids, the youngest aged eleven, the others fourteen and fifteen, altogether six of them, who were looking for bookings. They had played for charity to various groups, one of which I contacted to get a report. Well, they arrived with the most elaborate equipment, costing hundreds of dollars I am sure: a large drum, electric guitars, yards of cord, signs, cute stools, music stands, etc., and dressed very nattily in white slacks and coloured waistcoats. Their lead singer had pleurisy, so the girl who sang was very pretty but didn't have a very loud voice. After we'd shown the films and served supper downstairs, everyone carried their chairs upstairs (except the smaller kids, who sat on the carpet) and the group put on a twenty-minute program of popular songs for everyone. It was well received and I think the older teenagers (the majority of our children here now seem to be teenagers; altogether there were thirty-one children) seemed to identify with the group and perhaps were inspired to become members of a band or group too. Then they led us all in thirty minutes of Christmas carols.

By this time the younger ones were really closing in on the Christmas tree, a nice live pine that I had decorated the day before with the help of Andrew and Stan. Each child got a gift. I had had this party in mind when home in Canada, so had bought maple leaf broaches for the older girls and maple leaf tie pins for the older boys, and in Fiji had got beads for the younger ones and supplemented them with bits and pieces of action toys to make each present worth about $1.50 or $2.00. It is the one occasion of the year when we see the whole families of the staff, and I think it helps us realize what their home life is like.

Now that this major responsibility for Christmas entertaining is over, we have relaxed at several parties given by other people. For example, there was one out in the country where the wife raises basset hounds and has a very large and noisy kennel; one most elaborate Japanese dinner at the Japanese embassy, at which

297

the chief guest was Prince Mikasa, who is twenty-three, has a law degree from Japan, and has just finished an advanced English course here so that he can attend Australian National University next term; a pleasant "supper" at the home of the dean of the law school at 9:00 p.m. that turned out to be a dinner that began at 10:30; and a leisurely time last evening when we had in Arthur's secretary, Margaret Hall, who brought and showed excellent slides she had taken in the centre of Australia and in Fiji—they were really outstanding. She is going to be with us for three days at the Lodge in Kosciuszko.

EIGHT

1972

January 3, 1972

A » Sheila and I got back at about 5:45 p.m. from our six-hun-
dred-mile jaunt to Sydney to pick up a light fifty-pound aluminum boat and six-horsepower motor that Harry Horne insisted we should take up to Lake Jindabyne for our fortnight's
holiday. We thought that someone would bring the outfit up
from Sydney, but in the absence of such an offer decided to use
our New Year's weekend to do the trip ourselves. It is interesting that in the six years we have been here we have never driven
the three hundred miles to Sydney and the three hundred miles
back. And I don't mind confiding to you that we can go another
six years without repeating that drive. We drove the inside route
via Goulbourn, Nittagong, and Camden, leaving about 9:00 a.m.
and getting in about 3:30 p.m., with stops in Goulbourn to visit
an old National Trust home and in Nittagong to see a craft centre. The road twists and turns, and half the time there is only
one lane each way, which is a shocking reflection on the standard of roads between Sydney and Melbourne, Australia's main
cities. For the last twenty miles, through Sydney suburbs, we
were happy it was January 1, a Saturday afternoon, and without
significant traffic. We went for a swim and dinner with the
Hornes. Their son Kim, his girlfriend, a niece (who is a nurse),
and a companion of hers (also a nurse) were there too. This was

the anniversary of the death of their backward boy, Bernie. Probably they were better off with company, and we tried to be understanding. Sunday morning we left at nine o'clock to pick up the boat. Harry is handy at adjusting roof racks, and he secured the boat. We got it so well tied we didn't need to make an adjustment on the trip home. Then we crawled out of Sydney with the rest of the weekend South Coast traffic. It took us two hours to cover twenty miles—quite an experience. We had not been through Woolongong and Kiama and many other suburbs of Sydney that stretch down the coast to the south, so we were glad to see the area—but once is enough. Later we encountered better dairying country, south of Kiama and Dapto, and worked our way down to Nowra, where Herbert and Daisy have been. We got to Jackson's Garden Hotel at Ulladulla at 4:00 p.m. and went off immediately for a walk on the beach at Mollymook. While we were there it clouded over. We went to the golf club in hopes of getting dinner, but after waiting an hour we bought a stew and ate in our room.

This morning we had one of Burt Jackson's famous breakfasts. I had fresh snapper and Sheila had thin slices of lamb's fry and bacon. We left at about ten o'clock and toured the area, watching fish being unloaded from trawlers, etc. Then we drove home in a leisurely way, with a stop at a lookout over the Clyde River estuary for lunch, and another stop in Bungendore to see our friends Ash and Beth Davy on their property and to gather some mushrooms. We got back at about 6:00 p.m., after which Edith and a bowling friend and Sheila peeled and froze the mushrooms. We've dined on lamb chops and mushrooms and will now put ourselves in order for the coming week.

During the three workdays of last week I spent my time cleaning up the year's accumulation: personal reports, statistical returns, and all those old chestnuts that would look better under a 1971 dateline. During the four workdays of this week, before we go on a fortnight's leave, I hope to have made basic plans through until the end of February, including our Pacific Heads of Mission Conference in mid-February and the visit in late February of the Chief of the Defence Staff, General Fred Sharp.

s » Arthur has typed the generous share of the letter this week while I was finishing up arranging some large fern leaves we brought back, and a most peculiar fruit that seems to grow just once in a while in the heart of these burrawong fern trees. The fruit looks like a large pineapple, is green with shades of orange, and is said to be poisonous. Anyway, we now have one arrangement centred on this novelty, and I have taken the other two we found to a flower-arranging teacher friend of mine, who will make a superb arrangement with them.

January 30, 1972

s » As we have done several other years, we rented the VIP Lodge at Kosciuszko State Park for our holidays. It is becoming more popular with New South Wales cabinet ministers, so we could not get a booking as early as we would have liked. But we were lucky to get it for two weeks, from January 8 to 23. We had three sets of guests to share it with us this year. First to come up was Arthur's secretary, Margaret Hall, along with Judy Newman, a Canadian friend of hers who has been on a working holiday in Australia (working in hotels, mostly in the centre and on the Barrier Reef) and is now visiting Margaret here for a few weeks, and Edith. Each of the three of them was very keen to fish. It was the first time Edith had seen fishing on inland lakes, as she is used to sea fishing. She caught two fish, and brought one of them back for her sixty-sixth birthday celebration here in Canberra, so that pleased her. She and each of the other girls took a turn getting up at 5:30 a.m. to go out with Arthur at what he vowed was the best hour—or hours—for it. They would stay until after 9:00 a.m. and then come in for breakfast.

For the first time we had our own boat up there. Other years we have rented one by the day from the nearest caravan park, near Jindabyne. This time we used the small aluminum boat with the six-horsepower motor we borrowed from Harry Horne in Sydney. Arthur cleared out a place in the bay below the Lodge, and we had a good chain we locked it all up with at night, so we only had to bring up oars and fishing equipment. This meant that we were able to devote much more time to fishing this year. However, the boat could really only hold two people at a time, so it had to be on the relay system—one with Arthur in the early morning and another with him in the evening. Considering the hours of fishing that were put in, the catch over the two weeks was poor, but considering the sport and relaxation enjoyed by Arthur and all our guests the reward was great. We enjoyed about five good fish dinners up there and brought back ten fish for our freezer here, mostly brown trout, about two pounds each, but also a few rainbow trout. The biggest one caught was three and a half pounds, nothing like Art's six-pound one of last year. Besides feasting on trout, we received a gift of mushrooms from the chief ranger, who lived near us, and we managed to find the source of his supplies, a nearby paddock, and had mushrooms about five days in a row. We also learned an easy new way to cook them. Just wash them and put them in a dish in the oven at about 350 degrees, with no water or butter or anything, and in about twenty minutes they are done and delicious, without the calories from frying or other methods.

The three girls stayed three days, then for another four days we had Gordon and Elizabeth Upton, a couple from the Department of Foreign Affairs. She was born in Canada and went to McGill, but her parents were English and had retired in Canada. The Uptons brought their seventeen-year-old daughter, Kathy, who had just failed first year at ANU—but she didn't let that get her down, and was a very pleasant addition to the group. Then after three days on our own we had another Australian couple, Jess and Eric Keehn, for three days. I attend a lot of classes—French, art, etc.—with Jess, and Eric is an assistant secretary in the Department of the Interior. Just last year they sold their cottage at the coast, because their children are all grown up now, and they were typically Australian in that they had never thought of going to the mountains in the summer holidays—they had always gone to the sea coast—so it was a whole new country for them. With each set of guests we went on a lot of day expeditions and got good exercise walking. Altogether a good holiday and a good change.

February 6, 1972

s » This has been the hottest week of the summer. Every day it has been about 80 degrees. It is rather ironic, because this was the week all the children went back to school after their so-called "summer" holidays of the past two months, which have been chilly, and the wettest on record in many parts. Actually it was no hotter up in Queensland, where we were Monday and Tuesday, than here in Canberra the rest of the week.

Plane service to Brisbane, the capital of Queensland, has improved greatly, and luckily we made very close connections, so it only took two and a half hours from here to there, with a change of planes in Sydney. We left early Monday, the Australia Day holiday, and arrived in time to make our final arrangements before lunch with the chef at the Tower Hill Motel, where we were staying, to be hosts at a dinner that night in their ninth-floor restaurant, the Room at the Top, which has a lovely view over the city and the Brisbane River. We did not advertise the fact and I don't think anyone noticed, but we were thirteen for dinner, because Mr. Sawchyn, the general manager of the Winnipeg Ballet, felt that he should be with his company, which we quite understood given that it was opening night. Our guests were the Deputy Premier of Queensland and his wife, Sir Gordon and Lady Chalk; the Minister of Education and Cultural Affairs, Mr. Fletcher, and Mrs. Fletcher, whom we know from previous Canadian exhibition openings there; Rt. Honourable Frank Ford, now aged eighty-two but still very much there, and a keen friend of Canada, having been high commissioner in Ottawa at one time—he was prime minister of Australia for a few days once, so is a useful contact still; his daughter and son-in-law, a Brisbane architect; the Vice-Chancellor of the University and Mrs. Zelman Cowan; and Michael Edgley, the managing director of the theatre booking agency that has taken the chance of bringing the ballet to Australia as a commercial venture, a young chap of twenty-eight, and his twenty-one-year-old fiancée, Jeni King.

We were delighted with the premiere of the Royal Winnipeg Ballet. Brisbane has never before been selected as the city for such an important premiere—it's nearly always in Sydney or Melbourne—so they were flattered. A lot of free seats were given for the first night, and I am sure there isn't the theatre-going population to support a full house there every night for two weeks, but nonetheless the house was full and the audience warm and appreciative—and well they might be, as it was an excellent program. They began with *Aimez-Vous Bach*; it showed their technique and their classical skill, but it was lightened with humour. Then there was a complete contrast, a very dramatic piece called *Fall River Legend*, based on the axe-murder by Lizzie Borden and the murder trial that followed. It was more like a mood-play than a ballet. Then a Russian piece, and finally *Strike Up the Band*, a humorous take on the musical instruments in a band, using Gershwin melodies. We stayed for a champagne-and-chicken-sandwiches reception afterwards in the foyer of the theatre. It was given by the club called the Brisbane Firstnighters, who make a point of attending opening nights and obviously get a discount by doing so. We met some of the forty-five members of the Ballet, and the artistic director, etc. The next day Art had calls on the Premier, the Deputy Premier, and others, and we both had lunch out at the Staff Club of the University of Queensland with Professor and Mrs. Cowan and several of the professors there who have some connection with Canada. Then to the plane, and back here to Canberra in time for Art to go to the opening and dinner of the Rural Outlook Conference.

I was happy I did not have to go to that, because I was busy setting up the display of the Canadiana that I had borrowed from a variety of people in the office, mostly Eskimo carvings and some sports equipment peculiar to Canada, such as snowshoes. We put it in the end bedroom, because we are so snowed under with papers in the study, where I usually set up such a display, that I could not face moving all that junk before starting. All was admired at a Commonwealth wives meeting Wednesday morning.

February 13, 1972

A » As Sheila has been away since Thursday afternoon taking part in a seminar on Canada organized by the Extension Department of the University of New England in Armidale for the Country Women's Association of New South Wales, and will only return at 4:40 this afternoon (Sunday), I thought that I should get on with the weekend letter.

President and Madame Suharto of Indonesia and a large entourage including Foreign Minister Malik spent four days in Australia this past week. As dean of the diplomatic corps Sheila and I were more involved than others, including a ceremonial arrival last Sunday night and departure Tuesday morning. In between we went to a reception with three hundred others, the opening of the new Indonesian chancery, and a white tie dinner at Government House. With a population of 115 million living immediately to the northwest, and with the common frontier with Papua New Guinea, Indonesia is of evident importance to Australia. This was recognized back in 1950, when Australia sympathized with Indonesia's struggle for independence from the Netherlands, although there were setbacks during the dispute over Netherlands New Guinea or West Irian and during the confrontation with Malaysia in President Sukarno's time. The Australians have put some of their best diplomats into Djakarta and have pursued a generally enlightened and flexible policy. This has paid off, and the visit of President Suharto was a considerable success, marked only by minor protests about Indonesia's detention without trial of suspected communists.

John and Rhie Dougan (he is our High Commissioner in Wellington and they are long-time friends of ours) arrived on a sentimental visit on Wednesday. We gave a reception Wednesday night to enable them to meet some of their many friends from their service here from 1958 to 1961. In the evening we gave a small dinner at the Carousel Restaurant on Red Hill, attended by Secretary of the Cabinet and Peg Bunting, and the new counsellor of the New Zealand high commission, Bruce Brown, and his wife. The Dougans stayed with us, and their daughters with friends. They were invited out to all their meals after Sheila left, and then took off Saturday morning in our car for a trip to the Snowy Mountains. John is a great fisherman.

Beginning tomorrow, February 14, we are to have a three-and-a-half-day conference of our Pacific heads of missions, with five officers from Ottawa, for a total of sixteen. The first of these to arrive, at noon on Saturday, were Ralph and Jane Collins from Peking and, from Ottawa, Arthur Andrew, director general of the Bureau of Asian and Pacific Affairs. I took Ralph for a two-hour drive around the city yesterday afternoon and had a good chat about living conditions in Peking and the extent of access they have to Chinese officials. I gather that recreation facilities are minimal and diplomats are restricted to the immediate environs of Peking. Peking is drab grey and brown. However, if the Chinese want to be nice—and this is their current attitude to Canada—they can be quite agreeable, although they stick to the party line. I had David and Annabelle Anderson—David is responsible for Asia in the Department of Foreign Affairs here—in for dinner with our visitors, and we talked until late.

Later this afternoon I'm going out to meet Sheila, and more visitors. Some of the visitors may dine with us tonight. Then we head into a busy week, with meetings, entertainment, and perhaps some enlightenment on our future.

Cyclone Daisy has been battering the Queensland coast with winds up to 210 miles an hour and torrential rain. We have had some side effects. The electricity union in Victoria is striking for a fourth week of leave, causing blackouts, closing factories, etc. Tomorrow the state premiers come to Canberra on their annual exercise to beg for more money from the federal government. I wonder if Valentine's Day will help sweeten the atmosphere? The premiers consider raising state taxes politically unpopular, so prefer to ask the wealthier Commonwealth government to meet their needs.

February 20, 1972

s » When I returned last Sunday afternoon from the seminar on Canada at the University of New England, I was very pleased to find that Arthur had already written the weekend letter, because I was dead beat. I found a weekend in an academic atmosphere very stimulating but very demanding, because I was the only lecturer living in residence with the sixty-one people who had registered for the course, so I was involved in questions and discussion solidly for three days — early and late and at mealtimes. Actually they were fortunate to have two Canadian professors on the University staff, and they were the ones who gave two of the other lectures — which were on problems of agriculture and industry in Canada, and on ethnic groups in Canada. The third lecturer was married to a Canadian and had travelled in Canada. Still, all of them lived in Armidale, not in the residences. Besides, I expected just one session of one and a half hours and some of the discussion period to follow, but in the end was questioned for all of that second hour and a half, and I was made chairman and had to take a stab at all the questions the others could not answer. All this meant that I returned almost hoarse. All the display and exhibition materials we had sent ahead and I organized the first day were greatly appreciated, and helped establish the atmosphere. It was an experience I think I learned much from, and since the Country Women's Associations will be studying Canada for all of 1972 I will have a lot more contact with some of these people when they return to their separate districts in the state.

I ended up on the same plane from Sydney to Canberra as four of the people coming to the heads of missions conference for Pacific Rim countries that Art told you about last week. They came from eleven countries and various government departments in Ottawa: Al Johnson from Treasury Board, Tom Burns from Industry Trade and Commerce, Jacques Guerin from the International Development Agency, and Arthur Andrew and Bill Barton from External. So it was a pretty high-powered gathering of officials. The only two wives were Jane Collins from China and Velma Clark from the Philippines — plus Rhie Dougan the week before, who had gone to Sydney by the time the conference started. I had small ladies' lunches at the Commonwealth Club, and we had a large reception for about a hundred at the office, and then thirteen here for a stag dinner. I think Arthur found it a useful exercise to compare notes with so many fellow heads of missions and to be in closer touch with government thinking in Ottawa.*

This week we are planning for a Canadian art exhibition and the visit of the Chief of the Defence Staff and Mrs. Sharp—and next week, a week of performances here of the Winnipeg Ballet. Already opening night has been sold out in little Canberra, which shows how good the reviews and the publicity about the tour have been in Brisbane and Melbourne.

One of the travel expense regulations over which I quarrelled with the financial administration in Ottawa from early in my posting as high commissioner to Australia related to the authority of the head of mission to approve travel expenses incurred by staff.

Each post is allocated a sum of money each year for staff travel within the post's territory. The position taken by the financial authorities in External Affairs, after reference to Treasury Board officers, was that the spending authority applied only to officers' travel approved in advance by the head of mission. The head of mission or other officer could, if appropriate, take his wife to stand beside him and look pretty. However, they would not approve a wife's travel expenses if she went alone to speak to a women's organization, or to a school or college. Sheila liked to go off and speak to women's groups and educational groups, and she spoke well. So we covered her single travel costs ourselves.

We also had a female consular clerk who had served in Europe during the Second World War with the Canadian Women's Army Corps. She was a good speaker and liked to go out to talk to women's clubs about her war experiences and life in Canada. Ottawa would not pay her travel expenses, so I did.

During the conference of heads of missions of Pacific Rim countries I raised this question with Al Johnson, Secretary of the Treasury Board. Al said, "Write a telex addressed to me as Secretary of the Treasury Board and I'll look into it." The result was a change in the regulations so that heads of missions were now authorized to approve the travel expenses of spouses or staff, in order to make the most effective use of them.

Too bad this Pacific Rim heads of mission conference was held only a few months before I completed my tour in Australia and the South Pacific. (A.M. 2008)

February 26, 1972

s » This has been the week of the Pacific Forum meeting here in Canberra, a gathering of prime ministers of all the independent countries of the Pacific Islands: Fiji, Tonga, Nauru, Western Samoa, New Zealand, and Australia. The first such meeting was held in New Zealand last year. We have been interested of course because of our accreditation to Fiji, and the fact that Ratu Mara's earlier unofficial visit here was cancelled because of the shipping strike in Fiji, so this is his first visit here. The Australians have organized things for the visitors very much at the last minute, so we have had to try to fit those functions in with Canadian commitments of months' standing.

The first such commitment was the opening here in Canberra of the West Coast Art display in the National Library. Art had already seen it and opened it in Melbourne. In this small group of paintings collected by the Vancouver Art Gallery, only two are representational. All the rest are very modern, especially one sculpture painting consisting of fourteen ceramic apples and two pieces of turf joined by a chain, which is titled "Fourteen Rotten Apples." Arthur made the speech at the opening, and tactfully did not dwell too much on the present display, but rather offered a comparison of Australian and Canadian art in general and the general history and development of each. He has had several letters and comments on how good his speech was, so that is pleasing. We had about seventy people there at 5:45 p.m. in the foyer of the National Library and served just wine and cheese. Then afterwards we took the National Librarian out to dinner up at the Carousel Restaurant. He had introduced Arthur, and it's in his building the display will be until March 15. Also with us were his wife and two visiting librarians we had got involved with. To make it a three-ring circus, between the exhibit and the dinner we worked in a reception at Fiji House to meet the Fiji Prime Minister and Adi Lady Lala. We took in tow to it a Canadian businessman from Toronto—a director of the Bank of Nova Scotia, and on the board of the YMCA, United Church Missions, etc. He was also the person who had arranged and hosted the golf game for the Fiji Prime Minister when he was in Toronto.

The most important visitor of the week was General Fred Sharp, Chief of the Canadian Defence Staff, and because he came in an Armed Forces plane from Canada, via Fiji and New Zealand, he had a large and high-powered group travelling with him, several of whom brought their wives—such people as Dr. L'Heureux, Chief of the Defence Research Board, and Mrs. L'Heureux, and General and Mrs. Reid. They were only in Canberra twenty-four hours, from noon Thursday to noon Friday, but in that time had good talks with their opposite numbers here, and were entertained, etc. Colonel Corry had a large reception, and afterwards we had a dinner for twelve here, which went well, and the Sharps stayed on for a good talk after the other guests had left. I drove Mrs. Sharp and Mme. L'Heureux sightseeing after lunch the first day, and two of the other army wives the next morning. All week I have been trying to save my throat by cutting out such activities as tennis so that my cold would be under control for this important visit—and it did last, so I was lucky. Tomorrow I will go with Art to watch the Commonwealth versus Australia cricket match, but I do not get too excited by cricket, so I will not waste my voice cheering there. The staffs of the various high commissions supply the one team, and as senior high commissioner of course we have to support it. With Pakistan out of the Commonwealth now it is hard to scrape up enough players, so we have roped in seventeen-year-old Donald Corry and the sixteen-year-old Anstis boy as the only Canadians available.

March 2, 1972

s » Dear Norah: As you know, Daddy and I believe that travel is part of one's education. We have tried to include you and Kenneth as much as possible when you've been with us abroad, and to pay for your travel to and from us when we've been apart. We intend to continue doing so until each of you is established with a job. We consider this part of your graduate education. Last year when Kenneth went to Russia, we paid for his travel expenses—his transport, as distinct from his food or lodging or recreation. He submitted estimates of charter flights, etc., and on that basis we sent him a check for $500, which he did not have to repay.

We would like to do something similar for you for your travel in Europe. You were very keen to buy your return ticket to England from Canada, and we appreciated that. Now, for your further travel, we feel we should help. We do not know if you plan to go via camper van as you once mentioned, or by plane (charter flights, basically), or by train or bus. By this time you likely will have made some plans. We would appreciate it if you could estimate what your travel on the continent will cost for the next few months. We would be glad to send a cheque for at least $500 and, depending on your plans, up to $1,000. We look forward to hearing your plans.

love
Mummy

I subscribe to all this too and wish you a good time!
Dad

March 5, 1972

s » When Bill Barton, one of the assistant undersecretaries of External Affairs, was out here early last month he told Arthur that his name was to be put up for reassignment likely by Canadian summer, and in view of this both Arthur and I were to get thorough medical checkups so that our names could be put forward for a variety of posts. With all the possible combinations and commutations, nothing definite can be said now. Therefore we have both had hour-long medicals with Dr. Scott Finley, and had other time-consuming things done such as chest X-rays and cardiographs. Fortunately we seem a pretty healthy pair. This means I have been getting lots of attention and medical advice for my cold —one bottle of cough medicine is literally the size of a bottle of wine. Evidently medical records show that in Canberra one is more likely to have colds that hang on for a long time than in most other places, and mine certainly supports those statistics.

The visit of the Royal Winnipeg Ballet to Canberra has gone very well so far. We had all the officers and wives from our office and about forty other people at the opening night on Friday. Afterwards, these plus the executive of the Canadian-Australian Association, a few press, and the forty-five people connected with the ballet company all came to the chancery at 11:00 p.m. for a "champagne reception." To help decorate the office, we followed Art's idea to have large black silhouettes of three dancers cut out and placed against the bare walls high up in the foyer, and I had gorgeous big yellow dahlias from the garden of one of Edith's friends, roses from our own garden, and gladioli from the florist to help with colour. As everyone had been in evening dress and black tie for the opening, it was quite a gala occasion. The Australians are making a film on the future of Canberra, chiefly dealing with their National Capital Development Commission, and the TV crew from it came to shoot pictures of our reception, just as they had done for the opening the week before of the West Coast Art exhibition. Likely in the finished production there will only be a shot or two of each and a few remarks made by Arthur at the art exhibit, but the crew had their bright lights and equipment strung up all over the place and took a lot of film. Besides the ballet performers, who mixed very freely and easily with the crowd in spite of the fact that they had been up since six o'clock that morning to leave Melbourne, our chief guests were Minister of the Interior and Mrs. Ralph Hunt. Because Canberra has no city government, he is the local equivalent of a mayor. They stayed on until about 1:00 a.m., so must have been enjoying themselves.

Last night we went to the same program of the ballet a second time, because Deputy Prime Minister Doug Anthony and his wife had said that they could not come opening night but would like to come the following night. We had one other couple with them. Again we were struck by the professional competence of the entire company, and the excellent, varied program they put on. We will be going a third time this coming Wednesday, but it will be a different program from this one, which we have seen both in Brisbane and here. On that night the Governor General is to be the guest of honour. We will have a dinner beforehand for a few people and meet the Governor General at the theatre. It is amazing how much red tape and protocol is involved just in having the Governor General to a performance.

Arthur has been involved with a rifle team that is out here from Canada to take part in a shoot with Australians and New Zealanders this week. The MacKinnons had a reception for them on Thursday, and Art went to their shooting range this morning and will go to another part of the meet on Tuesday. It is mostly outdoors in the wind, so I have not gone because of my cold.

We are now off for the Rogers', where the whole ballet company of forty-five are coming for a barbecue—on this their one day off.

Flash! Flash! We were delighted to receive a happy phone call this morning from Kenneth to tell us that he has accepted the offer of a job as an assistant professor of sociology at the University of Guelph, to begin in September. We think that this location in Western Ontario, near so many academic centres, will be an excellent place for him. Since we know that jobs are not plentiful, we are very pleased indeed that he has been able to get such a good one. He is to teach nine hours a week, and is now corresponding about which courses he will be responsible for. It certainly is happy news.

March 12, 1972

s » Arthur has been working very hard and very late most nights getting reports done and material prepared, so I am glad he decided to take one day off this Sunday to try a bit of fishing at Burrinjuck Dam with Eric Conybeare and the boat we still have on loan from Harry Horne. It means that I have had a very quiet day around the house, the very best thing possible for this cold of mine, which lingers on and on. Last night at the formal dinner we went to at the British high commission to bid farewell to the Chief of the Air Staff, who has been appointed the new governor of Queensland, I had such a coughing fit I had to leave the table. I think that this one day without any talking has really helped my throat.

313

The Winnipeg Ballet gave two performances on their last day in Canberra, a matinée at 5:00 p.m. and an evening performance at 8:45. We had a dinner for twelve before this performance, and were joined at the theatre by the Governor General, Sir Paul Hasluck. He was most enthusiastic. He went backstage and talked to all the leading dancers, and had good talks with the few Australians in the company, especially Petal Miller, who comes from the same suburb of Perth as he does. We preferred the other program they put on this week, and the audience was warmer in their response, I think. We had all sorts of changes in our dinner list at the last minute, but managed to get replacements who worked in well.

March 15, 1972

s » Dear Norah: We were glad to get your letter. We feel as parents we should let you know our feelings and communicate them to you. We also appreciate that you are an adult and do not always agree with our ideas, and that you have your own life to live, so make your own decisions.

We are enclosing a cheque for $500 Canadian, as we still feel we would like to share in your travel on the continent. This is part of our policy, or philosophy, or call it what you will. We did it for Kenneth, and we would like to do it for you. We would also still like you to estimate your travel on the continent and, as we said before, we will be glad to supplement this with up to another $500 if you give us some idea of your expenses and where you will be travelling. If you literally do not know at all where you are planning to go, and therefore want to do the further instalment in retrospect, that is OK with us. But I would think it would be easier if you knew ahead, and had the money ahead. At least this first instalment will start you on your way.

Daddy is having a list of the Canadian officers in our posts in Western Europe made, and he'll indicate the ones we know well so that you will have contacts if you need them. He will mail it on the weekend.

We would like to have some general idea where our dear darling daughter is travelling, so would appreciate your keeping in touch with us as you go from country to country.

We hope that you and Eddie really enjoy the experience in Europe as much as you both seem to have enjoyed England. We wish you both heaps of fun and interest.

love
Mommy

March 19, 1972

s » We have had two important Canadian visitors this week, and our activities have revolved around them. The first was Dr. Lloyd Barber, Commissioner for Indian Claims for Canada and deputy chancellor of the University of Saskatchewan, who is accompanied by his wife. I don't know what the statistics prove, but it seems to me that Canadian families are getting much, much larger. Mrs. Lang, the young wife of the minister who was out here has six children, Mrs. Barber has six children, and our other visitor this week, John Carson, has six children. Mrs. Barber had left hers in the care of her mother, and as they had been a week in New Zealand before coming here and will be another three weeks in Australia, the granny will be well acquainted with all six, especially the eighteen-month-old, by the time they return to Canada. I drove Mrs. Barber around sightseeing most of Monday, and we had lunch at Gaye Applebaum's. Her husband, Bob, is going with the Barbers when they tour the Northern Territory to compare Aborigines in Australia and Indians in Canada with respect to the way they are treated and the legal aspects of dealing with them. We gave a dinner for them on Tuesday, which included some good discussions, as we had the head of the Institute for Aboriginal Affairs and the deputy secretary of the department that looks after the Northern Territory.

Since his arrival at noon Wednesday we have been involved with the Chairman of the Public Service Commission of Canada (what we used to call the Civil Service Commission), John Carson. He lost his wife through cancer this past year. We found him a very pleasant guest, and he performed very ably at his chief function in Canberra, an address to the Royal Institute of Public Administration. His talk, called "The Continuing Challenge of Change," showed how the Canadian civil service is adjusting and adapting itself to questions related to minorities in Canada—first the French-speaking minority, then women in the civil service, then recently admitted immigrants, then Indians and native peoples. His whole speech was thoughtful, and yet he shone best in the question period afterwards, in which the Australians asked very probing questions about Canadian experience with dissent in the service, retirement (which now is being encouraged throughout the Civil Service at age 55 instead of 60 or 65), and taking the load off the management decision-makers at the top of the service. We had good chats with him, both at dinner *à trois* Wednesday evening and for twelve on Friday evening, as well as a relaxed day with him yesterday, Saturday, when we took him sightseeing. We included a young nephew of his, who is in Canberra now on a round-the-world working holiday tour, and who obviously fell deeply in love with India during his three months there and found it very stimulating, He was rather disappointed in Australia, though he has a good research job here in the Department of Statistics (he has an honours degree in economics from Queen's). It was the most perfect summer day we have had in Canberra for months—up to 82 degrees—so some of them swam at the Rogers' pool, and all enjoyed a pleasant chops-and-sausages barbecue at lunch there before he had to leave on the late-afternoon plane. I must say that one of the advantages of serving abroad is that we see VIPs in such concentrated doses that we really get to know them, and have a great deal more exposure to them than we would ever experience in a whole year in Ottawa. When the person is an attractive, clever, modest, gentle Canadian like this one, it is very pleasant.

We were pleased to be included in a unique ceremony on Friday. Sir Kenneth Bailey is in hospital with cancer, and it has completely taken over his whole frail body, so no one really expects him to get out of the hospital. His mind, though, is still very keen and active. The University of Melbourne, his first alma mater, wishing to award him an honorary degree, constituted a synod in the hospital boardroom to confer it.

March 26, 1972

s » All this week a seven-man trade delegation from Ottawa has been out here having exploratory trade talks with their Australian counterparts. Most of the negotiation has to do with changes in the Australian-Canadian trade agreement of 1960 to allow for changes in Britain's position as it enters Europe. Arthur has been part of the negotiating team, along with Ben Shapiro, the commercial counsellor here, and Harry Horne, the commercial counsellor from Sydney. These meetings were not supposed to produce a definite treaty, they were just intended to get the talking started. The next round will likely be in Canada. Anyway, the talks seemed slow to get started, and you can imagine how rushed Arthur has been to be there daily, morning and afternoon, and at social dinners and luncheons for the guests (which would have exhausted me in themselves), plus trying to put in an appearance at his own office and cope with the most urgent matters there. As a result he was up to his neck in work, and I'm very glad that long before these trade talks were scheduled he had made arrangements to go fishing this weekend. It will be a complete change, and it will help him keep his sanity and perspective to get out on Lake Eucumbene with just rainbow and brown trout to worry about.

Edith had a fall on the garden steps on Tuesday and sprained her ankle badly. The first doctor's appointment she could get was for 6:15 p.m., which I took her to. He didn't think it was broken, so he strapped it up and arranged for an X-ray at the hospital the next morning. It was very swollen and black and blue, but the X-ray showed no break. The doctor said she would be laid up for two weeks. She was a surprisingly good patient, and literally stayed in bed three days, but this afternoon went out for a little drive with Mrs. Robey, her chief friend, and—oh yes—also went with me this morning to place some bets so that she would have some interest in listening to the races this weekend. Except for her hurt ankle she has been uncannily lucky the past couple of weeks, having won $35.00 at bingo and $45.00 at racing, and was only one word from winning a big several-thousand-dollar crossword-like puzzle contest. Having her in bed made me scurry a bit to get prepared for the ten-man trade lunch here on Wednesday, and tea for twelve Canadian office wives on Thursday after we had made a visit to the local Australian law courts in their handsome new building. There will just be social bowling over Easter, not competition bowling, so I hope Edith will be her usual active self by the middle of the month, when we return from New Guinea.

Arthur and I leave Wednesday night, the 29th, for Sydney, to be ready for the early-morning flight to New Guinea on Thursday the 30th. We will have just one night in Port Moresby and then we'll spend Good Friday and Easter weekend with the Canadian Montfort Missionaries in the Daru area. Bishop Deschamps has suggested that it will be a good time to see everyone there and to visit the various sites up the swampy Fly River. (I have started taking my malaria pills today.) Later we will have a few days in the Highlands and in Lae seeing some of the fifty Canadian University Students Overseas volunteers and some other Canadian projects and interests. We will fly back to Sydney on April 12, and Art will stay over there for the opening of a mine. I'll return to Canberra a day ahead of him, just in time for a big charity ball on April 14 that I'm involved with. The office will forward our mail as usual.

April 16, 1972

A » Our fortnight's visit to Papua New Guinea gave us a good opportunity to assess the changes that have taken place over the six years since we first went there, in August 1966, with Ken and Norah. I suppose that the most striking impression is the number of bright and attractive young Papua New Guineans now beginning to take their places in the public life of the country. Six years ago there was no University, Institute of Technology, or High School Teachers College. Now all of these have graduated classes, and many other students are coming along in specialized fields. Some of the recently elected members of the House of Assembly are articulate and well informed. Of course the scene is spotty, but it is promising. Then there has been a great improvement in roads and bridges. There is considerable light manufacturing in towns such as Lae and Port Moresby. With Bougainville Copper now starting to export copper concentrate, there is the prospect of better revenues. These things make it much easier for the House of Assembly to think in terms of self-government soon. What they will decide is still uncertain, because the division on independence between the more radical Pangu party and the more conservative United party has yet to be settled. The trend should appear later this week when the new House opens.

There are now six projects that have drawn aid or will draw aid from CIDA and Canadian voluntary agencies. All of these have been started in my time. I was glad to see them, because personal impressions strengthen written representations. We also have fifty-six CUSO volunteers whom we met in various parts of the country. They make a good impression for Canada.

I presented law books and more general books to the University of Papua New Guinea. This is the second presentation I have been pleased to be able to make.

I must tell you the way one district commissioner, Jim Sinclair of Goroka, described me in pidgin to some natives. He said, "This numba one big fella, half-caste bilong America." When asked about the half-caste, he said they all know about America, and he was trying to convey the impression that Canada was like America but a little different. There was also an amusing pidgin description of an organ: "All same boxus; you fightum teeth bilong him; him cry out loud plenty too much."

s » Arthur stayed over in Sydney an extra day on the way back to attend the opening of the first asbestos mine in Australia, located at Barraba, north of Tamworth, in New South Wales. A Canadian company has a 58-percent interest in the mine. I returned in order to continue my involvement in the charity costume ball to provide cyclone relief for Townsville, Queensland, which was held at the Turkish embassy Friday night. The army came through very generously, providing us with a marquee, tables, chairs, tablecloths, etc.; one of the big department stores let us have decorations (red plastic roses in strings by the hundreds) that they had used at Christmastime; and the Japanese on the committee organized a team of Japanese flower arrangers to do live arrangements in the front hall and on each of the small tables. Just the physical manual labour that goes into the work of a ball is better appreciated by me now, especially by the time we had spent three hours the day after, taking down all the decorations, which were strung up with tough plastic. About 190 people attended, of whom about one-third were in costume, some quite amusing; we stuck to just evening dress. I'll let you know later how much money we actually made. Anyway, all the members of the committee are tired out and resolve never to serve on another ball committee!

In New Guinea we were especially impressed with the good work done by the Catholic Montfort Missionaries in the Fly River area of West Papua. It is not just their young and enthusiastic Bishop Deschamps; all the people on the five of their eight mission stations that we visited seemed imbued with devotion. They are doing very practical work, whether nursing, or teaching, or helping with agricultural or fisheries projects. In a way I admire even more the various lay missionaries attached to such places, such as the two young Australian volunteers, nurses at one of the most isolated spots, who do bush patrols, which involve walking many, many miles in country thick with leeches, over many flooded streams, carrying all their own supplies, in near 100-degree heat and humidity. I must say I prefer the climate up in the Highlands, around Goroka and Mount Hagen, where it was actually cool enough at night for people to light fires. There was a bad air crash while we were in New Guinea that killed seven missionaries belonging to the Summer School of Linguistics, which we had been scheduled to visit but did not because of the mishap. I must say that a flight at up to 14,500 feet altitude to cross the mountains from the Western District to the Highlands in a small four-seater plane belonging to the mission was an experience I would not care to repeat—although it was interesting, and the pilot was excellent.

April 25, 1972

s » This is being typed Saturday afternoon instead of Sunday, because I expect to be involved in the first Canadian Invitation Tennis Tournament, organized by the Rogers, the Corrys, and the Anstises. It involves twenty-four players and was to have been held today, but it teemed rain today so it was postponed till Sunday. Arthur left with Eric Conybeare after dinner last night for a weekend of fishing at Lake Eucumbene, a recreation he doesn't think can be equalled. There'll be two other men there, and besides fishing they hope to repair the roof and fix up the cottage they have had the use of on several fishing weekends. Winter will soon be here—it was in the twenties this morning—so I am glad I gave him three blankets, a large casserole of stew, etc.

I am glad to be on hand today, because at the moment there is a tree surgeon at the gorgeous weeping willow tree over our patio. It has several obviously dead branches, and rather than have Andrew risk life and limb climbing up, we thought it time to get a professional to do the job. As you know, once let loose they want to do all sorts of trimming at great expense, so as a Canadian taxpayer I am watching like a hawk that they do the maximum possible for the original economical quote. They know that I value the tree more than the residence! The plan is now that as soon as we leave, the Canadian government will remake this whole house, leaving the part we now live in for family living, and adding entertainment rooms in the area where the garages are now. It will take at least six months to build, maybe a year, so the new high commissioner will have to be housed elsewhere. We are glad we will not be the ones to live through this upset, but think it is a better idea than a completely new residence on the other site at a most exorbitant price.

I am very pleased that the Townsville Cyclone Relief Ball committee will have a cheque for $1,800 to present to the member of Parliament for the Townsville area in Queensland in a small ceremony at the Turkish embassy this Wednesday. All the frustrations, bickering, anxious moments, frayed tempers, and other crises of the past three months are now forgotten, and some of the committee are saying, "We should have another ball for another charity." Those are not my sentiments. I'm so relieved it is over. I'm the one who has been writing the letters to the mayor of Townsville, etc.

Wednesday we had a full, interesting day, because we both went to Sydney, taking the 9:30 a.m. flight there and the 7:00 p.m. flight back. Arthur spent the morning at the Sydney office while I shopped long enough to buy a pair of shoes. Then I met him on the top floor of Farmer's Department Store, where they have a gallery called the Blaxland Gallery. There we held the opening ceremony for the same exhibition of art from Canada's West Coast, collected by the Vancouver Art Gallery, that you remember Art opened here in Canberra a month ago. In a busy store like that it should get a fair crowd during the two weeks it will be there, especially as the New South Wales Gallery is closed for renovation. John Sims, our External Affairs information officer attached to the Sydney office, had the bright idea of adding Indian wood plates with legends, some Eskimo carvings, and the large totem pole from our Canberra office, which brightened up the whole display area. We had lunch afterwards with the manager of the store, his wife, and several directors. I felt that Arthur spoke very easily and well at both that ceremony and the presentation of Canadian books he made in the afternoon at Macquarie University. It is the only Australian university that we had not visited before. It is very new. The buildings, on the outskirts of Sydney, were only started in 1965, it was opened in 1967, and it graduated its first students in 1969. The style of the buildings, in reinforced concrete, is very simple but good, and they have had the good fortune to receive all sorts of generous bequests, and loans of original Australian paintings. We were quite impressed with the whole atmosphere and setup.

April 26, 1972

s » Flash! Flash! Our big news has arrived: we have been posted. We were notified in a telegram today that the department is going to announce our appointment in Canada tomorrow. Arthur is to be Permanent Representative and Ambassador of the Delegation of Canada to the North Atlantic Council, usually referred to in brief as Ambassador to NATO. The headquarters of NATO was moved from Paris to Brussels about three years ago, as you remember, so that is where we will be for the next two or more years. NATO ranks high among present commitments, so it is one of Canada's most senior posts. It is a much higher-ranking post than Australia, so this is a promotion for Arthur. He has always had a good deal to do with NATO and with military personnel—when he was head of the Defence Liaison (1) Division in Ottawa, and on the Canada-United States Permanent Joint Board on Defence, etc.—and he has got along very well in such fields.

The way the department has handled the series of appointments that will presumably all be announced tomorrow seems very odd to us. We would have liked more notice here to say the least, rather than this sudden deadline, which meant that this afternoon Art had to inform the secretary of the Department of Foreign Affairs here and call in the officers of our mission and notify them. We would like to have been able to break it to them and to you, all our family, before it became public knowledge, but the department doesn't always think of such things.

Art was only asked about a month ago by Ed Ritchie, the undersecretary, if he would let his name stand for this post. That was where they felt we could best serve the interests of the whole department. Although perhaps we had expected and been led to expect that China or some other Asian post, such as Japan or India, was more likely to be in the books, as a career officer we are glad to go where management thinks best. It will be interesting and important to serve in Europe for a change. I must say I don't relish the prospect of having to conduct most business in French, but at least in the French atmosphere it will be more practical to learn the language rather than just playing with it, as we have done for so many years. Maybe we will have a bit of a crash course before we go.

We do not know about the timing of all these appointments, but understand they are to take place during "Canadian summer." We would expect to leave Australia between the middle and end of July, call in at Fiji en route back, and be in Canada during August and in Belgium sometime in September, but we have sent a letter to the department today asking that they tell us what sort of timing they have in mind.

As you can imagine, a thousand and one things will now have to be done. We are off to Fiji in two days, so not everything will be cut and dried and settled before we leave. Arthur is still busy writing reports about the Papua New Guinea trip; three stenographers have been busy all day today, and Miss Hall came in yesterday, the Anzac Day holiday. Anyway, we wanted you, the family, to know as soon as the news was public. Our successor here cannot be announced until the Australians give their agreement, but we imagine that that will happen in a few days too. When things start to move, they sure move. With an election in the offing it is much better that External gets its appointments made beforehand; otherwise they may get delayed for ages.

May 14, 1972

s » We were fortunate in the timing of our Fiji trip. The day we arrived was the end of their election campaign, and the counting on Sunday returned Ratu Maru and his Alliance party by 30 to 19. All except one of the cabinet ministers who ran were re-elected, so we know most of the important people there. Because of the first South Pacific Festival of Arts, which was held in Suva for two weeks starting May 6, there were VIP visitors from all of the fifteen countries and territories of the Pacific that were contributing dance and music and art and poetry, etc., to the festival. The opening ceremony in Albert Park in the heart of Suva was attended by five thousand. It had been raining every day that week, and Saturday was no exception, and when it rains in Suva it teems and teems, so you can imagine the state of the field. At 7:00 p.m., when festivities started, the sky was clear, and all the participants had agreed that they preferred to go ahead, come what might. A heavy shower came after the first half-hour, but not one person left their seat and not one performer missed a step of the dance. Their vitality and enthusiasm was marvellous. The ground got really muddy and churned up. Three members of the Fiji band lost shoes in the morass. Most of the dancers were in bare feet, so that didn't matter so much, but some had beautiful costumes that of course got very muddy at the bottom, and at one stage in the Tongan dance the performers lay right down on their backs on the muddy ground in their lovely tapa cloth costumes; one could not help admiring such good sportsmanship. Most of the rest of the three-and-a-half-hour performance was fine. There was infinite variety in the songs and dances put on by the Indian, Fijian, and Chinese communities of Fiji, and by the others from Tonga, Samoa, Cook Islands, Gilbert and Ellice Islands, by the Australian Aborigines, New Zealand Maoris, and New Caledonians, by the Solomon Islanders, New Hebrideans, and Papua New Guineans. Monday and Tuesday evenings, at 5:00 p.m. and 8:00 p.m. each night, we saw further shows put on by some of these groups. We saw Tongans, Gilbert and Ellice Islanders, Solomon Islanders, and New Caledonians, each very different and each well presented.

We were lucky to get out on Wednesday, because there was a strike against Qantas and a walkout of all traffic officers at Nandi airport, which prevented all planes from leaving on the following two days. Also, they had had five bomb scares in four days, so security searches were very strong. We ended up on the Air India flight with two extra people aboard, and had to get that straightened out before we could take off!

Art has really worked at all his different Canadian aid schemes, and although there are many delays and frustrations, he will be seeing results in several places before we leave in July. We visited the Agriculture School, a school for trades training that has received aid from B.C., and sites of possible welfare and community centres that may get Canadian International Development Aid. Of course there are a lot of reports and follow-up work to be done now that he has returned here to Canberra.

Although the name of our successor is not official yet, our appointment was announced in Canada, and most people here now know of our departure. It is hard to realize that we have only approximately two months left here. Art says I should ease down and start to think of packing, etc., but we just seem to be running to stay in the same place, catching up on the backlog of the two weeks away. Arthur has had to work this weekend on a speech to open an exhibition tomorrow of Canadian contemporary prints, which is not an easy subject. As dean of the corps we get involved in many time-consuming events that cannot be sidestepped.

May 20, 1972

s » Tuesday night we were out at the Rogers' for dinner, and one of Arthur's fishing cronies, Eric Conybeare, was there, so they planned to have one more last fling at fishing before Art leaves and before winter sets in completely. Hence this morning, Saturday, he and Eric and Sir Leonard Huxley, another regular, and one different buddy, Alan Fleming, the National Librarian, have left, and will return after supper tomorrow evening. As a result I have had a quiet day, indoors in the study the whole time, trying to get some sorting of material done so that I can begin work on my speeches for the Country Women's Association in June. Now that we know we are moving, any kind of sorting means throwing out lots of stray material, and this type of organizing can really eat into one's time with little to show for it. The only consolation is that the more I manage to throw out or to consolidate the less I will have to pack!

Poor Edith got an attack of her old tummy trouble, diverticulitis, while she was in Sydney, so she was never able to bowl, and because they could not find a substitute her whole team was out of the competition. However, she saw an old doctor friend in Sydney and got fixed up by the time of her return Wednesday night. It was disappointing.

This has been our week of art—not the man, the culture. On Monday Arthur opened an exhibition of contemporary Canadian prints at the Menzies Library at ANU. He had to bone up on the lingo of lithographs, woodcuts, etchings, silkscreen prints, and all the different processes, and managed to digest it all so that he gave a very good outline of the various processes at the opening of his speech. What is more, he did not use a single note, unlike the American Ambassador, who, at the opening of a similar exhibition of American prints in books two days later, just read a speech that was obviously prepared by someone else. Then on Thursday morning, as a conclusion for the series of lectures on Australian art I have been attending at ANU, the wife of the Dutch Ambassador and I arranged a showing of films at the National Library. We had an excellent new one about the Canadian Group of Seven that has just come out here for a showing at the Festival of Townsville next month, and the Dutch had one about a very modern Dutch painter, Abel, who does not paint, but "hits" —that is, he slaps at the huge canvases with such vim and vigour the whole picture shakes, even though there is a scaffolding behind it. One has to see the madman to believe such a presentation. And to think he gets paid for the results!

For the last three years, the new crop of foreign service cadets entering the Australian Department of Foreign Affairs has come to our office for three days' exposure to how a similar office abroad runs. I have a session beforehand for the female cadets, the wives of any married male cadets, and the wives of our Canadian officers here. This year twenty-five people turned up. First we had an information session at the office, then adjourned to the residence for tea and a meeting—sitting on cushions on the living room floor—at which I gave a ten-minute talk on what a young wife should try to do abroad, and each of the other Canadian wives had about three minutes about a different field. And they all asked questions. They are a bright, attractive group of young Australians, and I am sure they will do well at home or abroad. Wednesday noon the Rogers had a working lunch for them all, a Chinese-style buffet, and Friday night the Applebaums had a cocktail reception. So they have had work and play.

May 28, 1972

s » We have just had the administrative officer, Derek MacKinnon, in to try with Arthur to locate the place where the awful stinking smell of dead mouse or mice is coming from. We got a couple of dead bodies out of traps near the furnace, and the general odour of the house since about last Thursday has been that of roast or stewing mouse. As you may remember from our previous experiences in this old house, we don't want to have to open up floors if we can help it for the sake of two more months, but we got to the point where we could stand it no longer. Arthur and Derek found what they think is the source, under the floor in Art's upstairs study, but it will require a carpenter tomorrow, Monday, to get in deeper.

This has been the week of the visit of the Prime Minister of Fiji, Ratu Sir Kamisese Mara, and Adi Lady Lala Mara on their first official visit to Australia. As dean of the corps we were at the airport to meet them Monday morning. Raman and Papa Nair, the Fiji High Commissioner and his wife, said we were honorary Fijians during the visit here, and so included only us, with all their office staff, at a lunch at their house on Monday noon, which was very friendly, and that night we were again included as dean of the corps in the big official dinner at Government House. I sat next to the Prime Minister, Mr. McMahon, which was also interesting. Next day, while the Fiji Prime Minister was the speaker at the Press Club lunch, which Art attended, I had a luncheon here in honour of Adi Lady Lala that included Mrs. McMahon, Mrs. Anthony, the wife of the Deputy Prime Minister, who had attended the Fiji Independence, and others with connections with Fiji. The hit of the lunch was pumpkin soup served in the pumpkin shell. We had two, so each one served six people. I had seen it done in Malaysia, but of course I called it an Iroquois Indian dish, which it also is. Then for the main course we had two rainbow trout Arthur had caught and two other good-sized ones caught by Alan Fleming, who was on the same expedition with Arthur. Arthur was further involved with the permanent secretary of the Fiji Department of External Affairs that night at a reception and a dinner. Next morning we bade farewell to all of them at the airport on their way to Melbourne and a further six days in Australia. Since then I have driven Mrs. Nair and another Fijian to a Commonwealth Day lunch, where the film on the Independence of Fiji was shown, and again yesterday I took her to a Pan-Pacific tea while Arthur was playing in a men's

Canadian tennis team against a similar team from the British high commission. By good fortune the Canadians won by twenty points. As it is only in the fifties here now and quite windy, he went with his old white flannels, a winter coat, and a blanket to keep him warm between sets—and used them all. Women joined the men for a lunch of soup and sandwiches in the middle of the day at the Rogers'.

I have been working on the speeches I have to give to the Country Women's Association over the next month. I am very pleased that another Canadian wife here, the wife of the Army standardization officer, Joan Anstis, has also willingly agreed to make some speeches to these groups. I really enjoyed the first one she did, this week. Out of it she has got involved in another club in a nearby town, and has been invited to visit two properties. All of this pleases her—and naturally me too.

There is an exhibition of photographs of the Canadian Parliament Buildings taken by Malak on display in the King's Hall of Parliament House, so of course Art had to scurry around during the week to get a suitable speech prepared to open it. This is the last week the Australian Parliament sits until late August. He was thanked by the president of the Senate. I must say we can understand and appreciate such photographs much more readily than we can some of the pictures sent in exhibitions.

June 4, 1972

s » Last week I wrote you about the start of the anti-mice campaign. It turned out to be an anti-rat campaign. We had a carpenter here for two days working with the administrative officer, probing around under the floor of Arthur's study upstairs and in the ceiling of the small garage. We think that all the holes are plastered and that the menace is now over. This weekend, while we were away in Young, fortunately for us—but not for Edith, who likes her weekends off—we had a crisis with the heating system. The furnace went off; I thought it was something to do with the switch, but evidently it happened because the oilman had not come regularly as per his contract, and there was not one drop of oil in the tank, so the furnace had burned itself out and done all sorts of damage to itself in the process.

Monday and Tuesday we had film showings at the office — on Monday for a group of about fifty from External Affairs and from External Territories, who administer Papua New Guinea, and French-speakers from my French class and the French embassy; on Tuesday for fifty Canadian graduate students and their wives from ANU — to see the film made for Radio-Canada by Bertolino and shown trans-Canada last March, about the work of the Montfort Catholic Missionaries in the Western District of Papua New Guinea. The text is in French. It emphasizes the primitive early tribal customs and beliefs of the people and shows little of the constructive work of the missions. However, the photography is outstanding, and as a documentary of the social and archaeological background of customs that will soon have died out it is a unique film. We served drinks and coffee and hot sandwiches and small pizzas, so all stayed for good talk after the hour-long film.

Thursday night at the office, we had a diplomatic corps farewell for the Russian Ambassador. It was not an easy one for Arthur. While he was making his speech an interpreter simultaneously translated it for the benefit of the Ambassador, and then the Ambassador's speech of reply was translated piecemeal. The farewell for ourselves will be next. There was an announcement in the Australian press this week about our appointment, and about Jim McCardle's coming here. We have had good letters both from our successors here, Jim and Lanny McCardle, and from our predecessors in Brussels, Ross and Pippa Campbell, who have been appointed to Japan. This week's announcements list about thirty-five heads of missions who have been switched or appointed, so no wonder a few of them take a little understanding. On the whole they are good.

Friday I gave my hardest speech here — hardest because it was in Canberra, where I knew several in the audience and where the audience is more sophisticated and better informed and expect better speakers than in most smaller country towns. This was to the Country Women's Association.

Immediately afterwards Arthur and I motored in the Datsun about one hundred miles to Young in New South Wales to be the guests at a Canada Ball, held in the town hall and sponsored by the Anglican Church there. Ten debutantes were presented to Arthur. In such country towns, this old-fashioned custom still commands great support. Three hundred attended the ball. They had gone to no end of trouble with Canadian decorations—had had the debutantes dressed in white, of course, but with red bouquets, six children dressed in very effective red Mountie uniforms, and two small flower girls in red. One lady had painted a huge scene of the Rockies, with pine trees, snow, a Mountie, and an Indian, as a backdrop for the band! The menu featured Saskatoon slaw and Arctic ice cream with maple syrup. We toured the district and saw properties the next day.

A » I'd like to add a side-story to Sheila's account of the debutante ball. A Canadian war bride of an Australian airman was the co-ordinating hostess for this event. He had been chosen to go to Canada to take aircrew training under the Commonwealth Air Training scheme. When he left Australia it was still their summer, so he was wearing summer fatigues. As they neared Vancouver they felt the weather getting cooler, so they were issued Australian wool long johns. He said he had never felt so itchy before.

Posted to an air training base in Alberta, he found the local farmers very hospitable, and was invited out to a farm dinner. Having been plied with beer before the meal by his farmer host, in mid-meal he had to go to the bathroom. The housewife motioned for him to go through the kitchen and out the back door. He complied, and to his consternation found he was standing on a little path in ten inches of snow. He saw a shack fifty feet away and went to explore it. It was dark, and there was just a black hole, but in view of his bowel pressure he made use of this black hole as well as he could and returned to the farmhouse.

En route he met the farmer's wife dressed in a heavy coat and carrying a bundle of newspapers. "You've forgotten the toilet seat," she declared, opening up her bundle to show him what she had been protecting from the cold.

They returned to the warm farmhouse kitchen, where she explained that during the winter they kept the toilet seat behind the kitchen stove.

Every time he finished another bottle of beer at that debutante ball he would declare, "Canada! So damned cold they keep the toilet seat behind the kitchen stove!"

June 12, 1972

s » The Australians always celebrate the Queen's birthday with a holiday, and special things are planned for the weekend, such as cracker fireworks displays, the annual parade of the Duntroon military cadets, and a big reception given by the Governor General.

Arthur is attending a three-day seminar down in Melbourne sponsored by the Australian Institute of International Affairs, on China and the World Community. They have some good speakers lined up, and even though he is posted to Europe now he is still interested in that part of the world. However, as dean of the corps he had to come back to Canberra for a white tie evening affair at Government House Saturday night, and it was a good thing, because although there were 350 guests and most of the people just had supper served buffet style, we were escorted in by Governor General and Lady Hasluck. Such is the power of protocol, each presided over a small table of twelve.

Tuesday here at the residence, in recognition of the fact that Canadian wives have been invited as a group to both the British high commission and the American embassy, I arranged a return function, inviting only the wives of the bottom ten junior officers of each of the two missions, as they have such large organizations here that the juniors are the ones who do not get invited out so much. After coffee, I had the young Australian wife of one of their Foreign Affairs officers give a talk on prehistoric Australia. Josephine Flood has been doing a lot of research in connection with the ANU, assisted by a grant from the Council for Aboriginal Affairs. She has conducted excavations looking for remains of early settlement in areas quite close to Canberra. She has made quite a study of the Bogong moth, which migrated in huge swarms and were favourites of the Aborigines—in places they were almost a staple of their diet—and by following them she has found sites where the Aborigines stayed in or near caves for the Bogong season. She had many slides to illustrate her forty-minute talk. Everyone was fascinated, and went away quite convinced that on their next outing if they kept their eyes peeled they too would be able to find a stone or some other sign of earlier settlement.

Wednesday I attended the last meeting for me of the senior Commonwealth wives, at which, as the wife of the senior Commonwealth high commissioner, I preside. Our likely successor in the diplomatic corps as dean will be, as we have been, also the senior Commonwealth representative. This will be the Malaysian High Commissioner, Dato Donald Stephens, and his wife, Datin Stephens, or, as we all call her, June. I had to make a little speech outlining the past history of the organization and suggesting plans for how it should carry on. There are so many changes in the diplomatic corps that such an organization has many changes in personnel; consequently, some people are just not here long enough to know its basic principles. We saw two very good films on Malaysia, especially one recent one that showed more of Eastern Malaysia.

Friday was my more important talk—to the Country Women's Association out in Gunning. I drove the fifty-nine miles from Canberra on a lovely bright sunny day through good sheep country. I have been taking antibiotics and cough-suppressing medicine all week as prescribed by Dr. Scott Finley at the beginning of the week. I felt that my voice was much better and really under control, but I had some really bad coughing bouts in the middle of the speech, which was embarrassing. Also, the competition in the audience was quite intense. This being a small country town, many of the women had brought small children—a lot of toddlers and small babies in bassinets. Each and every baby had a good cry at some point in my speech. However, the one that really started me laughing, not coughing, was a small boy who, when I was showing a film on Canadian ballet that uses eerie pipe music, started to mimic it in a shrill screech—and he was quite exact, if not on key.

June 25, 1972

s » At the beginning of the week we were a bit involved with the first official visit of the Prime Minister of New Zealand, John Marshall, and his wife. Protocol has changed its policy, and no longer wants the dean of the diplomatic corps at the airport, so we were spared that, although we thought it strange. We did go to a dinner in their honour at Government House, and I was fortunate to sit between Prime Minister McMahon and the Deputy Prime Minister, Doug Anthony, and Art between their wives. I also went to a ladies' lunch in honour of Mrs. Marshall the following day at the New Zealand residence, and we both went to a government reception at Parliament House. Marshall made a good impression here. He handled press and tricky questions very well, and is a pleasant, reasonable sort of man, not pretentious in the manner of his predecessor, Sir Keith Holyoake.

Tuesday morning I left by plane for Albury, about two hundred miles south of Canberra on the Murray River, in New South Wales, just across from Victoria. I was met by the president of the Murray District Country Women's Association, Mrs. Gelbart, who was also my hostess for the night, and Mrs. Moll, the international secretary, who had taken part in the seminar at Armidale with me. They were very good at showing me the sights, after which we went to the meeting, which was attended by more than a hundred, in the brand-new Theatre Centre. I spoke for about forty minutes, they asked questions for twenty, and then we showed two short Canadian films. They had dug up one lone male who had played the part of a Mountie in *Rose Marie* about ten years ago, and he was on hand to meet everyone. It is uncanny how *Rose Marie* keeps cropping up here as an accepted portrayal of Canada. They had a doll contest that I had to judge—half marks for authenticity and half marks for sewing skill. There were Mounties, Eskimos, Indians, skiers, Miss Canadas, and fur trappers. Many of them were excellent. I chose an Eskimo. The girl had tanned her own rabbit skin to make the garments.

The name of the village twenty miles out of Albury where I stayed was Burrimbuttocks! Have you ever heard such a funny name! The garden of the homestead has won the *Sydney Morning Herald* award as the best homestead garden for the last three years. The family was pleasant. They had an electric blanket on the spare bed, which saved me, because half the windows of the house were kept half-open and were so heavy I could not close them. Fresh! You don't linger in a bathroom like that! Next day we carted fresh water from their property to the village school, which because of the drought is without water, and I spoke to the children on Canada very informally out in the courtyard. Then we drove eighty-three miles to Wagga Wagga, where there was a large luncheon meeting of the CWA. The first part was to celebrate their fiftieth anniversary in Australia, and the second part their International Day. The subject of the latter was the country they have been studying this year, Canada. I spoke for about thirty minutes and answered questions for another thirty. We left at 3:00 p.m. sharp to drive the eighty-three miles back to Albury airport.

There my troubles began. The plane from Melbourne, due at 5:35, did not come until 7:35. In those two hours I tried to charter a private plane and did all in my power to get moving so that I would be in time for the dinner in our honour at Government House that night at 7:30, all to no avail. You sure feel helpless waiting for a plane in the airport. Anyway, I contacted Arthur, who went ahead, and I arrived at Canberra Airport at 8:35 p.m. Andrew, our driver, met me, and I tore home, changed into evening dress, and was at Government House by nine o'clock, in time for the end of the turkey course. I don't think many people have dared to turn up late at Government House, but I must say that both Sir Paul and Lady Hasluck were very understanding about it all. They had invited all of the twenty people we had suggested in response to their inquiry, which was very thoughtful.

July 2, 1972

s » Last Sunday we started our celebrations in connection with Canada Day by attending the annual barbecue of the Australian-Canadian Association of Canberra. It was out at the Cotter River

Dam, about fifteen miles from Canberra. People wore slacks and warm clothes, and in the middle of the day, thanks to the fires of the barbecue and the sun, it was a fresh but pleasant outing for families. There were lots of small children, and there were races, peanut butter scramble, and treasure hunts. The president took the occasion to present us with a book from the Association, because we would not be able to be at their ball on Saturday here.

Friday of course was our biggest reception of the year, for which Edith has been cooking for the past two weeks and for which 776 people were invited. The number was almost identical to last year's, because even though we added "to say goodbye" as well as celebrate Canada Day, we knew we had to hold the line or all would be squashed, and the numbers once lifted would get out of hand. Before the reception 462 had accepted, but as it was a blustery rainy night, and a Friday night at the end of the week, we had just about four hundred turn up, which is the number we were reckoning on for catering, drinks, etc., all along. As well we had fifty members of the Dickson High School Choir, who won the contest at the recent Eisteddfod, singing one Canadian and one Australian song. They had very sweet voices, and earned their Cokes and hot dogs by their contribution. We cannot have a toast here, by Australian tradition, because we share the same queen, so it is nice to have something like the choir to mark the special occasion. We were fortunate to have received from the vice-president of B.C. Packers, who was out here recently, a beautiful fresh Canadian salmon, which we had had lightly smoked by a butcher here, and was a contrast to the more heavily smoked Canadian salmon that I had already bought. The most touching thing for me was when, at the end of the reception, after I had paid the eighteen waiters and three cloakroom assistants, the five regular waiters and waitresses whom we have used the most stayed behind and presented us with a box made of Australian woods with a map of Australia on it and a silver plaque on the bottom with their names and best wishes. Because it was so unexpected to get a gift from them I was really moved and pleased. They also gave Edith a bottle of whisky, which I thought was also kind and thoughtful. We have been fortunate to have such a pleasant and efficient group of people to work with here. Never once in six years have I had one fail to turn up.

On Saturday at 11:30 a.m. we left for Melbourne to celebrate Canada Day there with about two hundred Canadians and Australians at the Annual Canadian Club and Women's Canadian Club dinner dance. They are the only capital that has two separate clubs. On arrival we had lunch with Trevor and Margaret Pyman, Australians we have kept in touch with since Ottawa days. He is in the Civil Aviation Department, so Arthur has had much to do with him regarding air agreements. Kevin Osmond, the Canadian commercial counsellor in Melbourne, and his wife Winifred arranged a little drinks party at their residence for all the officers and wives at the Melbourne office before we went to the dance. They presented us with a bark painting, for which Arthur has just now gone off to borrow saw and carpentry equipment again from Allan Roger so that he can get it glued and mounted before the bark warps—quite a big job, but it improves the painting, because it will not crack as badly afterwards. This morning we looked in at the Melbourne Arts Centre for an hour before catching our flight. We returned to find that Edith has caught the flu, probably tired out from all the preparations last week. I too have a bit of a cold, so we'll get to bed early to prepare for our third-to-last week in Australia, which will include a speech and four black-tie dinners.

July 9, 1972

s » The packers are coming at 8:30 a.m. tomorrow to begin the process of packing. They will pack the books in the study and the paintings and ornaments. They will return again Friday, so I'm not just sure how quickly they will move, and whether things like this typewriter will have been taken away to include in the lift van to go to Belgium. But I think this will be our last typed letter.

Monday night all the other high commissioners gave us a joint farewell dinner at the residence of the Malaysian, who is the next senior and will take over from us, both as senior high commissioner and, more importantly, as dean of the diplomatic corps. Donald Stephens, the Malaysian, and his wife June are both very friendly people and will do a good job for sure. They have a spacious house and will be able to do all the entertaining there at home. They had the twenty-two at the dinner with no problem.

We are very pleased with what is to be our gift from the diplomatic corps, a screen made by Alison Willis, who does the bark paintings that we had her demonstrate in Canberra for the first time about three years ago. Because this has led to a great deal of business for her, she has always been very friendly and generous since. Therefore for three hundred dollars, which is the amount that the whole diplomatic corps usually pays for a farewell gift for one of its members, she has made a four-panel screen that is like four of her large bark paintings joined together, and each is covered with non-reflective glass. Her husband has done all the carpentry work, and has done an excellent job of finding wood and doing a small fret-saw pattern all over the back, which gives it a very artistic appearance. We could not have a more Australian-looking gift than the gum trees and sprawling fences and countryside that she has depicted. She has even worked in two kookaburras, two koalas, and two kangaroos. She has spent about a month working on it, and the price for anyone else I'm sure would be about $500. It was Arthur's idea originally, and we were not sure just how it would turn out, but the result surpasses our expectations, and certainly suits us better than the usual inscribed silver cigar box or silver salver. There is a small silver plaque on it saying that it is a gift from all the corps. Mr. and Mrs. Willis came for lunch when they delivered it.

We were at the Netherlands Ambassador's for a black-tie dinner Wednesday night—they too are leaving—and another dinner at Government House on Thursday night, because the Governor General has gone overseas and the Governor of Victoria is here acting as administrator. Nothing like being farewelled twice at Government House! I was also given a very nice farewell lunch by the ladies of the Australian-Canadian Association, which was in addition to their general farewell, but they are so kind and genuine, I was pleased.

On Friday at 7:25 a.m. we went to Sydney. Luckily there was no fog to delay the plane. We had arranged for a final tour of the Sydney Opera House, because it is one of the architectural wonders of the world. We had not seen through it for four years, and it will not be opened until October 1973, so there are still many problems to solve. It is a most impressive and imaginative building, but carrying through Utzon's plan has been difficult and the price soars and soars, but it is helped by the lottery. We made a farewell call on the Governor of New South Wales. Art had a lunch with business people that Harry Horne had arranged, and we both went to a farewell reception for the fifty or so Canadian and local staff at all the Sydney Canadian government offices. Art was presented with a didgeridoo, and in the evening we went to a pleasant restaurant with the officers and their wives, a party of about twenty. It was good food, there was a good floor show with Spanish dancers, and all in all they put on a gala celebration to bid us farewell. They gave me a boomerang. Saturday night we attended the Sydney Australian-Canadian dinner dance, a well-arranged function, and returned to Canberra at noon today, Sunday.

July 16, 1972

s » The packers did not make as much headway as I had hoped on Friday morning when they were here, but the dividend of that is that I have kept the typewriter out until Monday, partly to start an inventory list today. The Monday session is supposed to finish us, but I suspect we will have a few more cartons and suitcases to go in the lift van by about Wednesday or Thursday. Our major shipments will go by sea to Belgium, a smaller shipment to Ottawa will go in our storage there, and a third, mainly suitcases, will go by air freight to Ottawa. With us of course we can take sixty-six pounds each on the plane. Because we are flying Canadian Pacific and know the people concerned well in both Sydney and Fiji, our only worries are in Canberra, where it is Trans-Australia Airlines, not CP, and in Vancouver, where we do not know the people. But we hope for a lenient interpretation of exact weights! One unknown factor is the gifts we keep being given.

Most are small and reasonable to pack, but we still remember our leaving Japan and trying to pack in my overnight bag some very brittle pottery soup bowls we were given at the last minute, several of which got broken as a result of being jammed in.

Wow! Is Edith ever lucky! She went to Housie-Housie, i.e., Bingo, on Thursday night and won the jackpot, which was $178, and then today she placed a bet on the horse races and won another $20. She will take the pension she gets from the Canadian government all in one lump sum, because when in receipt of the Australian old age pension there is a limit of $10 a week she may have from outside sources, whereas it doesn't matter if she has many thousands in the bank. She plans to do some catering and some babysitting so that she will not get too bored after retiring at the end of the month. She is such an active person I think she will find her one-room flat constricting, and she will get restless after she has rested up a while.

Arthur feels a great weight off his mind, because he has made his last speech here—to the diplomatic corps at the farewell reception for us on Thursday night. There was a big turnout and he spoke well. Everyone was most impressed with the bark painting screen we had commissioned as our gift, and many now think that it is the gift they also want when they leave. I think Mrs. Willis could make more in her art as a full-time job than she and her husband can from their property, with the uncertain prices of sheep and cattle. After the reception we went to dinner with one couple from Australian External Affairs. The strike of oil workers here is now in its third week, so that many people have run out of oil. Others are rationing themselves, and still others expect to run out this week. Fortunately this Australian house has an open fireplace. I sat next to it the whole time. Many schools were without heat this week, and most government offices had the heat on for just two hours in the morning. As the high this week in Canberra has been about 55 or 57 degrees each day, you can imagine how chilly it is. The talk is that the strike may end by Tuesday. Most cars are limited to three gallons of gas, and some stations have run out, so we hope that there will be enough to hand over the Datsun on Wednesday with a reasonable amount in it. Our next worry is the planes running out of petrol—horrible thought!

Last night we went to the home of our administrative officer and his wife, Derek and Molly MacKinnon, where all the office staff had assembled for a staff farewell for us. There were about forty-five people. We had a very pleasant cold buffet, and were given a book. This week the officers at the office and their wives will have a farewell dinner for us.

We will write next from Fiji.

The man who broke new ground

Bruce Juddery, The Canberra Times, July 17, 1972

Arthur Menzies does not look very Machiavellian. He is, on the contrary, a short, somewhat stocky Canadian of normally serious but affable demeanour.

In his six and a half years as Canada's High Commissioner in Canberra, however, he has earned high marks in some quarters as an "operator." There are not many diplomats who can persuade their governments to extend their interests (and aid) to totally new areas.

Mr Menzies' area has been the South Pacific. Since October 1970 he has been High Commissioner to Fiji, which he visits about four times a year, as well as to Australia.

He keeps a watching brief on the rest of Melanesia as well. He was last in Papua New Guinea at Easter, and has visited the other centres of the region—New Caledonia, the New Hebrides and the Solomons—about once every couple of years.

Mr Menzies will not be making any more visits to the South Pacific, at least not in his present capacity. On Friday he leaves Canberra for the very different atmosphere of Brussels, where he is to be Canada's Ambassador to the North Atlantic Council—in other words, NATO.

He has a low-key, dry sense of humour. "I arrived here in November 1965," he recalls. "I got the job because my name was Menzies." A few weeks later his namesake, Sir Robert, was sufficiently confident that he was leaving the country in the very best of hands, to be able to retire.

Despite the apparently placid state of Australian-Canadian relations, one gathers it has not always been an entirely comfortable tour of duty. When the Menzies arrived, Australia for the first time was getting involved in a major war in which Canada was not one of its allies, and some people in Canberra nursed a bitter notion of betrayal.

A few years later, while Hasluckian Cold War orthodoxy still ruled in Canberra, the Canadians began talking to the Chinese in Stockholm. Beneath the surface that also was an unhappy period in Canadian-Australian affairs. In Canberra Mr Menzies had to carry the can for what some saw as his government's perfidy.

The High Commissioner himself prefers not to talk about such matters. He is happier with the routine of relations between Australia and Canada, and there is much more to these than one might expect.

He has travelled a lot in Australia, accepting a good many speaking engagements and other "PR activities," as he admits them to be. Mrs Menzies, though not on Ottawa's payroll, has also been heavily committed. This year the NSW Country Women's Association is studying Canada and she has been in great demand as a speaker.

The similarities between his own country and Australia— federalism and Commonwealth membership, emptiness and mineral wealth—are readily apparent. The amount of work these congruencies create for the sparsely staffed High Commission on Commonwealth Avenue are less obvious.

"I think they provide an enormous basis, now that we have each become more confident, for a vast exchange of views about how we govern ourselves, about our economic problems," he says with something that, after six and a half years, comes close to fervour.

Whether one is talking about Aborigines, Indians or Eskimos, many of the problems are similar. "I've been very active in encouraging exchanges in this field. We had a minister out here last year and we have two Australian teachers going up to the North-West Territories shortly."

There are similar constitutional issues. "Your Northern Territory, our North-West Territories and the Yukon, are comparable internal territories where the legislative councils are battling to get more power and the problems are quite comparable — division of powers, finances, the Federal Government's infrastructure."

Offshore minerals, fisheries, petroleum, pollution, all these are problems shared in common. Ottawa expects its Canberra office to keep it informed about Australian approaches to them.

A lot of the High Commission's work is economic. "We had a team out here in March for discussions concerning the 'derived British preferences', preferences which stem from the British agreements with Canada, Australia and New Zealand, and what we can do about them when Britain goes into the EEC."

There will be more talks soon, in Ottawa about "which of these do we wish to keep between ourselves and which do we wish to, you might say, bargain off in the next round of GATT negotiations, particularly with our bigger trading partners, the EEC, the US and Japan."

Other issues are more mundane. "We've just introduced legislation in Canada — it's an amendment to the Criminal Code — to permit off-course betting, to allow some of the provinces to introduce TAB. We had the Attorney-General of Ontario out here just a few months ago to look at these things."

Mr Menzies calculates that his mission is one of the three or four busiest in Canberra. He himself writes his own speeches and reports to Ottawa providing employment for two stenographers.

For a diplomat, the High Commissioner's antecedents are impeccably cosmopolitan. He was born in 1916 in China, where his father was a missionary. His high school was the Canadian Academy in

343

Kobe, Japan, and his degrees come from the University of Toronto and from Harvard.

Understandably, he was cast as an Asian expert when he joined the Canadian Department of External Affairs in 1940. He was sent to Havana just after the war but in 1950 he was back in Japan, first as head of Ottawa's liaison mission in Tokyo, then as chargé d'affaires. In 1958–61 he was first High Commissioner to Malaya, concurrently Ambassador to Burma.

"Before coming out here I was the head of our defence planning division in the department in Ottawa. I got into the hot seat just before the Cuban missile crisis, a very lively introduction to the job. I had military assistance, UN peace-keeping missions, NATO, North American defence and other things of this kind to look after." He also was one of Canada's representatives on the Canada-US Permanent Joint Board on Defence.

It was, of course, a sort of training for his new job with NATO, to which he appears to be looking forward. "Of course, it's a demanding and interesting prospect, especially since there has been some breakthrough recently in terms of the SALT agreements, the German treaties, Berlin access and so forth, and there will be some talks beginning in the northern autumn on what the Russians like to call a European security conference and we like to call 'mutual and balanced force reductions' ."

It is all a long way from the South Pacific. "Part of the fun that I have had over the past two or three years, as a side light you might say to my responsibilities in Australia, has been trying to inform the Canadian Government about the emergence of four independent Commonwealth countries in the South Pacific and the influence this has had on the achievement of the South Pacific identity, and the influence it has had on moves toward independence by the other territories of the area."

He has had results. In 1970 Canada allocated $118,000 in aid to the South Pacific, in 1971 $400,000 and this year some $567,000. This is less than the Australian allocation— $495,000, $543,000 and $1 million respectively in the last three financial years—but perhaps the wonder is that Canada has contributed at all.

"In attempting to establish Canada's distinct and separate national identity, we look for ways in which we can operate in the foreign affairs fields, distinctly from the US," Mr Menzies explains.

"Secondly, we don't have the immediate regional demands that Australia has upon it in respect to Papua New Guinea, Indonesia and South-East Asia and we are therefore perhaps better able to spread ourselves to other parts of the world."

On top of that, the Commonwealth membership of the new South Pacific countries provided Mr Menzies with a strong selling point. "I think there is quite a strong consciousness in Canada of the new Commonwealth. Because of our position alongside the US, Canadians felt intellectually separated off from a sense of dependence on Britain earlier than Australia did. This is just a fact of history...."

Even so, the notion that Canada should invest aid in the region took some selling. "The process by which governments take an interest in new areas is cautious and the Canadian Government has long been known for Scottish influence," the High Commissioner notes, dryly.

"So I am pleased," he adds, "not so much with the volume of the aid, but the multiplicity of contacts that have been achieved." So, no doubt, are the new nations of the South Pacific.

Canadian Development Assistance to the South Pacific

Having invested considerable time and effort in promoting Canadian development aid to the South Pacific islands, especially following my accreditation as the first Canadian High Commissioner to Fiji after it attained independence in 1970, I decided to produce a short paper describing this assistance, which I completed in 1972, for the record. I was helped by my colleague Allan Roger, Political Counsellor, to ensure that the paper would be as inclusive as possible in describing direct

CIDA and B.C. funding, as well as the assistance given by private charities with matching grants from CIDA. (A.M. 2008)

Canadian assistance in the development of the South Pacific has grown both in volume and variety in the two years since Prime Minister Trudeau announced in May 1970 an initial grant of (Can.) $250,000 to the University of the South Pacific in Fiji. In June of the same year the section dealing with the Pacific in "Foreign Policy for Canadians," a full review of foreign policy for the 1970s, stated the intention of the Canadian government to initiate a modest program of technical and economic cooperation in the South Pacific. This intention has been given substance through a number of programs: Canadian International Development Agency (CIDA) grant aid and technical assistance, "people to people" cooperative programs supported by the Non-Governmental Organizations Division of CIDA, Canadian University Service Overseas (CUSO) practical technical assistance, and the Commonwealth Scholarship and Fellowship Plan. In addition, grant aid from the British Columbia Aid to Developing Countries Fund has been devoted to various projects in the South Pacific.

CIDA regards the South Pacific as a region of eligibility for Canadian development assistance. This means that if a sound project is envisaged by which Canada can contribute effectively to regional development, the project will be considered on its merits in competition with projects put forward from other regions or countries of eligibility. The existence of a number of regional organizations in the South Pacific facilitates this approach. Assistance to the University of the South Pacific (USP), which is an institution that serves the region, is being provided in three ways. Scholarships to enable students from the various island nations and territories of the Pacific to attend the USP were granted to eleven islanders for the 1971 academic year and fifteen for the 1972 academic year. These scholarships cover fees, board, and travel, as well as the territorial contribution to the general running expenses of the University. A Canadian has been appointed Manager of the University's Resource Centre, with responsibility for printing books prepared under the UNDP (UNESCO) secondary school curriculum development project and other university publications, and for binding library books and training local staff to run the Resources Centre on a continuing basis. Lastly, it is intended that a significant Canadian contribution will be made in the field of Marine Biology within the University's School of Natural Resources to emphasize the importance of fisheries to the island peoples of the South Pacific.

A second regional institution, the South Pacific Commission (SPC), has received assistance from Canada since 1970. Four short-term consultants have been assigned to provide leadership at seminars organized by the SPC in such fields as development planning, community welfare, trade statistics, and education policy. As the SPC is a bilingual organization, Canadian observers attending the last three South Pacific Conferences have indicated that it might be beneficial to draw on Canadian bilingual facilities in requesting consultants. Beyond the SPC, but within the scope of the Commission's educational development program in Polynesia, CIDA provides two trained teachers for service in Western Samoa.

Under its terms of reference, the Non-Governmental Organizations (NGO) Division of CIDA contributes toward the cost of development projects undertaken by Canadian voluntary organizations in developing countries. A number of these cooperative development ventures have been begun in the South Pacific region and others are being processed. From "Miles for Millions" walks the Canadian YWCA raised $100,000 as a contribution to the $400,000 cost of construction of a new YWCA national headquarters building in Suva, Fiji, which incorporates recreational, residential, and vocational training facilities. The NGO Division of CIDA has provided a matching grant of $100,000 in support of this project. Similarly, the YMCAs of Greater Vancouver raised $90,000 toward the $270,000 cost of construction of a YMCA recreational and vocational training centre at Mt. Hagen in the Western Highlands of Papua New Guinea. Again a matching grant was obtained from CIDA.

In the Western District of Papua New Guinea, the Canadian Montfort Catholic Mission, with sixty missionaries working in eight stations, has undertaken a number of educational, medical, social, and economic development projects to improve the livelihood of the people of this remote area. With the cooperation of the Canadian Catholic Committee for Development and Peace (CCCDP), the Canadian Montfort Missions, and other contributors, a substantial sum of money has been raised in support of these projects. For its part, the NGO Division of CIDA has contributed $27,000 for medical programs and $32,000 for the Daru Youth Centre, which provides recreational facilities and functional literacy training for unemployed youths. Additional medical and community fishing projects developed by the Montfort Fathers are being considered for CIDA support. In a similar undertaking, the Franciscan Missionaries of Mary, with the support of their community in Canada and the CCCDP, have raised funds for the construction of a hospital and a domestic school for girls at Seim in the East Sepic district of Papua New Guinea. The NGO Division of CIDA has contributed $6,000 to this imaginative project.

Since CUSO sent its first volunteers to Papua New Guinea in 1970, the numbers have grown from ten in that year to thirty-two in 1971 and seventy-three in 1972. These volunteers, more properly called "co-operants," offer practical expertise in a wide variety of vocations, ranging from teaching and curriculum development to local business development, local Government Council engineering, and agricultural extension work. Through CIDA assistance in the funding of CUSO, $275,000 will have been provided for such development assistance in Papua New Guinea by the end of 1972. The CUSO Board of Directors agreed in July 1972 to extend its programs to other areas of the South Pacific.

A number of post-graduate students from Fiji, Papua New Guinea, and other South Pacific islands are studying in Canada under the Commonwealth Scholarship and Fellowship Plan. Canada was honoured to receive under this program one of the first graduates of the University of Papua New Guinea, who is now completing a master's degree in Political Science at the University of Victoria in British Columbia. About five such South Pacific scholars are in Canada at any one time. It is estimated that the cost of travel, fees, board, and lodging amounts to a minimum of $30,000 per year for each of these five students.

In October 1969, when the Colombo Plan Conference was held in the city of Victoria, on Vancouver Island, the Honourable W.A.C. Bennett, Premier of the Province of British Columbia, announced the establishment of a five-million-dollar fund, the interest from which was to be used for agricultural education in developing countries and for disaster relief. Since then the B.C. Aid to Developing Countries Fund has been generous in its assistance to selected projects in Fiji. Two annual grants of $30,000 each have been made to the SPC's Community Education Training Centre, near Suva, where home economics teachers and women's welfare workers from all over the South Pacific receive ten-month training courses in practical home economics for women in rural areas. Grants totalling $39,540 have been made for the construction and equipping of an agricultural machinery maintenance workshop at the Fiji School of Agriculture. Two grants, one of $16,000 and the other $31,500, have been made to the Navuso Agricultural School to supply trucks and buildings for the adult farmer training program. A grant of $31,000 has been made for motor mechanics and electrical maintenance workshops at the Marist Training Centre and Agricultural College in Taveuni, Fiji. The B.C. Aid Fund has also contributed to the Mt. Hagen YMCA project and the Port Moresby Community Development Workers Training Program in Papua New Guinea.

As a result of discussions initiated in July 1971 during the visit to Canada of the Prime Minister of Fiji, Hon. Ratu Sir Kamisese Mara, CIDA is now endeavouring to recruit a senior fisheries officer to direct the Fisheries Division of the Fiji Ministry of Agriculture, Fisheries, and Forests. Other projects in the region that are currently being considered for assistance from CIDA, the B.C. Aid Fund, and other Canadian sources include a fishing project involving communities on the Fly River, in Papua New Guinea, a boys' home and market garden training farm at Ba, in Fiji, the training of community workers by the Port Moresby Community Development Group, a youth recreation and vocational centre at Raiwaqa, in Suva, a community centre in Aoba Island, in the New Hebrides, a Technical Centre at St. Michel School in Santo, New Hebrides, and possible assistance to the Malaita Development

Company in the British Solomon Islands, where a representative of Canadian Executive Service Overseas served briefly in 1971. Additional assistance to the SPC is also expected.

Total grants from Canadian governmental sources for development assistance in the South Pacific have grown from approximately $118,000 in 1970 to $400,000 in 1971 and nearly $600,000 in 1972, for a three-year total of over $1,000,000. While this sum is not large in relation to the needs of the area, or in comparison with the assistance given by countries that have a long record of association with the South Pacific, or in relation to the total amount of Canadian overseas development assistance, it does represent, through the wide number of contacts established, an expression of Canadian interest in the emerging countries of the South Pacific. As indicated, government aid in many instances complements assistance from Canadian voluntary organizations, whose work in the South Pacific area is further evidence of the concern of Canadians for the welfare of their Pacific neighbours, the five million people who live in the thousands of islands strung across the ten million square miles of the South Pacific.

August 1972 · *Fiji*

A » After packing a lift van of possessions for shipment to Brussels and an air freight shipment to Ottawa, we left Australia on July 21, and arrived in Nandi, Fiji, at 3:15 a.m. the next morning for a farewell visit. We paid final calls on Prime Minister Sir Kamisese Mara and other cabinet ministers, but devoted most of our time to giving a final pat to the many aid and development projects we had launched in Fiji.

Sheila and I had established a long-term friendship with Ruth Lechte, an Australian who was the South Pacific representative for the International YWCA, and Anne Gilwillie, her Canadian associate. Ruth was the driving force behind the new YWCA building just being erected in Suva. I presented a Gestetner duplicating machine to Mrs. J.N. Kamikamika, President of the Suva YWCA (and wife of the Secretary to the Cabinet), for use in the office secretary course in the vocational training section.

Another appealing project was the Raiwaqa Youth Centre, established to provide recreation and vocational training for youth in a new suburb of Suva. I had been in touch with the Service Committee of the Rotary Club of Vancouver about their $11,000 grant.

There were a number of residential areas on the main island of Viti Levu and others in which the communities wished to provide youth recreation facilities, apprenticeships in the building industry, and market garden training for boys who were reaching the end of compulsory education at the age of fifteen. Only one in three wanted to go on to higher education. The challenge was to get in touch with service clubs in Canada whose contribution would be matched by the Non-Governmental Division of CIDA.

We visited the Fiji School of Agriculture, for whose construction and equipment the Honourable W.A.C. Bennett, Premier of British Columbia, had made a gift of $30,000 at a luncheon in Victoria on July 27, 1971, at the time of the Fijian Prime Minister's visit to Canada. I recommended an additional gift of (Fiji) $7,500 to complete the inventory of essential training equipment.

I was also pleased to learn that the B.C. Dental Association was prepared to donate surplus dental equipment, provided CIDA could find sea transport, say on a South Pacific voyage of HMCS *Provider*.

August 1972 · *Vancouver*

We took a few days leave before we left the hospitable shores of Fiji on August 1 to travel by CPA airliner to Vancouver, where we were welcomed by our daughter Norah and her boyfriend, Ed Langevin. The Department of Trade and Commerce office in Vancouver had made up a program of appointments with local businessmen and volunteer agencies interested in talking to me about Australia and the South Pacific. Business Writer Mike Grenby of the *Vancouver Sun* interviewed me and wrote an article that was published on August 5.

Man on the move:
Coal, the South Seas — he's at it for Canada

Mike Grenby, The Vancouver Sun, August 5, 1972

I don't want you to get the idea, said the high-commissioner-now-ambassador, "that all there is to the job is wearing striped pants and sipping cocktails."

Coming from a man who has travelled perhaps three million miles around the Pacific in Canada's foreign service, the statement really wasn't too necessary.

Arthur Menzies, 55, is a short, somewhat stocky man. He's just finished a tour of duty as Canadian high commissioner to Australia for the past six years and eight months; if someone suggested it to you, it wouldn't be hard to picture him wearing formal striped pants and sipping cocktails at a reception in Canberra's fashionable diplomatic district.

But if nobody suggested it to you, and all you had to go on was the impression he's made during a general conversation, you'd be far more likely to picture him as an energetic man actively out to further Canadian interests in a part of the world he knows best.

Menzies was born in China and educated in Japan and Toronto and at Harvard. He joined the department of external affairs in 1940 and has spent most of his time since then involved in the Pacific area.

Although he doesn't like to admit it, Menzies, who speaks Chinese and Japanese, has probably done as much as anyone to help shape Canada's foreign policy in the Pacific.

Based in Australia, he's travelled some 100,000 miles a year around the Pacific: "I was on the road at least 25 per cent of the time," he says.

Menzies is now in Vancouver enroute to his new posting as Canada's ambassador to the North Atlantic Council in Brussels. In an interview with The Sun Friday, he touched specifically on competition and co-operation between Canada and Australia as well as on the significance of the emerging South Pacific countries.

"Australia is important to Canada as a trading partner," he said.

"While the two countries may be competitors, Australia is also Canada's second most important market (after the U.S.) for manufactured goods. In addition, the two countries have a mutual interest in more orderly marketing of the products in which they compete."

Menzies noted that Canada and Australia together supply two-thirds of the important minerals that Japan imports.

"Because we are probably the most politically and socially stable suppliers, we can influence world markets," he said. "There has been consultation between the two countries, but there should be much more."

For example, he said, Australia, like Canada—and particularly like B.C.—is interested in developing its secondary industry; it wants to process more of its raw material, rather than simply exporting it.

"But Australia is afraid that if it put in more copper smelters, the Japanese would then turn more to Canada for the copper concentrates," said Menzies.

"Japan wants to continue to operate its own smelters and through its purchasing agreements with the concentrate suppliers, get these suppliers in effect to subsidize Japan's efforts to reduce the pollution caused by the smelters.

"If Canada and Australia got together and consulted with the other raw material producers, especially the developing countries, we could all work up a pretty strong position in this matter of further processing of minerals in our own countries.

"And don't think that this can be accomplished simply by the passing of government regulations. It takes consultation between government and industry within the countries as well as co-operation between the countries themselves."

Turning to coal, which both Canada and Australia sell heavily to Japan, Menzies said that Australia is beginning to feel the added cost of supplying services to new coal mining developments.

"At present," he said, "Australia is able to sell some high-grade coal at only 51 per cent of the price other supplier countries have to charge.

"But Australia is just beginning to discover the social implications of the exploitation of its mineral resources—the need to supply new facilities such as schools and hospitals in previously largely uninhabited areas.

"Australia is beginning to turn to the mining companies for help in the costs of providing these facilities."

Canada, on the other hand, because of its greater population, (22 million vs. 12.5 million), already has more of this supporting infrastructure.

"These developments in Australia could help Canada's competitive position as long as our costs don't go up as much," he said.

Menzies noted that Canada, thanks to the earlier development of its economy and the greater availability of cash from the U.S., is in a stronger economic position: Canada has a GNP of $100 billion and exports of $18 billion against Australia's GNP of $38 billion and exports of $5 billion, giving Canada a much higher per capita result.

Commenting on the South Pacific islands, which cover some 10 million square miles of ocean, Menzies said that now is the opportune time for Canada in particular to establish a viable presence in this area.

"Should the South Pacific be neglected just because it isn't strident in its demands?" he asked.

"Now, while the atmosphere is pleasant and agreeable, is the time to establish a people-to-people contact and help set the stage for a more stable world situation—before the agitators set to work and breed trouble, rioting and revolution.

"While there is a certain

amount of philanthropy involved, it also makes good business sense to take the trouble to establish relationships.

"Even though the contacts may be small and numerous, they could eventually add stability to Canada's export business and lessen its dependence on the U.S." The Pacific islands have a total population of 5 million, he added.

Menzies said tourism provides one of the prime opportunities for overseas investment, with some of the islands also offering mineral development potential.

The major event of my visit to Vancouver was a talk on "Canada and the South Pacific" that I gave on August 8 to a luncheon meeting of two hundred members of the Rotary Club. Here is its substance:

The popular Canadian view of the South Pacific was based on James Michener's *Tales of the South Pacific* and the Broadway and Hollywood musical that was made out of it. This is the image that tourist promoters project. After victory was achieved in Europe during the Second World War, the Japanese invasion of the South Pacific and the American intervention to drive them back attracted world attention. Then, after Japan's defeat, the South Pacific sank back into colonial obscurity, disturbed only by French nuclear explosions off Muraroa Atoll.

The South Pacific embraces the islands of the Pacific south of the equator other than Australia and New Zealand, and some atolls in the Western Pacific east of the Philippines. These islands add up to 200,000 square miles of land in ten million square miles of ocean. The region extends from Papua New Guinea in the west to Pitcairn Island (but not Easter Island) in the east and from Norfolk Island in the south to Guam and the Trust Territory of the Pacific (but not Hawaii) in the north. It is inhabited by

355

Polynesians, Melanesians, and Micronesians. The island communities of the South Pacific are scattered over an area of ocean three times the size of Canada. Each community is widely separated from its neighbours. Many of these islands are coral atolls surrounded by reefs, and their soil is generally poor, suitable only for growing coconut palm and root vegetables. The larger islands in the southwest support agriculture, timber, and mining.

The Polynesians, Melanesians, and Micronesians moved in from the west fifteen hundred to five thousand years ago in great sailing canoes that traversed great stretches of open water, five thousand miles from east to west and fifteen hundred miles from north to south. European exploration began in the sixteenth century with the Spaniard Mendaua, who was followed by Captains Cook, Bligh, and Vancouver. The explorers were followed by missionaries, whalers, traders, slavers, guns, and European diseases. The historian J.C. Beaglehole remarks that the islands were "more or less exploited, more or less missionized, and less rather than more administered," right up to the time of the Second World War. After the Americans, Australians, and New Zealanders fought savagely to drive the Japanese from the South Pacific, the area and its people were neglected, because of preoccupations with regions of greater population and greater strategic significance.

In 1947 the South Pacific Commission was formed by the colonial powers as a forum for consultation on common problems of health, and economic and social development. It operated on a restricted budget, because France and the U.S.A. did not wish to see their territories move quickly. Modest United Nations programs and direct development aid were begun. Broader issues were discussed in the South Pacific Conference meetings at the ministerial level.

Before the Europeans arrived the islanders had been self-sufficient, relying on root crops, coconuts, bananas, and reef fishing for subsistence. The Europeans introduced plantation agriculture, to produce coconuts, sugar, coffee, cocoa, tea, and bananas. Tropical timber was cut, and mining for phosphate, bauxite, gold, and copper was begun. Tuna fishing flourished, but it was mainly done by Japanese and Taiwanese trawlers. Transportation over the vast stretches of ocean, whether by small inter-island mixed freight and passenger vessels or by aircraft, and radio communications were a constant challenge.

Fiji became the regional hub, under the dynamic leadership of Ratu Sir Kamisese Mara. The University of the South Pacific in Fiji became a centre for the training of local leaders, and the University of Papua and New Guinea played a similar role. In addition to missionaries, various voluntary organizations such as the YMCA and YWCA, Canadian University Service Overseas, and comparable volunteer organizations from Australia, New Zealand, the United Kingdom, and the U.S.A. helped to organize and educate the five million people of the South Pacific islands (three and a half million of whom live on Papua New Guinea) to adapt to the modern world. I'm glad that service clubs like the Rotary Club of Vancouver, with the support of the Non-Governmental Division of the Canadian International Development Agency of Canada, are helping in the development of the human resources of the South Pacific.

August 1972 · *Quebec City*

A » On August 13, 1972, we flew from Vancouver to Quebec City to take a three-week French immersion course preparatory to our posting to Brussels, Belgium, as Permanent Representative of Canada to the North Atlantic Council—or, in short, Canadian Ambassador to NATO.

We had arrived in Australia on November 15, 1965, a fortnight before my forty-ninth birthday, and had stayed for six years and eight months, until July 21, 1972. These were years of good health for Sheila and me. We travelled extensively to explore the vast continent, to talk to friendly Australians about Canada, and to learn about the challenges faced by Australia in its domestic and foreign policies. We escorted Prime Minister and Mrs. Harold Holt to Expo 67 in Montreal, and welcomed a visit to Australia by Prime Minister Pierre Trudeau in May 1970. Many other Canadian cabinet ministers, academics, and business leaders visited Australia. I took an interest in the development toward independence of Papua and New Guinea. En route to and from Vancouver we stopped for fuelling in Fiji, and I took an interest in its progress toward independence. I was appointed first Canadian High Commissioner to Fiji after it achieved independence in 1970. This encouraged me, initially through an interest in the newly established University of the South Pacific in Suva, to widen my interest in the broad expanse of the South Pacific.

Altogether, it was a great experience, and Sheila and I will remember it with great affection.

INDEX

Hulme, Mr. 55
Hummel, Marion 175, 231, 240, 278
Humphrey, Hubert H. 134
Humping My Bluey (McInnes) 167
Hunt, Ralph and Mrs. 246, 257, 312
Hunter River valley 104
Hutchinson, Bob 111
Huxley, Sir Julian 33–4
Huxley, Sir Leonard and Molly 128, 266, 290, 293, 326
Huyck Factory 67

I

India 132, 283, 284
Indian Brotherhood of Canada 255
Indonesia 36, 136, 173, 282–3, 294, 305
International Communications Satellite Consortium 70
International Development Research Centre (IDRC) 218
International Grains Agreement 143, 153
International Monetary Fund 293
irrigation 64, 67–8, 166, 238
Isa, Mount 81
Isbister, Claude and Mrs. 131, 132
Israel 279–81

J

Jackson, Burt 300
Jahn, Mr. 134
Jamieson, Stuart and Mrs. 86, 293
Jansen, Andrew and Mrs. 23, 142, 235, 246, 283, 297, 321, 335
Jarvis, Esmond 143, 291
Jay, Douglas 81

Jaycee Clubs 112, 159
Jenolan Caves 265
Jess, Cameron and Linda 113
Jindabyne 118–19, 301: Jindabyne, Lake 119, 231, 299
Johnson, Al 307, 308
Johnson, Lyndon Baines 116–17, 133, 134
Johnston, Sir Charles and Lady Johnston 45, 224, 260–1
Jones, Terry 160
Judge, Margaret 170

K

Kaiser, Edgar and Mrs. 109–10
Kamikamika, Mrs. J.N. 351
Kangaroo Valley 96
Karsh, Malak 329
Karsh, Yousuf 88, 102
Katoomba 266
Kavic, Lorne 138, 185
Keehn, Eric and Jess 302
Kekkonen, Sonja 89, 90, 161, 163
Kendrew, Sir Douglas 169
Kennedy, Robert, assassination of 134
Kent, Duke and Duchess of 169
Kenwood Mills (Arnprior, ON) 67
Ker, I. 112
Khancoban 108
Khoman, Thanat 187
Killen, Mr. 193
King, Leslie 122
Kirkland-Casgrain, Marie-Claire 287, 289
Kniewasser, Andy 158
Koop, Dr. 103

N

Rockhampton 157, 159, 203
Roger, Allan and Gene 136, 147,
    155, 159, 181, 197, 198, 230,
    236, 243, 254, 262–3, 269,
    283, 291, 321, 326–7, 329, 337
Rome 178–9
Rose Marie (film) 334
Ross, Andy 249
Rotary Clubs 66, 67, 70, 88, 105,
    124, 169, 191, 201
Royal Australia Air Force (RAAF)
    82, 121, 123, 203
Royal Canadian Mounted Police
    (RCMP) 69, 334
Royal Commonwealth Society 71,
    111–12, 115, 152, 165, 170
Royal Easter Agricultural Fair
    58–9, 101, 254
Royal Institute of Public
    Administration 316
Royal Military College (Duntroon)
    129, 196, 234, 285, 332
Royal Winnipeg Ballet 303–4, 308,
    312–14
Rum Jungle 82
Rusk, Dean 73–4
Russell, Kay 238
Rylah, Mr. 102

S

SEATO Foreign Ministers
    Conference 72–4
Salamonie, Joanisie 160, 164–5
Sanders, Robert 244
Sandys, Duncan 36
Sawchyn, Mr. 303
Schlink Pass Road 119

Scotland, influence in Australia
    and Canada 41
Sculthorpe, Peter 142
Seaborn, Blair 21, 185
Selassie, Haile 130
Sellers, Roy and Mrs. 267
Separation Tree 51–2
Shann, Mr. and Mrs. 86
Shapiro, Ben and Tillie 283, 291,
    295, 317
Sharp, Fred and Mrs. 240, 242,
    246, 250, 300, 308, 310
Sharp, Mitchell 128, 185, 187–8,
    277
Shebib, Donald 268
sheep 157, 161, 196, 266: Breeders
    of British Sheep 211;
    sheepdogs 29–30, 103–4
Shortliffe, Glen, Newton, and Scott
    173
Silcock, Prof. 154
Simon Fraser University 138
Sims, John 217, 322
Sinclair, Ian and Mrs. 116
Sinclair, Jim 319
Singapore 97, 172
Sir Colin MacKenzie Sanctuary
    (Healesville) 52
Skelton, Alex and Janet 175, 177–8
Skelton, Herbert and Daisy 126,
    175, 190, 278, 300
Skelton, Oscar Douglas 61, 113, 182
Slater, Mrs. Dyson 267
Slater, Naomi. *See* Mrs. Peter Hayden
Slink Pass 94
Slyfield, Philip, Jinny, and
    Christopher 26, 93, 140

Australia and the South Pacific: Letters Home was typeset by Dennis Choquette, winter 2009. The type is Scala, designed by Martin Majoor. The book was printed, Smyth sewn, and cased in at Tri-Graphic, Ottawa. The paper is acid-free and forest friendly.

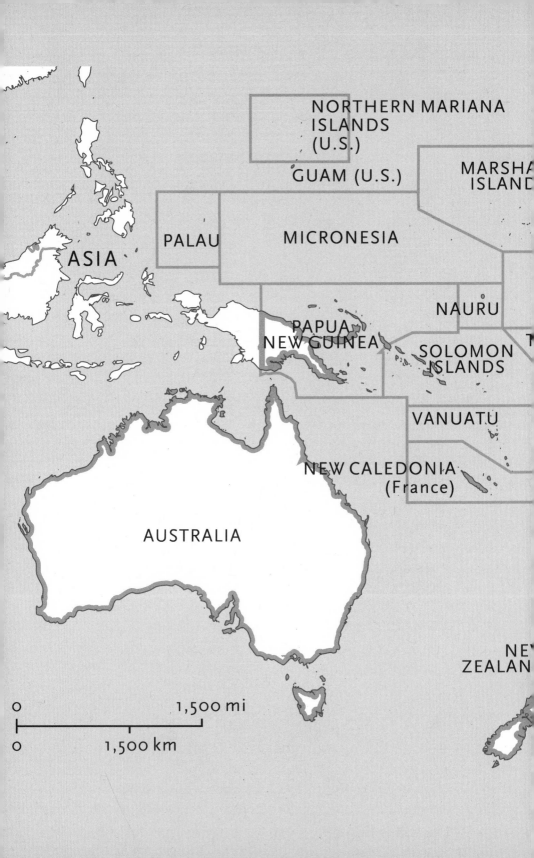